THE PENGUIN DICTIONARY OF

Economics

G. BANNOCK, R. E. BAXTER
AND R. REES

ALLEN LANE / THE VIKING PRESS

ALLEN LANE
Penguin Books Ltd
17 Grosvenor Gardens, London s w 1 w 0 b d

THE VIKING PRESS
625 Madison Avenue, New York, N.Y. 10022

First published in paperback, 1972
This hardback edition, 1977

Copyright © Penguin Books Ltd, 1972

ISBN 0 7139 1038 0 (Great Britain)

ISBN 0 670 27224 8 (United States of America)
Library of Congress Catalog Card No. 77–77776

Set in Monotype Times
Printed in Great Britain
by Richard Clay (The Chaucer Press) Ltd,
Bungay, Suffolk

FOREWORD

'... no dictionary of a living tongue can ever be perfect, since while it is hastening to publication, some words are budding, and some falling away'
— SAMUEL JOHNSON, *The Dictionary of English* (1755)

The general aim of this book is to provide a companion (not an oracle) to two sorts of users of economics. First, it is intended to be of use to the general reader who wants to follow economic discussion in the press or elsewhere and to the increasing number of people who need a knowledge of economic terms and concepts in their daily work – town planners, trade unionists, civil servants, teachers, journalists, politicians and businessmen among them. Secondly, it is aimed at students up to the second year of a university course in the subject.

We have tried to eschew an examination-crammer treatment, and to write as far as possible as practitioners of the art, to recognize controversy where it exists and to indicate wherever possible the practical applications of the terms and concepts defined. Economics, and economic theory in particular, cannot be mastered solely by reference to a dictionary or any other single book, and it is not always an easy subject to express in simple language. For these reasons, our entries on the more technical terms are not intended to be fully comprehensible to the layman. We have, of course, done our best, and the length of our entries is related more to the space required for exposition than to our assessment of their relative importance.

To avoid repetition, and in the interests of brevity and coherence, the entries are elaborately cross-referenced, small capitals indicating where reference to another entry will help understanding. There is less difference between British and American terminology in economics than in many other subjects, and, except in institutional matters, it is hoped that our dictionary will have equal value to British and American readers. In some instances where a term has a specialized meaning in the United States, or is little used in this country, we have inserted '(U.S.)' after the term concerned.

Our subject is a large one, and we have had to be highly selective in our treatment of it. Words in common usage are not included unless they have a specialized meaning in economics. Economic theory,

5

including international, monetary and welfare economics, has been treated fairly comprehensively. We have also given considerable emphasis to the history of economics in keeping with our view that the subject is a developing, lively one. Individual economists, however, are included only where they have made a definable contribution to the contemporary corpus of economic thought. Even so, entries have been confined to contributions at the expense of biographical information. We have been even more cautious in the inclusion of contemporary economists, except where they figure in continuing controversy; this has inevitably meant leaving out many distinguished members of the profession. We have given comprehensive treatment of the terms used by statisticians and econometricians that have practical relevance as well as those used in business finance. In a book of this length, it is not possible to do justice to the full flowering of concepts, institutions and terminology in financial and business economics, public finance, international trade, payments and development, but we hope that, institutions apart, nothing important has been omitted.

We have made little attempt to erase all the differences in style and treatment of the entries for which we were individually responsible, but we have tried to ensure consistency. We remain jointly responsible, of course, for errors and omissions, on which we should welcome comment from readers for incorporation in future editions.

Among the many people who have helped us, we should like to mention Mrs Carol Laid, who typed much of the manuscript, Miss J. M. Smith, who also contributed to the research and editing of the whole work, and Judy Rees and Kay Siddiqui, who read part of the manuscript and made valuable comments.

G.B.
R.E.B.
R.R.

London, December 1971

LIST OF ABBREVIATIONS

A.D.B.	Asian Development Bank
A.P.C.	Average propensity to consume
A.P.S.	Average propensity to save
A.S.P.	American selling price
B.I.S.	Bank for International Settlements
B.N.E.C.	British National Export Council
B.S.O.	Business Statistics Office
C.A.C.M.	Central American Common Market
C.I.C.	Capital Issues Committee
c.i.f.	Cost, insurance, freight
C.S.D.	Civil Service Department
C.S.O.	Central Statistical Office
D.C.E.	Domestic credit expansion
d.c.f.	Discounted cash flow
D.E.A.	Department of Economic Affairs
E.C.A.	Economic Cooperation Administration
E.C.A.F.E.	Economic Commission for Asia and the Far East
E.C.G.D.	Export Credits Guarantee Department
E.C.S.C.	European Coal and Steel Community
E.D.C.	Economic Development Committee
E.D.I.T.H.	Estate Duties Investment Trust
E.E.C.	European Economic Community
E.F.T.A.	European Free Trade Association
E.M.A.	European Monetary Agreement
E.P.U.	European Payments Union
F.A.O.	Food and Agricultural Organization
F.H.A.	Finance Houses Association
f.o.b.	Free on board
G.A.T.T.	General Agreement on Tariffs and Trade
G.D.P.	Gross domestic product
G.F.C.F.	Gross Fixed Capital Formation
G.N.I.	Gross national income
G.N.P.	Gross national product
H.H.F.A.	Housing and Home Finance Agency
H.P.	Hire purchase
I.B.A.	Industrial Bankers Association

7

I.B.R.D.	International Bank for Reconstruction and Development
I.C.F.C.	Industrial and Commercial Finance Corporation
I.C.I.	Imperial Chemical Industries
I.C.O.R.	Incremental capital output ratio
I.D.A.	International Development Association
I.F.C.	International Finance Corporation
I.H.A.	Issuing Houses Association
I.L.O.	International Labour Organization
I.M.F.	International Monetary Fund
I.R.C.	Industrial Reorganization Corporation
I.R.R.	Internal rate of return
I.S.I.C.	International Standard Industrial Classification
I.T.O.	International Trade Organization
L.A.F.T.A.	Latin American Free Trade Association
M.I.D.A.S.	Maritime industrial development areas
M.P.C.	Marginal propensity to consume
M.P.S.	Marginal propensity to save
M.R.S.	Marginal rate of substitution
N.B.P.I.	National Board for Prices and Incomes; see also P.I.B.
N.D.L.B.	National Dock Labour Board
N.E.D.C.	National Economic Development Council
N.E.D.O.	National Economic Development Office
N.N.I.	Net national income
N.N.P.	Net national product
N.R.D.C.	National Research Development Corporation
O.E.C.D.	Organization for Economic Cooperation and Development
O.E.E.C.	Organization for European Economic Cooperation
P.A.Y.E.	Pay-as-you-earn
P.I.B.	Prices and Incomes Board; see also N.B.P.I.
P.O.S.B.	Post Office Savings Bank
P.P.B.S.	Programme, planning, budgeting systems
R. & D.	Research and development
R.P.M.	Resale price maintenance
S.D.R.	Special drawing rights
S.E.T.	Selective employment tax
S.I.C.	Standard Industrial Classification
T.D.C.	Technical Development Capital Ltd
T.D.R.	Treasury deposit receipt

U.N.C.T.A.D.	United Nations Conference on Trade and Development
U.N.R.R.A.	United Nations Relief and Rehabilitation Administration
V.A.T.	Value added tax

The use of single and double arrows (⇨ ⇨) in the text indicates, respectively, *see* and *see also* where a point is either amplified or complemented in another entry.

A

'A' shares. ⬦ SHARES.

Above the line. 1. Promotional expenditure incurred by a firm on selling its products or services by means of direct advertising, such as through television commercials, newspaper advertisements and posters. Below-the-line expenditure includes all other promotional sales expenditure, such as that incurred by special offers, free gifts and in-store displays. **2.** A now obsolete distinction made in the BUDGET (1947–63) between government payments and receipts authorized by Parliament to be made out of current revenue and those (below the line) for which it is authorized to borrow or which it may use to service DEBT. The distinction is thus roughly, although not precisely, as in the national accounts, between CURRENT ACCOUNT and capital account. Above-the-line expenditure includes CONSOLIDATED FUND services, e.g. judges' salaries, and defence expenditure debt service paid out of TAXATION; and above-the-line receipts all taxation revenue. Below-the-line expenditure includes LOANS to NATIONALIZED INDUSTRIES, and debt service paid out of interest; below-the-line receipts include repayments or interest on loans made by the government. The reason for the distinction is that expenditure above or below the line has different economic implications, the former being financed out of taxation and miscellaneous revenue receipts while the latter is not. The TREASURY normally budgets for a surplus above the line for DEMAND MANAGEMENT purposes, and to finance a deficit below the line. Any net EXCHEQUER cash deficit which occurs when the below-the-line deficit exceeds the above-the-line surplus is financed by borrowing.

Abstinence theory of interest. ⬦ INTEREST, ABSTINENCE THEORY OF.

Accelerated depreciation. ⬦ CAPITAL ALLOWANCES.

Acceleration principle. The hypothesis that the level of INVESTMENT varies directly with the rate of change of output or sales. Given technological conditions, and the relative prices of CAPITAL and LABOUR, a certain size of CAPITAL stock will be required to produce a particular rate of output. If this rate of output should change, then, other things being equal, the desired size of the capital stock will also change. Since net investment is, by definition, the amount by which capital stock changes, it follows that, on the assumptions made, the amount of investment depends on the size of the change in output, or the rate of change of output. At its simplest, the hypothesis asserts that investment will be proportional to the rate of change of output, at all levels of output. However, under more realistic assumptions the relationship, although still holding, may cease to be a simple proportional one. There may, for example, be spare capacity over some range of increasing output, so that the capital stock does not have to be increased until full capacity is reached; or the CAPITAL INTENSITY of production may vary as the level of output varies, as when at higher levels of production it becomes economic to install fully automatic machinery. In addition, the relation will be influenced by EXPECTATIONS, time lags, etc. As well as being very important in explaining the determination of investment expenditure in the economy, the acceleration principle also plays an important part in theories of the TRADE CYCLE, e.g. the ACCELERATOR-MULTIPLIER MODEL, and the theory of ECONOMIC GROWTH, e.g. in the HARROD-DOMAR MODEL. ⇨ CLARK, J. M.; ACCELERATOR COEFFICIENT.

Accelerator coefficient. The amount of additional CAPITAL stock required to produce a unit increase in sales. A key element in the ACCELERATION PRINCIPLE, this is the coefficient which relates the level of INVESTMENT to the change in sales. Thus, if I_t is investment in time t, and Y_t and Y_{t-1} are output or sales in times t and $t-1$ respectively, then we have: $I_t = V(Y_t - Y_{t-1})$, where V is the accelerator coefficient. Thus, the value of V tells us the strength of the effect that a change in output or sales will have on the level of investment. The simplest form of the theory takes V as a constant determined basically by technology. However, we might also expect V to be affected by interest rates, wage rates, and the degree of CAPACITY UTILIZATION. ⇨ CAPITAL-OUTPUT (RATIO).

Accelerator-multiplier model. A MODEL of the TRADE CYCLE based on the interaction of the ACCELERATION PRINCIPLE and the MULTIPLIER. A change in INVESTMENT causes, through the multiplier, change in NATIONAL INCOME. This change in national income determines, through the acceleration principle, a level of INVESTMENT. If this level is different from the level previously attained, there is a further change in investment, a further change in income, and so on. It is possible to show by a mathematical analysis of this process that it may cause national income to vary cyclically over time.

Accelerator theory of investment. ⇨ ACCELERATION PRINCIPLE.

Accepting house. An institution specializing in accepting or guaranteeing BILLS OF EXCHANGE. Most acceptance houses have taken on other functions as the use of bills of exchange has declined, returning to their original, wider, function of merchant banking (⟡ MERCHANT BANKS). There are some eighteen accepting houses in the City of London represented on the Accepting Houses Committee, a body that ensures policy coordination between them, the TREASURY and the BANK OF ENGLAND.

Account. 1. A record of financial transactions in the form of STOCKS or flows. ⟡ BALANCE OF PAYMENTS; BALANCE SHEET; CURRENT ACCOUNT; SOCIAL ACCOUNTING. **2.** The period in which STOCK EXCHANGE transactions take place and after the end of which settlement must be made. Up to the end of an account, transactions are made without payment and account dates are thus of vital importance to speculators. There are twenty-four account periods in a year, two of them extending to three weeks, the rest being a fortnight in duration.

Account day. The day on which all transactions made during the previous ACCOUNT at the STOCK EXCHANGE must be settled. It is normally the Tuesday week after the end of the account, and is also known as *settlement day*, and more rarely as *pay day*.

Accrued expenses. The cost of services utilized in advance of payment and written into a company's accounts as such.

Active balance. An old-fashioned term for a BALANCE OF PAYMENTS surplus on CURRENT ACCOUNT.

Activity analysis. ⟡ LINEAR PROGRAMMING.

Activity rate. ⟡ PARTICIPATION RATE.

Actuary. Someone trained in the calculation of RISK and PREMIUMS for ASSURANCE purposes.

Administered prices. Prices which are set consciously by a single decision-taking body, e.g. a MONOPOLY firm, a CARTEL, a government agency, rather than being determined by the free play of MARKET forces.

Ad valorem tax. ⟡ TAX, AD VALOREM.

Advances. Loans (⟡ BANK LOAN).

Adverse balance. A deficit in the BALANCE OF PAYMENTS.

Advertising. The publicizing of goods and SERVICES, which can take a variety of forms – display advertising in the press and on billboards, motor vehicles, products themselves; classified advertisements and publicity on television, radio and the cinema. Advertising may be used for noncommercial purposes – for example, charities or the state – but in economics it is usually used loosely as a synonym for the whole range of methods of sales promotion. In practice, sales promotion also includes free gifts, competitions, TRADING STAMPS and special displays in shops and so on, while the still wider function of MARKETING includes travelling salesmen, sales outlets owned by manufacturers and other techniques for furthering sales, so that advertising is strictly speaking only one element in what is called the marketing mix. Expenditure on advertising varies between trades and tends to be significantly higher in consumer than in capital goods and highest of all in fast-moving consumer goods trades such as soap and cigarettes.

The significance of advertising in economic theory is that it permits product DIFFERENTIATION and hence may create a BARRIER TO ENTRY. Under PERFECT COMPETITION, all products are identical in any given MARKET and knowledge is assumed to be perfect so that advertising is excluded by definition. Advertising is, however, taken into account in the theory of MONOPOLISTIC COMPETITION, where a relatively small number of firms with differentiated products is assumed to exist. Under these conditions, new competition may be deterred by the high cost of establishing a new brand in the face of competition from existing producers. It does not, of course, follow that advertising is socially undesirable and, arising mainly from the impracticability of measuring the effects of advertising, there is considerable controversy about its role. GALBRAITH believes that advertising is a powerful method of influencing consumers and that its role in controlling demand is an indispensable requirement of modern CAPITAL-INTENSIVE production methods. The traditional view in economics is that consumers must be informed of the availability of products and that this informational role is essential. There is more argument about the desirability of persuasive advertising, although it is generally recognized that the two types of advertising are not easy to distinguish in practice. It is argued that, on the one hand, advertising helps to create mass markets, and hence permits the exploitation of the ECONOMIES OF SCALE, and, on the other, that under OLIGOPOLY, in particular, market forces do not always prevent excessive and wasteful use of advertising.

Aggregate concentration. ◇ CONCENTRATION.

Aggregate demand. The total DEMAND for goods and SERVICES in the economy. It is conventionally broken down into: (a) the demands of HOUSEHOLDS for consumer goods and SERVICES; (b) the demands

14

of firms and the government for INVESTMENT GOODS; (c) the demands of both central and local government for goods and services; and (d) the demands of consumers and firms in other countries for goods and services in the form of EXPORTS. Since aggregate demand determines the level of production and hence employment, analysis of the determinants of these components of aggregate demand is the core of the Keynesian (⟐ KEYNES) analysis of NATIONAL INCOME and employment determination (⟐ EMPLOYMENT, FULL). ⟐ SOCIAL ACCOUNTING.

Aggregated rebate. ⟐ DEFERRED REBATE.

Aggregate supply. The total SUPPLY of goods and SERVICES in the economy available to meet AGGREGATE DEMAND. It consists of domestically produced goods and services plus IMPORTS.

Agricultural Mortgage Corporation. Set up to make LOANS to farmers against MORTGAGES on their land by the Agricultural Credits Act 1928. The capital of the corporation was originally supplied by the BANK OF ENGLAND and the joint stock banks (⟐ COMMERCIAL BANKS), but the corporation also issues state-guaranteed DEBENTURES. The corporation's loans are irrevocable, except in cases of default, and are usually made through the local branches of the commercial banking system.

Aid. ⟐ UNITED NATIONS CONFERENCE ON TRADE AND DEVELOPMENT; DEVELOPING COUNTRY; FOREIGN INVESTMENT.

Allen, Sir Roy George Douglas (1906–). Educated at Sidney Sussex College, Cambridge, Sir R. G. D. Allen began lecturing at the London School of Economics in 1928. During the Second World War he moved from the U.K. TREASURY to Washington as Director of Records and Statistics of the British Supply Council and of the combined Production and Resources Board. In 1944 he was appointed Professor of Statistics in London University. His publications include *Mathematical Analysis for Economists* (1938), *Statistics for Economists* (1949), *Mathematical Economics* (1956) and *Macro-Economic Theory – A Mathematical Treatment* (1967). In 1934 he published an article in *Economica* with Sir J. R. HICKS which demonstrated the use of the INDIFFERENCE CURVE based on ORDINAL UTILITY as an analytical tool in the theory of consumer behaviour. ⟐ ALLEN REPORT; E. SLUTSKY.

Allen Report. The Report of the Committee of Inquiry into the Impact of Rates on Households (1965), under the chairmanship of Professor R. G. D. ALLEN. This committee found that the impact of rates was regressive. Although only 2·9 per cent of total disposable HOUSE-

HOLD income (⟡ DISPOSABLE INCOME) was taken by rate taxation, the burden was as much as 8·2 per cent of the income of households earning less than £6 per week, and 6·2 per cent on between £6 and £10 per week. The committee made recommendations for the easing of the impact of rates such as that their payment could be made on a monthly basis. This and other measures to ease the burden were included in the Rating Act of 1966.

Allocation, resource. ⟡ RESOURCES; ECONOMIC EFFICIENCY.

Allocative efficiency. ⟡ ECONOMIC EFFICIENCY.

Allotment letter. A letter addressed to a subscriber to an issue of SHARES informing him of the number of shares that he has been allotted and – where payment was not made with the application – the amount due.

American loan. ⟡ WASHINGTON AGREEMENT.

American selling price. ⟡ GENERAL AGREEMENT ON TARIFFS AND TRADE.

Amortization. Provision for the repayment of DEBT by means of accumulating a 'sinking fund' through regular payments which, with accumulated INTEREST, may be used to settle the debt in instalments over time, or in a lump sum. The term is also used as a synonym for DEPRECIATION.

Annual allowances. ⟡ CAPITAL ALLOWANCES.

Annuity. 1. A constant annual payment. **2.** A guaranteed series of payments in the future purchased immediately for a lump sum. Annuities are described as 'certain' where payment is specified for a fixed number of years. A 'life' annuity payment continues until the death of the person for whom it was purchased. Annuities may be 'immediate', where payment commences on purchase, or 'deferred', where payment starts at a future specified date. The British government sold annuities until 1962, but they are now only available from INSURANCE companies, whose pension schemes (⟡ PENSION FUNDS) are often annuities purchased with accumulated contributions and INTEREST. The price of an annuity is based on the PRESENT VALUE of the stream of income payments it provides, and it varies with RATES OF INTEREST and, in the case of life annuities, the age and sex of the person who will draw the annuity. In the autumn of 1970, for example, a man aged fifty would receive £116·50 each year until his death on the purchase of an annuity for £1,000. A man aged eighty would receive £241 for the same cost, and a woman £207·50.

Anti-trust (U.S.). Anti-MONOPOLY or restrictive practices in the context of uncompetitive market conditions. The term TRUST originally referred to large amalgamations of firms, but anti-trust laws in the U.S. are analogous to monopolies and restrictive practices legislation in Britain and apply to single firms, large and small, as well as to what are called CARTELS in other countries. The U.S. anti-trust laws prohibit mergers or acquisitions which might tend to lessen competition or create a monopoly as well as a number of restrictive practices such as PRICE DISCRIMINATION, EXCLUSIVE DEALING and tying contracts. Although restrictive practices legislation in Britain (▷ RESTRICTIVE TRADE PRACTICES ACTS) makes certain types of business practice illegal, the creation of monopoly as such by acquisition, for example, is not illegal and the approach of the MONOPOLIES COMMISSION is far more pragmatic than the corresponding institutions in the United States.

Appreciation. Increase in the value of an ASSET; the antonym of DEPRECIATION. Appreciation may occur through rising PRICES as a result of INFLATION, increased scarcity or increases in earning power. ▷ CURRENCY APPRECIATION.

Appropriation account. A business account showing how net PROFIT is distributed between DIVIDENDS, reserves, PENSION FUNDS, etc.

Arbitrage. The practice of switching short-term funds from one INVESTMENT to another in order to obtain the best return. An arbitrage flow of funds will take place between two financial centres if the difference in their RATES OF INTEREST is greater than the cost of covering against the currency exchange RISK. The latter is reflected in the difference between the spot exchange rate and the forward exchange rate (▷ FORWARD EXCHANGE MARKET). The source of these arbitrage flows may come from dealers who specialize in this business. Arbitrage may also take place between BONDS or BILLS OF EXCHANGE with different maturity dates when the interest rates diverge. Arbitrage in itself is not speculative. For instance, there are two alternative methods for a holder of sterling to speculate on a revaluation (▷ EXCHANGE RATE) of the franc. The first is to buy francs spot in Paris and invest in bills on the Paris market; the second is to buy forward francs and invest sterling in the London market. The choice between the two will depend on the actual interest rates prevailing in each market.

Arc elasticity. ▷ ELASTICITY.

Area-volume relationships. ▷ ECONOMIES OF SCALE.

Arithmetic mean. ▷ AVERAGE.

Arithmetic progression. A series in which each VALUE differs by a constant from that of the preceding value, e.g. x, $(a + x)$, $(2a + x)$, ... $(an + x)$. ⟣ GEOMETRIC PROGRESSION.

Articles of association. ⟡ MEMORANDUM OF ASSOCIATION.

Asian Development Bank (A.D.B.). The Bank set up in November 1966 following the recommendations of the United Nations Economic Commission for Asia and Far East. It was formed 'to foster economic growth and cooperation in the region of Asia and the Far East and to contribute to the acceleration of economic development of the DEVELOPING COUNTRIES of the region'. It hopes to encourage economic and financial cooperation among the regional members. About 60 per cent of the total subscribed CAPITAL of $1,100 million has been contributed by the nineteen countries within the United Nations commission region, which include the three developed countries of Japan, Australia and New Zealand. The remaining non-regional members include the U.S., which subscribed $200 million (as did Japan), West Germany, Canada, the U.K. and Switzerland. The bank intends to operate as a viable BANKING institution, charging realistic RATES OF INTEREST, and to encourage a flow of capital to the region from outside sources (⟡ COLOMBO PLAN).

Assets. A business accounting term. On the BALANCE SHEET of a company, everything that the company owns and which has a money value is classified as an asset, total assets being equal to total LIABILITIES. Assets fall into the following categories, roughly in order of the extent to which realizing their money value would disrupt the company's business: (a) *Current assets:* CASH, bank deposits and other items that can readily be turned into cash, e.g. bills receivable, STOCK and work in progress, marketable SECURITIES. (b) *Trade investments:* INVESTMENT in subsidiary or associated companies. (c) *Fixed assets:* LAND, buildings, plant and machinery, vehicles and furniture, usually at cost less DEPRECIATION written off. (d) *Intangible assets:* goodwill, patents, etc. The assets of an individual are those possessions or the liabilities of others to him, which have a positive MONEY value.

Assurance. That branch of INSURANCE under which a contract is made to pay a CAPITAL sum on a specified date or on the death of the person assured. The former contract or policy is called term or endowment assurance, and the latter whole-of-life. Both types of policy may be with or without PROFITS. By paying a higher PREMIUM, the policy-holder can receive a share of the PROFITS earned by the life fund. Policies may also be linked in some way to

EQUITIES so that the final payment is determined by the stock market prices current at the time ($\diamond$ UNIT TRUST). Because life assurance is an important source of private SAVINGS, the premiums attract relief from TAXATION. This fact has encouraged BUILDING SOCIETIES to issue term policies, the premiums for which are invested in their own business. The tax saving enables the saver to obtain a high YIELD.

Atomistic competition. The type of MARKET STRUCTURE in which very large numbers of small firms compete independently. $\diamond$ PERFECT COMPETITION.

Austrian School. A tradition of economic thought originating in the work of CARL MENGER (1840–1921), who was Professor of Economics at Vienna until 1903. He was succeeded in the Chair by VON WIESER (1851–1926) and BÖHM-BAWERK (1851–1914). Menger's principal achievement was the construction of a marginal utility theory of value ($\diamond$ VALUE, THEORIES OF). His work was developed by Von Wieser, who, in addition, clearly formulated the important concept of OPPORTUNITY COST. Böhm-Bawerk's main contributions were in the fields of CAPITAL and interest rate theory ($\diamond$ RATE OF INTEREST). The Austrian tradition has been continued in the work of VON MISES and F. A. HAYEK. $\diamond$ W. S. JEVONS; S. M. LONGFIELD.

Authorized capital. The amount of share CAPITAL fixed in the MEMORANDUM OF ASSOCIATION and the articles of association of a company as required by the Companies Acts ($\diamond$ COMPANY LAW). Also known as *nominal capital* or *registered capital*.

Auto-correlation. CORRELATION between the error terms in a regression model ($\diamond$ REGRESSION ANALYSIS). Its effect is to invalidate one of the assumptions which underlines the ordinary least-squares procedure ($\diamond$ LEAST SQUARES REGRESSION), and thus to make necessary a modification of that procedure.

Autonomous investment. That portion of total INVESTMENT which is not determined by economic factors such as the RATE OF INTEREST the rate of change of sales, or profitability of investment, but rather by factors which can be considered exogeneous to the economic system ($\diamond$ EXOGENEOUS VARIABLE). An example would be investment which is carried out to take advantage of some INNOVATION or technical discovery. The importance of autonomous investment in economic theory is that changes in it may spark off economic fluctuations, and may influence the behaviour of the TRADE CYCLE in ways which are not explained by MODELS based on explanations of investment in terms of endogeneous factors (rate of interest, rate of change of sales, etc.).

Average. A single number intended to be representative of a set of numbers, by showing a 'central' value around which the numbers are grouped. Thus, a batsman's scoring average is meant to indicate his typical performance over a season; the average wage of a group of workers is meant to suggest the wage which those workers typically tend to earn. Necessarily, some or even all of the numbers may differ from the average – a batsman may in fact never score his 'average' number of runs; a worker may never earn his 'average' wage (cf. the statement that the average number of persons per HOUSEHOLD in the U.K. is $3\frac{1}{2}$). Nevertheless, the average is useful if it gives us an idea of the value about which the actual numbers are closely grouped, or, as statisticians say, a measurement of the 'central tendency' of the data.

There are in fact several ways of calculating an average from a set of numbers, and these different ways will frequently give different values. It is misleading to say 'the average . . . is' without specifying exactly what type of average is being used. The types of average most frequently encountered are:

(a) *The arithmetic mean:* This is the 'average' most commonly met in everyday use: the set of numbers is summed, and the answer divided by the number of numbers. If a batsman has had ten innings, then his 'average' or mean score is found by adding up the ten scores, and dividing by ten. The 'mean' wage of a group of 500 workers is found by summing their individual wages, and dividing by 500. And so on. The mean gives a good representation of the typical values of the numbers when the numbers are *evenly* dispersed around it: that is, when the numbers are reasonably closely clustered with no extreme values very much greater or very much smaller than the rest. If there are such extreme values, the mean tends to give an inaccurate representation of the typical values taken by the numbers. Thus, suppose we calculated the mean weekly wage of five men, who earned respectively: £15, £17, £18, £20 and £20.

Then the mean is given by: $\left(\dfrac{15 + 17 + 18 + 20 + 20}{5}\right) = £18$ p.w.

Suppose, on the other hand, that the fifth man had earned £55 per week. The mean wage would then be £25 per week, which is much less representative of the whole set of numbers – almost all the men earn quite a lot less than this. Hence, the mean in that case would not be very satisfactory.

Certain types of data often exhibit such extreme values, e.g. wages, and incomes generally (▷ INCOME DISTRIBUTION), size of firms in an industry (▷ SIZE DISTRIBUTION OF FIRMS), size of cities in a country, etc. Hence, the mean is often rejected as the appropriate measure of the average for these, and other types of average tend to be used.

Note also that the usefulness of the mean depends on how *closely* the numbers are grouped around it. In the mean wage example given above, the actual wages are quite closely grouped around the mean of £18. Suppose the wages of the five men were, however, £8, £11, £18, £26 and £27. Then the mean is again £18 per week, but now this is much less of a typical value, because the numbers are much more widely dispersed. In fact, whenever a mean value is given, it should be accompanied by a measure of how closely or widely the numbers are dispersed around it (▷ VARIANCE and STANDARD DEVIATION).

(b) *The median:* A type of average which is often used when the mean is inappropriate. The median of a set of numbers is that number which has the same number of values less than it as there are greater than it. To find the median, the set of numbers is first arranged in ascending order of size, like the first set of values of weekly wages given above. If the number of values in the set is odd, then the median is found immediately as the middle number; there are five values in the set of wage rates, and the middle value is the third number, i.e. £18. On the other hand, if the number of values is even, then none of those values is the 'middle number'. If, for example, there were four numbers, the second number would have one number below it and two above; the third number would have two below and one above. The solution in the case of an even number of values is to take the two adjacent central values (the second and third when there are four numbers, the tenth and eleventh when there are twenty numbers, and so on), and take their mean as the median. To illustrate: suppose the set of wage rates contains the four numbers £15, £17, £18 and £20. The two middle numbers are £17 and £18.

Their mean is $£\left(\dfrac{17 + 18}{2}\right) = £17\cdot5$. Hence, £17·5 is the median wage rate. It has two numbers below it (£15 and £17) and two above it (£18 and £20).

In calculating the median, therefore, the middle value of the set is taken as typical or representative of the whole set. The advantage

21

this has over the mean is that it ignores extreme values. Thus, in the case described above where the fifth wage rate was £55 p.w., the median would still be £18 p.w., whereas the mean rises to £25 p.w. In fact, we could make the two values above the median as high as we liked, or the values below the median as low as we liked: as long as the number of values remains as five, the median is £18 and remains unchanged. It follows that, when there are extreme values among the higher values in the set, the mean will tend to be pulled above the median; when there are extreme values among the lower values in the set, the mean will tend to be pulled below the median. In each of these cases, the median will tend to give a more accurate representation of the whole set of data.

(c) *The mode:* This is the value in the set of numbers which occurs most frequently. Thus, in the set £15, £17, £18, £20 and £20, the mode is £20. If we deleted the last £20, then the set would have no mode. If we increased the set of numbers to six by adding in a value of £15, the set would have two modes (it would be 'bi-modal'), one of £15, and one of £20. The mode is frequently of interest for its own sake: it may be interesting to know the wage which is earned more frequently than any other, the size of family which is encountered more than any other, etc. However, in some circumstances it is possible that the mode will be much less representative of the whole set of data than the mean or median, whereas when it is representative, its value is very close to the values of the latter. The mean or median tend therefore to be more generally used in statistical work.

(d) *The geometric mean:* This is calculated as the n'th root of the product of n numbers. Thus, the geometric mean of 1 and 4 is $\sqrt{1 \times 4} = \sqrt{4} = 2$. Similarly, the geometric mean of 1, 2, 3, 13·5 is $\sqrt[4]{1 \times 2 \times 3 \times 13\cdot5} = \sqrt[4]{81} = 3$. The geometric mean is chiefly used in calculating average growth rates over a period of time. Suppose that NATIONAL INCOME has grown by 4 per cent in one year, 2 per cent in the next year, and 1 per cent in the third year, and that we wish to find what the average annual rate of growth has been over these three years. The solution is not found by taking the arithmetic mean of the growth rates, but rather by taking the geometric mean, i.e. by finding $(\sqrt[3]{4 \times 2 \times 1})$ % = $(\sqrt[3]{8})$ % = 2%. Although calculating the geometric mean from the definition could be very cumbersome when the number of growth rates is large, the procedure is simplified by noting that the logarithm of the geometric mean is found by taking the arithmetic mean of the logarithms of the growth rates. ⟡ WEIGHTED AVERAGE.

Average cost pricing. The method of setting prices in which PRICE is set equal to AVERAGE COST. Since total revenue is equal to price multiplied by quantity, and total cost is equal to average cost multiplied by quantity, average cost pricing ensures that total costs will always be covered by revenue. ⟡ MARGINAL COST PRICING.

Average costs. The total COSTS of producing a given number of units of output divided by that number of units. May also be referred to as 'unit cost'. It is usual to distinguish between LONG-RUN and SHORT-RUN average costs. In the case of LONG-RUN average costs, total costs are calculated on the assumption that all INPUTS have been adjusted to the minimum cost levels for the given level of output. In the case of short-term average costs, however, over most ranges of output only some of the inputs will be at their most efficient levels, and therefore, in general, short-run average costs will be above long-run average costs. ⟡ AVERAGE COST PRICING.

Average productivity. Output of a good divided by the number of units of a particular FACTOR OF PRODUCTION required to produce it. The most usual measure is the average productivity of LABOUR found by dividing output by numbers employed or man-hours. Measures of average productivity are used as indicators of productive efficiency. They suffer from the limitation that inter-firm productivity comparisons may be misleading if the firms have different labour and CAPITAL intensities (⟡ CAPITAL INTENSIVE).

Average propensity to consume (A.P.C.). For the economy, this is the total value of expenditure on consumption goods and SERVICES divided by the value of NATIONAL INCOME. It is, therefore, the proportion of national income devoted to CONSUMPTION. Similarly, the average propensity to consume of an individual is the proportion of his INCOME which is devoted to consumption. Since income can either be spent or saved, the lowest value the A.P.C. can take is zero (all income is saved) and the highest is one (all income is spent). It is generally asserted that the higher level of income of either an economy or an individual, the lower the A.P.C., and the greater the proportion which will be saved. ⟡ CONSUMPTION FUNCTION; MARGINAL PROPENSITY TO CONSUME.

Average propensity to save (A.P.S.). The complement of the AVERAGE PROPENSITY TO CONSUME. The A.P.S. is defined as the proportion of INCOME of an individual or the whole economy which is not spent on consumption goods and services, i.e. which is saved (⟡ SAVING).

It is therefore measured as 1 – A.P.C. It is generally asserted that as the income of the individual or the economy rises, so a higher proportion of the income is saved, i.e. the A.P.S. rises. ⟡⟩ CONSUMPTION FUNCTION.

Average revenue. The total revenue received from the sale of a given number of units of output, divided by that number of units. Since total revenue is defined as PRICE multiplied by the number of units sold, average revenue and price are necessarily identical.

Avoidable costs. Those COSTS of production which would not be incurred if a given output were not produced. They are closely related to VARIABLE COSTS or PRIME COSTS, which are the direct costs of producing additional units. However, the costs avoided by not producing an additional unit of output may not only be the direct costs, but also any costs arising indirectly in other parts of the firm's production system. Moreover, total avoidable costs need not equal total variable costs, since, if a firm ceased production of a good altogether, it may 'avoid' costs which must be incurred if any output is to be produced, but which do not vary with output, e.g. lump-sum royalty payments on a particular process. ⟡⟩ MARGINAL COST PRICING.

B

'Back door'. When the DISCOUNT HOUSES are short of funds they can, as a last resort (⟡ LENDER OF LAST RESORT), go to the BANK OF ENGLAND and sell their holdings of TREASURY BILLS at the discount of BANK RATE. This is a 'front door' operation. However, when bank rate is very high and the discount houses are in temporary difficulties, the government BROKER may buy bills from them at the market rate to ease the pressure on their LIQUIDITY. This operation is called 'back door'.

Backwardation. 1. In a COMMODITY market, the amount by which the spot PRICE (including the cost of stocking over time) exceeds the forward price. ⟡ SPOT MARKET and FORWARD EXCHANGE MARKET. **2.** On the STOCK EXCHANGE, a sum of MONEY paid by a BEAR to a BULL for the right to delay delivery of SECURITIES sold forward at a fixed price. A bear will have sold securities to a bull for delivery on a certain date in the expectation that, by that date, the market price will have fallen. If they do not, in fact, fall, he may consider it worthwhile to pay a backwardation so as to defer delivery of the shares until the next account period.

'Bad money drives out good'. Before paper MONEY (⟡ BANK-NOTE) became universally accepted as a means for settling DEBTS, precious metals were the most common forms of money. Gold and silver coins were struck bearing a FACE VALUE equivalent to the value of their metal content. Debasement of the coinage occurred when the face value was kept above the value of the metal content of the coinage. The holders of the correctly valued coinage became unwilling to exchange for the debased coinage because they would obtain less metal in exchange than if they bought direct. The result was that the 'good', undebased coinage did not circulate. The process is referred to as GRESHAM'S LAW.

Bagehot, Walter (1826–77). Bagehot graduated in mathematics at University College, London, and was called to the Bar in 1852. After a spell as a banker in his father's business, he succeeded his father-in-law as editor of *The Economist* newspaper in 1860, a post he held until 1877. He was an influential commentator on current economic affairs and a prolific writer who is often quoted today. His publications include *Universal Money* (1869), *Physics and*

25

Politics (1872), *Lombard Street. A Description of the Money Market* (1873) and *Postulates of English Political Economy* (1876).

Balance of payments. A tabulation of the CREDIT and debit transactions of a country with foreign countries and international institutions, drawn up and published in a similar form to the INCOME and expenditure ACCOUNTS of companies. These transactions are divided into two broad groups: CURRENT ACCOUNT and capital account. The *current account* is made up of visible trade (i.e. merchandise EXPORTS, RE-EXPORTS and IMPORTS) and invisible trade (i.e. income and expenditure for SERVICES such as BANKING, INSURANCE, tourism and shipping, together with profits earned overseas and interest payments). The balance on current account is the difference between the NATIONAL INCOME and national expenditure in the period.

Current Account	£m
Imports (f.o.b.)	7,882
Exports/re-exports	7,885
Visible balance	+ 3
Interest, profits, dividends	
Debit	869
Credit	1,381
Net balance	+512
Transport	
(net balance)	− 58
Government	
(net balance)	−486
Other*	+608
Invisible balance	+576
Balance on current account	+579
Investment and other capital flows (Capital Account)	
Inter-government loans	
(net balance)	−128
Other official long-term capital	
(net balance)	−26
Other Overseas investment	
(net balance)	+819
Total investment and other capital flows	−615
Balancing item	+93
Total currency flows	+1,287

* Includes travel, banking, insurance, royalties, etc.
(Source: *U.K. Balance of Payments 1971*, H.M.S.O., London.)

The *capital account* (*investment and other capital flows*) is made up of such items as the inward and outward flow of money for INVESTMENT and international grants and loans. The U.K. has traditionally had a DEFICIT on visible trade – that is, she has imported more goods than she has exported. However, in the past this has been more than compensated for by the surplus which she has earned on invisible account. Indeed, from the middle of the nineteenth century up until 1931, the U.K.'s balance on current account was always in surplus (except for the period during the First World War, and perhaps to a minor extent in 1926). Even after 1931, up until the Second World War, the deficits were relatively small. In the 1940s the U.K. was forced to liquidate many of its overseas assets and to borrow substantial sums to pay for the war, with the result that, although on average the current balance continued in surplus, the immediate post-war years saw considerable changes. After 1958, the current balance tended downwards into deficit until 1968. The table shows the composition of the balance of payments for the U.K. in 1970.

The overall deficits or surpluses are brought into balance by movements in the GOLD AND FOREIGN EXCHANGE RESERVES or sterling liabilities (⊳ STERLING AREA). The transactions between foreigners and residents are carried out through the EXCHANGE EQUALIZATION ACCOUNT which operates to keep the EXCHANGE RATE for sterling within the agreed limits. A balance of payments surplus means that there is a net demand for sterling greater than the supply during the period, and conversely for a deficit. If the market for sterling were free, the demand and supply would be brought into balance by means of an alteration in the exchange rate (i.e. the price of sterling relative to other currencies or gold). With fixed exchange rates, the central authority must achieve balance either by (if in surplus) buying foreign currency or gold in exchange for sterling, or by (if in deficit) selling gold or foreign exchange for sterling. The success of this policy depends on the size of the gold and dollar reserves (⊳ RESERVE CURRENCY) and whether the deficit/surplus is persistent or temporary. A deficit in the balance of payments is not necessarily a bad thing, any more than a surplus need be a good thing. It is a form of borrowing which could be used to enhance domestic savings to boost investment to the benefit of future growth. On the other hand, if the deficit is occasioned, for instance, by an excess of AGGREGATE DEMAND over supply in the domestic market, it will persist until the home market has reached EQUILIBRIUM, and if the overseas borrowing is used to finance immediate

27

consumption rather than investment, will yield little benefit in the form of higher rates of growth in the future.

There are many measures which can be taken in an attempt to correct a DISEQUILIBRIUM in the balance of payments. If the imbalance is expected to be temporary, borrowing (or lending) from other countries or international institutions, either through direct arrangements or through adjustments in the level of interest rates, may be possible (◊ INTERNATIONAL MONETARY FUND). Import TARIFFS, import QUOTAS, IMPORT DEPOSITS and EXPORT INCENTIVES could be applied in order to affect the visible trade balance quickly, but such measures are subject to the GENERAL AGREEMENT ON TARIFFS AND TRADE. Other measures include EXCHANGE CONTROL and operations designed to ease the strain on the balance of payments by adjusting the level of aggregate demand in the home economy. This latter, together with interest-rate policy, has been the main method pursued by U.K. governments from devaluation in 1949 to devaluation in 1967 (see STOP-GO). Changes in the exchange rate, under the fixed system which operated from the BRETTON WOODS agreement of 1944 to the exchange rate adjustments of 1971, were regarded as the final long-term solution.

Balance of trade. The BALANCE OF PAYMENTS on CURRENT ACCOUNT.

Balance sheet. A statement of a company's WEALTH on a given date; not to be confused with the profit-and-loss account (◊ DOUBLE-ENTRY BOOKKEEPING), which records changes in the company's WEALTH over a year. A balance sheet is in two parts: (a) on the right-hand side ASSETS and (b) on the left LIABILITIES. The assets of the company are set out against the claims of the persons or organizations owning them, so that the two sides of the balance sheet are equal. This does not, of course, mean that the shareholders owe as much as they own – they are included among the claimants. In the U.S., and increasingly in Britain, in economic analysis, it is more usual to present the balance sheet in vertical form with fixed and current assets at the top. Current assets are then deducted from total assets to give net assets. This total is then broken down to show how these assets are financed, i.e. SHARE capital, COMPANY RESERVES and LOAN CAPITAL. ◊ NET WORTH.

Balanced budget. The central government BUDGET is in balance when current receipts are equal to current expenditure. Broadly, that is to say, taxes on INCOME and expenditure, etc., are sufficient to meet payments for goods and services, interest on the NATIONAL

DEBT, etc. In practice, the U.K. budget has generally been in deficit since the end of the Second World War; during the inter-war period the balancing of the central government budget was deemed a sign of good 'housekeeping'. KEYNES, however, showed how the budget surpluses and deficits could be used to regulate the economy. It should be remembered that a balanced budget does not necessarily have a neutral effect on the economy. For instance, if the government raised taxes on the rich to give assistance to the poor, the budget would have a MULTIPLIER effect and generate additional incomes overall. This is because the propensity to save of the rich is higher than that of the poor (▷ AVERAGE PROPENSITY TO SAVE).

Balancing allowance. ▷ CAPITAL ALLOWANCES.

Bancor. The term J. M. KEYNES applied to the CURRENCY which he proposed a new central international bank should create and put into circulation for the payment of DEBTS between countries. ▷ KEYNES PLAN. His proposal was rejected at the 1944 BRETTON WOODS Conference, which established the INTERNATIONAL MONETARY FUND. However, the beginning of 1970 saw the introduction of a similar international currency in the allocation of SPECIAL DRAWING RIGHTS through the I.M.F.

Bank advances. ▷ BANK LOAN.

Bank bill. ▷ BILL OF EXCHANGE.

Bank, clearing. ▷ CLEARING BANKS.

Bank clearings. ▷ CLEARING HOUSE.

Bank, commercial. ▷ COMMERCIAL BANK.

Bank credit. ▷ CREDIT.

Bank deposits. The amount of money standing to the CREDIT of a customer of a bank. Bank deposits are ASSETS of its customers and LIABILITIES of the bank. Deposits may arise from the payments of CASH or a CHEQUE to a bank for credit to a customer, or by transfer into an account from another account, including a LOAN from a bank to its customer. Bank deposits are simply I.O.U.s written in the books of the bank. They do not necessarily reflect actual holdings of cash by the bank. Since bank deposits are used in the settlement of debts, they are MONEY in the economic sense, so that by creating deposits banks create money (▷ BANKING). A deposit may be on CURRENT ACCOUNT or DEPOSIT ACCOUNT. These two types of account are known as DEMAND DEPOSITS and TIME DEPOSITS in the U.S. Bankers' deposits are deposits by a COMMERCIAL BANK at the CENTRAL BANK.

Bank for International Settlements (B.I.S.). An institution, with head

29

offices in Basle, set up on the basis of a proposal by the Young Committee in 1930. The original purpose was to enable the various national CENTRAL BANKS to coordinate through their own central bank the receipts and payments arising mainly from German war reparations. It was hoped, however, that it would develop beyond this, but many of the functions which it might have performed were, in fact, taken over by the INTERNATIONAL MONETARY FUND after the Second World War. Since then, the B.I.S. has acted like a bank for the central banks by accepting deposits and making short-term loans. It has, however, in recent years played a more active part in attempting to mitigate the effects of international financial SPECULATION. In 1968, for instance, the level of funds passing through the B.I.S. increased by nearly 50 per cent. In addition, the bank has carried out financial transactions for the ORGANIZATION FOR EUROPEAN ECONOMIC COOPERATION, ORGANIZATION FOR ECONOMIC COOPERATION AND DEVELOPMENT, EUROPEAN PAYMENTS UNION, EUROPEAN MONETARY AGREEMENT, EURO-PEAN COAL AND STEEL COMMUNITY and the I.M.F. Although the major functions of a central bank for central banks are performed by the I.M.F., the monthly meetings of the directors of the B.I.S. held in Basle have been a useful means of central-bank cooperation, especially in the field of off-setting short-term monetary movements of a speculative kind. The board is made up of the representatives of the central banks of the U.K., France, West Germany, Belgium, Italy, Switzerland, Netherlands and Sweden. Other countries' representatives, e.g. from the U.S., Canada, Japan, however, attend meetings regularly. ⟨⟩ BRUSSELS CONFERENCE.

Bank, industrial. ⟨⟩ INDUSTRIAL BANK.

Bank loan. A LOAN by a bank, normally for a fixed period of two to three years or more for a specific purpose, usually to a commercial concern. In England, unlike Continental Europe, the COMMERCIAL BANKS have not regarded it as their function to make long-term loans to industry, especially until recent years. Loosely, the phrase bank loan is also used to include OVERDRAFTS and PERSONAL LOANS. In this broader sense, bank loans are more commonly known as *bank advances*. ⟨⟩ TERM LOAN.

Bank-note. A note issued by a bank undertaking to pay the bearer the FACE VALUE of the note on demand. Bank-notes in England had their origin in the receipts issued by London goldsmiths in the seventeenth century for gold deposited with them for safekeeping. The whole practice of BANKING has its origin in the activities of these goldsmiths, who began lending money and whose deposit receipts came to be used as money. Later the goldsmiths issued bank-notes, and so did the banks that developed later still. Today only the BANK OF ENGLAND and the Scottish and Irish Banks in the U.K. are allowed to issue bank-notes. Since 1931, when bank-notes became inconvertible to gold, the promise on a bank-note to 'pay the bearer on demand' has simply been an undertaking that the note is legal tender. Thus, the Currency and Bank Notes Act of 1954, which regulates the issue of bank-notes in Britain, refers to the FIDUCIARY ISSUE. Only four denominations of notes are now issued to the general public, the largest being the £20 note. Most other developed countries issue notes of much larger denominations than this, probably because the use of CHEQUES is less developed elsewhere than in Britain. ⟫ BANKING AND CURRENCY SCHOOLS.

Bank of England. The CENTRAL BANK of U.K. Set up in 1694 as a JOINT STOCK COMPANY by Act of Parliament, the bank was a private company formed by a group of London merchants to lend MONEY to the state and deal with the NATIONAL DEBT. The Bank of England Act of 1946 brought the bank into public ownership. The Bank of England is the government's banker and is also the principal organ for implementing the state's financial and monetary policies (⟫ BANKING). It is managed by a governor, a deputy governor and a court (board) of sixteen directors (four full-time executive directors) appointed by the Crown for periods of five and four years. The bank is obliged by law to accept directives from the TREASURY, although the governor has a statutory right to be consulted. In its turn, the bank has wide statutory powers to direct the general affairs of the COMMERCIAL BANKS. Under the Bank Charter Act of 1844 (⟫ BANKING AND CURRENCY SCHOOLS), the Bank of England is divided into an issue department and a banking department. The issue department is responsible for the issue of BANK-NOTES and coins, which it buys from the ROYAL MINT, against its holdings of government SECURITIES and a relatively small amount of gold, coin and other securities. The banking department's liabilities consist of: bankers' DEPOSITS, i.e. deposits of the commercial banks, including SPECIAL DEPOSITS; deposits of government departments, including the EXCHEQUER, which receives the proceeds of TAXATION; the Post Office Savings Bank (⟫SAVINGS BANKS), etc.; and the bank's own CAPITAL, held by the Treasury since nationalization. The Bank of England also holds deposits from a small number of private customers. The principal assets of the banking department are government securities, discounts and advances, notes and coin. The ASSETS and LIABILITIES of the Bank of England are set out in the bank return issued every Wednesday. The bank also publishes an annual report and a quarterly bulletin. Besides its management of the national debt and the other activities mentioned above, the bank manages the EX-CHANGE EQUALIZATION ACCOUNT and conducts transactions between Britain and the rest of the world, including other central banks and international financial institutions such as the INTER-NATIONAL MONETARY FUND. ⟡ BANK RATE; CREDIT CONTROL; SECURITIES MANAGEMENT TRUST.

Bank overdraft. ⟡ OVERDRAFT.

Bank rate. The RATE OF INTEREST at which the CENTRAL BANK will lend to the banking system; which, in practice, means the rate at which it will rediscount 'ELIGIBLE PAPER' presented by the DISCOUNT HOUSES, or make LOANS to them (⟡ LENDER OF LAST RESORT). Short-term interest rates are geared to the bank rate through the banking system. Movements in bank rate, which are normally announced on Thursdays, are intended to have the following two types of effect.

The first effect is that upon the level of short-term interest rates in the MONEY MARKET and hence, through the related effects, on long-term rates and so upon the level of economic activity. It is in assessing the strength of these effects that there is some controversy among economists, even where the BANK OF ENGLAND succeeds in making bank rate effective by open-market operations (⟡ BANKING). If the CAPITAL MARKET thinks that a new, high bank rate is likely to last for some time, long-term rates will also move up and in this way businessmen will be discouraged from investment by the high rate of interest. They will also be deterred from holding stocks of raw materials and finished and semi-finished goods. Through the effect of the MULTIPLIER, this will tend to depress economic activity. This effect depends, however, primarily on expectations about the duration of the new, higher interest-rate level, on how important a consideration interest rates are in investment decisions, and on the level of economic activity generally – hence the controversy about the effectiveness of bank rate as such. The current consensus of opinion places more emphasis on the money supply than on interest rates as instruments of economic policy. ⟡ QUANTITY THEORY OF MONEY.

The second effect of bank rate is upon international capital movements. In recent years, changes in bank rate have mainly been motivated by BALANCE OF PAYMENTS considerations. If interest rates in London, as a result of an increase in bank rate, become higher than in other financial centres, money will be attracted for investment. In some instances the level of domestic activity and balance of payments considerations will present conflicting objectives to the monetary authorities, in so far as the level of interest rates are concerned. In recent years, this dilemma has presented itself to the U.S. monetary authorities, who were confronted on the one hand with unemployment at home, which required lower interest rates; and on the other hand with a balance of payments deficit, which required higher interest rates. In Britain, the bank rate has been raised and lowered frequently in the interests of both domestic and overseas payments: at the time of devaluation in 1967 it was raised to 8 per cent although from 1932 onwards it was kept down to 2 per cent to stimulate economic activity after the GREAT DEPRESSION. ⇨ CHEAP MONEY.

Banker's draft. A CHEQUE drawn by a bank as opposed to a bank's customer. Banker's drafts are drawn at the request of a customer, and that customer's account is debited when it is drawn. They are regarded as CASH since they cannot be returned unpaid and are used when a creditor is not willing to accept a personal cheque in payment.

Banking. The business of accepting DEPOSITS and lending MONEY. Banking defined in this way, however, is carried out by some other FINANCIAL INTERMEDIARIES that perform the functions of safeguarding deposits and making LOANS. BUILDING SOCIETIES and FINANCE HOUSES, for example, are not normally referred to as banks and are not regarded as being part of the banking system in the narrow, traditional sense. The banking system is normally understood to include the COMMERCIAL BANKS (joint stock banks), the CENTRAL BANK, the MERCHANT BANKS or ACCEPTING HOUSES and the DISCOUNT HOUSES (which are not banks as such), but to exclude the SAVINGS BANKS and INVESTMENT BANKS. The key to this confusing distinction between *banking* and *the banking system* is that the latter is the principal mechanism through which the money supply of the country is created and controlled. The deposits of some types of bank, e.g. the Post Office Savings Bank, cannot be used in the settlement of debts until they are withdrawn, but a deposit in a commercial bank can be used to settle debts by the use of

CHEQUES or transfers. When the manager of a branch of one of the joint stock banks opens an OVERDRAFT account for a customer, the loan creates a deposit; that is to say, a book debt has been incurred to the customer in return for a promise to repay it. Whether or not the overdraft is secured by COLLATERAL SECURITY, such as an INSURANCE policy, or some other ASSET, the bank has added to the total MONEY SUPPLY. In BALANCE SHEET terms, the deposit is a claim on the bank – that is a LIABILITY – while the customer's promise to repay it or the collateral security is an asset to the bank. The limitation on the bank's ability to create deposits is their obligation, if they are to remain in business, to pay out CURRENT ACCOUNT deposits in cash on demand. Since the bank's customers meet most of their needs for money by writing cheques on their deposits, the cash holdings the banks need are only a small fraction of their total deposits. This ratio between their deposit liabilities and cash holdings is called the CASH RATIO. By convention, in Britain, the cash ratio is 8 per cent. Banks also hold LIQUID assets (BILLS OF EXCHANGE, loans at call and other loans to the money market) of a further 20 per cent of their total deposits, the cash and liquid asset ratios together being called the LIQUIDITY RATIO. In many countries the minimum banking reserve ratios are fixed by law, but in Britain these ratios are fixed by convention growing out of experience. This gives advantages in flexibility in that the banking system does not set in a violent squeeze on LIQUIDITY when, for example, public requirements of CASH rise sharply and temporarily at weekends. The object of the banker is, of course to keep his reserves as near as possible to the minimum, since no return at all is earned on holdings of cash and a very low return in the money market. The banking system is based on confidence in the system's ability to meet its obligations. In the short run, no bank is able to meet all its obligations in cash, and if demands upon it exhausted its cash reserves, the bank would be obliged to close its doors. Runs on banks have not occurred in a developed country since the U.S. bank failures in the 1930s, but in 1967 the Intra-bank in the Lebanon was closed as the result of a 'run'.

Banking systems in the advanced countries, and especially in Britain, have now developed and concentrated to the point where bank failure, or the necessity to control new entrants to the banking system, no longer present any problems. Indeed, many people argue that the banks are insufficiently competitive. Banking in these countries has also developed by acquisition or internal growth to include many other services, e.g. credit cards (⟡ CREDIT ACCOUNT), HIRE PURCHASE, merchant banking, which were previously the sole province of more specialized institutions.

The supply of money is a basic tool of economic policy, and a government exerts control over the creation of credit by the banking system through its finance ministry. In Britain this function is performed by the TREASURY, and the BANK OF ENGLAND. Deposits at the central bank are regarded by the commercial banks as cash, and in Britain about half of the 8 per cent cash ratio is, in fact, held in this form. By buying and selling securities in the open market (open-market operations), the central bank can directly affect the level of the commercial banks' deposits with it, and hence, through the mechanism of the cash ratio, the money supply. An important element in public confidence in the banking system is that the central bank invariably acts as a 'LENDER OF LAST RESORT'. By its willingness to lend, the central bank ensures that, in times of temporary tightness in the availability of cash, the commercial banks are not forced to call in loans from the money market on a large scale, and thus perhaps to create a crisis. In Britain, the Bank of England does not, by convention, lend to a commercial bank but to the discount houses, so that the BANK RATE is, in practice, the RATE OF INTEREST at which the Bank of England will discount first-class securities. In varying the bank or discount rate, the central bank has another important weapon with which to influence the money supply. An increase in this rate forces the discount houses to raise the rates at which they are willing to do business, since, if they did not do so and were forced to go to the bank to discount bills, they would incur heavy losses should a large differential occur between their rates and the bank rate. For similar reasons, the commercial banks will also raise their lending and deposit rates. Thus, an increase in bank rate applies upward pressure to the whole structure of interest rates, and in doing so tends to check an increase in the money supply although the extent to which it would do so without the back-up of other measures, such as open-market operations, is a matter of controversy among economists. The effect of changes in the money supply on the price level and on output is also a matter of controversy (⟡ QUANTITY THEORY OF MONEY). The Bank of England's control over the banking system is increased by its legal powers over the commercial banks' operations, by the system of SPECIAL DEPOSITS and, since September 1971, by the new system of CREDIT CONTROL. ⟫ BANK-NOTE (for the origin of banking); CREDIT SQUEEZE.

Banking and Currency Schools. The representatives of the two sides of opinion in a controversy which centred on Sir Robert Peel's Bank Charter Act of 1844. This Act effectively limited the creation of BANK-NOTES to the BANK OF ENGLAND and regulated their issue. The *Banking School* argued that, given that bank-notes were convertible into gold, there was no need to regulate the note issue because the fact of convertibility would prevent any serious over-issue. Moreover, it was pointless to try to regulate the issue of bank-notes because the demand for currency would be met by an expansion of BANK DEPOSITS, which would have the same effect as an expansion of the note issue. The *Currency School*, on the other hand, argued that the check offered by convertibility would not operate in time to prevent serious commercial disruption. Bank-notes should be regarded as though they were the gold specie they in fact represented, and consequently the quantity at issue should fluctuate in sympathy with the BALANCE OF PAYMENTS. ⟫ BANKING; FIDUCIARY ISSUE; GOLD STANDARD.

Bankruptcy. A declaration by a court of law that an individual or company is insolvent, that is, cannot meet its DEBTS on the due dates (⟫ INSOLVENCY). A bankruptcy petition may be filed either by the debtor, or by his creditors requesting a receiving order. An inquiry into the debtors' affairs is then conducted by, in Britain, the official receiver, an official of the Department of Trade and Industry, who retains temporary control of the debtor's financial affairs. If he thinks fit, the receiver may call a meeting of the debtor's creditors, and if they wish it, declare the debtor bankrupt. The debtor's assets are then realized and distributed among his creditors. In the case of a company it goes into LIQUIDATION. Until he is discharged, i.e. has paid off his debts and has been declared a discharged bankrupt in law, a bankrupt may not incur CREDIT in excess of £10 without making it known that he is an undischarged bankrupt, nor may he serve as a director in a limited company without permission from the court.

Banks, joint stock. ⟫ COMMERCIAL BANKS.

Bargaining theory of wages. A theory of the determination of wages which sees them as the outcome of a bargaining process between representatives of management and LABOUR. It places primary emphasis on the analysis of the bargaining process, rather than on the general analysis of SUPPLY and DEMAND for labour. Nevertheless, these two approaches are not incompatible, since we can regard demand/supply conditions as establishing the general context within which bargaining takes place, and the bargaining process itself as being the means by which the EQUILIBRIUM is attained. ◊ COST-PUSH INFLATION.

Barriers to entry. Features of technological or economic conditions of a MARKET which raise the costs of firms wanting to enter the market above those of firms already in the market, or otherwise make new entry difficult. For example, a high degree of product DIFFERENTIATION creates a barrier to entry since a new entrant might have to spend a very great deal on advertising and sales promotion in order to overcome the brand loyalty of consumers to existing brands. Similarly, the existence of marked ECONOMIES OF SCALE in the industry may require the new firm to enter at a very large scale of output, if it is not to suffer a cost disadvantage. But the need to capture a large part of the market may cause a fall in PRICES and PROFITS, and make the entry unprofitable. We would expect the nature of barriers to entry of an industry to be an important determinant of the profits earned in the industry. Hence, with very low barriers, we would expect profits in the long run to approach normal profits. On the other hand, high entry barriers will strengthen MONOPOLY power and may permit high profits to be made. Other important sources of entry barriers are patents, EXCLUSIVE DEALING contracts with suppliers or distributors, and VERTICAL INTEGRATION. On the other hand, entry barriers will be less effective when there is rapid expansion in demand, or technological change.

Barter. Direct exchange of goods and SERVICES without use of MONEY. Thus, if you have a particular quantity of some good, and require some quantity of another good, in a barter system, you either find someone with matching requirements (who wants what you have or has what you want), or make one or more intermediate transactions to obtain the good required by the person who possesses the good you want. Such a system is obviously cumbersome, particularly in an economy where specialization (◊ DIVISION OF LABOUR) is carried quite far, since specialization increases the need for an EXCHANGE ECONOMY to enable satisfaction of the whole range of requirements. Some form of money, in terms of which the VALUE of each good is expressed, and which can be exchanged for any COMMODITY therefore becomes essential to any highly developed economy.

Base period. The time period used as the base from which to calculate an INDEX NUMBER, or a growth rate. Thus, currently, the *Index of Industrial Production* is calculated with 1963 as its base year: industrial output in each year is expressed as a percentage of that in 1963; the growth rates of NATIONAL INCOME of the Western industrial economies could be compared on the basis of the annual average rate of growth between 1950 and 1970, in which case 1950 is the base period for the comparison. The main consideration in choosing a base period for any particular measurement is that it should be a fairly typical or normal period in respect of the forces which influence the numbers under consideration. If the base-period value is unusually low, subsequent growth rates will be exaggerated, and the converse will be true for an unusually high base-date value.

Basic rate, base rate. The RATE OF INTEREST which forms the basis for the charges for OVERDRAFTS or deposit rates of the COMMERCIAL BANKS. ⇨ CREDIT CONTROL.

Basing-point pricing system. A form of price system used in industries characterized by: (a) a relatively small number of sellers; (b) marked differences in location between buyers and sellers; (c) a product which has high weight and bulk relative to its VALUE, so that transport costs constitute an important proportion of the final price; (d) high capital intensity (⇨ CAPITAL-INTENSIVE); and (e) a tendency for marked cyclical and regional fluctuations in DEMAND. Perfect examples of industries with these characteristics are cement and iron and steel, both of which in the U.S. and the U.K. use or have used a basing-point pricing system. The system works in the following way: some number (varying from one to all) of the plants in an industry are designated 'bases', and a base PRICE is set, which is price 'at the factory gate', so to speak. A standard system of freight charges is then laid down, which may vary with distance from the base, e.g. £1 per ton-mile for deliveries within a five-mile radius, 87½p per ton-mile for deliveries of between five and ten miles, 75p per ton-mile for deliveries of between ten and fifteen miles, etc. All base prices, and the standard freight charges, are known to each seller. Given a buyer at any location, each seller calculates the price he quotes as the base price at the base nearest to the buyer, plus standard freight charges from that base to the buyer. Prices are always delivered prices, i.e. the buyer always pays delivery charges as part of the price and does not effectively have the option of arranging his own transport and paying the price exclusive of transport costs. The inevitable result of the system is that all sellers will quote identical delivered prices to a buyer at any given location.

A major advantage of the system to the firms using it is that it ensures that prices will be uniform in an uncertain and unstable environment, and it thus restricts both deliberate and accidental price competition. This may be particularly important in an industry with high OVER-HEADS and prone to the development of EXCESS CAPACITY from time to time. It also permits firms to obtain business in areas outside their main MARKET areas, without having to reduce prices within their main market areas, which implies in effect PRICE DISCRIMINA-TION as between nearer and more remote customers. To see this, suppose that a firm is forty miles further away from a customer than the base nearest the customer. Freight charges included in the delivered price are calculated from the base to the customer, and so the firm's actual transport costs are likely to be much higher. In effect, therefore, the firm is reducing its price to the new customers. This ability to gain new business, while not losing profits on business the firm can be more sure of, has been considered by some economists to be the major attraction of the system.

Basle facility. ⟡ STERLING AREA.

Bear. A STOCK EXCHANGE speculator who sells STOCKS or SHARES that he may or may not possess because he expects a fall in prices and, therefore, that he will be able to buy them (back) later on at a PROFIT; the antonym of BULL. A bear who sells SECURITIES that he does not possess is described as having 'sold short'. If he does possess the securities he sells, he is described as a 'covered' or 'protected' bear.

Bearer bonds. BONDS, the legal ownership of which is vested in the holder, no TRANSFER DEED being required. An endorsed CHEQUE, or a cheque made payable to a bearer, or a BANK-NOTE are similar in nature to bearer SECURITIES. Bearer securities normally have dated interest COUPONS attached to them which can be presented to the issuer of the security for payment.

Bearer securities. ⟡ BEARER BONDS.

'Beeching Plan'. The report by the British Railways Board entitled *The Reshaping of British Railways* which, published in 1963, has become known as the 'Beeching Plan' after the Railways Board chairman Dr (now Lord) Beeching. The report set out proposals for the closure of unremunerative branch lines and stations in order to specialize in the services 'in which the railways' merits predominate and in which they can be competitive'. The report pointed out that only 1 per cent of the total passenger and ton-miles carried by British Railways was carried over one third of its route mileage, and over 95 per cent of their traffic used only half the number of stations. All closures are subject to public inquiry and the veto of the Secretary of State for the Environment. Under the 1968 Transport Act, the government will give grants to British Railways in order for them to continue to operate unprofitable passenger services which the government consider to be socially necessary. In addition, the board will receive financial assistance to bridge the gap before it can close down its other surplus facilities.

'Beggar-my-neighbour' policy. ◊ RECIPROCITY.

Behavioural assumption. An assumption, or hypothesis, about the way in which individual economic units – consumers, firms, suppliers of FACTORS OF PRODUCTION – behave, and most especially about their motives, and the way in which they respond to differences between expected and actual outcomes. Examples of such assumptions are the PROFIT-maximizing assumption in the theory of the firm (◊ FIRM, THEORY OF), the UTILITY maximization assumption in the theory of consumer demand, and the assumption that firms respond to unexpected INVENTORY accumulation by cutting back production in the macroeconomic theory of income determination (◊ MACROECONOMICS). ◊◊ BEHAVIOURAL THEORY OF THE FIRM.

Behavioural theory of the firm. A theory which attempts to improve upon the standard economic theory of the firm (◊ FIRM, THEORY OF) by taking account of the fact that many present-day firms are large, complex organizations, with hierarchical managerial BUREAU-CRACIES. The theory rejects the classical assumption that firms wish to maximize PROFIT, and indeed rejects the idea that firms wish to maximize anything. Rather, it sees the firm as being composed of a number of sub-groups – managers, workers, shareholders, customers, suppliers – each of which has its own set of goals, and these goals may well be in conflict with each other (higher wages mean higher PRICES, lower profits, etc). As a result, the actual goals adopted by the organization will represent a compromise which more or less resolves the conflict, and so cannot maximize any one thing. The theory also considers the processes by which these goals are revised over time, and, again unlike the traditional theory of the firm, makes uncertainty and the search for information important determinants of the firm's behaviour. Thus, the theory stresses the effects which the processes of decision-taking and the organization of the firm have on the decision it makes. The development of the theory owes a great deal to the insights provided by organization theorists, industrial psychologists and sociologists, and is associated primarily with the work of H. A. Simon, March and R. Cyert, and the Carnegie Institute of Technology in the U.S. Although it is accepted as being descriptively realistic, the theory has not replaced the traditional theory of the firm. Largely, this is because the behavioural theory is much more difficult to handle and has yet to show that it can yield predictions about MARKET behaviour and the overall pattern of RESOURCE allocation which are as accurate as the traditional theory. ⟡ INDUSTRIAL ORGANIZA-TION, ECONOMICS OF.

Below the line. ⟡ABOVE THE LINE.

Benefit-cost analysis. ⟡ COST-BENEFIT ANALYSIS.

Benelux. The CUSTOMS UNION between Belgium and Luxembourg on the one hand and the Netherlands on the other, agreed in principle before the end of the Second World War and set up in 1948. The union abolished internal TARIFFS and with some difficulty reduced import QUOTAS between the three countries, who adopted a common external tariff. The aim of the union, reiterated in a final treaty which was ratified in 1960, was the eventual merging of the fiscal and monetary systems of the member countries. There is free movement of LABOUR and CAPITAL within the union and a common policy with other countries. In 1958, Benelux joined the EUROPEAN ECONOMIC COMMUNITY.

Bentham, Jeremy (1748–1832). The leading philosopher of UTILITAR-IANISM. Self-interest was deemed the sole stimulus to human endeavour and the pursuit of happiness an individual's prime concern. The purpose of government should be to maximize the sum of the happiness of the greatest number of individuals.

Bernoulli, Daniel (1700–82). ⟡ BERNOULLI'S HYPOTHESIS.

Bernoulli's hypothesis. A hypothesis, first formulated by D. Bernoulli, that the decision of an individual on whether or not to accept a particular gamble depended on the UTILITY which he attached to the sums of MONEY involved, and not just the sums themselves. For example, consider the following gamble: we toss a coin; if it comes up heads, I pay you £10, if tails, you pay me £9. The PROBA-BILITY of getting a head is $\frac{1}{2}$, as is the probability of getting a tail. Hence, the 'expected value' to you of the gamble is given by: $\frac{1}{2}(£10) - \frac{1}{2}(£9) = £0.50$. This has the interpretation that if we played this game a large number of times, on average you would end up winning £0.50 per game. Hence, we would expect you to accept the gamble, and, indeed, be prepared to pay anything up to £0.50 per game for the right to be allowed to play. However, Bernoulli observed several paradoxes which arose from this view, and it appeared to be refuted by experience – people did reject gambles whose expected values were positive. This could be rationalized in the following way. Suppose the MARGINAL UTILITY of INCOME is diminishing, so that it is quite possible that the gain in utility from winning £10 is smaller than the loss in utility from losing £9. For example, suppose we could measure these utilities as a gain of 4 units and a loss of 5 units respectively. Then, in deciding whether or not to accept the gamble, our individual would find that the utility he can expect to get from the gamble is negative, i.e. that $\frac{1}{2}$ (4) – $\frac{1}{2}$ (5) $= -\frac{1}{2}$, and hence he would reject the gamble.

This emphasis on utility values rather than the absolute money values now plays an extremely important role in the economic theory of RISK and UNCERTAINTY, and the Bernoulli hypothesis has turned out to be of fundamental importance.

Beveridge, William Henry (Lord Beveridge) (1879–1963). Director of the London School of Economics from 1919 to 1937, Lord Beveridge's work in economics arose from a continuous interest through his life in the problem of UNEMPLOYMENT. His major contribution to the subject was published in *Unemployment* (1931). He was a major influence in the setting up of labour exchanges, and his 1942 report, *Social Insurance and Allied Services*, which became known as the BEVERIDGE REPORT, led to the extension of the welfare services. His definition of full employment, which he gave in *Full Employment in a Free Society* (1944) as being reached at a level of 3 per cent unemployed, became a reference point for subsequent government policy. ⟡ DECASUALIZATION; F. W. PAISH; J. C. L. S. DE SISMONDI).

Beveridge report. Lord BEVERIDGE (then Sir William Beveridge) prepared a report in 1942 at the request of the government on *Social Insurance and Allied Services*, which was based on three aspects of a plan for social security. These were: (a) a system of children's allowances; (b) a comprehensive health service; and (c) full EMPLOYMENT. His report to the government covered the first two of these aspects. On the basis of contributions from income, he proposed a system of social security to yield higher unemployment benefits, children's allowances, medical attention and pensions in order to prevent any individual's INCOME from falling below subsistence level. The Beveridge Report was the basis for the Family Allowances Act of 1945 and the National Health Service and National Insurance Acts of 1946. In 1944, Lord Beveridge published on his own initiative *Full Employment in a Free Society*, which he described as an attempt to cover the third aspect of his 1942 report, that of full employment.

'Big 5'. The five largest COMMERCIAL BANKS in Britain – Midland, Barclays, Lloyds, Westminster and National Provincial, now, following the MERGER of the last two, known as the *Big 4*.

Bilateral flow. An expression referring to a flow of funds from the government to the PRIVATE SECTOR of the economy in exchange for goods or SERVICES; as opposed to a unilateral flow, such as pension payments or TAXES, in which there is no corresponding flow of goods or services in exchange.

Bilateralism. The agreement between two countries to extend to each other specific privileges in their INTERNATIONAL TRADE which are not extended to others. These privileges may, for instance, take the form of generous import QUOTAS or favourable import duties (◇ TARIFFS). In so far as such agreements tend to proliferate, and in that they impose artificial restraints on the free movements of goods between countries, in the long run they could have an unfavourable effect on INTERNATIONAL TRADE compared with MULTILATERALISM, under which there is no discrimination by origin or destination. Bilateralism became widespread in the inter-war period as countries tried to protect themselves from the fall in international trade during the depression. In 1932, the U.K. signed a series of bilateral agreements with other Commonwealth countries in Ottawa (◇ COMMONWEALTH PREFERENCE). After the Second World War, there was a fear that a restrictionist policy would be followed by the Commonwealth and Western European countries in order to protect themselves from the influence of the U.S., which had emerged from the war in a relatively strong position. However, the GENERAL AGREEMENT ON TARIFFS AND TRADE was established in 1947 on multilateral principles, and has since been pursuing a policy designed to eliminate bilateralism and other restrictions on international trade. The Communist countries of the U.S.S.R. and Eastern Europe conduct their international trade predominantly in terms of bilateral agreements in which quotas are set on both sides. Exchange agreements of this kind enable these countries to set their international trade requirements into their national plan objectives (◇ PLANNED ECONOMY).

Bill broker. A firm or individual that deals in TREASURY BILLS and

BILLS OF EXCHANGE on the London MONEY MARKET. Normally a bill broker is a DISCOUNT HOUSE. ⟡ BROKER.

Bill of exchange. An I.O.U. used in INTERNATIONAL TRADE by which the drawer makes an unconditional undertaking to pay to the drawee a sum of MONEY at a given date, usually three months ahead. In principle, a bill of exchange is similar to a post-dated CHEQUE, and like a cheque it can be endorsed for payment to the bearer or any named person other than the drawee. A bill of exchange has to be 'accepted' (endorsed) by the drawee before it becomes negotiable. This function is normally performed by an ACCEPTANCE HOUSE, but bills may also be accepted by a bank (it is then known as a *bank bill*) or by a trader (*trade bill*). Once accepted, the drawee does not have to wait for the bill to mature before getting his money; he can sell it on the MONEY MARKET for a small discount (⟡ DISCOUNT HOUSE; ELIGIBLE PAPER). Bills of exchange, also referred to as *commercial bills*, were first developed in inland trade by merchants who wished to resell goods before making payment for them (⟡ INLAND BILL OF EXCHANGE). They later became of great importance in international trade, but with the development of other means of CREDIT, their use has tended to decline although there has been a resurgence in the use of domestic or inland bills and the total value of bills outstanding in the money market is still around £700 million at any one time. In the U.S. bills of exchange are called *notes*.

Bill of lading. A document giving details of goods shipped, the ship on which the goods are consigned and the names of the consignor and consignee. Bills of lading are normally sent ahead of the ship and give proof of title to the consignor. Copies of the documents are held on the ship and by the exporter.

Bill of sale. A document that gives evidence of transfer of ownership but not of possession of goods. It is not often used nowadays, but was once a common method of raising a LOAN on the security of personal possessions, the borrower retaining possession of goods until the DEBT is repaid. ⟡ MORTGAGE.

Birth rate. The crude birth rate is the average number of live births occurring in a year for every 1,000 population. The birth rate of the U.K. fell steadily from about thirty-five per 1,000 population in the 1870s to about twenty in the 1920s. It fell dramatically to about sixteen in the 1930s and rose equally dramatically in 1947 to nearly twenty-one. After falling back from this exceptionally high figure, it was on an upward trend from the early 1950s until the mid 1960s, since which time it has fallen. It is still uncertain whether this drop reflects a permanent change in attitudes to family size. Other statistical measurements which are computed for the study of population trends include: (a) the *fertility rate,* which measures the average number of live births per 1,000 for all women between the ages of fifteen and forty-four, a statistic which has in fact exhibited similar trends in the U.K. as the crude birth rate (it reached a level of 84·3 in 1970); and (b) the rate specific for age of mother in which the number of live births per 1,000 is given for different age groups of mother. There has been growing anxiety of the social and economic consequences of the rapidly expanding size of the world population. At the present rate of growth, the current world population of 3,300 million people will be doubled in less than forty years. A major factor in this growth has been the extension of life expectancy achieved by modern medicine, but high birth rates have also played an important part. Measures of family control are being taken, particularly in critical DEVELOPING COUNTRIES such as India, in order to try to achieve a growth in population more in line with available economic and social resources (◇ T. R. MALTHUS).

Blue book. The informal name for the annual publication, *National Income and Expenditure* which presents the U.K.'s national accounts statistics. The Blue Book, which is prepared by the Central Statistical Office, appears in the late summer each year and shows estimates of the main aggregates of the national accounts for the previous year and a run of ten years before that. In addition to the summary tables of INCOME, output and expenditure that break down the NATIONAL INCOME and national product estimates, more detailed statistics are given for the public, personal and company sectors of the economy. Useful information is also given which is not strictly part of the system of social accounts (◇ SOCIAL ACCOUNTING), such as the distribution of personal income before and after TAX and trading profits by industry. Quarterly and more recent estimates of the main components of national income and expenditure are published in the *Monthly Digest of Statistics* and elsewhere. The Central Statistical Office also prepares the National Income and Balance of Payments White Paper giving preliminary estimates of the main components of the national income as well as the BALANCE OF PAYMENTS accounts each year immediately before the BUDGET.

Blue chip. A first-class EQUITY share, the purchase of which hopefully entails little RISK, even of sharp declines in EARNINGS, in economic recessions (◇ DEPRESSION). The term is, of course, applied as a matter of subjective judgement. In the U.K., I.C.I., Unilever and Shell equities, for example, are commonly regarded as blue chip.

Böhm-Bawerk, Eugen von (1851–1914). A member of the AUSTRIAN SCHOOL, who took over the Chair of Economics at Vienna from VON WIESER. His analyses of the rate of INTEREST and CAPITAL have had an important influence on the development of these aspects of economic theory. His major publications include *Capital and Interest* (1884) and the *Positive Theory of Capital* (1889). The nature of the rate of interest could be found, he argued, in the three propositions: (a) that people expect to be better off in the future; (b) that people put a lower valuation on future goods than on present goods – 'jam today is better than jam tomorrow' – these two 'psychological' factors making people willing to pay to borrow against their future income to spend on consumption goods now (⟡ TIME PREFERENCE); and (c) the technical proposition that goods in existence today are technically superior to goods coming into existence at some future date because today's goods could be capable of producing more goods during the interval. (⟡ INTEREST, PRODUCTIVITY THEORIES OF; I. FISHER). Capital is associated with roundabout methods of production. In order to reap a harvest, you could send workers into the fields to pluck the ears of corn. A more efficient method is to spend capital on making scythes and then use these to cut the corn. An even more efficient method is to spend even more capital manufacturing reaping machinery and use this to harvest your corn. Progress is achieved through the use of LABOUR in more roundabout methods of production; a widening of the gap between INPUTS and outputs (⟡ INPUT-OUTPUT ANALYSIS). Capital supplies the necessary subsistence to labour during the 'waiting time' before new consumer goods are produced (⟡ WAGE FUND THEORY). This waiting time is extended to yield increased productivity until, in equilibrium, productivity is equated with the RATE OF INTEREST. This theory was later developed into a theory of the TRADE CYCLE by members of the Austrian School (⟡ K. WICKSELL; L. VON MISES; F. A. VON HAYEK).

Bolton Committee. A committee of inquiry set up by the President of the (then) Board of Trade in 1968 under the chairmanship of John Bolton to report on the role of small firms in the British economy. The committee reported in November 1971 that there were one and a quarter million small firms in the U.K. economy contributing some 24 per cent of the net output of the private sector, or 19 per cent of the GROSS NATIONAL PRODUCT. The small-firm sector was in secular decline, both in number and in its share of economic activity. Quite apart from the social and political value of small firms, thd committee distinguished a number of important economic functions performed by them (while recognizing their organic role and the difficulty of distinguishing single functions). Two of these functions – 'as a breeding ground of new industries and the source of dynamic competition' – were regarded as of crucial importance, and it could not be assumed that the ordinary working of market forces would necessarily preserve a small-firm sector large enough to perform them. The report found that the small-firm sector in the U.K. was significantly smaller than in other advanced countries, but the committee judged that the decline 'has not yet reached a stage at which deliberate discrimination in favour of small firms on the part of the government would be justified'. The committee recommended, and this was subsequently accepted by the government, that a small-firms division should be established in the Department of Trade and Industry to monitor the health of the small-firm sector. The committee made a number of recommendations for improving the availability of statistical information on small firms, including a census of ENTERPRISES and many other matters including TAXATION, industrial training, form filling, competition policy, disclosure (◊ PRIVATE COMPANY), industrial development and planning controls. The committee concluded that the MACMILLAN GAP had been filled, although it was 'important to remember that the role of (financial) . . . institutions, however adaptable and sensitive to market needs . . . is necessarily limited . . . (and) can never take the place of personal wealth and ploughed-back profits'. The causes of the decline in the small-firm sector were identified as increasing taxation, increased importance of MARKETING economics, the increasing role of the state, the emergence of the giant corporation, improved transport and communication and other technological factors.

Bond. 1. A form of fixed-interest SECURITY mainly issued by central or local governments, e.g. DEFENCE BONDS. Bonds are usually a form of long-term security, but they may be irredeemable and may be secured or unsecured. ◊ PREMIUM SAVINGS BONDS. In the U.S. the term bond includes DEBENTURES. **2.** A term also used to describe goods in a warehouse on which customs duty (◊ TARIFFS) has not yet been paid.

Bonus issue, or rights issue, scrip issue, capitalization issue (U.S. stock dividend, stock split). Virtually synonymous terms describing

SHARES given without charge to existing shareholders in proportion to the shares already owned. A *scrip issue* does not add to the CAPITAL EMPLOYED by the firm, but is made where the capital employed has been increased by withholding profits, and is, therefore, out of line with the ISSUED CAPITAL. Consequently, it is a purely bookkeeping transaction. DIVIDENDS, for example, will, after a scrip issue, be divided among a larger number of shares, so that the dividend per share will fall in proportion to the number of bonus shares issued. ⬦ NEW ISSUE MARKET.

Book value. The value of ASSETS in the BALANCE SHEET of a firm. This is often the purchase price, and may be less than the market value.

Bowley, Sir Arthur Lyon (1869–1957). A statistician and mathematical economist, who became Professor of Mathematics and Economics at University College, Reading (1907–13), Professor of Statistics at the University of London (1919–36) and Director of the University of Oxford Institute of Statistics (1940–4). His economic textbook *Mathematical Groundwork for Economists*, was published in 1924, but his major contributions were in the field of NATIONAL INCOME accounting and wages and INCOME. ⬦ *Three Studies on the National Income* (with J. Stamp) (1938) and *Wages and Income in the U.K. since 1860* (1937).

Branch banking. A BANKING system, most highly developed in the U.K., where the small number of COMMERCIAL BANKS have a large number of branches all over the country. Other developed countries, especially the U.S. have a much larger number of commercial banks with fewer branches. ⬦ FEDERAL RESERVE SYSTEM.

Brassage, mintage. A charge made by a mint for converting metals into coin. The Royal Mint no longer makes such a charge.

Bretton Woods. An international conference was held at Bretton Woods, New Hampshire, in the U.S. in July 1944 to discuss alternative proposals relating to post-war international payments problems put forward by the U.S., Canadian and U.K. governments. The agreement resulting from this conference led to the establishment of the INTERNATIONAL MONETARY FUND and the INTERNATIONAL BANK FOR RECONSTRUCTION AND DEVELOPMENT. ⬦ KEYNES PLAN.

British Export Board. An organization set up at the end of 1971 to take over the functions of the BRITISH NATIONAL EXPORT COUNCIL and the export promotional activities of the Department of Trade and Industry, later called the British Overseas Trade Board.

British National Export Council (B.N.E.C.). A council which took over in 1964 the coordination of the export promotional activities of the Western Hemisphere Exports Council (formerly the Dollar Exports Council), the Export Council for Europe, the Council for Middle East Trade and the Commonwealth Exports Council. Its membership consisted of representatives both from the relevant government departments and from industry. The council channelled Department of Trade and Industry aid to trade organizations such as chambers of commerce. This aid covered financial assistance for trade missions, overseas market research and the distribution of buyers' guides. The council's functions were taken over by the BRITISH EXPORT BOARD at the end of 1971, but continued in a limited form in 1972.

Broker. An intermediary between a buyer and a seller in a highly organized market, e.g. a STOCKBROKER, INSURANCE BROKER, or a market operator working on his own account, e.g. a PAWN-BROKER, BILL BROKER. On the STOCK EXCHANGE, a broker is the intermediary between a JOBBER and the public.

Brokerage. Commission charged by a BROKER. It is characteristic of the broking profession that they operate only in highly organized markets where margins are relatively small. A STOCKBROKER, for example, charges about 1 per cent on the price of the SHARES he buys and sells, although today he will usually also specify a minimum absolute COMMISSION since normal commission on dealing with a £50 parcel of shares would not cover his costs.

Brussels Conference (1920). An international conference at Brussels which with that at Genoa in 1922 obtained agreement that every country should have a CENTRAL BANK through which to control its financial affairs. This was a necessary preliminary to the establishment of the BANK FOR INTERNATIONAL SETTLEMENTS at Basle.

Buchanan report. A report published in 1963 entitled *Traffic in Towns*, prepared under the guidance of Sir Colin D. Buchanan, Professor of Transport at Imperial College, London. Professor Buchanan was given the following terms of reference by the Minister of Transport in 1960: 'to study the long-term development of roads and traffic in urban areas and their influence on the urban environment'. The rapid growth of expenditure on the purchase of motor-cars was outstripping the expenditure by local and central governments on the environment necessary to accommodate this traffic. Moreover, the vehicle population was expected to grow by a multiple of four by the end of the century. There was a need for transportation plans for large urban areas. These plans would incorporate forecasts of the growth of the demand for transport in the area and would indicate how this demand would be divided between the private and public sectors. The report suggested alternative ways of regulating the increase in traffic in order to bring it into line with the available facilities; for instance by (a) permits and licences; (b) pricing road space within a zone; (c) parking controls; and (d) subsidization of public transport. Professor Buchanan was also a dissenting member of the ROSKILL COMMISSION.

Budget. An estimate of INCOME and expenditure for a future period as opposed to an account which records financial transactions. Budgets are an essential element in the planning and control of the financial affairs of a nation or business, and are made necessary essentially because income and expenditure do not occur simultaneously.

In modern large-scale business, the annual budget, which is normally broken down into monthly and weekly periods, is a complex document that may take several months to prepare. The starting-point will be an estimate of sales and income for the period, balanced by budgets for purchasing, administration, production, distribution and research costs. There will also be detailed budgets of CASH FLOWS and CAPITAL expenditure. These are often also made for periods of further than one year ahead, so that borrowing requirements and capacity requirements can be assessed (▷ CAPITAL BUDGET-ING). A *flexible budget* is one based on different assumed levels of plant activity.

The national budget sets out estimates of government expenditure and revenue for the financial year, and is normally presented by the Chancellor of the EXCHEQUER to the British Parliament early in April. In his statement, the Chancellor reviews economic conditions and government expenditure for the past year, makes forecasts for the coming year and announces proposed changes in TAXA-TION. With the increasing importance of government expenditure in the economy, the annual budget is an important instrument in government economic policy. Fiscal changes have less to do with planned expenditure and more to do with decisions to modify the budget surplus (or more rarely deficit) in the interest of demand management (▷ BALANCED BUDGET). Economic conditions sometimes require interim budgets, although the government normally has sufficient discretionary powers to make the necessary changes in fiscal monetary policy. ▷▷ ABOVE THE LINE.

Budget deficit. ▷ BALANCED BUDGET.

Budget surplus. ⟡ BALANCED BUDGET.

Budgetary control. A system of budgetary control checks actual INCOME and expenditure against a BUDGET so that progress towards set objectives may be measured and remedial action taken if necessary. Budget control statements comparing actual and estimated expenditure are issued weekly or monthly. These statements will be issued in considerable detail to departmental heads, and in less detail to higher management. Budget control statements must, if any necessary remedial action is to be taken in time, be issued as soon as possible after the close of the period to which they relate, and for this reason need not be of the same accuracy as accounting statements and may be based partly on estimated data. The development of computerized accounting procedures has greatly facilitated budgetary control.

Building society. An institution that accepts DEPOSITS, upon which it pays INTEREST and makes LOANS for house purchase secured by MORTGAGES. Building societies, which are unique to Britain, grew out of the Friendly Society movement in the late seventeenth century and are non-PROFIT-making. Their activities are regulated by the Building Societies Act of 1874, which set up a Registrar of Building Societies. Subsequent Acts have tightened controls over the societies' financial management. The societies accept deposits which can be withdrawn on demand up to a limited amount or at one month's notice, or 'shares', which may be subject to a longer notice of withdrawal. Interest on building society deposits is paid by special concession net of ordinary INCOME TAX, the society paying the tax to the Inland Revenue. Traditionally, the societies' deposits are fed by regular small savings and the average holdings are under £1,000. Loans are made to persons wishing to purchase their homes, or more rarely to builders, and administrative costs are financed by the difference between the borrowing and lending rates. The loans are repaid on regular monthly instalments of CAPITAL and interest over a period of years, usually on a REDUCING BALANCE basis. Building societies' RATES OF INTEREST must bear a close relationship to rates charged or obtained elsewhere, since they compete with other institutions for funds, but their rates are relatively stable and are only altered when a sustained imbalance occurs between the rates at which deposits come in and loans are made. Investors in building societies may put their money into shares or into deposit. The former have no relation to EQUITY shares, but are simply a form of deposit for which slightly more restrictive withdrawal terms are rewarded by a higher interest rate. Special interest-rate incentives are provided for regular savers. Originally highly localized in their operations, the building societies, of which there are many hundreds in the U.K., are now extending their activities on a national basis and are expanding rapidly. ▷ ASSURANCE; FINANCIAL INTERMEDIARIES. For the U.S., ▷ HOUSING AND HOME FINANCE AGENCY.

Built-in stabilizers. Institutional features of the economy which, without explicit government intervention, automatically act to dampen down fluctuations in EMPLOYMENT, NATIONAL INCOME, etc. Examples of these are the fact that: (a) unemployment benefits, national assistance payments, etc., automatically increase in total when unemployment increases, and fall in total when unemployment falls, and thus this part of government expenditure adjusts automatically in the desired directions to offset in part changes in other components of AGGREGATE DEMAND; and (b) government taxation falls in total as national income falls, and rises as national income rises, both because the incidence of INCOME TAXES changes and because, with changes in CONSUMPTION expenditures, indirect taxation (▷ DIRECT TAXATION) also changes. Since an increase in taxation tends to restrain expenditure, while a fall in taxation stimulates it, we again have 'automatic' factors counteracting inflationary and deflationary pressures in the economy (▷ INFLATION; DEFLATION). The effectiveness of these built-in stabilizers must not be exaggerated, however. They rarely have sufficient force to render positive corrective policies unnecessary.

Bull. A STOCK EXCHANGE speculator who purchases STOCKS and SHARES in the belief that prices will rise and that he will be able to sell them again later at a profit (▷ SPECULATION); opposite of BEAR. The market is said to be *bullish* when it is generally anticipated that prices will rise.

Bullion. Gold, silver or other precious metal in bulk, i.e. in the form of ingots or bars rather than in coin. Gold bullion is used in international monetary transactions between CENTRAL BANKS and forms partial backing for many CURRENCIES (▷ GOLD STANDARD). A *bullion market* is a GOLD MARKET.

Bureaucracy. The phenomenon of large-scale administrative organization involving a rigid hierarchy of authority, the use of committees to coordinate and take decisions, the adoption of standard operating rules and procedures to classify problems and find solutions, and the emphasis on communication of information by written means.

The nature and growth of bureaucracy has been of considerable interest to sociologists, social psychologists, etc., because of its importance as a form of social organization, and because of the types of social behaviour which tend to develop. Economists have been less concerned with the study of bureaucracy as such, regarding it merely as an aspect of the problem of diseconomies of scale (⟡ DISECONOMY): as the scale of activities increases, so the administrative superstructure expands, presenting real difficulties of maintaining efficiency of operation. However, the pejorative connotations of the term in everyday speech – often being used as a synonym for inefficiency, unwieldiness, lack of humanity and inertia – are not part of the formal definition; rather, this is just a term for a particular form of organization. Moreover, bureaucracy is not regarded as unique to central and local government. It is the case that these organizations were the first to attain the sorts of size at which bureaucratic features become marked, but it is increasingly the case that industrial companies are, as a result of growth, encountering similar problems of large-scale organization and control. This is, in fact, becoming recognized in economics, and is largely responsible for the interest in organization theory and the development of the BEHAVIOURAL THEORY OF THE FIRM.

Business cycle. ⟡ TRADE CYCLE.

Business finance. The provision of MONEY for commercial use. The CAPITAL requirements of business may be divided into short and medium term, or long term. Short-term capital consists of the current LIABILITIES of a business plus medium-term capital. The main sources of short- and medium-term capital (for a company) can be further subdivided into internal and external:

Internal: RETAINED EARNINGS, including ACCRUED EXPENSES and tax reserves. ⟡ CASH FLOW; CORPORATION TAX; SELF-FINANCING.

External: Temporary LOANS from sister companies, directors and others; FACTORING; BILLS OF EXCHANGE; trade creditors and expense creditors; and short-term TRADE INVESTMENTS.

Short-term capital should, of course, only be used for investment in relatively liquid ASSETS (⟡ LIQUID) so that it is readily available to discharge the liability if necessary. Thus, these sources of short-term capital may be used for finished goods in stock and work in progress, trade debtors, pre-paid expenses, cash in hand and at the bank.

Correspondingly, the main sources of long-term liabilities or capital can be subdivided in the same way:
Internal: Reserves, retained earnings and DEPRECIATION provisions.
External: Share capital, i.e. ORDINARY SHARES, PREFERENCE SHARES, long-term loans including MORTGAGES, LEASE-BACK arrangements and DEBENTURES.
Long-term capital may be used for long-term investment in fixed assets – land, buildings, plant, equipment and machinery, etc.; in goodwill, patents and trademarks; and in long-term trade investments. The main institutional sources of business finance are the COMMERCIAL BANKS, the MERCHANT BANKS, the FINANCE HOUSES, the DISCOUNT HOUSES, factoring companies and the institutions concerned with new issues (⟡ NEW ISSUE MARKET). A number of other institutions specialize in providing TERM LOANS and RISK CAPITAL, and especially for innovation and smaller businesses, e.g. the NATIONAL RESEARCH DEVELOPMENT CORPORATION, INDUSTRIAL AND COMMERCIAL FINANCE CORPORATION, ESTATE DUTIES INVESTMENT TRUST and TECHNICAL DEVELOPMENT CAPITAL LTD.

Business saving. That part of the net revenue of a firm which is not paid out as interest, DIVIDENDS or TAXATION, but rather is kept in the business as reserves and DEPRECIATION allowances or to finance new INVESTMENT. Sometimes called *retentions*. ⟡ SELF-FINANCING.

Business Statistics Office (B.S.O.). A government department, administratively part of the Department of Trade and Industry (but responsible to the CENTRAL STATISTICAL OFFICE for policy), established in 1969. The B.S.O. will gradually become the focal point for the collection and publication of industrial statistics. The CENSUS OF PRODUCTION, *Business Monitor,* and the Census of Distribution are already the responsibility of the B.S.O., which is developing a new system of production statistics based on annual sample surveys.

Business taxation. ⟡ CORPORATION TAX.

Buyer's market. Essentially a MARKET in a situation of EXCESS SUPPLY, so that buyers are relatively scarce and able to obtain favourable terms.

By-product. Some material or product which is the outcome of a process designed primarily to produce another product. The opportunity COST of a by-product is virtually zero. There is, therefore, an incentive to find uses or markets for by-products, e.g. blast-furnace slag, which is sold for road building. If such a use cannot be found, it becomes a *waste product.*

C

Call. An unpaid portion of the price of a SHARE. This may arise when an applicant for a new share issue pays only part of the price of the share on application and the remainder on allotment or when the issued shares of a company are not fully paid up (⟡ PAID-UP CAPITAL).

Call option. A contract giving a right to buy SHARES from the dealer making the contract at the price ruling at the time during a specified future period, usually three months. Call options carry a COMMISSION to the dealer on the price of the shares traded. The opposite of *put option* (⟡ OPTION).

Cambridge School. A term referring to that group of English economists who came under the influence of ALFRED MARSHALL (1842–1924). Marshall was appointed Professor of Political Economy at Cambridge in 1885, a post he retained until his retirement in 1908. His major work, *The Principles of Economics* (1890), was in the tradition of the CLASSICAL SCHOOL. He was succeeded at Cambridge by A. C. PIGOU (1877–1959), who held the Chair until he retired in 1944, when D. H. ROBERTSON (1890–1963) took over the professorship.

Cantillon, Richard (1680(?)–1734). An Irish international banker, who wrote *Essai sur la nature du commerce en général*, which was not published until 1755 but had circulated from about 1730. This work was one of the first synoptic descriptions and analyses of the economic process. His views on the importance of agriculture, based on its receipt of pure RENT, and his analysis of the circulation of wealth foreshadowed the PHYSIOCRATS and the TABLEAU ÉCONOMIQUE.

Capacity utilization rate. The ratio of actual output of a plant, firm or economy to its full-capacity output. ⟡ EXCESS CAPACITY.

Capital. The stock of goods which are used in production and which have themselves been produced. A distinction is normally made between *fixed capital*, consisting of durable goods such as buildings, plant and machinery; and *circulating capital*, consisting of stocks of raw materials and semi-finished goods, components, etc., which are used up very rapidly (⟡ CIRCULATING CAPITAL). In addition, the word capital in economics generally means *real capital* – that is, physical goods. In everyday language, however, *capital* may be used to mean money capital, i.e. stocks of MONEY which are the result of past saving. Two important features of capital are (a) that its creation entails a sacrifice, since resources are devoted to making non-consumable capital goods instead of goods for immediate consumption; and (b) that it enhances the PRODUCTIVITY of the other FACTORS OF PRODUCTION, LAND and LABOUR, and it is this enhanced productivity which represents the reward for the sacrifice involved in creating capital. Hence, we can surmise that new capital is only created as long as its productivity is at least sufficient to compensate those who make the sacrifice involved in its creation. ⟡ HUMAN CAPITAL; INVESTMENT.

Capital account. ⟡ BALANCE OF PAYMENTS.

Capital allowances. Reductions in TAX liability which are related to a firm's CAPITAL expenditure. In most countries, expenditure on new capital assets is encouraged by various kinds of allowances and annual DEPRECIATION is recognized as an expense of the business in calculating tax liability. The taxation authorities' methods of depreciating an ASSET are not necessarily the same as those used by the company in the published ACCOUNTS. Where a company may claim depreciation for tax purposes at will, e.g. to write off the whole of the cost of an asset against tax in a single year, or to spread it over twenty years as it chooses, this is known as *free depreciation* or *depreciation at choice*.

In Britain annual (sometimes called *wear and tear*) allowances at specified rates on a reducing balance system, e.g. 20 per cent per annum on the written-down value of the asset, are admitted as depreciation expense for most assets except industrial buildings. Alternatively, for buildings and certain other assets with a long life, the straightline system of depreciation expense is adopted, e.g. an annual allowance of 4 per cent on cost.

However, other allowances are also admitted, mainly with the object of encouraging new INVESTMENT. The system of capital allowances has been subjected to very many changes and modifications in Britain. Investment grants (now abolished) were paid in cash by the authorities for certain capital expenditures, and initial allowances in some but not all cases. An initial allowance on the cost of an asset could be claimed in addition to the annual allowance in the first year only, thus providing *accelerated depreciation* for tax purposes. The system of initial and annual allowances, however, is not intended to permit more than 100 per cent of the cost of an asset to be written off against tax. At the end of its planned life and disposal, a balancing charge or allowance is made on an asset so that, ultimately, tax relief equivalent to the net capital cost of the asset over its life is given, and no more. ⇪ INVESTMENT INCENTIVES.

Capital, authorized. ⇕ AUTHORIZED CAPITAL.

Capital budgeting. The process of budgeting CAPITAL expenditure by means of an annual or longer-period capital BUDGET. Planned and actual CASH FLOWS and capital expenditures can be compared. In recent years, the methods of selecting INVESTMENT projects for inclusion in the capital budget have been extensively refined (⇕ INVESTMENT APPRAISAL).

Capital charges. Charges in the ACCOUNTS of a company or individual for interest paid on CAPITAL, DEPRECIATION or repayment of LOANS.

Capital, circulating. ⇕ CIRCULATING CAPITAL.

Capital consumption. Either (a) the using up of CAPITAL in the production of new goods, or (b) the sale or LIQUIDATION of capital ASSETS in order to increase current consumption. Both result in a diminishing stock of capital for an economy, firm or individual. In the former case, capital consumption corresponds to what is loosely termed 'DEPRECIATION' – the wear and tear on machines, and their resulting loss of VALUE, which occurs in the process of production. In the NATIONAL INCOME accounts, capital consumption is a category of expenditure which is based on depreciation allowances made by firms in their accounting records (⇕ CAPITAL ALLOWANCES), and which is subtracted from gross national income or product to obtain net national income or product. Conceptually, it represents an allowance for replacing capital used up in the process of production, but in practice, it will be strongly influenced by accounting conventions for estimating depreciation, which do not accurately reflect actual capital consumption.

Capital, cost of. 1. The cost, measured as a RATE OF INTEREST, of the CAPITAL employed by a business weighted according to the proportions of different sources of capital used. **2.** The marginal cost of capital, i.e. the cost of raising new capital. **3.** In INVESTMENT APPRAISAL, the cost of capital is used in DISCOUNTED CASH FLOW calculations, either directly in the discounting procedure (⇕ net PRESENT VALUE), or as a standard of comparison with the INTERNAL RATE OF RETURN. That is to say, it is the minimum rate of return which a firm would consider on a new INVESTMENT project, and would be ideally equal to the rate of return which the firm's shareholders could obtain on comparable investments outside the company. According to A. J. Merrett, the current long-term rate at which shareholders can invest in EQUITY shares is 7 per cent in REAL TERMS or 10 per cent in money terms net of taxes which involves the firm in earning about 14 per cent of net CORPORATION TAX on its new SHARE issues.

Capital employed. The CAPITAL in use in a business. There is no universally agreed definition of the term. It is sometimes taken to mean NET ASSETS (i.e. fixed plus current assets minus current LIABILITIES), but more usually BANK LOANS and OVERDRAFTS are included and other adjustments made for purposes of calculating the return on *net capital employed* (⇨ RATE OF RETURN), such as the exclusion of intangible assets and the revaluation of TRADE INVESTMENTS at market prices. ⇨ INVESTMENT APPRAISAL.

Capital expenditure. The purchase of fixed ASSETS (e.g. plant and equipment), expenditure on TRADE INVESTMENTS or acquisitions of other businesses and expenditure on current assets (e.g. stocks); to be distinguished from CAPITAL FORMATION.

Capital formation. NET INVESTMENT in fixed ASSETS, i.e. additions to the stock of real CAPITAL. *Gross fixed capital formation* includes DEPRECIATION, repairs and maintenance expenditure; *net capital formation* excludes them.

Capital gains. A realized increase in the value of a capital ASSET, as when a share is sold for more than the price at which it was purchased. Strictly speaking, the term refers to CAPITAL appreciation outside the normal course of business. The 1962 Finance Act imposed INCOME TAX on such capital gains for assets sold within six months of purchase ('*short-term gains*'). In the 1965 Act, the time limit was extended to twelve months and a separate long-term gains tax was introduced; there is now a single tax rate for all capital gains. The tax does not cover gains arising from the sale of personal belongings, including cars or principle dwelling houses, but it does cover gains from the sale of STOCK EXCHANGE securities, with the exception of GILT-EDGED SECURITIES, after one year. The tax for individuals is 30 per cent of the gain, although CAPITAL LOSSES may be set against tax liability. Capital gains arise from changes in the supply and demand for capital assets, but also from INFLATION, and it can be argued that it is inequitable to tax the latter element. Capital gains are taxed in a similar way in other countries, including the U.S., and companies as well as individuals are liable (⇨ CORPORATION TAX).

Capital gearing. ▷ GEARING.

Capital goods. ▷ CAPITAL.

Capital-intensive. A capital-intensive process of production is one which uses proportionately more CAPITAL relative to the quantities of other INPUTS. A nuclear power plant is a capital-intensive method of producing electricity, compared with a conventional coal-burning plant, because the cost of LABOUR and fuel is a smaller proportion of total costs in the first instance than in the second instance. As labour costs rise, almost all processes are becoming more capital intensive (▷ FACTORS OF PRODUCTION).

Capital, issued. ▷ ISSUED CAPITAL.

Capital Issues Committee (C.I.C.). A non-statutory body that advises the TREASURY on applications from overseas borrowers to make issues on the British CAPITAL MARKET. After the Second World War and until 1959 the C.I.C. also effectively controlled larger domestic issues in the interests of general economic policy. The C.I.C. grew out of the Foreign Transactions Advisory Committee set up in the 1930s to control the export of CAPITAL.

Capital loss. A reduction in the MONEY value of an ASSET, opposite of CAPITAL GAIN.

Capital, marginal efficiency of. ▷ INTERNAL RATE OF RETURN.

Capital, marginal productivity of. ▷ INTERNAL RATE OF RETURN.

Capital market. The market for longer term loanable funds as distinct from the MONEY MARKET, which deals in short-term funds. There is no clear-cut distinction between the two MARKETS, although in principle capital market LOANS are used by industry and commerce mainly for fixed INVESTMENT. The capital market in any country is not one institution, but all those institutions that canalize the SUPPLY and DEMAND for long-term capital and claims on capital, e.g. the STOCK EXCHANGE, banks and INSURANCE companies. The capital market, of course, is not concerned solely with the issue of new claims on capital, but also with dealings in existing claims. The marketability of SECURITIES is an important element in the efficient working of the capital market, since investors would be much more reluctant to make loans to industry if their claims could not easily be disposed of. All advanced countries have highly developed capital markets, but in DEVELOPING COUNTRIES the absence of a capital market is often as much of an obstacle to the growth of investment as a shortage of savings, and governments and industrialists in these countries are obliged to raise capital in the international capital market, i.e. that composed of the national capital markets in the advanced countries. ⟡ BUSINESS FINANCE; PUBLIC FINANCE.

Capital movements. ⟡ FOREIGN INVESTMENT.

Capital, nominal. ⟡ AUTHORIZED CAPITAL.

Capital-output ratio, incremental (I.C.O.R.). The increase in the CAPITAL STOCK of a firm, industry or economy, over a period, divided by the increase in output over that period. It is the ratio of NET INVESTMENT to change in output. For a given increase in output, the size of the change in capital stock will be determined by technological conditions and relative FACTOR prices, e.g. the higher are wages and the lower the RATE OF INTEREST, the greater will be net investment for a given increase in output. If the I.C.O.R. can be taken as roughly constant over a particular period, then multiplying it by the expected change in output gives the expected level of net investment, and this fact leads to the accelerator theory of investment (⟡ ACCELERATION PRINCIPLE), with the I.C.O.R. identified as the ACCELERATOR COEFFICIENT. Accordingly, I.C.O.R.s play an important part in the theories of the TRADE CYCLE and ECONOMIC GROWTH. I.C.O.R.s are frequently used by economists in analysing the relative growth experience of different countries. In these cases, figures of percentage increases in GROSS INVESTMENT from national accounts data are used and divided by the percentage increase in GROSS NATIONAL PRODUCT. Such a ratio is more properly called a *gross incremental capital-output ratio*. One other related ratio is the *average capital-output ratio*, in which the total depreciated capital stock (⟡ DEPRECIATION) is divided by total output.

Capital, registered. ⟡ AUTHORIZED CAPITAL.

Capital reserves. ⟡ COMPANY RESERVES.

Capital, sources of. ⟡ BUSINESS FINANCE.

Capital stock. The total amount of physical CAPITAL existing at any one time, in a firm, industry or economy. It is extremely difficult to obtain a satisfactory measure of this in practice. Clearly, it is impossible to aggregate the physical amounts of different types of capital, but this then raises the problem of defining a useful MONEY measure. Strictly, the VALUE of the current capital stock is the PRESENT VALUE of the stream of INCOME which it will generate in future, but it is clearly impossible to measure this with any real precision. Hence, we are often thrown back on the valuations of ASSETS shown in firms' BALANCE SHEETS (which need bear little relationship to any economically meaningful value), or valuations made for INSURANCE purposes, etc.

Capital structure. The sources of long-term CAPITAL of a company. A company's capital structure is determined by the numbers and types of SHARES it issues and its reliance on fixed-interest debt (⟡ GEARING). A company's choice between different sources of finance will be determined by their cost, the type of business it is, its past and expected future earnings, TAXATION and other considerations. ⟡ BUSINESS FINANCE; CAPITAL, COST OF.

Capital, working. ⟡ WORKING CAPITAL.

Capitalism. The political economic system, based on private property and private PROFIT, censured by KARL MARX for its exploitation of labour. ⟡ FREE MARKET ECONOMY.

Capitalist economy. ⟡ CAPITALISM.

Capitalization. 1. The amount and structure of the CAPITAL of a company. **2.** The conversion of accumulated PROFITS and reserves into ISSUED CAPITAL. **3.** *Market capitalization* is the market value of a company's issued SHARE capital, i.e. the quoted price of its shares multipled by the number of shares outstanding.

Capitalization issue. ⟡ BONUS ISSUE.

Capitalized ratios. Ratios which describe the CAPITAL STRUCTURE of a company, by indicating the proportion of each type of SECURITY issued.

Capitalized value. The CAPITAL sum at current RATES OF INTEREST required to yield the current earnings of an ASSET. For example, if the earnings of an asset were £5 per annum and the appropriate rate of interest were 5 per cent, its capitalized value would be £100. Capitalized value does not represent a satisfactory means for the VALUATION of most capital assets, since the capitalized value of an asset would not necessarily compensate an owner for the loss of the asset.

Carry-over. Postponement of settlement of ACCOUNT on the STOCK EXCHANGE until the following period involving payment of INTEREST on the account. Also called *Contango* (⟡ BACKWARDATION).

Cartel. A group of firms which enter into an agreement to set mutually acceptable PRICES for their products, and this is often accompanied by output and INVESTMENT quotas. The rules of the cartel will be embodied in a formal document, which may be legally enforceable, and penalties will be laid down for firms which violate it. The essence of a cartel is that it is a formal system of collusion, as opposed to a set of informal or tacit agreements to follow certain pricing policies. Currently, cartels are illegal in the U.K. and the U.S., it being held that their general effect is to restrict output, raise prices, and, in general, create MONOPOLY conditions in industry. On the other hand, cartels have been legalized at certain times, especially in Germany in the inter-war period, when they were seen as a means of achieving gradual 'rationalization' of an industry suffering from EXCESS CAPACITY or of achieving sufficient strength to compete more effectively in INTERNATIONAL TRADE.

Cash. 1. Coins and BANK-NOTES. **2.** LEGAL TENDER in the settlement of DEBT.

Cascade tax. ⟡ TURNOVER TAX.

Cash flow. The flow of MONEY payments to or from a firm. Expenditure is sometimes referred to as a 'negative' cash flow. The *gross cash flow* of a business is the gross PROFIT (after payment of fixed INTEREST) plus DEPRECIATION provisions in any trading period, i.e. that sum of money which is available for INVESTMENT, DIVIDENDS or payment of taxes. The *net cash flow* is retained EARNINGS and depreciation provisions before or after TAX. Net cash flows of a particular project are usually defined as those arising after taxes have been paid, expenditure on repairs and maintenance carried out, any necessary adjustments made to WORKING CAPITAL, and account is taken of any residual value of ASSETS at the end of a particular project's life or other miscellaneous income accruing to the project or business. This term is important in INVESTMENT APPRAISAL. 'Cash flow statement' is often used synonymously with 'statement of SOURCES AND USES'. ⟡ BUDGET.

Cash ratio. 1. The ratio of a bank's CASH holdings to its total deposit LIABILITIES. ⟡ LIQUIDITY RATIO; BANKING. **2.** For an individual firm, the proportion of its current liabilities that are accounted for by cash in hand, including BANK DEPOSITS, and sometimes payments due from customers.

Cassel, Gustav (1866–1945). ⟡ PURCHASING POWER PARITY THEORY.

Census. An official count or enumeration, usually providing social, demographic (⟡ POPULATION) or economic information. The first censuses were probably made to assess the TAX BASE, and date at least from Roman times. Censuses of population have been taken regularly in Britain since 1801, and there are now censuses of PRODUCTION and distribution and other matters with varying regularity. (⟡ BUSINESS STATISTICS OFFICE).

Central American Common Market (C.A.C.M.). A common market of the five Central American states – Guatemala, El Salvador, Honduras, Nicaragua and Costa Rica – agreed in the General Treaty of Central American Economic Integration signed in December 1960. This treaty came into operation in June 1961, and a head-quarters was established in San Salvador. There is an economic secretariat, which has offices in Guatemala City, an economic council and an executive council. FREE TRADE between the member countries was expected to be established by June 1966. In the event, although duties have been eliminated on about 95 per cent of products, duties on many of the remaining products, particularly agricultural, are likely to continue. An agreement on the Equalization of Import Duties and Charges was made in September 1959, and subsequent agreements have established a common external TARIFF on all but a small number of products, such as petroleum and motor vehicles. The member countries have agreed to harmonize fiscal incentives granted to industries, if they effectively contribute to the growth of the region. In 1961, the Central American Bank for Economic Integration was formed to finance industrial projects in the region, housing and hotels. In 1964, the five CENTRAL BANKS agreed to the establishment, in the long term, of a common CURRENCY. However, C.A.C.M. suffered a set-back on the withdrawal of Honduras at the end of 1970 and the imposition of import duties on a number of commodities by Costa Rica in 1971. ⇨ CUSTOMS UNION.

Central bank. A bankers' bank and LENDER OF LAST RESORT (⇨ BANK OF ENGLAND). All developed and most DEVELOPING COUNTRIES have a central bank that is the instrument of the government's function of controlling the CREDIT system. Central banks, such as the Bank of France, the Federal Reserve Bank and the Bank of Canada, control the note issue (⇨ BANK-NOTE), act as the government's bank, accept DEPOSITS from and make LOANS to the COMMERCIAL BANKS and the MONEY MARKET, lead the interest rate structure (⇨ RATE OF INTEREST) through establishing the rate at which loans of last resort will be made, and conduct transfers of MONEY and BULLION with central banks in other countries. ⇨ BANK FOR INTERNATIONAL SETTLEMENTS; FEDERAL RESERVE SYSTEM.

Central bank of central banks. ⇨ BANK FOR INTERNATIONAL SETTLEMENTS; INTERNATIONAL MONETARY FUND; KEYNES PLAN.

Central planning. ⇨ STATE PLANNING.

Central Statistical Office (C.S.O.). Part of the Cabinet office; responsible for the coordination of work throughout the government statistical service. The C.S.O. collects from departments the statistics relating to the national economy and analyses them as a basis for government economic and financial policy. It is responsible for preparing the national accounts (⟡ SOCIAL ACCOUNTING).

Certificate of incorporation. A document issued by the Registrar of Companies certifying the legal existence of a company after certain legal requirements for registration have been met. ⟡ COMPANY LAW.

Certificate of origin. A certificate required by a customs authority to accompany imported goods which can claim preferential TARIFF rates by virtue of their country of origin. Such certificates are required in U.K., as a member of the EUROPEAN FREE TRADE ASSOCIATION. The certificates are prepared for exporters and issued by associations such as the local chambers of commerce approved by the Department of Trade and Industry. They are intended to prevent non-member countries from exporting into a high tariff country through a low tariff country.

Chamberlin, Edward Hastings (1899–). After a period at the University of Michigan, Professor Chamberlin joined Harvard as a tutor in 1922 and became a full Professor of Economics there in 1937. His publications include *Theory of Monopolistic Competition* (1933), *Towards a More General Theory of Value* (1957) and *The Economic Analysis of Labour Union Power* (1958). In *Theory of Monopolistic Competition* he proposed a new emphasis for economic theory which broke away from the old concepts of pure or PERFECT COMPETITION or pure MONOPOLY. These two cases he saw as special limiting ones. In between was 'monopolistic competition', which was the condition under which most industries, in fact, operated. Each firm pursued a policy of product DIFFERENTIATION by special packaging or advertising so that it created a 'pen-umbra' of monopoly around its product. He also analysed the problem of selling costs, e.g. advertising. ⟡ MONOPOLISTIC COMPETITION; J. V. ROBINSON.

Charge account (U.S.). ⟡ CREDIT ACCOUNT.

Chartist (U.S.). A stock-market analyst who predicts share-price movements solely from a study of graphs on which individual SHARE prices and price indices are plotted.

Cheap money (U.S. easy money). A deliberate MONETARY POLICY of keeping RATES OF INTEREST low, either, as from 1932 onwards in Britain, to stimulate borrowing and economic recovery, or, as during the Second World War, to reduce the cost of government borrowing. In most of the 1930s and 1940s, BANK RATE was 2 per cent, and that rate could not, therefore, be used as a flexible instrument of monetary policy during that period. The cheap money era came to an end in 1951.

Check trading. The practice whereby a company, generally a FINANCE HOUSE, sells a voucher or check on CREDIT. The purchaser repays the DEBT by agreed regular instalments and with INTEREST. The purchaser exchanges the check for goods at certain shops. The finance house reimburses the retailer at the face value of the check, less a discount. It is a very old-established method of CONSUMER CREDIT financing, especially in the north of England. It has, however, in recent years come into prominence as a method of avoiding HIRE PURCHASE regulations. The latter do not apply to check trading because (a) the finance house does not sell goods, it only extends credit; and (b) the retailer does not sell goods by instalments. ⇨ CROWTHER COMMITTEE.

Cheque. An order written by the drawer to a COMMERCIAL BANK or CENTRAL BANK to pay on demand a specified sum to the bearer, a named person or corporation.

Chicago school. ⇨ M. FRIEDMAN; QUANTITY THEORY OF MONEY.

C.i.f. Cost, insurance and freight, or charged-in-full. The U.K. Overseas Trade Accounts records IMPORTS in terms of their value c.i.f. (charged in full) and exports F.O.B. (free-on-board). In order to determine the VISIBLE TRADE balance for the BALANCE OF PAYMENTS accounts, the import figures are adjusted to an f.o.b. basis. The insurance and freight element, which accounts for about 10 per cent of the total import bill, is included in the balance of payments as INVISIBLES.

Circular flow of income. ⇨ INCOME, CIRCULAR FLOW OF.

Circulating capital. Funds embodied in STOCKS and work in progress or other current as opposed to fixed ASSETS. A now little-used synonym for WORKING CAPITAL.

Civil Service Department (C.S.D.). ⇨ TREASURY, THE.

Clark, John Bates (1847-1938). Educated at Amherst College, and Heidelberg and Zürich Universities, Clark taught at Amherst until, in 1895, he was appointed Professor of Economics at Columbia University. He held this post until his retirement in 1923. His major publications include *Philosophy of Wealth* (1885), *Distribution of Wealth* (1899), *Essentials of Economic Theory* (1907), *The Control of Trusts* (1901) and *The Problem of Monopoly* (1904). He is regarded as the founder of the marginal productivity theory of distribution in the U.S. (▷ DISTRIBUTION, THEORY OF).

Clark, John Maurice (1884-1963). The son of JOHN BATES CLARK. He succeeded his father to the Chair of Economics at Columbia University in 1926. His publications include *Economics of Overhead Costs* (1923) and *Essays in Preface to Social Economics* (1963). In an article, 'Business Acceleration and the Law of Demand', in the *Journal of Political Economy* in 1917, he formulated the ACCELERATION PRINCIPLE, one of the basic theories upon which has been constructed modern dynamic macroeconomic theory (▷ MACROECONOMICS).

Classical economics. The classical period of economics ranges from ADAM SMITH'S *Wealth of Nations*, which was published in 1776, to JOHN STUART MILL'S *Principles of Political Economy* of 1848, and was dominated by the work of DAVID RICARDO. The French PHYSIOCRATS had lain stress on the position of agriculture in the economy, claiming that this sector was the source of all economic wealth. Smith rejected this view and drew attention to the development of manufacturing and the importance of labour PRODUCTIVITY. Ultimately LABOUR was the true measure of VALUE. Ricardo took up this idea and propounded a theory of relative prices based on costs of production in which labour cost played the dominant role, although he accepted that CAPITAL costs were an additional element. Capital played an important role, not only by improving labour productivity, but also by enabling labour to be sustained over the period of waiting before work bore fruit in consumable output. This was the idea of the wages fund (▷ WAGE FUND THEORY). Wages were dependent on two forces: (a) the demand for labour, derived from the availability of capital, or savings, to finance the wage bill; and (b) the supply of labour, which was fixed in the short run, but in the long run was dependent on the standard of living. The latter was related to the level of subsistence. This was not regarded as merely the basic necessities required to keep the workers alive and to reproduce themselves. It was determined by custom, and was accepted to be increasing as real living standards improved. T. R. MALTHUS, in his theory of population, pointed to the need for restraint because of the presumption that there was a natural tendency for the growth of population to outstrip agricultural output. Ricardo analysed the implications of the productivity of land at the margin of cultivation. The Physiocrats and Adam Smith had attributed agricultural RENT to the natural fertility of the soil, but Ricardo refuted this. Rent existed because of the poor fertility of the final increment of land taken under cultivation. Because of competition, PROFITS and labour costs must be the same everywhere and therefore a surplus must accrue to all land that was more fertile than that on the margin. This surplus was rent. The presumption of competition was the foundation of classical thought. The Classical Economists believed that, although individuals were each motivated by self-love and personal ambition, free competition ensured that the community as a whole benefited. As Adam Smith put it, 'It is not from the benevolence of the butcher that we expect our dinner, but from [his] regard to [his] own interest.' As a consequence, they concluded government interference should be kept to a minimum. The Classical Economists gave little attention to macroeconomic problems (▷ MACROECONOMICS), such as the TRADE CYCLE. Most of the classicists accepted J. B. SAY's Law of Markets, the gist of which purported to maintain the impossibility of any severe economic recession (▷ DEPRESSION) arising from an overall deficiency in AGGREGATE DEMAND. Malthus disputed this. He argued that increased savings would not only lower consumption but would also increase output, through increased investment. However, his view was not accepted. The Classical Economists, including Malthus, held a theory in which savings were equated with investment through changes in the RATE OF INTEREST (▷ A. TURGOT). Classical Economists continue to influence economists both in the U.K. and in other countries to this day. Indeed, J. S. Mill's book was used as a school text until the end of the nineteenth century. ALFRED MARSHALL in his *Principles of Economics* of 1890 assimilated the old classical economics with the new marginalism of JEVONS, MENGER and WALRAS. The great controversy which raged in the years of the Great Depression of the 1930s between the neo-classical economists and the advocates of deficit spending on public works, was resolved when the classical macroeconomic theory gave way to the new economic revolution set in train by J. M. KEYNES.

Classical School. The tradition of economic thought that originated in ADAM SMITH and developed through the work of DAVID RICARDO, T. R. MALTHUS, J. S. MILL down to A. MARSHALL and A. C. PIGOU (▷ CLASSICAL ECONOMICS).

Clearing banks. Members of the London Bankers' CLEARING HOUSE. Often used as a synonym for COMMERCIAL BANKS or joint stock banks.

Clearing house. **1.** Any institution that settles mutual indebtedness between a number of organizations. **2.** The London Bankers' clearing house sets all claims among its eleven members (i.e. CHEQUES paid into banks other than those upon which they are drawn) against one another, and each day a balance is struck and the differences in total indebtedness paid by cheque on the BANK OF ENGLAND. The sums involved often exceed £1,000 million per day. The clearing house is situated off Lombard Street near all the main London offices of the CLEARING BANKS. Similar institutions exist in other countries, e.g. the New York clearing house. There is also a settlement department at the STOCK EXCHANGE which matches final buyers and sellers of stocks known as actively traded *clearing stocks*.

Clearing stocks. ⇨ CLEARING HOUSE.

Close company (U.S. closed company). A company that is effectively controlled by five or fewer shareholders. The purpose of close company tax legislation, introduced in Britain with CORPORATION TAX under the 1965 Finance Act, is to prevent the avoidance of surtax (⇨ INCOME TAX), which cannot be levied on shareholders who choose to retain PROFITS in their business. Close companies in Britain are compelled to distribute all of their investment income and 60 per cent of their trading profits unless they can show that its retention is necessary for the development of the business. A company in which the public hold 35 per cent or more of the EQUITY is not treated as a close company. ⇨ CORPORATION TAX.

Closed economy. An economy assumed not to take part in INTERNATIONAL TRADE, so that it has no EXPORTS or IMPORTS. Though no such economy exists in the real world, the assumption is a useful simplification when examining how total expenditures on CONSUMPTION and INVESTMENT and government expenditure and TAXATION interact to determine the levels of NATIONAL INCOME and EMPLOYMENT. It reflects the typical device used in economics of starting off with a highly simplified model and gradually introducing additional complications.

Closed-end trust (U.S.). An INVESTMENT TRUST.

Closing prices. Price of a COMMODITY, e.g. SECURITIES on the STOCK EXCHANGE, at the end of a day's trading in a MARKET.

Cobb-Douglas production function. A particular type of PRODUCTION FUNCTION of the form:

$$Q = b_0 x_1^{b_1} x_2^{b_2} \ldots x_n^{b_n}$$

where Q is output, $x_1 x_2 \ldots x_n$ are FACTORS OF PRODUCTION, and b_0, b_1, b_2 ... b_n are PARAMETERS. This function is given this name in economics because it was used by Cobb and Douglas in an article in the *American Economic Review* in 1928 which attempts to explain the relative constancy of the shares of CAPITAL and LABOUR in the NATIONAL INCOME. This function, particularly in its special form where $b_1 + b_2 + \ldots + b_n = 1$, is widely used in economics, not only in the theory of INCOME DISTRIBUTION, but also in the theory of PRODUCTION and the theory of ECONOMIC GROWTH. ⟡ L. EULER.

Cobweb theorem. An analysis of the question of whether, in a MARKET in which the amount currently supplied depends on what the price was in some previous period, price will tend to converge to an EQUILIBRIUM, or diverge from an equilibrium, if it is ever out of it. The analysis was first developed in the context of certain agricultural markets (it was for some time referred to as the 'hog cycle' phenomenon). Suppose farmers plant now an acreage of a particular crop, which, given climatic conditions and the absence of stocks, determines the amount of the crop which will be supplied after the harvest. If the acreage devoted to the crop depends on the price at the time of sowing, then supply at a given time depends on the price one period earlier. In this case, if the market is ever out of equilibrium, there will be a series of fluctuations in prices, which may get smaller and smaller and eventually converge to an equilibrium, or larger and larger and never converge. At time period 1, price will be at a particular level, farmers will plant accordingly, and in one period's time will put the resulting crop on the market. Suppose, however, that at that time demand is higher than it was previously, so that the available supply is insufficient to meet the demand at the old price, and price must rise to 'ration off' available supply among buyers. Then, at time period 2, farmers will plant a larger acreage of the crop than they did previously, because price is now higher, and so, in one period's time, a larger supply will be forthcoming on the market. This supply will be more than that required to satisfy demand at the price which prevailed at period 2, and so price must fall to induce buyers to take up the extra supply. Less will therefore be sown at time period 3, and so less will be put on the market at time period 4, and so price must rise again. And so the process continues. The important question is: do the price changes become smaller each time, or larger each time? If the former, then the market will converge to equilibrium – eventually, the amount put on the market will be just equal to the amount buyers are prepared to take at the price which existed last period. If the latter, the price simply oscillates infinitely. It is possible to formulate in precise terms the conditions under which each occur, and in fact the analysis of these conditions was one of the earliest examples of dynamic analysis in economics (◇ ECONOMIC DYNAMICS). The importance of the Cobweb Theorem is as one of the earliest and easiest examples of dynamic analysis, which raises in sharp but relatively simple form many of the basic problems of dynamic analysis. Also, despite its assumptions that individual producers act in an uncoordinated way (no longer true even of agricultural markets), form their expectations in a very naïve way (by considering only one price – that prevailing at the time of planting), and do not learn as their expectations are continually proved wrong, the analysis does shed light on the reasons for price fluctuations in certain markets. It obtains its name, the 'cobweb' theorem, because if the movements of prices and quantities are plotted on a conventional SUPPLY and DEMAND diagram, the pattern of lines looks much like a cobweb.

Cohen committee. ◇ COUNCIL ON PRICES, PRODUCTIVITY AND INCOMES.

Collateral security. A second SECURITY (in addition to the personal surety of the borrower) for a LOAN. BANK LOANS, other than PERSONAL LOANS, are normally made against the security of STOCKS and SHARES, property or INSURANCE policies.

Collusion. Overt cooperation between oligopolists (◇ OLIGOPOLY) to set common policies. These policies generally involve setting agreed PRICES, and may also involve assigning market QUOTAS and coordinating INVESTMENT plans. Since collusion precludes price competition, and tends to promote inefficiency and a low rate of innovation it has been criticized by economists. ◇◇ CARTEL.

Colombo Plan for Cooperative Economic Development in South and South-East Asia. A plan for the economic assistance for the DEVELOPING COUNTRIES of Asia agreed in 1950 with special concern for the re-establishment of economic activity on a sound basis in the aftermath of the Second World War. The member countries include U.S., U.K., Australia, Canada, New Zealand and Japan as well as individual Asian countries. The consultative committee publishes an annual report describing the economic progress and aims of the developing countries in the plan and the nature and level of technical assistance given. In 1968, this assistance reached a level of $200m. About 60 per cent of this sum was spent on the provision of experts, about 30 per cent on technical equipment and the rest on training. In 1968, the U.K. contributed $8 million to aid under the plan. ⇨ ASIAN DEVELOPMENT BANK.

Comecon. ⇨ COUNCIL FOR MUTUAL ECONOMIC AID.

Command economy. ⇨ PLANNED ECONOMY.

Commercial banks. Privately owned banks receiving DEPOSITS and making LOANS, in the U.K. through a large number of branches (⇨ BANKING; BRANCH BANKING). Formerly and still sometimes called *joint stock banks* and also incorrectly CLEARING BANKS, since not all the commercial banks in the U.K., e.g. the Scottish banks, are members of the London Bankers' CLEARING HOUSE. In the U.S. these banks are referred to as *member banks* and in Western Europe as *credit banks* to distinguish them from INVESTMENT BANKS. In most countries, the commercial banks are concerned mainly with receiving DEPOSITS and making short-term LOANS to private individuals, companies and other organizations. The banks also provide a number of other services to their customers: trustee and executor facilities, the supply of foreign currency, the purchase and sale of SECURITIES and, more recently, CREDIT TRANSFER, PERSONAL LOAN and credit card facilities (⇨ CREDIT ACCOUNT). The banks have also, in recent years, diversified into other financial services in competition with the FINANCE HOUSES and the MERCHANT BANKS, e.g. VENTURE CAPITAL.

In Britain, the number of commercial banks has been greatly reduced in recent years, and in addition to the BIG 4 there are only two other English banks of any size – Coutts and Williams & Glyn. The Scottish and Northern Ireland banks are separate from the English banking systems, although their methods of working are very similar. There are, of course, a substantial number of foreign banks in Britain, some of them with branches outside London, and their number has greatly increased in recent years.

The commercial banking system is most highly developed in the U.K., where a relatively small number of banks have a large number of branches throughout the country, enabling them to offer a country-wide service and to spread their risks widely while enjoying the benefits of large-scale organizations. In the U.S., and to a lesser extent in Western Europe, branch banking is less widespread. In the U.S. unit banking, where the bank's operations are confined to a single office, is more common, although some banks have a limited number of local branches.

The TREASURY, through the BANK OF ENGLAND, has wide powers

to control the activities of the commercial banks in the interest of national monetary policy and has not hesitated to use these powers in recent years, especially concerning the level of advances (▷ BANK LOANS; CREDIT SQUEEZE) made by the banks. Until recently, competition between the commercial banks was mainly restricted to the services they offer, since OVERDRAFT and deposit rates were identical and bank charges very similar. The abandonment of ceilings on bank advances in favour of the new system of CREDIT CONTROL in 1971, however, was carried out on the understanding that the banks would end their agreement not to compete in RATES OF INTEREST. The banks no longer base their deposit and overdraft rates on BANK RATE, but publish their own base rates, though it is still too early to be clear how the nature of competition between banks will change as a result.

Commercial bills. ▷ BILL OF EXCHANGE.

Commission. A percentage of the VALUE of a transaction taken by an intermediary as payment for his services, e.g. BROKER'S commission, estate agency's commission.

Commodity. 1. In economics, synonymous with a good. **2.** An article of trade (▷ COMMODITY EXCHANGE).

Commodity control schemes. ▷ INTERNATIONAL COMMODITY AGREEMENTS.

Commodity exchange. A MARKET in which COMMODITIES are bought and sold. It is not necessary for the commodities to be physically exchanged; only rights to ownership need be. London has important commodity markets arising partly from her industrial and colonial history, and partly from the nature of her foreign trade. The commodity exchanges in London cover a wide variety, such as tea, coffee, wool, cotton, rubber, non-ferrous metals and furs. The old practice of auctioning commodities from warehouses in which samples could be inspected beforehand has become less important. An efficient system of grading and modern systems of communication have enabled the practice of 'c.i.f. trading' to develop. A buyer can buy a commodity in the country of origin for delivery C.I.F. to a specified port at which he can off-load for direct delivery to his own premises. This method saves warehousing costs and auction charges. However, many auctions still take place in London, e.g. tea, wool and furs. The market not only enables commodities to be sold 'spot' or for delivery at some specified time and place (▷ SPOT MARKET), but it also includes a market in 'FUTURES'. This latter enables merchants to avoid the effect of price fluctuations by buying for forward delivery at an agreed price, which will not be affected by intervening changes in the 'spot' rate.

Commodity shunting. The practice of buying a commodity with one CURRENCY and selling it for another in order to circumvent EXCHANGE CONTROL regulations, which prevent direct foreign exchange CONVERTIBILITY. The practice became embarrassingly prevalent in sterling in the early 1950s when transferable sterling was not convertible into dollars. For example, platinum was bought with sterling in London and shipped to Kuwait for resale for dollars (the so-called 'Kuwait gap'). The practice ceased when its *raison d'être* was removed by the BANK OF ENGLAND officially supporting the black market RATE OF EXCHANGE for transferable sterling, until the latter's discount on the official rate was eliminated.

Commodity Stabilization Agreements. ⟡ INTERNATIONAL COM-MODITY AGREEMENTS.

Common Market. ⟡ CUSTOMS UNION; EUROPEAN ECONOMIC COMMUNITY.

Commonwealth preference. Under the Finance Acts of 1919 and 1957 and the Import Duties Acts of 1932 and 1958 and various regulations made under these Acts, certain imports into the U.K. are charged customs duties (⟡ TARIFFS) at reduced rates or are admitted free of duty, provided that the products have been grown entirely in the Commonwealth or Eire or at least 25 per cent of the value of manu-factured goods is attributable to a Commonwealth country. There are some exceptions to this rule, so that, for instance, some articles must contain at least a 75 per cent Commonwealth contribution. Other members of the Commonwealth reciprocate and wholly or partly extend the preferential system to some or all of the other Commonwealth countries. The preferential system was confirmed in a series of bilateral trade agreements concluded between Common-wealth countries at Ottawa in 1932. In principle, the preferential system is contrary to the MOST FAVOURED NATION CLAUSE accepted by the GENERAL AGREEMENT ON TARIFFS AND TRADE, by which no special privileges in trade should be established between countries without these privileges being made available to all. Many Commonwealth preferential rates are levied in terms of a fixed amount per unit rather than a percentage of value. The result has been that INFLATION has reduced the preferential margin in real terms. At the same time, U.K. exports to Commonwealth countries have become relatively less important in the U.K.'s total trade, and the U.K. membership of the EUROPEAN FREE TRADE

ASSOCIATION has further undermined the preferential position enjoyed by Commonwealth members in the U.K. market. This is not to say that the U.K. preferential treatment is not now significant. Commonwealth countries have a protected market in the U.K. for many food and raw material exports. The fact that the 'Imperial preference system', as it was once called, is even now of importance to certain Commonwealth exporters to the U.K., has given it considerable significance in negotiations for British membership of the EUROPEAN ECONOMIC COMMUNITY (▷ BILATERALISM).

Company law. The law governing the establishment and conduct of incorporated business enterprise. It originally developed from the PARTNERSHIP, and has its origins in common law and, from the eighteenth century onwards, in a series of company and other Acts. The first companies were created by Royal Charter, and the whole basis of company law is that certain benefits are conferred (in these first instances, that of a MONOPOLY in many cases) in return for certain obligations. The Act of 1720 created the Statutory Company with LIMITED LIABILITY, making possible, for example, the establishment of the early British railway companies. By 1825 the expansion of business had made the creation of companies by separate Acts of Parliament too cumbersome, and in that year a new Act made it possible to form JOINT-STOCK COMPANIES by registration with a Registrar of Companies. It was not until 1862, however, that limited liability was extended to certain private as well as public companies. Company law has continued to evolve under successive Acts as the needs of business have developed and altered. Other laws, such as the Prevention of Fraud Act, also apply to companies. Under present law (deriving principally from the 1967 Companies Act) there are three classes of company: (a) limited and (b) unlimited private companies; and (c) public limited companies. Compared with the two other forms of business unit, the SOLE PROPRIETOR and the partnership, INCORPORATION confers advantages for financing and, in certain circumstances, TAXATION, in addition to limited liability, where appropriate. (An unlimited private company does not have limited liability, i.e. its owners are responsible for company debt to the full extent of their fortune.) However, companies, unlike individuals or partnerships, are obliged to make public certain information about their business. As a result of the recommendations by the Jenkins Committee, both private and public limited companies are obliged to file certain information for public inspection, and to circulate accounts to their shareholders. Until

1967. certain PRIVATE COMPANIES, 'exempt private companies', were not obliged to comply with all of the accounting and disclosure requirements.

A public company may have an unlimited number of shareholders and may offer SHARES for public subscription. Quoted companies are public limited companies whose shares are listed on a recognized STOCK EXCHANGE. Private companies place certain restrictions on the transfer of shares, may not offer shares to the public and may consist of no more than fifty members other than employees.

Company law sets out other provisions dealing with the powers, appointment and tenure of directors, the protection of investors, including minorities, ownership and control, winding-up and other matters.

Company reserves. PROFITS retained in the business and set aside for specified purposes. The Companies Act requires a distinction to be made in ACCOUNTS between revenue and CAPITAL reserves. The former, at the discretion of the board of directors, can be distributed as DIVIDENDS to EQUITY shareholders, but the latter may not. Capital reserves are created when new shares are issued at a PREMIUM over par or when the book value of existing assets is revalued to bring it into line with replacement costs or CAPITAL GAINS are made; in each case, the whole of the surplus is transferred to the capital reserve account. These reserves may later be transformed into issued capital (⟡ CAPITALIZATION).

Revenue reserves are created by transfers of undistributed profits into special accounts, e.g. asset replacement reserves or general reserves, out of which a dividend may be paid in a later year in which the company makes a loss. The bulk of company reserves are not kept in CASH, but are invariably invested in the business (ploughed back) or outside. In all cases, however, the sums in reserve accounts are always matched by ASSETS. Tax reserves and the balance on the PROFIT and loss account at any time are also classified as revenue reserves. A taxation equalization reserve may include tax allowances accruing under accelerated depreciation (⟡ CAPITAL ALLOWANCES), i.e. where DEPRECIATION for tax purposes is faster than depreciation written into the company accounts, and future tax liabilities on current revenue. The decision on how much profit to retain in the business and how much to distribute in dividends is, of course, entirely the responsibility of the board of directors. ⟡ RETAINED EARNINGS.

Company taxation. ⟡ CORPORATION TAX.

Comparative advantage. ⟡ DAVID RICARDO for the law of comparative costs; INTERNATIONAL TRADE.

Comparative cost. ⟡ DAVID RICARDO; INTERNATIONAL TRADE.

Comparative static equilibrium analysis. A basic method of analysis in economics. It begins by examining the EQUILIBRIUM of the subject of study – the individual consumer, the MARKET, the economy, etc. One of the underlying determinants of this equilibrium is then changed and the resulting new equilibrium examined. The new equilibrium position is then compared to the previous equilibrium position, and from this the effects of the change deduced. The accuracy of predictions based on such analysis will obviously depend on the appropriateness of the analytical MODEL used.

For example: in a study of the market for a particular good, the initial EQUILIBRIUM PRICE and quantity traded are determined by the equality of SUPPLY and DEMAND. The underlying determinants of this equilibrium are such factors as the level of buyers' INCOME, their tastes, PRICES of other products, technology, prices of FACTORS OF PRODUCTION, etc., and if one or more of these changes, one or both of the SUPPLY CURVE and the DEMAND CURVE will shift. Suppose that there is a rise in buyers' incomes. This will (unless the good is an INFERIOR GOOD) lead to an increase in demand at every price. This will cause price to rise, and the quantity supplied to increase, until the market is again in equilibrium. By comparing the new equilibrium with the initial one, we would see that price has risen and quantity traded has increased, and so we can predict that the effect of a rise in buyers' incomes is to raise price and increase the quantity bought and sold. The same technique could have been used for a change in any other underlying determinant.

The word 'comparative' is due to the fact that we compare two equilibrium positions; the word 'static' is due to the fact that they are static equilibrium positions, i.e. in the absence of any change in the underlying determinants, the equilibrium positions would be maintained for all time – there is no built-in process of time-related change in the model.

Note that to be able to apply this kind of analysis, we first have to assure ourselves that the system under study does move to an equilibrium position after some change. Also, the method of analysis tells us nothing about the behaviour of the system between the two equilibrium positions or how long it takes to move from one equilibrium to another – for this we need a DYNAMIC ANALYSIS.

Comparative statics. ▷ COMPARATIVE STATIC EQUILIBRIUM ANALYSIS.

Compensation principle. A test of whether or not SOCIAL WELFARE is increased by some economic change. Virtually all economic policy measures involve making some people better off while others are made worse off. Suppose we wish to decide whether a given change increases total social welfare, but do not want to make value judgements about the desirability of making some people better off and some worse off. We might then apply the compensation principle, which states that, if the gainers from the change could fully compensate the losers from the change, and still be better off than they were before the change, then the change can be deemed desirable, even if the compensation is not actually paid.

For example, suppose the change in question is the construction of a reservoir in a valley containing a small number of farms, the purpose of the reservoir being to supply water to a near-by town. If the people who benefit from the reservoir, i.e. the urban population, could in principle fully compensate the losers, i.e. the farmers, and still feel that they will be better off as a result of the reservoir, then the reservoir should be built.

Though in this example the principle seems quite plausible and clear-cut, it is not difficult to think of types of economic policy measures for which the principle would be inapplicable. Unless compensation is actually paid, we cannot say that the change is desirable since some people actually are being made worse off. Also, in practice, it may be difficult to find if the gainers *could* compensate the losers and still be better off. Finally, we might ask if we really want a criterion of the desirability of economic change which tries to avoid value judgements about INCOME DISTRIBUTION (in fact, the idea that it is a good thing to make some people better off and no one else worse off is itself a value judgement which, though a fairly mild one, may not be acceptable in all circumstances). Economic policy is ultimately the responsibility of a political authority, which will generally have explicit value judgements about the desirability of making various groups of people better or worse off, and which will be accountable through the political process for the judgements it makes. Hence, the compensation principle may be superfluous. ▷ SOCIAL WELFARE FUNCTION.

Compensatory finance. Synonym for DEFICIT FINANCING. ▷ UNITED NATIONS CONFERENCE ON TRADE AND DEVELOPMENT.

Competition. ▷ ATOMISTIC COMPETITION; PERFECT COMPETITION.

Complementary demand. Two or more products are said to be complementary in DEMAND when an increase in demand for one is generally associated with an increase in demand for another. Examples are: bread and butter; motor-cars and petrol; cigarettes and cigarette lighters. The complementarity stems from the nature of consumer tastes, which result in some products being habitually consumed together, e.g. bread and butter; or from some technical relationship which makes one necessary if the other is to be enjoyed. It follows that complementarity need not exist for all time – tastes may change, or technology may alter (e.g. electric power-driven motor-cars). Goods having such complementarity are called *complementary goods.* ⬦ COMPOSITE DEMAND.

Complementary goods. ⬦ COMPLEMENTARY DEMAND.

Composite demand. The DEMAND for a product which arises from several uses of the product. Thus, leather may be demanded for making shoes and briefcases; sheet-steel may be demanded for making car bodies and tin cans, etc. ⬦ COMPLEMENTARY DEMAND.

Compound interest. INTEREST which is not only calculated on the original CAPITAL invested, but also on the interest earned in previous periods, e.g. a capital of £100 invested at 10 per cent would yield $\frac{10}{100} \times 100 = £10$ in the first year, $\frac{10}{100} \times (100 + 10) = £11$ in the second year, etc. This contrasts with *simple interest*, in which the interest is calculated on the original capital only, for all years.

Concealed discount. ⬦ TRADE DISCOUNT.

Concentration. The degree to which a relatively small number of firms account for a significant proportion of output, employment, etc., in an industry. An industry is concentrated where a small number of large firms account for a high proportion of these things. An industry is highly concentrated, for example, if 80 per cent of employment is in the four largest firms; an industry with low concentration would be one which contained a hundred firms each of approximately the same size. The degree of concentration is therefore a characteristic of the SIZE DISTRIBUTION OF FIRMS in the industry. As such, it is one important aspect of MARKET STRUCTURE.

Interest in the degree of concentration which exists in an industry arises because it is an important determinant of the way firms behave, and of the resulting levels of prices, outputs, and PROFITS. Consider three standard models of PRICE THEORY: PERFECT COMPETITION; OLIGOPOLY; and MONOPOLY. The first is characterized by a large number of small firms, i.e. by a very low degree of concentration, and since it is so small relative to the total market, each firm takes the market price as given and adjusts to it. As a result, price is equated to MARGINAL COST, which is a necessary condition for an optimum allocation of resources (⇨ ECONOMIC EFFICIENCY). In oligopoly, on the other hand, there is a high degree of concentration: a small number of firms control a large percentage of sales, net ASSETS, etc. Firms may adopt policies of COLLUSION, spend large amounts on ADVERTISING and other forms of NON-PRICE COMPETITION, restrict entry of new sellers and adopt other policies which tend to run counter to the interest of consumers, while prices will tend to exceed marginal costs. Finally, in monopoly there is complete concentration. In this case, economic theory suggests that price will exceed marginal costs, that there may be a tendency to inefficiency and greater profits than normal profits. Hence, in each of these cases, the degree of concentration is an important determinant of the economic efficiency of the market. Attempts have also been made to measure the concentration in the economy as a whole, sometimes referred to as *aggregate concentration*. ⇨ CONCENTRATION RATIO.

Concentration ratio. A single number which attempts to indicate the degree of CONCENTRATION which exists in an industry. Various types of concentration ratio exist:

(a) The percentage of total industry sales, employment or some other measure of size, held by the largest three, four or eight firms. The greater this percentage, the more concentrated the industry.

(b) The smallest number of firms whose sales, employment or some other size measure sum to a given percentage of the total industry sales, employment, etc. – normally 60, 75 and 80 per cent. The smaller this number, the more concentrated the industry.

(c) The *Herfindahl Index*, so named after the American economist, Orris C. Herfindahl, who devised it. This takes the value of sales, employment or other size measure for each firm, expresses each of these as a proportion of total industry sales, employment, etc., squares each of these proportions, and then sums them. The formula for the index is:

$$H = \sum_{i=1}^{n} \left(\frac{X_i}{X} \right)^2$$

where H is the Herfindahl Index, X_i is the value of the size variable for the i'th firm ($i = 1, 2, \ldots n$), and X is the total value of the variable for the industry. The largest value H can take is 1, and this is when one firm has 100 per cent of sales, etc., in the industry. The smallest value H can take is $1/n$ (n is the number of firms in the industry), and this occurs when the firms in the industry are all of exactly equal size. These properties of the index accord well with our intuitive ideas of concentration.

No attempt to summarize a complicated concept in a single statistic can be entirely successful, and concentration ratios are no exception. They cannot be better than the data on which they are based, and, because of difficulties of data collection and industry definitions in the presence of multi-product ESTABLISHMENTS, a given concentration ratio may, as calculated, be somewhat inaccurate. More importantly, the first two types of ratio listed above suffer from the conceptual weakness of not relating to the whole SIZE DISTRIBUTION OF FIRMS, but rather to just a single point on it. For example, if we calculated that, in each of two industries, the four largest firms accounted for 60 per cent of total sales, we may conclude that there is an 'equal degree of concentration' in the industries. However, it would surely make for a difference in behaviour of firms in each industry, if, in one industry, three large firms accounted for the remaining 40 per cent, while, in the other, twenty firms of varying size supply this proportion. The Herfindahl Index, on the other hand, avoids this problem, since it incorporates the size of each firm, but, at the same time, the data on which to calculate the index is not usually forthcoming in sufficient quantity. Despite their limitations, of which several more exist than can be mentioned here, concentration ratios can be extremely useful in industrial economics, particularly in investigating relationships between such factors as PROFITS, ADVERTISING, RESEARCH AND DEVELOPMENT, on the one hand, and MARKET STRUCTURE on the other. Awareness of their limitations is, however, important in interpreting the conclusions of these studies.

Confirming houses. An agency in Britain which purchases and arranges the export of goods on behalf of overseas buyers.

Conglomerate. A business organization generally consisting of a HOLD-ING COMPANY and a group of subsidiary companies engaged in dissimilar activities. The organization generally grows by MERGER or TAKE-OVER, and bases its success on its central management expertise. ⇨ INTEGRATION.

Consolidated fund. Sums standing to the account of the EXCHEQUER (for which it is often used synonymously) into which the proceeds of TAXATION are paid and from which government expenditures

($\Diamond$ BUDGET) are made. Prior to 1787, different funds were maintained for various purposes and taxation receipts divided among them, but after that date the various funds were consolidated. *Consolidated fund standing services* is an item in the British budget which includes expenditure authorized by specific legislation. This expenditure, such as servicing the NATIONAL DEBT, is paid out of the consolidated fund and, unlike SUPPLY SERVICES, does not have to be voted annually in Parliament.

Consolidated stock. $\Diamond$ CONSOLS.

Consols. Abbreviation for *consolidated stock*: unredeemable government stock first issued in the eighteenth century as a consolidation of the NATIONAL DEBT. Consols bear an interest of $2\frac{1}{2}$ per cent and have a total nominal value of £267 million.

Conspicuous consumption. CONSUMPTION of goods which is ostentatious and intended to impress, so that the satisfaction derived from the consumption arises from the effect on other people, rather than from the inherent utility of the good itself. Such aspects of consumer psychology as these, and their implications for orthodox consumer theory, were most fully analysed by Thorstein Veblen in his book *Theory of the Leisure Class* (1899).

Consumer credit. Short-term LOANS to the ordinary public for the purchase of specific goods. Consumer credit takes the form of CREDIT by shopkeepers and other suppliers, CREDIT ACCOUNTS, PERSONAL LOANS and HIRE PURCHASE. OVERDRAFTS, money lenders and other private sources of borrowing are not referred to as consumer credit, either because they are not tied to the purchase of specific goods or because they are long-term loans, e.g. MORTGAGES. $\Diamond$ BANKING; CHECK TRADING; CREDIT; FINANCE; FINANCE HOUSES.

Consumer surplus. The difference between the total amount of MONEY an individual would be prepared to pay for some quantity of a good, and the amount he actually has to pay. If we were to ask an individual consumer to tell us the maximum amount he would be prepared to pay rather than go without some quantity of a particular good, we should generally find that this exceeds the amount of money he actually does pay, i.e. PRICE per unit of the good multiplied by the quantity. This is because there is a 'surplus' of satisfaction or UTILITY from the consumption of the good which is not completely swallowed up by the total expenditure on the good. The money value of this 'surplus' satisfaction is the consumer surplus. A rigorous analysis of the nature of consumer surplus was first put forward by A. MARSHALL. Its existence stems essentially from the tendency for MARGINAL UTILITY to diminish as consumption of a good is increased. The sum of total expenditure on a good, and the consumer surplus derived from it, will give a money measure of the total utility derived from its consumption. The concept of consumer surplus is of some importance in economics, particularly in WELFARE ECONOMICS. ⟡ A. J. E. J. DUPUIT.

Consumer expenditure. Total expenditure in the economy as a whole on goods and SERVICES for immediate CONSUMPTION. It constitutes about two thirds of the NATIONAL INCOME.

Consumer goods. ⟡ GOOD.

Consumers' preference. A term used to denote the relative strengths of consumers' wishes to consume various goods and SERVICES. In a FREE MARKET capitalist economy, resources are said to be allocated 'according to consumers' preference'. The way in which consumers divide up their total expenditure among the goods and services available is determined by their relative preferences (as well as by PRICE). Total expenditure on each good or service then determines the output required from the firms producing it. This in turn determines (in conjunction with technological methods of production and prices of FACTORS OF PRODUCTION) how much of the scarce resources of the economy are used in producing each good. Thus, the greater is consumer preference for a good, the greater the demand for it, and hence the greater the amount of resources absorbed in its production. Similarly, changes in preferences will cause changes in relative demands and reallocation of RESOURCES, from goods now less preferred, as compared to the original position, to goods now more preferred. ⟡ REVEALED PREFERENCE; INDIFFERENCE ANALYSIS.

Consumers' sovereignty. This is said to exist when, within the limitations set by conditions of supply, RESOURCES are allocated in line with CONSUMER PREFERENCE, as opposed to, say, state direction. The amount of 'sovereignty' possessed by each individual consumer is, of course, determined by his INCOME.

Consumption. 1. The total expenditure in an economy on goods and SERVICES which are used up within a specified, usually short, period of time, generally a year (plus, by convention, all expenditure on defence). This expenditure will therefore not only include consumer goods and services, but also the raw materials, etc., used in production processes. It constitutes about 80 per cent of the NATIONAL INCOME. **2.** The actual physical process of using a good or service: e.g. one 'consumes' the services of a house by living in it; one 'consumes' the services of a pair of shoes by wearing them.

Consumption function. The relationship between total consumption expenditure in the economy, and total consumers' INCOME. The relationship was first defined by J. M. KEYNES, and played a central part in his economic analysis. He suggested that, owing to a 'fundamental psychological law', as income rose, CONSUMPTION would rise, but the rise in consumption would (except in very poor countries) be less than the rise in income, because some of the increase would also be saved (⟫ MARGINAL PROPENSITY TO CONSUME and AVERAGE PROPENSITY TO CONSUME). This relationship plays an important part in the Keynesian model of INCOME DETERMINA-TION, giving rise to the important concept of the MULTIPLIER. In subsequent study of the relationship, most work has centred on refining the concepts of income and consumption, measuring and quantifying the effects of changes in income on consumption, and extending the relationship to take into account other determinants of consumption. In attempting to quantify the relationship, it was found that there is often considerable short-run variation in consumption which is not accounted for by changes in income, but that when income and consumption are measured in terms of longer-run averages (say five years), there is a close relationship (⟫ LINEAR RELATIONSHIP). The variation in consumption which was unaccounted for by variation in income suggested that other influences would also be important, e.g. the COST and availability of consumer CREDIT, the value of the WEALTH possessed by the consumer.

Contango. Synonym for CARRY-OVER.

Continuation. Synonymous with CARRY-OVER.

Continuous variable. A VARIABLE which is capable of taking any fractional VALUE; that is, between any two values of the variable, however close together, we can always find an infinite number of other values of the variable. For example, between the value 2·7 and 2·8, there lie an infinite number of values which we may find by writing numbers to as many decimal places as we wish.

Contract curve. A concept of great importance in WELFARE ECON-OMICS and BARGAINING THEORY. It is defined as the locus of points at which any change in the allocation of RESOURCES or INCOME cannot make one person better off without making some-one else worse off. ⟫ ECONOMIC EFFICIENCY; F. Y. EDGEWORTH.

Conversion. Issue of a new STOCK to replace another. This may arise where a DEBENTURE is convertible into EQUITY shares or where holders of GOVERNMENT STOCK at or near redemption are offered a new stock in exchange for existing stock.

Convertible debenture stock. ⇨ DEBENTURE.

Convertibility. A CURRENCY is said to be convertible when it may be freely exchanged for another currency or gold. During the Second World War sterling was inconvertible, and it was made a condition of the WASHINGTON AGREEMENT of 1946 that it should be made fully convertible by July 1947. In fact, the sterling area's GOLD AND FOREIGN EXCHANGE RESERVES were not able to support the demand for conversion and convertibility lasted little more than five weeks. Two types of sterling emerged: (a) that earned by the dollar-area countries, which was convertible; and (b) transferable sterling, which was used to finance trade inside the STERLING AREA and which was not officially convertible. In fact, black markets grew up in which transferable sterling was converted into dollars at a discount. In February 1955, the BANK OF ENGLAND began officially to support the black market RATE OF EXCHANGE to bring it into line with the official rate. This meant, in fact, that the convertibility of transferable sterling was admitted. By the end of 1958, sterling was fully convertible for non-residents. ⇨ COMMODITY SHUNTING; DOLLAR POOL; FOREIGN EXCHANGE MARKET; SECURITY STERLING.

Corporate income tax (U.S.). ⇨ CORPORATION TAX.

Corporate planning. A business function concerned with the formulation of long-term objectives and the development of plans to achieve them. Corporate planning has become more and more formalized as business units have grown larger and more diversified. J. K. GALBRAITH argued in the *New Industrial Estate* that the enormously large CAPITAL requirements of modern technology require that the consumer and the MARKET become subservient to the planning needs of the large corporations which have come increasingly to characterize the modern economy.

Corporation tax. A tax (⇨ TAXATION), at present (1971–2) at a single rate of 40 per cent, levied on the PROFITS of all companies and unincorporated associations. It is calculated after INTEREST and all inland revenue allowances (⇨ CAPITAL ALLOWANCES), but before DIVIDEND distribution. The company also has to deduct INCOME TAX at the standard rate from dividends, and account for it to the tax authorities. This tax is regarded as being paid by the shareholder who may claim any adjustment should he not be liable to income tax or pay tax at less than the standard rate. Should these dividends be received by another company, then that company is not liable to corporation tax on them, and the tax deducted may be set off against income tax deductions from its own dividends, for which it has to account to the tax authorities. Dividends received by companies, from which tax has been deducted in this way, are known as FRANKED INVESTMENT INCOME.

In the United States, a similar tax, called *corporate income tax*, is levied on companies, but it has a progressive element. Corporation tax was introduced in Britain by the 1965 Finance Act for the 1966/7 fiscal year. Prior to that year, a profits tax of 15 per cent and income tax at the current standard rate were levied on trading profits, and shareholders were also taxed in the ordinary way on dividend INCOME. Corporation tax is designed to encourage the retention of earnings by companies, and thus to stimulate INVESTMENT. Under the previous system, assuming a standard rate of income tax of 43 per cent, then if a company retained all its profits and distributed nothing, it paid 58 per cent in tax (15 per cent plus 43 per cent). Under corporation tax it pays only 42½ per cent (40 per cent in 1971–2). It is not, in fact, clear whether or not corporation tax has encouraged retentions, and there is some controversy among economists as to whether or not it is desirable to do so. In 1971, the British government announced that it was considering changes to the corporate tax system. Either an 'imputation system' or a 'two-rate system' were the possibilities. Under the latter, corporation tax is payable at a lower rate on distributed profits but income tax is also deducted from dividends. Under the former, a single rate is applied, but part of it is allowed as a credit against shareholders' personal tax liability. Some economists argue that the allocation of capital RESOURCES is best determined by the CAPITAL MARKET, and would prefer to see a higher proportion of dividends distributed and then rechannelled back to investment via the capital market and this, it appears, is the object of the new proposals. Moreover, the possibility of TAX AVOIDANCE by individual investors liable to surtax in CLOSE COMPANIES has lead to the application of special rules to enforce distributions by these companies. Close companies have received special tax treatment since the 1920s, and the present law requires that a close trading company must distribute 60 per cent of its profits unless it is able to demonstrate that a higher rate of retention is necessary for the development of the business. For investment companies, the required standard is 100 per cent. Participators in companies that do not meet these requirements are liable to a *shortfall assessment* on the difference between their required standard of distributions and the actual distributions. This shortfall assessment is charged to surtax on the income of the participators or investors concerned. Close company tax law is somewhat complex, and there are also special provisions regarding LOANS to participators, INTEREST and salaries or fees paid to directors as well as special reliefs for small trading companies.

Companies are also liable to CAPITAL GAINS tax, but at the corporate tax rate of 40 per cent rather than the personal capital gains rate of 30 per cent. Special provisions allow capital gains taxation on the sale of productive ASSETS to be deferred (*roll-over*), where the proceeds are used to purchase new assets of the same type. There is also a special relief for persons of retirement age.

Individuals in business on their own (operating on own account), and members of PARTNERSHIPS, pay income tax on their individual shares of total profits (broadly defined in the same way as for companies). For an established business, tax is payable in any year on the profits earned in the accounting period that ended in the previous fiscal year (◊ FINANCIAL YEAR). Capital gains are chargeable at the 30 per cent rate.

Correlation. A statistical technique for determining the extent to which variations in the VALUES of one VARIABLE are associated with variations in values of another. For example, if we found that relatively high values of one variable tended to be associated with relatively high values of another, and also relatively low values tended to occur together, we would say that the variables were closely correlated or associated. Statisticians have made this notion precise, and have devised methods of measuring the degree of association, the most frequently used of which is the *correlation coefficient* (or, strictly, the *product-moment correlation coefficient*). This coefficient measures the degree of association on a scale which varies between -1 and $+1$, inclusive. If the sign of the coefficient, measured for a set of pairs of values of two variables is negative, this tells us that relatively high values of one variable tend to be associated with relatively low values of the other, and *vice versa*; i.e. there is an inverse association. If the sign of the coefficient is positive, this tells us that relatively high values of both variables tend to occur together, as do relatively low values (throughout this explanation we are using 'relatively high' and 'relatively low' in the sense of 'above average' and 'below average' respectively). The actual value of the number tells us how strong the association is. Thus, a value close to $+1$ tells us that relatively high values of one variable are very often associated with relatively high values of the other, and similarly for relatively low values. A value close to -1 tells us that relatively high values of one variable are very often associated with relatively low values of the other, and *vice versa*. On the other hand, a value close to zero, whether positive or negative, indicates that relatively high values of one variable are just about as often associated with relatively high as relatively low values of the other. Thus, stronger and stronger degrees of association are indicated as the coefficient varies from zero to ±1. The usefulness of correlation analysis lies in testing hypotheses about the relationships between variables. Thus, we could assert the following hypotheses: (a) the higher is household INCOME, the higher will be household expenditure; (b) the higher the rate of INTEREST, the lower the level of business INVESTMENT; (c) the greater the rate of cigarette smoking, the greater the incidence of lung cancer; and (d) the larger the size of the family, the shorter the duration of each child's full-time education (given the statutory minimum). These hypotheses could be tested by measuring values of the variables for households; years; groups of smokers (classified by consumption) and non-smokers; and families, respectively, and then by calculating the correlation coefficients. These would show us how closely the variables were associated in practice, and hence how confident we could be that the hypotheses were correct (or, at least, not clearly wrong).

Statisticians stress several limitations of correlation analysis in terms of the correlation coefficient here described, the most important of which is that the correlation coefficient does not itself prove anything about causation; it is possible for values of variables to be associated without there being a causal connection flowing from one variable to another. One reason for this may be that both variables are in fact determined by some third variable: changes in values of the latter cause changes in the former to be associated, without there being any causal relationship between them. An important special case of this is where time is the third variable: two variables may have strong time-trends which lead to their being highly correlated without there necessarily being a causal relation. Alternatively, a high correlation may arise for purely chance reasons, as, for example, the well-known high correlations between the number of storks nesting in Scandinavia and the birth rate in London. Thus correlation does not prove causation, and we are invariably thrown back on theoretical arguments for interpretation of the 'facts'. ⟡ MULTIPLE CORRELATION; PARTIAL CORRELATION; REGRESSION ANALYSIS; E. SLUTSKY.

Cost. Broadly, the measure of what has to be given up in order to achieve something. Two concepts of costs can be distinguished which may but need not be equivalent:

(a) *Opportunity cost:* In economics, it is considered appropriate to define cost in terms of the value of the alternatives or other opportunities which have to be foregone in order to achieve a particular thing. This will amount to the same thing as outlays (see below), if and only if the PRICES with which the outlays are calculated correctly reflect the value of alternative uses of the RESOURCES. If they do not, then the two concepts diverge, and, since opportunity cost is concerned with the real sacrifice involved in achieving something, it is the measurement of costs as 'outlays' which is incorrect (⟡ F. VON WIESER).

(b) *Outlays:* An accountant would define the cost of something as the total MONEY expenditure or outlays necessary to achieve it.

As an example of the meaning of opportunity cost, and the distinction between this and outlays, consider the situation in which a firm is considering expansion of output of one of its products. This involves it in purchasing certain INPUTS – raw materials, power, possibly some LABOUR, new machinery, etc. – and also, we assume, in diverting certain resources already possessed to the production of the GOOD – warehouse and factory space, etc. Assume also that the FINANCE for capital expenditure is provided out of RETAINED EARNINGS. The total cost of increasing production in terms of outlays would be the sum of expenditure on materials, power and new machinery, the WAGES of the additional labour assigned to this product and salary bill of extra managers assigned to it plus a proportion of OVERHEADS. The opportunity cost of the increased production, however, will consist of: (i) the outlays on the increased amounts of inputs bought in; (ii) the loss of PROFIT resulting from the fact that the production of other goods must be cut down in order to release warehouse and factory space, and divert it to the product whose output is being increased; (iii) the cost of financing the capital expenditure, which is equal to the RATE OF RETURN which the firm could have obtained on the funds used to expand production, if they had been used in the next most profitable opportunity open to the firm, whether internal or external.

The principle of opportunity cost involves asking what is actually foregone by choosing a particular alternative. This concept is preferred by economists, because it leads to a more rational process of decision-taking against which the returns from an alternative are compared to the real cost involved in undertaking it. In fact, the difference in approach to the meaning of cost, between the economist and accountant, may perhaps be attributed to the fact that the economist is primarily interested in optimal decision-taking, whereas the accountant has been traditionally more concerned with the ex-post recording and presentation of money flows.

Cost accounting, costing and cost control. Procedures by which the expenditure of a firm is related to units of output. Cost accounts, while they can be directly related to financial accounts, are concerned with the detailed elements of COST in identifiable output for purposes of PRICING, departmental budgeting and the control of manufacturing methods, material and LABOUR usage for these products rather than the overall financial results of the firm's operations. ⟡ COST.

Cost, average. ⟡ AVERAGE COSTS.

Cost, avoidable. ⟡ AVOIDABLE COSTS.

Cost-benefit analysis. A technique which attempts to set out and evaluate the SOCIAL COSTS and SOCIAL BENEFITS of INVESTMENT projects, to help to decide whether or not the projects should be undertaken. The essential difference between cost-benefit analysis and ordinary INVESTMENT APPRAISAL methods used by firms is the stress on the social costs and benefits. The aim is to identify and measure the losses and gains in economic welfare which are incurred by society as a whole if the particular project in question is undertaken. In calculating the benefits of constructing a new underground railway, for example, as well as the revenues from ticket sales, we would take into account the value of reductions in travelling-time to users, congestion costs to motorists, etc. Similarly, in calculating the costs of a new airport, in addition to the costs of land acquisition, construction and subsequent operation, the losses in welfare resulting from aircraft noise, spoilation of areas of scenic beauty, etc., would be included. As a result of this emphasis – on taking into account all significant costs and benefits and not just the costs and revenues received and incurred by the agency undertaking the project – a major problem in cost-benefit analysis is the evaluation of certain types of cost and benefit.

First is the problem of measurement in physical units. We may measure savings in travelling time in minutes and hours, and noise nuisance in decibels, but how do we measure the 'amount of pleasure' derived from a particular piece of scenery? Second is the problem of reducing all costs and benefits to a 'common denominator' so that they are comparable with one another. That is, to obtain an idea of the aggregate benefits and costs associated with a project, and to compare these for different projects whose costs and benefits are measured in different physical dimensions or none at all, it is helpful to reduce all magnitudes to some common 'unit of account'. Since the 'unit of account' most commonly used is MONEY, this generally becomes the problem of valuing costs and benefits in monetary terms. Questions which have to be answered are: What is the money value of time spent in travelling? What is the money value of the loss of visual amenity in the area in which an airport is located? In some cases, economists have developed ways in which such values may in principle be measured. Ultimately, however, many of these problems of valuation can only be resolved by political decision, which hopefully reflects society's evaluation of the costs and benefits which are not directly measurable in money terms (e.g. the value of a Norman church, or the valuation to be placed on reducing fatal accidents along a stretch of road).

This should not, however, be translated into the proposition that, since it is all a matter of politics anyway, the cost-benefit analysis is irrelevant and unnecessary, and itself a waste of RESOURCES. Careful itemization of all relevant classes of costs and benefits, the exclusion of irrelevant TRANSFER PAYMENTS, quantification of what can reasonably be quantified, and a full specification of the complete set of alternatives to the project under consideration, not only provides a much sounder basis for an eventual decision, but also permits an estimate to be made of the implicit money values that must be attached to particular non-monetary benefits and costs in order to justify a particular project. At the very least, one may then consider whether these values fall within some range of 'reasonableness', or are consistent with other such decisions. Thus, cost-benefit analysis should be viewed as a means of making the best possible information available to governmental decision-takers, rather than as a mechanical means of taking decisions.

Cost control. ⟡ COST ACCOUNTING.

Cost curves. Curves which relate TOTAL COSTS, AVERAGE COSTS or MARGINAL COSTS to rate of output.

Cost, marginal. ⟡ MARGINAL COST.

Cost of capital. ⟡ CAPITAL, COST OF.

Cost of living index. ⟡ RETAIL PRICE INDEX.

Cost, opportunity. ⇨ COST.

Cost, overhead. ⇨ FIXED COSTS.

Cost-plus. A method of PRICE-fixing in which the contractor charges the actual cost of the goods he supplies or the work he carries out plus either a percentage or an agreed absolute amount for his services. Used both during and after the Second World War for some government contracts, the cost-plus formula provides no incentive for the contractor to keep his costs to the minimum, and where the percentage service charge is applied, he actually has an incentive to inflate them. The justification for the cost-plus system is that for certain kinds of work, e.g. development contracts in advanced techniques, it is not possible to estimate costs in advance.

Cost-push inflation. INFLATION which is created and sustained by increases in costs of production, these increases being independent of the state of demand. The most common source of cost-push inflation is held to be the power of trade unions to gain wage increases (⇨ BARGAINING THEORY OF WAGES), which then lead to rises in PRICES, which in turn spark off further wage claims, etc. Critics of this theory argue that if trade unions succeeded in raising wages and prices at times when the level of AGGREGATE DEMAND has not risen by enough to justify this, there would be a tendency for UNEMPLOYMENT to increase, with subsequent deflationary effects in the economy (⇨ DEFLATION). Such a process could not continue indefinitely, and therefore cost-push certainly could not explain the persistent inflationary processes in virtually all West European economies since the Second World War. Either the price increases must be 'ratified' by stimulation of aggregate demand, to prevent the unemployment, or the inflation in fact is due to EXCESS DEMAND in the first place. This latter proposition essentially argues that advocates of the cost-push theory mistake the mechanism of adjustment for a motive force of the process. Suppose that when firms experience increased demand for their products, they do not raise prices, but instead attempt to increase output by increasing overtime, employing more workers, etc. This increased demand in the LABOUR MARKET then leads to increases in wage earnings and wage rates (these increases taking place in negotiations between unions and employers). As a result of these wage increases, firms are forced to raise prices. Clearly, however, the motive force for the price rises came from the demand increases: the wage negotiations are simply the mechanism by which excess demand is translated into wage and price increases.

The argument that inflation is caused either by ratification of wage increases, or simply by excess demand in the first place, has important implications for the control of inflation. If the purely cost-push theory is accepted, then either the government must sit back and allow unemployment to develop, or it can try to intervene in the bargaining process with political/administrative measures to restrain unions in their demands for inflationary wage claims. On the other hand, if the theories based on excess demand are accepted (⇨ DEMAND PULL), then the only really effective way to control inflation is to use monetary and fiscal policies to restrain the level of aggregate demand. It is probably true to say that, with the exception of the last few years, post-war inflation has involved both demand-pull and cost-push elements. ⇨ COHEN COMMITTEE; PRICES AND INCOMES POLICY.

Cost schedule. A table relating total costs of production to given levels of output from which schedules of MARGINAL COSTS and AVERAGE COSTS can be developed.

Costing. ⇨ COST ACCOUNTING.

Costs, fixed. ⇨ FIXED COSTS.

Costs, historical or historic. Actual costs at the time incurred. An ASSET in the BALANCE SHEET at historical cost is shown at the price actually paid for it, even though it might be worth more or cost more to replace. ⇨ DEPRECIATION.

Costs, selling. The expenses incurred in creating or maintaining the MARKET for a product. Distribution costs are normally excluded, but ADVERTISING, sales staff, sales campaign costs and sales office expenses are included.

Costs, prime. ⇨ PRIME COSTS.

Costs, social. ⇨ SOCIAL COSTS.

Costs, supplementary. ⇨ SUPPLEMENTARY COSTS.

Costs, total. ⇨ TOTAL COSTS.

Council for Mutual Economic Aid (Comecon). A council set up in 1949 consisting of the East European countries, viz. Bulgaria, Czechoslovakia, German Democratic Republic, Hungary, Poland, Romania and the U.S.S.R. with Outer Mongolia (Yugoslavia is an observer). Its aim is, by means of central planning, to develop the member countries' economies on a complementary basis for the purpose of achieving self-sufficiency. The result has been that trade with Western Europe has been kept to a fraction of requirements, in spite of the rejection by some of the East European member countries of the principle of total submission to the Comecon ideal of the central determination of their economic development. Romania, for instance, has refused to accept that she should specialize in agriculture. In 1963, the Romanians also prevented the setting up of a supra-national planning board for Comecon.

Council on Prices, Productivity and Incomes (Cohen Committee). A council set up in 1957 under the chairmanship of Lord Cohen (Lord Justice of Appeal, 1946–51) to study the problem of INFLATION and its relation to AVERAGE PRODUCTIVITY and to keep under review the development of the economy. It consisted of only three members – originally Sir Harold Howitt (chartered accountant) and D. H. ROBERTSON in addition to Lord Cohen – but invited written contributions for their consideration. Their first report, which appeared in February 1958, came out at a time when there was considerable controversy whether INFLATION was 'DEMAND PULL' or 'COST-PUSH'. The report was considered to have overemphasized the former. However, in its fourth and last report, which came out in July 1961, the council was able to write a more balanced review of the factors generating inflation. In 1959, Professor Phelps Brown replaced Professor Robertson, and in 1960 Lord Heyworth (Chairman of Unilever, 1942–60) became chairman and Sir Harold Emerson replaced Sir Harold Howitt. The council was wound up in 1962. ⟡ R. F. HARROD; F. W. PAISH; PRICES AND INCOMES POLICY.

Countervailing duty. A special additional import duty (⟡ TARIFFS) imposed on a COMMODITY to offset a reduction of its price as a result of an export subsidy in the country of origin. ⟡ DUMPING; EXPORT INCENTIVES.

Countervailing power. The idea, most fully developed by J. K. GALBRAITH, in his book *American Capitalism*, that excessive power held by one group can be balanced or neutralized by the power held by an opposing group, leading not to exploitation but to a workable and reasonably equitable economic or political system. Thus the power of large employers may be balanced by that of large trade unions, or of large food manufacturers by retail chains.

Coupon. A piece of paper entitling the owner to MONEY payment (as in BEARER BONDS), cut-price or free goods (gift coupons) or rations.

Cournot, Antoine Augustin (1801–77). Cournot was made Professor of Analysis and Mechanics at Lyon in 1834, and Rector of Grenoble University in 1835 and of Dijon University in 1854. His main economic work, *Recherches sur les principes mathématiques de la théorie* *des richesses*, was published in 1838. Other economic works were *Principes de la Théorie des richesses* (1863) and *Revue sommaire des doctrines économiques* (1877). In *Recherches*, Cournot set out in mathematical form the basic apparatus of the theory of the firm (◊ FIRM, THEORY OF) which, after being refined by A. MARSHALL, appears in elementary economic textbooks today. He was the first to set out the VARIABLES and functions facing a firm; DEMAND as a diminishing function of PRICE; COST CURVES and revenue curves. By the use of calculus, he demonstrated that a monopolist will maximize his profit at the output at which his MARGINAL COST was equal to his MARGINAL REVENUE. Cournot traced a direct logical line from the single seller (MONOPOLY) through two (DUOPOLY) or many (OLIGOPOLY) sellers to 'unlimited competition'. He showed how, in the latter case, the marginal cost equals the marginal revenue relationship of the monopolist because the price equals the marginal cost relationship of the firm in PERFECT COMPETITION. In doing so, he analysed the situation of duopoly and showed that, given that each seller assumed the other's output was unaffected by his own, they would each adjust prices and output until a position of EQUILIBRIUM was reached, somewhere between that reflected by the equations for monopoly and that for unrestricted competition. Nevertheless, in spite of the undoubted significance of his work, he had no influence on the mainstream of economic thought until his ideas were taken in and developed by Marshall.

Cover. The ratio of total to distributed PROFIT of a limited company. A DIVIDEND is said to be twice covered if it represents half the earnings of the company.

Covered bear. ◊ BEAR.

Crawling peg. ◊ EXCHANGE RATE.

Credit. Granting the use or possession of goods and services without immediate payment. There are three types of credit: (a) *Consumer credit:* credit extended formally and informally by shopkeepers, FINANCE HOUSES and others to the ordinary public for the purchase of consumer goods (◊ CONSUMER CREDIT.) (b) *Trade credit:* credit extended, for example, by material suppliers to manufacturers, or by manufacturers to wholesalers or retailers (◊ TRADE CREDIT). Virtually all exchange in manufacturing industry, services and commerce is conducted on credit. Firms may provide small discounts on accounts settled within say, one month. (c) *Bank credit:* credit consisting of LOANS and OVERDRAFTS to a bank's customers (◊ BANKING).

Credit enables a producer to bridge the gap between the production and sale of goods, and consumers to purchase goods out of future INCOME. Bank and other kinds of credit form part of the MONEY supply and have considerable economic importance. Hence, the use of credit restrictions, or CREDIT SQUEEZES, by governments to restrain the growth of total demand in times of rising prices. Credit restrictions can take the form of a limitation on the level of bank overdrafts or on the repayment periods and deposit requirements for HIRE PURCHASE agreements. In a credit squeeze, restrictions on the availability of credit are normally accompanied by higher RATES OF INTEREST. ⇨ DEAR MONEY; QUANTITY THEORY OF MONEY.

Credit account. 1. An account against which purchases may be made and paid monthly (U.S. – *charge account*). **2.** A form of revolving INSTALMENT CREDIT offered by some retail stores in which the consumer makes fixed regular monthly payments into an account and receives in return credit to purchase goods up to the limit of a certain multiple of the monthly payments, normally eight or twelve. A service charge, which is, in effect an INTEREST charge, is normally made as a percentage of the value of each purchase. **3.** Bank and agency credit cards in which the consumer pays his account monthly are also a form of credit account.

Credit banks. ⇨ COMMERCIAL BANKS.

Credit cards. ⇨ CREDIT ACCOUNT.

Credit control. A new arrangement for the control of all bank CREDIT in Britain, announced in September 1971 to replace 'credit ceilings'. Prior to the Second World War, the BANK OF ENGLAND controlled the volume of bank credit, and hence the MONEY SUPPLY, through the cash base, and also the ratio of cash to deposits of the COMMERCIAL BANKS. After the war, it controlled bank credit through the LIQUIDITY RATIO and SPECIAL DEPOSITS. In 1968, ceilings on bank advances were introduced, but these also appeared to be ineffective in restraining the growth in the money supply, and were, moreover, undesirable on the grounds that they inhibited competition between the banks. From 16 September 1971 the new system of credit control was introduced, which unlike the previous system of ratio control applied to all banks. Banks are now required to work on a day-to-day ratio of 'reserve assets' to 'eligible assets' of not less than $12\frac{1}{2}$ per cent. Eligible liabilities are defined as all sterling deposits made for a period of less than two years, plus funds obtained by switching overseas currencies into sterling. The new definition of reserve assets excludes CASH and SPECIAL DEPOSITS, and is different in other, more technical ways from the 'liquid assets' employed in the previous system of ratio control. All deposit-taking FINANCE HOUSES with eligible liabilities over £5 million are to be subjected to the same controls as banks, except that their minimum reserve ratio will be 10 per cent. Overseas banks are also included in the new system. The DISCOUNT HOUSES are treated differently from the rest of the banking system in that they are not subject to the reserve ratio on their deposits, but they have entered into a commitment to keep not less than 50 per cent of their assets in certain kinds of government securities.

Credit restrictions. ⇨ CREDIT SQUEEZE.

Credit sale. ⇨ CONSUMER CREDIT.

Credit squeeze. Government restriction on the expansion of bank CREDIT and FINANCE HOUSE credit as part of a policy to reduce the growth of AGGREGATE DEMAND. The U.K. government imposed a progressively severe credit squeeze following the 1967 DEVALUATION of sterling. In May 1968, the BANK OF ENGLAND requested banks to restrict loans to no more than 4 per cent above the level at the time of devaluation in November 1967. However, in the following November, the banks were asked to reduce their lending to 98 per cent of that level by March 1969. In the event, they were granted an extension beyond this date in which to achieve the reduction. At the same time, HIRE PURCHASE terms were made more stringent, both by increasing the percentage DEPOSIT, and by reducing the time within which the outstanding sums should be repaid. There has been some criticism of the efficacy of credit squeezes of this kind, arguments being put forward that more attention should be given to reducing the quantity of MONEY in the economy and as a result, in 1971, it was announced that credit ceilings would be abandoned and replaced by CREDIT CONTROL. ⇨ QUANTITY THEORY OF MONEY; RADCLIFFE REPORT.

Credit transfer, or Giro. A system in which a bank or post office will transfer MONEY from one account to another on receipt of written instructions. Several accounts, e.g. HOUSEHOLD or trade bills, may be included in a list which must state the location or account numbers of the payees. Credit transfers, which have been used by post offices in Europe for many years, were first introduced into Britain by the COMMERCIAL BANKS in 1961 and the Post Office in 1968. They are now rapidly being extended. Benefits to the customer include the saving on stamp duty payable on CHEQUES (since abolished in Britain), and economies in accounting procedures, though banks do make a charge for each item transferred.

Creditor nation. A country with a BALANCE OF PAYMENTS surplus. The KEYNES PLAN recognized that DISEQUILIBRIUM in international payments was as much the responsibility of creditor as of *debtor nations*. Under that plan, the International Clearing Union or international CENTRAL BANK would have given OVERDRAFTS to debtor countries and by so doing would have created deposits for the creditor countries in terms of its special CURRENCY called BANCOR, in a similar way to normal BANKING operations. However, not only would INTEREST be charged on the debtors' overdrafts but also on the creditors' deposits. Although the Keynes Plan was not accepted at the BRETTON WOODS Conference, the principle that a surplus country has 'obligations' has been accepted and a scarce currency clause written into the INTERNATIONAL MONETARY FUND agreement. Western Germany during the 1960s had a persistent balance of payments surplus. Accordingly, the DM. was revalued in 1961, and in 1968 adjustments in TURNOVER TAXES effectively increased the price of German EXPORTS and reduced the price of merchandise IMPORTS. These measures were followed in October 1969 by a further revaluation. ⟡ INTERNATIONAL LIQUIDITY.

Critical-path analysis. A technique concerned with finding the least-cost way of carrying out a task which consists of a number of activities, at least some of which have to be carried out consecutively. Hitherto, its main application has been in planning and controlling construction programmes for large industrial projects – power stations, oil refineries, etc. – though its applications are being extended to such problems as the design of clerical systems. It works by first setting out the way in which activities are related and finding the length of time required by each activity. Any sequence of activities which must be carried out consecutively defines a path, and the time taken to complete all the activities in a path is simply the sum of the separate activity times. The 'critical path' is then the path with the longest completion time. It is 'critical' in the sense that its length determines the time required by the whole task. Other paths which are not critical can be 'fitted in' around the critical path in such a way as to reduce COSTS, while the main effort at reducing activity time should clearly be directed at activities which are on the critical path.

Cross-elasticity of demand. The responsiveness of the quantity demanded of a particular good to changes in the PRICE of another good. It is measured by taking the proportionate change in quantity demanded of the first good and dividing this by the proportionate change in price of the second good. When this elasticity is positive, the goods are SUBSTITUTES (since a rise in price of one causes an increase in demand for the other), and when negative, they are complementary goods (◊ COMPLEMENTARY DEMAND). As with price elasticity of demand, cross-elasticity can be measured either by the point-elasticity formula or the arc-elasticity formula (◊ ELASTICITY). Finally, the numerical value of the elasticity will measure the closeness of the relationship between the two goods, a zero value denoting no relationship, a high positive or negative value denoting a close relationship.

Cross-section analysis. Analysis of statistical data relating to the same time period, as opposed to TIME-SERIES analysis, which studies data through time. The comparison of family expenditure on foods, for example, through the study of BUDGETS of numbers of families at different income levels might be expected to yield information about the relationship between INCOME and DEMAND for these foods. Time-series analysis would either look at the way a particular family's demand for food changed as its income changed, or would relate the total demand for foods per family to total average family income. Cross-section analysis does overcome some of the problems of time-series analysis, but the data may be difficult or costly to obtain.

Cross-subsidy. ◊ SUBSIDY.

Crowther Committee. The Committee on Consumer Credit set up under the chairmanship of Lord Crowther in July 1968 which published its report in March 1971. The committee's terms of reference were: (a) to inquire into the present law and practice governing the provision of CREDIT to individuals for financing purchases of GOODS and SERVICES for personal consumption; (b) to consider the advantages and disadvantages of existing and possible alternative arrangements for providing such credit, having regard to the interests of consumers, traders and suppliers of credit including depositors; (c) to consider in particular whether any amendment of the Moneylenders Acts is desirable; and (d) to make recommendations. The report includes the first comprehensive review of the structure and history of the consumer credit industry in the U.K. and analyses the whole range of economic, social and legal problems associated with consumer lending.

The committee found that there was no cause for alarm in the growth of the level of credit. There was no evidence of any significant degree of consumer insolvency, or to show that the growth of credit threatened economic stability. The credit industry should be left to develop within a free competitive MARKET subject only to legal controls to prevent abuse. The committee recommended that the confused array of different Acts relating to credit should be abolished and replaced by a single body of law based on the recognition that all credit was the same whether CHECK TRADING, HIRE PURCHASE or credit sale, etc. The committee proposed that a credit commissioner should be appointed to enforce the legal provisions through a licensing system.

In the committee's view, the control of hire purchase had little effect on total consumer expenditure but caused distortion, not only because it impinged more on some industries than others, but also on some types of credit more than others. It recommended therefore that powers to control hire purchase should be repealed.

Cum dividend. With DIVIDEND; the purchaser of a security quoted 'cum dividend' is entitled to receive the next dividend when due. The term 'cum', meaning 'with', is also used in a similar sense in relation to BONUS ISSUES, RIGHTS ISSUES, or INTEREST attached to SECURITIES, etc.

Cumulative preference shares. ⬦ PREFERENCE SHARES.

Currency. Notes and coin that are the 'current' medium of exchange in a country (⬦ MONEY SUPPLY.) Gold and, to a lesser extent, national currencies that act as RESERVE CURRENCIES, such as the dollar, are referred to as *international currency* because they are regarded as acceptable for the settlement of international DEBTS. BALANCE OF PAYMENTS problems have forced many countries to impose restrictions on the amount of currency which may be taken in and out of the country. ⬦ BANK-NOTE; DECIMAL CURRENCY; EXCHANGE CONTROL; EXCHANGE RATE; SOFT CURRENCY.

Currency appreciation. The increase in the EXCHANGE RATE of one CURRENCY in terms of other currencies. The term is usually applied to a currency with a floating rate of exchange; upward changes in fixed rates of exchange are called *revaluations*. For example, sterling appreciated from $3\frac{1}{2}$ to $5 during 1933 and from $2·4194 in August 1971 to $2·5293 in December 1971. Similarly, the Canadian dollar appreciated from a discount of 5 cents to parity with the U.S. dollar in 1951; it had been left to float in September 1950. ⬦ CURRENCY DEPRECIATION; DEVALUATION.

Currency depreciation. The fall in the EXCHANGE RATE of one CURRENCY in terms of other currencies. The expression is usually applied to floating exchange rates; downward changes in fixed rates of exchange are called DEVALUATIONS. When the U.K. came off the GOLD STANDARD in September 1931, sterling depreciated immediately from $4·86 to $3·97. It continued to depreciate until November 1932, by which time it had fallen by 30 per cent. The Italian lira depreciated $620 to $600 during its float between August and December 1971. ⋗ CURRENCY APPRECIATION; DEVALUATION.

Currency School. ⋗ BANKING AND CURRENCY SCHOOLS.

Currency notes. ⋗ TREASURY NOTES.

Current account. 1. The most common type of bank account, on which DEPOSITS do not earn INTEREST, but can be withdrawn by CHEQUE at any time (U.S. *demand deposit*). **2.** That part of the BALANCE OF PAYMENTS accounts recording current, i.e. non-capital, transactions.

Current assets. ⋗ ASSETS.

Current balance. The net position on the CURRENT ACCOUNT of the BALANCE OF PAYMENTS.

Current expenditure. Expenditure on recurrent, i.e. non-CAPITAL, items in business or private accounts.

Current liabilities. ⋗ LIABILITIES.

Current ratio. The ratio of the current LIABILITIES to the current ASSETS of a business. It is a measure of the extent to which current assets are being financed from long-term sources (⋗ BALANCE SHEET). Current assets normally always exceed current liabilities. The difference between the two is WORKING CAPITAL, which is normally financed from long-term sources. The amount of working capital required varies with the type of business and its commercial practices – e.g. on the proportions of its output sold for cash and on three months' CREDIT – so that the current ratio is not a universally useful guide to the solvency of a business. ⋗ LIQUIDITY RATIO.

Current yield. ⋗ YIELD.

Customs duties. ⋗ TARIFFS.

Customs drawback. The repayment of customs duties (⋗ TARIFFS) paid on imported goods which have been re-exported or used in the manufacture of exported goods.

Customs union. A customs union is established within two or more countries if all barriers (such as TARIFFS or QUOTAS) to the free exchange of each other's goods and services are removed and, at the same time, a common external tariff is established against non-members. This contrasts with a FREE TRADE AREA in which each member country retains its own tariffs *vis-à-vis* non-members (⇨ EUROPEAN ECONOMIC COMMUNITY, BENELUX, EUROPEAN FREE TRADE ASSOCIATION, CENTRAL AMERICAN COMMON MARKET, LATIN AMERICAN FREE TRADE AREA). At one time, it was generally accepted that customs unions unambiguously yielded economic benefits. Without the distortions imposed by tariffs, trade was directed in favour of the producer with advantageous costs (⇨ D. RICARDO). It was believed that as FREE TRADE was itself beneficial, in that it led to the optimal allocation of world resources, so a customs union, which was a step in that direction, must also be beneficial. However, Jacob Viner in *The Customs Union Issue*, published in 1950, pointed out that the creation of a customs union could have two effects: (a) a trade-creating effect, and (b) a trade-diversion effect. Although the former might be a gain, greater losses might be incurred by the latter. Take the example of two countries A and B and the rest of the world C producing a particular commodity for £50, £40 and £30 respectively. The home market of A is protected by a 75 per cent *ad valorem* import duty, so that A has no trade. Country A is devoting £50 of resources to the production of the commodity. Country A then forms a customs union with B and trade is created because it is cheaper for A to obtain the commodity from B than to produce it itself. There is a gain in so far as A is £10 better off. On the other hand, if Country A's original import duty were 50 per cent *ad valorem*, trade would then be taking place with the rest of the world, as this would be the least-cost source to A. In this case, if A forms a customs union with B it will switch its trade because it can obtain the commodity for £40 from B compared with £30 + 50% = £45 from C. This as trade diversion represents a move away from the optimum of RESOURCE allocation, because B is a higher real-cost source than C (⇨ SECOND BEST, THEORY OF). Whether, therefore, a customs union will yield overall gains from shifts in the location of production will depend on the superiority of trade creation to trade diversion. However, this type of analysis covers only a part of the problem; many other factors must be taken into account in assessing whether a customs union is beneficial. In particular, the removal of tariff barriers between countries will change the TERMS OF TRADE and therefore the relative volumes of the different commodities demanded. It will shift the commodity pattern of trade as well as the geographical origins of the commodities traded. Whether a community will finish up better off therefore depends on the price and income elasticities of demand for the commodities traded ($\diamond$ELASTICITY). An added benefit may accrue because the increase in the size of markets may enable ECONOMIES OF SCALE to be made. Finally, a protective tariff is initially imposed because home costs are high; but home costs may remain high because a protective tariff is imposed. Removal of the tariff may induce more efficient operation and lower costs.

Cycle, trade. $\diamond$ TRADE CYCLE.

Cyclical unemployment. UNEMPLOYMENT which results from the TRADE CYCLE. Downswings in the level of economic activity in the economy create unemployment which will be eliminated in the upswing. Cyclical unemployment clearly can be reduced by reducing the extent of the downswings in the trade cycle, and this is in fact what post-war economic policy in Britain has to quite a large extent succeeded in doing.

D

Dated securities. BONDS, BILLS OF EXCHANGE or other SECURITIES which have a stated date for redemption (repayment) of their nominal value. *Short-dated securities* are those for which the REDEMPTION DATE is near; *long-dated securities* are those for which it is a long time ahead.

Deadweight debt. A DEBT incurred to meet CURRENT EXPENDITURE, or which for any other reason is not covered by a real ASSET. Most of the NATIONAL DEBT is deadweight debt since it was incurred to finance war.

Dear money (tight money). A deliberate policy of keeping RATES OF INTEREST high. Dear money is often accompanied by restrictions on the availability of CREDIT, and it is aimed at reducing borrowing and economic activity usually in the interest of fighting INFLATION and/or attracting CAPITAL from abroad in the interests of the BALANCE OF PAYMENTS. ⟡ MONETARY POLICY; QUANTITY THEORY OF MONEY.

Death rate. The number of deaths occurring in any year for every 1,000 of the population is referred to as the crude death rate. It may be quoted for each sex and each age-group. The rapid growth in U.K. population in the early nineteenth century is attributed more to the decline in the death rate than to an increase in BIRTH RATE. A similar effect is to be observed in the highly populated DEVELOPING COUNTRIES of Asia.

Debentures, debenture stock. Fixed-interest SECURITIES issued by limited companies in return for long-term LOANS. Debentures are dated for redemption (i.e. repayment of their nominal value by the borrower to the holder) between ten to forty years ahead (⟡ REDEMPTION DATE). Very occasionally debentures may be irredeemable. There are two main types of debenture: (a) *mortgage debentures* which are secured by a MORTGAGE on specific ASSETS of the company; and (b) *floating-charge debentures,* where its assets are not suitable for a fixed charge (⟡ FLOATING DEBENTURES). Debenture interest must be paid whether the company makes a PROFIT or not. In the event of non-payment, debenture holders can force LIQUIDATION and rank ahead of all shareholders in their claims on the company's assets. The interest which debentures bear depends partly on long-term RATES OF INTEREST prevailing at the time and partly on the type of debenture, but will in any case, because of the lower risk involved, be less than borne by PREFERENCE SHARES. Debenture shares are most appropriate for financing companies whose profits are stable and which have substantial fixed assets, such as property companies.

Convertible debentures carry an option at a fixed future date to convert the STOCK into ordinary SHARES at a fixed price. This option is compensated for by a lower rate of interest than an ordinary debenture, but convertible debentures are attractive since they offer the investor, without sacrificing his security, the prospect of purchasing EQUITY shares cheaply in the future. For this reason, convertible debentures are issued at times when it is difficult to raise CAPITAL either by equity or fixed-interest securities.

Debt. A sum of MONEY or other property owed by one person or organization to another. Debt comes into being through the granting of CREDIT or through raising LOAN CAPITAL. *Debt servicing* consists of paying interest on a debt. Debt is an essential part of all modern, capitalist economies. (⟡ CAPITALISM). ⟡ NATIONAL DEBT.

Debt conversion. ⟡ CONVERSION.

Debt management. The process of administering the NATIONAL DEBT, i.e. providing for the payment of INTEREST, and arranging the refinancing of maturing BONDS.

Debt ratio. ⟡ GEARING.

Debtor nation. ⟡ CREDITOR NATION.

Decasualization. The abolition of the practice of the casual employment of workers; an expression first used by Lord BEVERIDGE. The report of the Royal Commission on the Poor Laws and Relief of Distress in 1909 emphasized that one of the most insidious causes of social distress was the practice of casual employment, and they made a special study of the docks as a leading example. At the same time, the Report of a Special Committee on Unskilled Labour said of the London docks that 'the central evil is the maintenance of a floating reserve of LABOUR for longer than is required to meet the maximum demands of employers'. With UNEMPLOYMENT in the docks averaging about 30 per cent between the two world wars, many schemes were prepared for registering workers to limit the size of the work force. Beveridge in his *Full Employment in a Free Society* recommended that the guaranteed wage introduced during the Second World War should be continued, and that this should be followed by permanent employment. In fact, in 1947 the Dock Labour Scheme set up a register of workers and dock work was defined for a number of scheme ports. Only workers on the register could be employed to do dock work. A minimum weekly wage was guaranteed. The scheme was administered by the National Dock Labour Board. When the DEVLIN REPORT was published in 1965, about 75 per cent of the dock labour force was still casually employed, the N.D.L.B. allocating labour from its 'pool' in response to the port employers' demands. These workers attended, and were hired, by the half-day. The Devlin Report recommended the abolition of the practice of casual employment, and this was accepted in return for the elimination of restrictive practices by the dockers, and was put into effect in September 1967.

Decentralized decision taking. ▷ FREE MARKET ECONOMY.

Decimal coinage. A CURRENCY system in which the basic unit is divided into multiples of ten. The U.K. government set up a Committee of Inquiry on Decimal Currency (the Halesbury Committee) in 1961, to advise on the introduction of a decimal currency to replace the existing pound, shillings and pence duodecimal system. The committee reported in 1963, a majority opinion favouring the retention of the pound, with a hundred sub-divisions valued at 2·4d. each. A minority view held that a system based on 10s. was preferable. The Decimal Currency Act of 1967 set up the Decimal Currency Board, which was required 'to facilitate the transition from the existing currency and coinage to the new currency and coinage provided by this Act'. The Act incorporated the majority view of the committee. The U.K. switched to a decimal currency, based on the pound, on the 15 February 1971. The new coinage consists of a new halfpenny ($\frac{1}{2}$p), a new penny (1p), a two new pence (2p), a five new pence (5p), a ten new pence (10p), and a 50 new pence (50p). There are no BANK-NOTES below the value of the pound. The 5p and 10p coins were introduced in April 1968, the 50p in October 1969 and the rest in February 1971. The old coinage is being phased out over a period of four years. The halfpenny was demonetized in August 1969, and the half-crown in January 1970. Other coins were demonetized within eighteen months of February 1971, with the exception of the old 6d. The latter will remain legal tender until February 1973 at a value of $2\frac{1}{2}$p, and then a decision will be taken on whether to retain the coin as part of the decimal system.

Decreasing returns. ▷ DISECONOMY; RETURNS TO SCALE.

Deemed disposal. The assumed realization of an ASSET in the calculation of liability for CAPITAL GAINS taxation or ESTATE DUTY. Shares in a company, for example, might be valued and tax charged on the difference between that value and the price originally paid for them, even where the shares did not change hands.

Defence bonds. A savings SECURITY issued by the British government from 1939 to 1964. Now superseded by the NATIONAL DEVELOPMENT BOND.

Deferred rebate. A rebate or discount on a purchase which is accumulated for a specified period to encourage customers to remain with a particular supplier. Also called *aggregated rebate*. ⟷ MONOPOLIES COMMISSION.

Deferred shares. A SHARE issued where ORDINARY SHARES have a fixed DIVIDEND and which entitle the holders to all PROFITS after prior charges have been met. Now virtually unknown.

Deficiency payments. Payments to British farmers, by the government, of the difference between the average FREE MARKET prices for certain agricultural products and those guaranteed in the annual price review. These subsidies have been paid since the 1947 Agricultural Act and have as their object the maintenance of domestic agricultural production for strategic, aesthetic and other reasons. Other countries support agriculture, although not necessarily in the same way. ⟷ FARM PRICE REVIEW; SUBSIDY.

Deficit. An excess of LIABILITIES over ASSETS, or of an expenditure flow over an income flow, e.g. BUDGET deficit, BALANCE OF PAYMENTS deficit.

Deficit financing. A deliberate excess of expenditure over INCOME. When carried out by governments, it is also known as *compensatory finance* or *pump priming*. Such deficit financing takes the form of a budgeted deficit financed by borrowing. It has the object of stimulating economic activity and EMPLOYMENT by injecting more purchasing power into the economy. In fact, with the growth of government expenditure, BUDGET deficits are now common even in times of full employment (⟷ EMPLOYMENT, FULL) so that deficit financing in the true sense would normally consist of increasing the deficit as a matter of policy. The use of deficit financing as a part of monetary policy was first advocated by J. M. KEYNES. ⟷ QUANTITY THEORY OF MONEY.

Deflation. 1. A reduction in the level of economic activity in an economy. Deflation will result in lower levels of NATIONAL INCOME, EMPLOYMENT, and IMPORTS, and lower rates of increase of wages and prices.

It may be brought about by MONETARY POLICIES, such as increases in RATES OF INTEREST and contraction of the money supply, and/ or by FISCAL POLICIES, such as increases in TAXATION (direct and indirect) or reductions in government expenditure. The aims of deflation may be to improve the BALANCE OF PAYMENTS, partly by reducing AGGREGATE DEMAND and thus imports, and partly by causing DISINFLATION and improving exports. **2.** The adjustment of an economic variable measured in MONEY terms by a price INDEX in order to give an estimate of the change in the variable in REAL TERMS.

Demand. The willingness and ability to pay a sum of MONEY for some amount of a particular GOOD or SERVICE. ⟁ DEMAND CURVE; A. MARSHALL.

Demand curve. A curve relating PRICE per unit of a product to the quantity of the product which the consumer wishes to buy. The demand curves of all consumers in the market can be aggregated to obtain the *market demand curve*, showing the total amount of the good which consumers will wish to buy at each price. The demand curve is usually drawn between axes with price on the vertical and quantity demanded on the horizontal, and is generally portrayed as sloping downwards from left to right. This reflects the so-called 'law of demand', which can be stated as: the lower the price, the greater the quantity of the product demanded. This 'law', to which there are important exceptions, is based on an analysis of the INCOME EFFECT and the SUBSTITUTION EFFECT of relative price changes. Important exceptions to the law are: (a) where price of the product is taken as an indicator of its quality, e.g. wine; (b) where the good is an article of ostentation, so that the higher its price the more people wish to own it, e.g. certain types of motor-car or fur coats; and (c) where there is a speculative element in the purchase of something, so that a price rise now leads to the expectation of a further price rise, and more of the good will be bought (e.g. STOCKS and SHARES; ⟁ GIFFEN PARADOX). In each of these cases, the demand curve will slope upwards from left to right. ⟁ MARGINAL UTILITY; A. MARSHALL.

Demand deposit (U.S.). Money on CURRENT ACCOUNT, i.e. a BANK DEPOSIT that can be withdrawn without notice.

Demand function. The relationship between the quantity of a GOOD which a consumer wants to buy, and all the quantitative factors which determine this demand, e.g. PRICE of the good, prices of complementary goods (⟁ COMPLEMENTARY DEMAND) and SUBSTITUTES,

INCOME, HIRE PURCHASE conditions, etc. By holding all these factors except one constant, at preassigned values, we can study the relationship between quantity demanded and this one factor by observing how the former varies with changes in the latter. The DEMAND CURVE is an example of this procedure, with everything held constant in the relationship except price and quantity demanded. Tastes, needs and habits of the consumer do not enter in as explicit VARIABLES in the demand function. Rather they determine the form the function takes. ⬫ E. SLUTSKY.

Demand for labour. The amount of a particular type of labour service (measured in man-hours or numbers of workers) which firms will wish to employ at given rates of remuneration of that type of labour service. The demand for LABOUR can be considered at two levels in economic theory: at (a) that of the individual firm; and (b) that of the whole economy.

(a) *The firm:* the traditional economic theory of the firm's demand for labour assumes that the firm wishes to maximize PROFITS (⬫ FIRM, THEORY OF). The firm will wish to employ a quantity of labour such that the contribution to REVENUE made by the last labour unit just equals the cost of that unit. The contribution to revenue made by increasing EMPLOYMENT by one unit depends on two things: (i) the increase in physical output; and (ii) the extra revenue received from sale of that increase in physical output. The former depends on the marginal productivity of labour (⬫ MARGINAL PRODUCTIVITY THEORY OF WAGES), which is determined by the nature of technology and the quantities of other INPUTS, especially CAPITAL, available to the firm. The latter depends on the conditions of DEMAND for the product, i.e. the intensity and elasticity of demand. The firm's demand for labour is thus determined by this whole complex of factors.

(b) *The economy:* We could represent the aggregate economy-wide demand for labour as the sum of demands of individual firms, and combine this with the aggregate supply of labour to determine EQUILIBRIUM wage levels. Among several difficulties with this procedure, however, one of the major ones is that since the level of this demand is derived from the overall demand for goods, which depends in turn on the levels of INCOME, and hence wage levels, we cannot ignore the interdependence between the equilibrium wage rate and the position of the labour demand curve. This problem is only properly resolved by integrating the supply and demand for labour with a full MACROECONOMIC model of the economy. This is necessary because, at the level of the whole economy, the assumption of a given and constant level of aggregate purchasing power made when considering the firm alone no longer holds. ⇨ WAGE FUND THEORY.

Demand price. The PRICE which buyers will be prepared to pay for a given quantity of a GOOD or SERVICE.

Demand management. ⇨ FISCAL POLICY.

Demand pull. The name given to the set of theories of INFLATION which begin with the hypothesis that AGGREGATE DEMAND for goods and SERVICES in excess of aggregate supply is the cause of inflation. The theories are generally contrasted with COST-PUSH theories of inflation. A great deal of work has been done to try to ascertain whether post-war inflation in the U.K. has been predominantly 'demand-pull'. The conclusion has been that it has. Although there have been cost-push elements (union bargaining strength has resulted in higher wage and price increases than would have resulted from the state of excess demand by itself), some degree of EXCESS DEMAND is a necessary precondition for inflation to persist in the long-run. This precondition has been amply fulfilled in the post-war U.K. economy with its high levels of both CONSUMPTION and government expenditure. ⇨ BUDGET; COHEN COMMITTEE.

Demand schedule. A table showing the quantities of a GOOD demanded at varying prices. From this information the DEMAND CURVE can be drawn.

Demand, theory of. The branch of economic theory concerned with analysing the determinants of a consumer's choice of a particular set of purchases from all those that are open to him. The theory is essentially concerned with analysing how the consumer's tastes, INCOME and the PRICES of the goods determine his pattern of puchases. From this analysis it is possible to predict how he will respond to such changes as increased income, reduced price of a good, changed tastes, etc. In addition, it is possible to deduce the shape of the DEMAND CURVE, and clarify what determines its ELASTICITY. The analytical apparatus of choice first developed in the theory of demand, and in particular the use of INDIFFERENCE ANALYSIS, has proved to be capable of very wide application right across the whole field of economics. The theory of demand is often criticized for its apparent aridity and 'unrealism', especially by those who are prepared to take its main conclusions as obvious anyway – e.g. much of demand theory seems to be concerned with showing that when price goes down a consumer or consumers of a good will want to buy more of it, though in its full generality, the theory says only that quantity demanded will rise, fall or stay the same following a price change! However, economists have never been content simply to take the demand curve as given, and prefer to investigate its foundations in the consumption decision of the individual consumer. ⟡ A. MARSHALL.

Demography. ⟡ POPULATION.

Department of Economic Affairs (D.E.A.). A government department established by the new Labour government after the General Election of October 1964, which was the ministerial responsibility of the Secretary of State for Economic Affairs. The department had a staff of about 550 and had overall responsibility for the work of the National Economic Development Office (⟡ NATIONAL ECONOMIC DEVELOPMENT COUNCIL). In 1965, the department published a five-year NATIONAL PLAN for the growth of the U.K. economy based on an expansion of the GROSS DOMESTIC PRODUCT of 4 per cent per annum. At the time, the plan was much criticized for aiming at a historically high growth-rate, and events, leading up to DEVALUATION in 1967, soon proved the plan's expectations unrealistic. In February 1969, the D.E.A. published a much less ambitious document, *The Task Ahead, an Economic Assessment to 1972*, in which alternative growth-rates of the economy were considered. The D.E.A.'s responsibility for PRICES AND INCOMES POLICY was taken over by the new Department of Employment and Productivity when it was set up in place of the Ministry of Labour in April 1968. The D.E.A. was wound up in 1969, and its functions transferred to other government departments.

Dependent variable. A VARIABLE whose value is determined by the value(s) taken by some other variable(s). For example, in the equation: $y = 2 + 3x$, once we assign a value to x, we have determined the value of y, and y is called the dependent variable. ⟡ INDEPENDENT VARIABLE.

Deposit. Money placed in an account at a bank and constituting a claim on the bank. The term 'bank deposit' includes deposits on all types of account, including CURRENT ACCOUNTS. ⟡ BANKING.

Deposit account. A bank account in which DEPOSITS earn INTEREST, and withdrawals from which require notice. In the U.K. the COMMERCIAL BANKS normally require seven days' notice of withdrawal and pay interest at 2 per cent below BANK RATE. Deposit accounts are called *time deposits* in the U.S. and *savings accounts* in France and other European countries. ⟡ BANKING.

Depreciation. 1. The reduction in VALUE of an ASSET through wear and tear. An allowance for the depreciation on a company's assets is always made before the calculation of PROFIT on the grounds that the consumption of CAPITAL assets is one of the costs of earning the revenues of the business and is allowed as such, according to special rules, by the tax authorities. Since depreciation can only be accurately measured at the end of the life of an asset (i.e. EX POST), depreciation provisions in company accounts require an estimate both of the total amount of depreciation and the asset life. Annual depreciation provisions are normally calculated according to two methods: (a) the 'straight-line method' where the estimated residual (e.g. scrap) value of an asset is deducted from its original cost and the balance divided by the number of years of estimated life to arrive at an annual depreciation expense to set against revenue; and (b) the 'reducing-balance method'. In this case the actual depreciation expense is set at a constant proportion of the cost of the asset, i.e. a diminishing annual absolute amount. There are other methods of calculating depreciation and also of dealing with the fact that, in periods of rising prices, the replacement cost of an asset may be very much greater than its original cost. This latter problem is dealt with by revaluing assets at intervals, or even annually, using special capital cost indices and adjusting depreciation charges accordingly. This is called *replacement-cost depreciation* as opposed to *historic-cost depreciation* (▷ COST, HISTORIC) when the original cost of purchase is retained throughout the period. It should be noted that OBSOLESCENCE is distinct from depreciation, in that the former is an unforeseen change in the value of an asset for technological or economic reasons. If an asset becomes obsolescent its undepreciated value is usually written off (depreciated) completely in the year of replacement. In some cases the life of an asset may be very difficult to determine because it is specific to the production of a product the demand for which is subject to rapid changes in taste or fashion, i.e. there is a high risk of product obsolescence. In these cases the life of the asset is written off over a very short period. The purpose of depreciation provisions in accounting is to ensure that the cost of the flow of services provided by capital assests is met in the price of the company's products; it is not to build up funds for the replacement of these assets to be available at a certain date. In practice, depreciation provisions are treated as part of the net CASH FLOW of a business and are used to repay LOANS, to purchase other fixed assets or to invest in other businesses; that is, they are put

111

to the use that will give the highest possble return. Much confusion is caused by this point, since what happens to depreciation provisions – which are, in effect, transfers of funds from fixed assets to current assets and sometimes back again – is not often clear from the BALANCE SHEET. ⟡ AMORTIZATION. Depreciation is accepted for tax purposes as a charge against profits, but this depreciation has to be calculated according to certain rules and does not necessarily bear any relation to the depreciation actually charged by the business in its accounts. ⟡ CAPITAL ALLOWANCES.

2. A reduction in the value of a CURRENCY in terms of gold or other currencies under FREE MARKET conditions and coming about through a decline in the DEMAND for that currency in relation to the SUPPLY. Corresponds to DEVALUATION under a fixed parity system. ⟡ CURRENCY DEPRECIATION.

Depreciation at choice. ⟡ CAPITAL ALLOWANCES.

Depressed areas. ⟡ DEVELOPMENT AREAS.

Depression. That state of the economy in which men and machinery remain unemployed persistently, as compared with a *recession*, during which UNEMPLOYMENT is of short duration. ⟡ J. M. KEYNES; TRADE CYCLE.

Derived demand. The DEMAND for a FACTOR OF PRODUCTION is said to be a derived demand. This is because both the intensity of demand, i.e. the height of the DEMAND CURVE, and the relationship between factor price and quantity demanded, are determined by the demand for the FINAL PRODUCT. Thus, the greater the demand for the finished product, the greater the demand for the factor of production.

Devaluation. The reduction of the official rate at which one CURRENCY is exchanged for another. The pound sterling has been devalued twice since the Second World War: in September 1949, when the rate of exchange against the U.S. dollar was reduced from $4·03 to $2·80; and again in November 1967, when it was reduced to $2·40. Under the original articles of the INTERNATIONAL MONETARY FUND, its member countries agreed to the stabilization of their EXCHANGE RATES in terms of the dollar and gold. Fluctuations about the agreed par rate of ± 1 per cent (widened unofficially to ± 2·25 per cent in December 1971) are permissible, but changes in the par rate itself should be agreed by the I.M.F. and made only in the face of serious BALANCE OF PAYMENTS problems. The U.K. government, therefore, has regarded devaluation as a means of correcting a balance of payments deficit only as a measure of last resort. They have in fact predominantly relied on DEFLATION of the home market and international borrowing. Devaluation can correct a balance of payments deficit because it lowers the price of EXPORTS in terms of foreign currencies and raises the price of IMPORTS on the home market. Devaluation does not necessarily succeed in its purpose. The immediate effect is similar to an unfavourable change in the TERMS OF TRADE. For the same resources devoted to the production of exports, less foreign exchange is earned with which to pay for imports. If the level of imports remained the same, more output would have to be diverted to exports and away from home consumption and INVESTMENT, simply to maintain the *status quo*. Devaluation could lead to a loss of REAL INCOME without any benefit to the balance of payments. The implicit expectation in a controlled devaluation therefore is that the price ELASTICITIES of demand and supply are such that the 'terms of trade' effect is more than offset by shifts of both foreign and domestic demand in favour of home production (▷ MARSHALL-LERNER CRITERION). If, therefore, the home economy is, at the time of devaluation, in a position of FULL EMPLOYMENT, additional government action is required to create the spare capacity needed to meet the increased demand on home production. Unless this is carried out, the excess demand will generate INFLATION, and possibly renewed deficits in the balance of payments.

Developing country. A country which has not yet reached that stage of ECONOMIC DEVELOPMENT characterized by the growth of industrialization and a level of NATIONAL INCOME sufficient to yield the domestic SAVINGS required to finance the INVESTMENT necessary for further growth (▷ W. W. ROSTOW). The developing countries are mainly agricultural primary producers based on relatively primitive subsistence farming methods, and they rely heavily on the EXPORT earnings from the sale of their primary products to the developed countries. Their attempts to obtain significant increases in their REAL INCOMES have been frustrated by the deterioration in their TERMS OF TRADE and the rapid expansion of their populations. Their trend growth of exports has been only about half that of world trade as a whole, and this has been reduced in real terms further by the fall in their terms of trade. Many ideas have been put forward to assist these countries to go some way towards bridging the gap between them and the developed countries (▷ UNITED NATIONS CONFERENCE ON TRADE AND DEVELOPMENT). In addition, these countries have a chronic over-population

113

problem. Overall, their national income has been growing at about 4 per cent per annum which is not far short of that of the developed countries as a whole. However, their POPULATION has been growing at about $2\frac{1}{2}$ per cent per annum compared with about $1\frac{1}{4}$ per cent for the developed countries. The result is that, in terms of income per head, their growth has been only about $1\frac{1}{2}$ per cent, i.e. about half that in the developed countries. The result is that the gap between the two is getting progressively wider. The countries which can be classified as developing countries do not have identical economic resources or even problems. Those of South America and Indonesia have substantial underexploited resources in arable land and mineral deposits, whereas countries such as Greece, Egypt and India are relatively poor in this respect. Again, population is concentrated in India, Pakistan and Indonesia, which together include about 45 per cent of the total population of the developing countries, and here the dangers of population growth are far more acute. In 1964, an International Trade Centre was set up by the members of GENERAL AGREEMENT ON TARIFFS AND TRADE jointly with those of the U.N.C.T.A.D. to assist in the promotion of exports of the developing countries. It gives free services to developing countries in the field of export training, market research and publications. ⟷ ASIAN DEVELOPMENT BANK; COLOMBO PLAN.

Development areas. Geographically defined areas of the U.K. which have UNEMPLOYMENT levels significantly above those prevailing in the rest of the country. Special government assistance is given to these areas in order to raise employment. Before the 1950s, these areas were generally known as *depressed areas.* ⟷ HUNT COMMITTEE; INVESTMENT INCENTIVES.

Devlin report. The report issued by the committee, set up by the Minister of Labour, under the chairmanship of Lord Devlin which was asked to investigate 'DECASUALIZATION and causes of dissension in the (ports) industry and other matters affecting efficiency of working'. It published its final report in August 1965. The report recommended the complete decasualization of the dock labour force. This report was followed in October 1966 by the report of a second Devlin Committee of Inquiry into dock workers' pay, which laid down, *inter alia*, guaranteed weekly wage levels for dockers, to come into effect on the implementation of decasualization.

Differentiation, product. The creation of real or imagined differences in essentially the same type of product, by means of branding, packaging, ADVERTISING, quality variation, design variation, etc. It is most prevalent in consumer goods industries, e.g. washing powders, cosmetics, motor-cars, cigarettes and alcoholic beverages. The purpose of product differentiation is to build up 'consumer loyalty' to one firm's product or brand. This may permit it to raise PRICE above undifferentiated versions of the same product, and make greater PROFITS. It also may ensure greater stability of sales, which facilitates production and sales planning. Some degree of product differentiation is quite likely to be in the consumer's interests since there will generally be a range of tastes and INCOMES which are best served by a range of product qualities and designs, e.g. in the motor-car industry the range of 'models', from expensive, high-quality, high-performance sports-cars and saloons to lower priced, mass-produced motor-cars, clearly meets a wide variety of tastes and incomes. Economists' objections to product differentiation usually centre on cases where it involves wasteful expenditures on advertising, packaging and design changes. It may also lead to too many brands, which prevents the realization of full ECONOMIES OF SCALE, and it creates BARRIERS TO ENTRY of new firms and allows firms to make excess profits. ⇔ MONOPOLISTIC COMPETI-TION; OLIGOPOLY.

Diminishing marginal productivity. ⇔ MARGINAL PRODUCTIVITY, LAW OF DIMINISHING.

Diminishing marginal utility. ⇔ MARGINAL UTILITY, LAW OF DIM-INISHING.

Diminishing returns, law of. The hypothesis that if one FACTOR OF PRODUCTION is increased by small, constant amounts all other factor quantities being held constant, then after some point the resulting increases in output become smaller and smaller. Before this point is reached output may increase by constant or by increasing amounts. It is assumed under this law that the units of the variable factor are identical, and that technological knowledge does not change. Since it assumes at least one fixed factor, the hypothesis relates to the SHORT-RUN. Although it is called a 'law', it is simply an assertion that economists make about the nature of technology in the real world, and would be refuted if it was found that, under the conditions it assumes (homogeneous inputs, fixed technology), returns did not in fact tend to diminish. However, logically it appears quite plausible. Keeping fixed the number of machines, e.g., and steadily increasing the number of workers, must mean that, at some point, adding another worker adds less to output than did the addi-tion of the previous worker; in the extreme, the variable factor may become so numerous relative to the fixed factor that further additions of the former add nothing to output, or even cause a decrease in output ('too many cooks spoil the broth'). The 'law' or hypothesis is important because it underlines the theory of SHORT-RUN COST CURVES and hence the short-run theory of the firm (⟐ FIRM, THEORY OF THE). ⟐ A. R. J. TURGOT.

Direct costs. ⟐ VARIABLE COSTS.

Direct investment. INVESTMENT by companies domiciled in one country in companies domiciled in another, e.g. by TAKE-OVER or by providing the initial CAPITAL for a new company or increasing that of an existing one; in the usual sense of the term it involves investor control and always managerial involvement. Governments normally prefer direct investment to PORTFOLIO investment from overseas because the former also involves a technological input. ⟐ FOREIGN INVESTMENT.

Direct taxation. TAXATION on individuals or companies which is paid directly by them or through their employer to the Inland Revenue. In general, direct taxation is levied on WEALTH or INCOME and is in contrast to *indirect taxation* which is levied on expenditure, e.g. PURCHASE TAX. In 1970–1 about 52 per cent of total U.K. tax receipts of the central government were derived from direct taxation. Direct taxation has a disadvantage compared with indirect taxation in that it can discourage individuals from seeking additional income, especially if, for social reasons, it is imposed in steps of progressively higher incidence. The disadvantages of indirect taxes are that they are regressive (a tax on a commodity is more of a burden to the poor than the rich) and, by raising prices, can lead to INFLATION.

Disclosure requirements. ⟐ PRIVATE COMPANY.

Discount. Generally meaning a deduction from FACE VALUE, i.e. the opposite of PREMIUM. Discount has a number of specific applications in economics and commerce: (a) A *discount for cash* is a percentage deductible from an invoice as an incentive for the debtor to pay within a defined period. (b) A deduction from the retail price of a GOOD allowed to a wholesaler, retailer or other agent. (c) A charge made for cashing a BILL OF EXCHANGE or other promissory note before its maturity date (⟐ DISCOUNT HOUSE; FACTOR). (d) The difference, where negative, between the present price of a SECURITY and its issue price. ⟐ DISCOUNTED CASH FLOW.

Discount house. 1. An institution in the London DISCOUNT MARKET that purchases promissory notes and resells them or holds them until maturity. There are twelve members of the London Discount Houses Association and a number of smaller, more specialized firms engaged in the same business. According to the RADCLIFFE REPORT, the CAPITAL employed by the major London discount houses in 1957 was some £35 million, and their borrowings up to £900 million, but they employed only some 400 people in total.

2. A 'cut-price' retail store selling goods at a DISCOUNT.

Discount market. The market dealing in TREASURY BILLS, BILLS OF EXCHANGE and short-dated BONDS and consisting of the BANKING system, the ACCEPTING HOUSES and the DISCOUNT HOUSES. Although the existence of discount houses as such is unique to the City of London, a MONEY MARKET, with which the discount market is virtually synonymous, is a feature of all financial centres. The discount houses originally dealt mainly in bills of exchange accepted by the MERCHANT BANKS, but over half of their assets now consist of treasury bills and a further third or more of GILT-EDGED SECURITIES or short bonds. The discount houses purchase these securities from the government and the PRIVATE SECTOR with MONEY borrowed from the banking system, including overseas banks in London, supplemented by their own CAPITAL. Their profit is made by borrowing at very short-term (normally twenty-four-hour call-loans) and lending by DISCOUNTING securities at slightly higher RATES OF INTEREST. In this way the discount houses take up the surplus LIQUIDITY of the banking system and lend it to the government and those issuing bills of exchange. The discount houses retain some bills to maturity; others are sold to the banking system as they near maturity. The discount houses perform a useful function in providing a flexible and smooth MARKET in short-term securities, and also play an important part in the mechanism by which the authorities exert control over the monetary system. The ability of the discount houses to borrow short and lend long depends on their knowledge that they can borrow from the BANK OF ENGLAND at any time ($\diamond$ LENDER OF LAST RESORT). This borrowing, which arises when the COMMERCIAL BANKS and overseas banks call in their loans, comes about through the bank discounting ELIGIBLE PAPER for the discount houses, in which circumstances the market is said to be 'in the bank'. There is an understanding that the discount houses will always take up the treasury bill weekly tender, and do so by a 'syndicated bid'. The rate at which this bid is made naturally reflects and influences the level of all short-term interest rates, which, therefore, the TREASURY authorities push up or down by varying the amount of the tender.

Discount rate. ⟡ BANK RATE; DISCOUNTING.

Discounted cash flow (D.C.F.). A method of appraising INVESTMENTS based essentially on the idea that the VALUE, to an individual or firm, of a specific sum of MONEY, depends on precisely when it is to be received. Given the existence of INTEREST rates and the possibilities of borrowing and lending, it is always better to receive money earlier rather than later; and to pay money later rather than earlier. For example, if the current annual interest rate is 10 per cent and I have £100 today, that could be worth £110 in one year's time, £121 in two years' time, £133·10 in three years' time, and so on. It follows that if I am to receive £110 in one year's time, that is not worth the same as £110 held today. £100 held today is worth £110 in one year's time; £110 in one year's time is worth only £100 today, since that is the amount which would grow to £110 in one year's time if I invested it at 10 per cent today. But since the value of a sum of money depends on when it is received, it follows that, in appraising investments, which typically yield PROFITS over future time, we cannot simply add up the profits accruing at different points in time. It is necessary first to correct for the 'time-value' of money, and this is done by DISCOUNTING, i.e. dividing by a suitable FACTOR to find what the present worth or PRESENT VALUE of a future sum really is. The result of this procedure will then be a discounted CASH FLOW, on the basis of which the true profitability of the investment can be assessed. There are several specific procedures based on the idea of discounted cash flow (⟡ NET PRESENT VALUE; INTERNAL RATE OF RETURN).

Discounting. 1. The application of a discount or RATE OF INTEREST to a CAPITAL sum or title to such a sum. Calculations of PRESENT VALUE or the price of a bill before maturity are made by discounting at the current appropriate rate of interest. **2.** The future effects of an anticipated decline or increase in PROFITS or some other event on SECURITY prices, commodity prices, or EXCHANGE RATES, is said to be discounted if buying or selling leads to an adjustment of present prices in line with expected future changes in these prices. **3. (U.S.)** The pledging of accounts receivable, i.e. sums owed by debtors, as COLLATERAL SECURITY against a LOAN. ⟡ DISCOUNT.

Discriminating duty. An import duty (⟡ TARIFFS) imposed at a level different from other comparable import duties such as to favour (or discourage) the importation of a particular commodity or imports from a particular country of origin. ⇔ COMMONWEALTH PREFERENCE; GENERAL AGREEMENT ON TARIFFS AND TRADE; MOST FAVOURED NATION CLAUSE.

Discriminatory prices. ⇔ PRICE DISCRIMINATION.

Diseconomy. An increase in long-run AVERAGE COSTS of production which comes about when the scale of production is increased. There is an important distinction between (a) internal diseconomies and (b) external diseconomies.

Internal diseconomies arise as the result of the expansion of the individual firm. Their main source is the possibility of increased administrative costs per unit of output, which in turn is a result of increased problems of coordinating activities on a greater scale, a lengthening of the management hierarchy and a growth of BUREAUCRACY. Though, logically, we expect that there must be scales of output at which such diseconomies occur, in practice it appears that large firms are capable of avoiding them by specialization in administrative functions, introducing mechanical and electronic equipment, e.g. computers, and delegating authority and responsibility to avoid delays and bottlenecks. There is, however, little empirical information available on internal diseconomies.

External diseconomies arise as a result of the expansion of a group of firms, this expansion creating cost increases to one or more of them. Such diseconomies are usually classified into: (i) Pecuniary: these are diseconomies arising from increases in prices of inputs caused by expansion in demand of firms which use them, e.g. expansion of the construction industry may cause wages of bricklayers to rise, thus creating an external pecuniary diseconomy to any one firm employing bricklayers (it is assumed that expansion by that firm alone would not have caused a rise in wages). (ii) Technological: this category tends to include all those not falling within the previous group. For example: as firms in particular areas expand, road congestion increases, due to increased deliveries, shipments, etc., and this increases the transport costs of all firms; similarly, expansion of a group of chemicals firms located along a river bank may lead to increased discharge of effluent into the river, thus increasing costs of cleaning and using the water to firms located downstream. ⇔ SOCIAL COSTS.

Disequilibrium. The state of a system in which EQUILIBRIUM has not been attained. That is, opposing forces are not in balance, so that there is a tendency for at least some of the ENDOGENEOUS VARIABLES in the system to change over time.

Disguised unemployment. A potential addition to the labour force which does not reveal itself unless opportunities are actually available. Consequently, it does not show up in UNEMPLOYMENT statistics. A major element of this are married women, who, if the opportunities existed, might take on jobs of various kinds – typing, clerical work, machine-minding in certain types of factory work, etc. – but otherwise do not register as unemployed. The likely extent of disguised unemployment in a given region or area may be gauged by comparing its PARTICIPATION RATE with other areas.

Dishoarding. The running down of stocks of GOODS or MONEY which have been accumulated by HOARDING.

Disinflation. The reduction or elimination of INFLATION. Should not be confused with DEFLATION.

Disinvestment. This occurs when items of CAPITAL equipment – machines, buildings, vehicles, etc. – are not replaced as they wear out, so that the stock is being reduced. This is then the opposite of INVESTMENT. ⟫ AMORTIZATION.

Disposable income. The residual of personal INCOME including TRANSFER PAYMENTS after all DIRECT TAXES and national insurance contributions have been deducted. For both the individual and the economy as a whole, this gives a measure of the amount available for expenditure on CONSUMPTION and SAVING.

Dissaving. The excess of CONSUMPTION expenditure over DISPOSABLE INCOME. Either the stock of WEALTH accumulated by past SAVING is being diminished, or borrowing against future INCOME is taking place. In either case, there is a net decrease in the ASSETS of the individual.

Distribution, Theory of. The branch of economics concerned with explaining how the prices of FACTORS OF PRODUCTION (land, LABOUR and CAPITAL), and hence the INCOMES they receive, are determined. It attempts to explain the way in which the total flow of GOODS and SERVICES available for consumption is distributed among people in the economy. The traditional approach is to analyse the question of distribution in terms of MARKET ANALYSIS: each factor of production is bought and sold in a MARKET. The conditions of the SUPPLY of and DEMAND for each factor will determine its EQUILIBRIUM PRICE (RENT, WAGES, INTEREST) and the EQUILIBRIUM QUANTITY utilized, and the product of these gives the total flow of income to that factor of production. Why does a dentist earn more than a dustman? would be answered in terms of the supply and demand conditions for each of these types of labour, and so factors such as the period of training, restrictions on entry, etc., would be taken as determining the conditions of supply and demand. Since, in the traditional theory, the DEMAND CURVE for a factor of production is determined by its MARGINAL PRODUCTIVITY, the theory is sometimes referred to as the *marginal productivity theory of distribution* (⇨ L. EULER).

There have, of course, been revisions to this theory over time. The existence of MONOPOLY and MONOPSONY in particular types of factor market has lent emphasis to the development of BARGAINING THEORIES of factor prices (in fact, such theories have been generally directed at the determination of wages). In addition, in contrast to the MICROECONOMIC approach of the traditional theory of distribution, N. KALDOR has put forward a macroeconomic theory of distribution which, though it does not explain the determination of the prices of factors of production, attempts to explain the relative shares of factors of production in national income, using an extension of the KEYNESIAN model of the economy. A major aim of this theory was to explain the observed constancy of the relative shares of wages and profits in national income over the past fifty years or so: although the traditional theory is not inconsistent with such constancy, the theory requires some rather special assumptions to give this result. In spite of this, Kaldor's theory does not seem to have received widespread acceptance, and has not supplanted the traditional theory. ⇨ M. FRIEDMAN; J. K. GALBRAITH; D. RICARDO.

Disutility. The opposite or negative of UTILITY. Theoretically, someone would have to be paid to 'consume' a GOOD which yielded disutility or would pay to reduce 'CONSUMPTION' of such a good, e.g. people install double glazing to reduce 'consumption' of noise from the road outside, or pay the local council to remove garbage, etc. Similarly, the fact that work tends to yield increasing disutility the more one does, explains why overtime rates are usually above normal hourly rates of pay.

Diversification. This occurs when a firm undertakes production of a new product, without ceasing production of its existing products. Diversification may take place for one or more reasons: (a) from a desire to spread risks or compensate for seasonal or cyclical fluctuations in demand; (b) because of the existence of spare management or productive capacity; (c) from a desire to grow faster and earn

121

greater PROFITS than are possible in existing markets, which may be declining or expected to decline; (d) following a decision to exploit to the full an innovation or research result; or (e) as a result of some specific opportunity which, though not necessarily planned for, may seem too good to miss. Diversification will often take place by MERGER with the acquisition of a firm in the industry into which the firm is diversifying, though this need by no means always be the case. Writers on diversification have stressed the fact that there are usually close links between existing products and products into which firms diversify – similarities of underlying technological characteristics, or MARKETING techniques, or very strong research and development expertise in the relevant areas of technology. In contrast to this is the pattern of diversification shown by HOLDING COMPANIES and financial trusts (▷ TRUST), and some so-called CONGLOMERATES, where the only common area of expertise is in financial management and control, and there is considerable diversity of products and technologies.

Dividend. The amount of a company's PROFITS that the board of directors decides to distribute to ordinary shareholders. It is usually expressed either as a percentage of the NOMINAL VALUE of the ORDINARY SHARE capital, or as an absolute amount per SHARE. For example, if a company has an issued CAPITAL of £100,000 in 400,000 25p ordinary shares and the directors decide to distribute £10,000, then they would declare a dividend of 10 per cent or $2\frac{1}{2}$p per share. A dividend is only the same as a YIELD if the shares stand at their NOMINAL VALUE. Some shareholders may not have bought their shares at PAR VALUE and might have paid, say, 50p each for them, in which case the yield would not be 10 but 5 per cent.

Dividends are declared at general meetings of the shareholders. Interim dividends are part payments of the annual dividend made during the year. Dividends are paid out of profits for the current year, or if profits are inadequate but the directors consider that a dividend is justified, out of reserves from profits of previous years. The profits after tax from which dividends are paid are those after payments to holders of PREFERENCE SHARES and DEBENTURES have been allowed for, the balance being split between dividends and reserves. Dividends are paid to shareholders after deduction of INCOME TAX at the standard rate, CORPORATION TAX where applicable having already been paid out by the company.

Cooperative Society dividends are distributed in proportion to the value of purchases of its members, e.g. a dividend of $2\frac{1}{2}$p is paid for every pound's worth of purchases by each member. ⬙ CUM-DIVIDEND; EX-DIVIDEND.

Dividend cover. The number of times the net PROFITS available for distribution exceed the DIVIDEND actually paid or declared. For example, if a company's net profits are £100,000 and the dividend was £5,000, then the dividend cover would be 20.

Dividend limitation. During the incomes policy in Britain (⬙ PRICES AND INCOMES POLICY), and at other times when WAGES have been 'frozen' in the interests of controlling INFLATION, the government also imposed a DIVIDEND limitation. In 1969, total ordinary dividends in respect of company account years were limited to not more than 3½ per cent above the amount declared for the previous year.

Dividend warrant. The CHEQUE by which companies pay DIVIDENDS to shareholders.

Dividend yield. ⬙ YIELD.

Division of labour. The specialization of workers in particular parts or operations of a production process. From the time of ADAM SMITH, the division of LABOUR has been a recognized source of ECONOMIES OF SCALE, and a basic reason for the development of an EXCHANGE ECONOMY. The techniques of division of labour which Adam Smith noticed in a pin-making factory have perhaps reached their ultimate development in modern motor-car assembly plants, where a particular worker's function may consist entirely of tightening a particular set of nuts. The advantages of division of labour were also clearly documented by Adam Smith – the increase in skill and speed of operation which comes through specialization, together with the time saved by workers not having to switch from one operation to another. In a broader sense, the division of labour has led to the modern exchange economy. Rather than attempting to produce each one of his needs for himself, the individual specializes on particular needs, e.g. hats, and purchases his other requirements from other specialists in exchange for hats through the medium of MONEY.

Dollar area. A group of countries whose sterling accounts could be freely converted into dollars during the post Second World War period of dollar shortage (⬙ DOLLAR GAP). These countries were the U.S. and her dependencies; Canada; Bolivia; Colombia; Costa Rica; Cuba; the Dominican Republic; Ecuador; El Salvador; Guatamala; Haiti; Honduras; Mexico; Nicaragua; Panama and Venezuela; Liberia and the Philippines. The U.K. BALANCE OF PAYMENTS statements recorded statistics of the sterling holdings of

123

the dollar area up to 1958, but the term has become less meaningful with the wider CONVERTIBILITY of sterling, and since that date has been abandoned.

Dollar certificate of deposit. ⟡ EURO-DOLLARS.

Dollar gap. The Second World War destroyed the productive capacity of Western Europe, and in the immediate post-war years the primary need was to replenish the devastated stock of capital ASSETS and raw materials. At the same time, consumers emerged from the war years with substantial MONEY balances which they had been prevented from spending. There was, therefore, at once both a high potential demand for all kinds of GOODS for consumption and INVESTMENT, and at the same time an inability of the countries of Western Europe to meet such demands from home production. European recovery had to be based on imports, and only the U.S. was in a position to supply the necessary goods. The BALANCE OF PAYMENTS of Western Europe plunged into deficit, primarily with the U.S., and gold and dollar reserves were rapidly exhausted, in spite of restrictions on IMPORTS. American aid was necessary to carry Western Europe over the post-war recovery period (⟡ EURO-PEAN RECOVERY PROGRAMME). The dollar gap lasted until the mid 1950s.

Balance of payments of O.E.E.C countries

(1,000m. $)

	1947	1948	1949	1950	1951	1952	1953	1954
Current account	−6·9	−3·6	−1·4	−0·5	−1·3	+0·8	+1·9	+2·2
Capital account	+4·9	+3·6	+2·5	+1·5	+0·4	+0·6	−0·4	−1·3
Of which economic aid	+5·8	+5·2	+4·6	+2·9	+2·3	+1·5	+1·0	+0·8

It was at one time thought that a world shortage of dollars would persist, but in recent years more concern has been expressed over a 'reverse dollar gap' or dollar glut. The U.S. balance of payments has moved into substantial deficit, especially since the escalation of the Vietnam war, and she has consequently suffered considerable losses to her gold reserves. A considerable increase has occurred in her DEFICIT on capital account arising from the growth in U.S. industrial investment overseas and her economic-aid programmes. In the ten years following the Second World War, the U.S. gold reserves averaged about $22,500m. and at the end of 1970 they stood at $10,732m. In 1971 the dollar was made inconvertible into gold (⟡ CONVERTIBILITY; INTERNATIONAL LIQUIDITY).

Dollar pool. Under the U.K. EXCHANGE CONTROL regulations, U.K. residents may not convert sterling into dollars for the purpose of PORTFOLIO investment. However, there exists a 'pool' of dollar securities held by U.K. residents, which originated prior to sterling inconvertibility, and U.K. residents are permitted to deal in the SECURITIES in this pool. In addition, the CURRENCY repatriated on the realization of dollar securities is available for further purchases of overseas investments. The rate at which the dollars in this pool exchange for sterling is above that in the official FOREIGN EXCHANGE MARKET. This premium is called the *dollar premium.* Investment institutions such as UNIT TRUST and INVESTMENT TRUSTS were requested to keep their foreign investment holdings at the level existing in May 1966 up until April 1969 when the government lifted this request. As a result, the dollar premium rose 60 per cent, only to fall during subsequent months to 20 per cent (⟡ PROPERTY CURRENCY).

Dollar premium. ⟡ DOLLAR POOL.

Domar, Evsey David (1914–   ). ⟡ HARROD-DOMAR MODEL.

Domestic bill of exchange. ⟡ INLAND BILL OF EXCHANGE.

Domestic Credit Expansion (D.C.E.). A measure of the change in the MONEY supply, which is adjusted to take into account the effects of changes in FOREIGN EXCHANGE reserves and government borrowing overseas. The normal definition of the money supply as notes, coins and BANK DEPOSITS also includes holdings of foreign exchange reserves. However, if we are primarily concerned with the changes in internal CREDIT availability (deposit creation by the banks, increased availability of notes and coin by the government), it is helpful to exclude changes in foreign exchange reserves, since these simply have a distorting effect on the measurements without any economic significance. Hence, the change in foreign exchange reserves, *less* the change in government overseas borrowing (which is regarded as simply a means of avoiding an equal change in reserves), is subtracted from the change in money supply, as conventionally measured, to get D.C.E. The measure achieved prominence when it was used in 1968 in an undertaking by the then Chancellor of the

EXCHEQUER to the INTERNATIONAL MONETARY FUND as a means of expressing the extent to which the increase in money and the availability of credit would be contained (◊ CREDIT CONTROL).

Double-entry bookkeeping. The accounting system in which every business transaction, whether a receipt or a payment of MONEY, sale or purchase of GOODS or SERVICES, gives rise to two entries, a DEBIT and a corresponding credit, traditionally on opposite pages of a ledger. The credit entries record the sources of finance, e.g. shareholders' CAPITAL, funds acquired from third parties or generated through current operations; the debit entries record the use to which that finance is put, e.g. acquisition of fixed ASSETS, STOCKS, financing of debtors and current operating expenses, etc. Since every debit entry has an equal and corresponding credit entry, it follows that if the debit and credit entries are added up they will (or should) come to the same figure, i.e. balance (◊ BALANCE SHEET). Confusion is caused by identifying credits and debits with gains or losses. While this is basically true in the very long run, the profit or loss over a short period of time is measured by selecting from ledger balances items of income and expenditure which are then used to produce a *profit-and-loss account* (U.S. *income and earned surplus statement*). ◊◊ BUSINESS FINANCE.

Double option. ◊ OPTION.

Double taxation. The situation in which the same TAX BASE is taxed more than once. Double taxation agreements between two countries are designed to avoid, for example, INCOMES of non-residents being taxed both in the country they are living in and in their country of origin.

Douglas, Major Clifford Hugh (1878–1952). ◊ SOCIAL CREDIT.

Dow Jones Index. An INDEX NUMBER of SHARE prices prevailing on the WALL STREET stock exchange.

Drawback. ◊ CUSTOMS DRAWBACK.

Dumping. Strictly, the sale of a COMMODITY on a foreign MARKET at a PRICE below MARGINAL COST. An exporting country may suffer the short-run losses of this policy in order to eliminate competition and thereby gain a MONOPOLY in the foreign market. Alternatively, it may dump in order to dispose of temporary surpluses without causing a reduction in home prices and therefore producers' INCOMES. The GENERAL AGREEMENT ON TARIFFS AND TRADE accepts the imposition of special import duties (◊ TARIFFS) to counteract such a policy if it can be established that dumping is taking place. The practice of dumping is prohibited under the terms of the EUROPEAN ECONOMIC COMMUNITY Treaty of Rome. Note that export prices which are lower than home market prices are not conclusive evidence of the existence of dumping. Rules to be followed by governments were agreed as part of the KENNEDY ROUND OF TRADE NEGOTIATIONS by the E.E.C., North America and the EUROPEAN FREE TRADE ASSOCIATION. In the U.K., these rules were embodied in the Customs Duties (Dumping and Subsidies) Act of 1969.

Duopoly. The MARKET situation in which there are only two sellers of a particular GOOD or SERVICE. The essence of this situation is that the actions of one seller affect the position of the other, and will induce some sort of response from him. Each firm cannot then predict the precise consequences of its own actions unless it can also predict the reaction of its competitor. This is the characteristic problem of OLIGOPOLY in an acute and simplified form, and so the duopoly model was often used to analyse oligopolistic situations. Without assuming something about the reactions of the two firms involved, it is impossible to find a determinate EQUILIBRIUM solution in the market. However, a problem is that there is a range of possible assumptions which could be chosen, most of which are of equal degrees of plausibility or implausibility, and which generally give different results. ⇨ A. A. COURNOT.

Duopsony. The MARKET situation in which there are only two buyers of a particular GOOD or SERVICE. It is thus the analogue of DUOPOLY on the buying side.

Dupuit, Arsène Jules Etiènne Juvénal (1804–66). A French civil engineer, whose main works relating to economics were *De la mésure de l'utilité des travaux publics* (1844) and *De l'influence des péages sur l'utilité des voies de communication* (1849). His studies of the pricing policy for public SERVICES such as roads and bridges led him to the idea of CONSUMERS' SURPLUSES and PRODUCERS' SURPLUSES. These terms were, in fact invented by MARSHALL, but the ideas were clearly brought out by Dupuit. He realized that the prices were not the maximum users would be willing to pay for services, except those users at the very margin who found it just worthwhile to pay. Consumers, therefore, benefited by the difference. Similarly, the producer selling the service obtains a surplus in so far as his fixed charge is related to his cost at the margin (⇨ MARGINAL COST) and this is greater than his AVERAGE COST. These concepts were refined by Marshall.

Durable goods. Consumer goods, like washing machines, motor-cars and TV sets, which yield SERVICES or UTILITY over time, rather than being completely used up at the moment of CONSUMPTION. Most consumer goods are in fact durable to some degree, and the term is often used in a more restricted sense to denote relatively expensive, technologically sophisticated goods – 'consumer durables' – such as the examples given above. The significance of the durability of these goods is that the conventional apparatus of demand analysis relevant to consumable goods is not directly applicable, and in fact the modes of analysis developed in capital theory are more appropriate (⭗ DEMAND, THEORY OF).

Dynamic economics. ⭗ ECONOMIC DYNAMICS.

Dynamic peg. ⭗ EXCHANGE RATE.

E

Earnings. 1. The return for human effort, as in the earnings of LABOUR and the earnings of management. In labour economics, wage earnings are distinguished from wage rates; the former include overtime, the latter relate only to earnings per hour or standard working week. Earnings may be quoted as pre- or post-tax (gross or net) and other deductions and in REAL TERMS or money terms. **2.** The INCOME of a business, part of which may be retained in the business and part distributed to the shareholders (▷ RETAINED EARNINGS). Earnings per SHARE (post-tax), which is a measure of the total return earned by a company on its ORDINARY SHARE capital, is calculated by taking gross income after DEPRECIATION, INTEREST, PREFERENCE SHARES and minority interests, deducting tax and dividing the resulting figure by the number of ordinary shares. Note that earnings per share are normally higher than the DIVIDEND per share. For example, a firm may earn 10p per share but may only pay a 5p or 20 per cent dividend on its 25p ordinary shares.

Earnings yield. ▷ YIELD.

Econometrics. The application of mathematical and statistical techniques to economic problems. Econometric studies proceed by formulating a mathematical MODEL. Then, using the best data available, statistical methods are used to obtain estimates of the PARAMETERS in the model. Methods of STATISTICAL INFERENCE are then used to decide whether the hypotheses underlying the model can be rejected or not. Econometrics is thus concerned with testing the validity of economic theories, and providing the means of making quantitative predictions. ▷▷ CORRELATION; REGRESSION ANALYSIS.

In addition, side by side with the empirical application of econometric methods, a body of statistical and mathematical theory has been developed, which is essentially concerned with the particular difficulties encountered in applying statistical methods to economic theory and data (▷ AUTO-CORRELATION; MULTICOLLINEARITY). Thus, it becomes possible to speak of 'econometric theory', and 'applied econometrics', of which the latter may still appear rather abstract to the layman.

Economic Cooperation Administration (E.C.A.). An Act for the appro-

129

priation of $6,098m. for foreign aid was signed by President Truman in 1948 and the E.C.A. was set up under Paul G. Hoffman, President of the Studebaker Corporation, to administer the fund. Under the programme, the U.K. received $2,694m. The E.C.A. was superseded by the *Mutual Security Agency* in 1951, the *Foreign Operations Administration* in 1953 and the *International Cooperation Administration* in 1955. ⟡ EUROPEAN RECOVERY PROGRAMME.

Economic development. The process of growth in total and PER CAPITA INCOME of DEVELOPING COUNTRIES, accompanied by fundamental changes in the structure of their economies. These changes generally consist of the increasing importance of industrial as opposed to agricultural activity, migration of LABOUR from rural to urban industrial areas, lessening dependence on imports for the more advanced producer and consumer goods, and on agricultural or mineral products as main exports, and finally a diminishing reliance on aid from other countries to provide funds for INVESTMENT and thus a capacity to generate growth themselves. Associated with this economic process will tend to be important social and political reform, such as revisions in the system of land tenure, and a greater democratization of political systems, but the latter are by no means inevitable. The main objective of economic development is to raise the living standard and general well-being of the people in the economy. ⟡ ECONOMIC GROWTH, STAGES OF.

Economic Development Committee (E.D.C.). ⟡ NATIONAL ECONOMIC DEVELOPMENT COUNCIL.

Economic dynamics. That part of economics which is concerned with analysing the movement of economic systems through time. The 'economic system' concerned may be a MARKET, a firm, the economy as a whole or even a whole set of interrelated economies. The essence of any 'dynamic' analysis in economics is that it is concerned with movement through time. The non-dynamic, or 'static' approach in economics analyses a system in terms of its EQUILIBRIUM: we try to specify the relationships between the VARIABLES in the system, set out the conditions which the system must satisfy for equilibrium to exist, e.g. SUPPLY equal to DEMAND, MARGINAL REVENUE equal to MARGINAL COST, SAVING equal to INVESTMENT, and then examine the characteristics of the system when it is in equlibrium. This equilibrium is 'timeless', or static, in the sense that it does not change with time, it is fixed for all time, unless one of the underlying relationships in the system changes (⟡ STATIC ECONOMICS). This is obviously unrealistic. In reality, everything is

changing with time. Nevertheless, the static approach has been extremely useful in the clarification and solution of economic problems, and in fact the basic approach of attempting to define an
equilibrium situation for the system under consideration has carried
over into dynamic economics. Dynamic economics proceeds by
setting up relationships which are explicitly time-dependent, i.e.
which contain variables assumed to change through time. In MICRO-
ECONOMICS, for example, the COBWEB THEOREM provides an
example of a dynamic analysis, in which the paths over time of
PRICE and output in a particular market are analysed. In the theory
of ECONOMIC GROWTH, the factors causing NATIONAL INCOME
to change over time, and the determinants of its rate of change,
are analysed. Similarly, in the theory of TRADE CYCLES, the
determinants of the extent of cyclical fluctuations in National
Income over time are examined. However, right throughout dynamic
economics, the instinct to search for some kind of equilibrium is still
strong. In the Cobweb Theorem, for example, we are primarily
interested in the question of whether price and output will eventually
reach values at which they will remain constant, or continue to
oscillate without limit. In GROWTH THEORY, the main question
has been, is it possible for the economy to grow continuously at
some constant rate (the equilibrium rate), and if so, what determines
that rate? The advantages of economic dynamics do not therefore
lie in the fact that it abandons the notion of equilibrium. Rather, they
lie in the fact that there are many problems in which we are interested,
the essence of which is that they involve changes over time (in fact,
the question of whether static equilibrium position will ever be
achieved is one such problem), and so only a dynamic analysis can
give the answers we require. ⇨ J. C. L. S. DE SISMONDI.

Economic efficiency. This can be broken down into two parts: (a) productive efficiency; and (b) allocative efficiency. Suppose we ask
an engineer to write down all the possible quantities of INPUTS
which could be combined to make a given quantity of some particular
GOOD. We could first of all eliminate all those combinations of inputs
which involved more of every input than the other combinations,
but this would very probably leave us with a number of possible
combinations. If the engineer had taken into account the best known
technology in writing out the 'production possibilities', we could
say that the set of input combinations remaining was the technologically most efficient set, but we would have no technological
grounds for choosing any one of them. This is where the concept of

131

economic efficiency comes in. If we now took the PRICES of the inputs, and found the total COST of each input combination (by summing the products of price and input quantity for each combination), economic efficiency would be achieved by choosing that combination which costs least. Thus, economic efficiency in production relates output to cost, using data on input quantities and prices, and attempts to minimize cost for a given level of output, or, equivalently, to maximize output for a given level of cost. ⇨ LINEAR PROGRAMMING.

Allocative efficiency relates to the way in which scarce RESOURCES are allocated among the goods and SERVICES produced by the economy. Resources are said to be allocated efficiently when it is not possible to change the allocation of resources, increasing quantities of some goods and reducing quantities of others, without making someone worse off than before. That is, if it is possible to reallocate resources and make some people better off (in the sense that they prefer the second situation to the first) while making no one else worse off, then the existing pattern of resource allocation is not efficient. This criterion of efficiency is called the Pareto criterion, after the economist and sociologist V. F. D. PARETO. If a particular allocation of resources is efficient in this sense, then it is called 'Pareto-optimal'. That branch of economics known as WELFARE ECONOMICS has been largely concerned with the attempt to establish the necessary conditions which must be fulfilled for an efficient allocation of resources. The main practical result of the analysis of allocative efficiency has been a set of propositions about the ways in which certain features of actual economies – MONOPOLIES, MONOPSONIES, indirect taxation (⇨ DIRECT TAXATION) etc. – impair allocative efficiency and the policy implications these entail. ⇨ X-EFFICIENCY.

Economic growth. The steady process of increasing productive capacity of the economy, and hence of increasing NATIONAL INCOME. The analysis of economic growth has played an increasingly important part in economics in the last two or three decades. On the one hand, awareness of the problems of DEVELOPING COUNTRIES, and the inapplicability of conventional tools to these problems, has led to the development of a whole body of theoretical and descriptive economics concerned with them. On the other hand, the shift of emphasis away from the problem of persistent UNEMPLOYMENT in advanced industrialized capitalist economies (⇨ CAPITALISM) towards the problems of FULL EMPLOYMENT has naturally led to the question of what determines the rate at which the economy grows over time. No definitive answers have yet emerged, but the general emphasis is on the rate of growth of the LABOUR FORCE, the proportion of national income saved and invested and the rate of technological improvements (including increasing skill of the labour force, and managerial efficiency), as being the main determinants. The economic theories of growth have been rather abstract and formalistic, and much more attention has been paid to the logical and mathematical properties of the various growth MODELS than to their empirical relevance, which is fairly low (⇨ HARROD-DOMAR MODEL). The everyday concern with economic growth arises out of the fact that the greater the rate of growth of the economy, the greater, other things being equal, the increase in the level of well-being (⇨ WELFARE ECONOMICS). Hence comparisons between the growth rates of the U.K. and other countries have long since given the impression that the level of well-being is not increasing as rapidly as it might be, which has in turn led to the search for new policies to stimulate growth. Several economists, chief among whom is E. J. Mishan, have however pointed out the possible fallacies in this. The U.K. economy may be growing more slowly than others because we prefer to consume more now rather than later, i.e. we have a high rate of TIME PREFERENCE. This is perfectly rational, in the sense that a high preference for current as opposed to future consumption is, on economic grounds alone, no more reprehensible than a low preference. Hence, the idea that we should consume less, in order to save and invest more, and grow as fast as other countries, is both crude and paternalistic. Dr Mishan has also criticized the preoccupation with economic growth on the grounds that unless SOCIAL COSTS incurred are allowed for, e.g. the costs of environmental pollution, the welfare benefits may be illusory.

Economic growth, stages of. The five stages of economic growth which all economies are considered as going through in their development from fairly poor agricultural societies to highly industrialized mass-consumption economies. These five stages were defined and analysed by W. W. ROSTOW in his book *The Stages of Economic Growth*. The five stages in question are:

(a) The traditional society, in which adherence to long-lived economic and social systems and customs means that output per head is low and tends not to rise.

(b) The stage of the establishment of the pre-conditions for 'take-off' (see below). This stage is a period of transition, in which the traditional systems are overcome, and the economy is made capable of exploiting the fruits of modern science and technology.

(c) The take-off stage. 'Take-off' represents the point at which the 'old blocks and the resistances to steady growth are finally overcome', and growth becomes the normal condition of the economy. The economy begins to generate its own INVESTMENT and technological improvement at sufficiently high rates so as to make growth virtually self-sustaining.

(d) The 'drive to maturity', which is the stage of increasing sophistication of the economy. Against the background of steady growth, new industries are developed, there is less reliance on IMPORTS and more exporting activity, and the economy 'demonstrates' its capacity to move beyond the original industries which powered its take-off, and to absorb and to apply efficiently the most advanced fruits of modern technology.

(e) The fourth stage ends in the attainment of the fifth stage, which is the age of high mass consumption, where there is an affluent population, and durable and sophisticated consumers' GOODS and SERVICES are the leading sectors of production.

As a broad and imaginative description of the process of economic growth, this characterization of the stages of growth is interesting and possibly useful, having much the same flavour as KARL MARX'S famous theory of the evolution of society from feudalism to bourgeois CAPITALISM and finally to communism. It also leads directly to a policy conclusion which was already favoured by many: aid should be given to the economies at the pre-take-off stages, in an attempt to get them to the take-off stage. Once this is achieved, these economies will have their own dynamic and momentum, and hence aid becomes much less necessary. The theory has had only limited impact among professional economists concerned with the problem of ECONOMIC DEVELOPMENT. Partly this is because Rostow's analysis of exactly what factors were responsible for take-off, and subsequent self-generating growth tended to be vague, ambiguous and incomplete. Also the theory is framed in such general terms that it can be made consistent with virtually any past growth situation. Partly also perhaps, the broad sweep of the historian's vision, with the implication of the inexorability of the historical processes, is not of very much help in trying to solve the particular development problems of particular economies.

Economic imperialism. The assertion of influence of one country over another based on economic advantage. An emergent underdeveloped country has need for INVESTMENT capital which it cannot hope to finance from its own SAVINGS. Being also a primary producer, it must depend on the advanced industrial nations for its EXPORTS. The former, therefore, can exert authority both through VISIBLE TRADE and the flow of investment capital.

Economic rent. The excess of total payments to a FACTOR OF PRODUC-TION (land, LABOUR or CAPITAL) over and above its total TRANS-FER EARNINGS. For example, a film-star might receive an annual INCOME of £20,000. If he were not a film-star, his occupation might be a shoe salesman earning £1,000 a year. If this was the only alternative, any income over £1,000 a year would be more than enough to make him stay a film-star. Hence, we could calculate that his economic rent was £19,000 a year. ⇨ QUASI-RENT.

Economic sanction. A measure, taken in respect of some economic activity, which has the effect of damaging another country's economy. Examples would be: a complete embargo of trade between countries; refusal to permit BANK DEPOSITS held in the country imposing the sanction to be drawn upon by the government and residents of another; etc. An example of the aims and nature of economic sanctions was provided by the measures taken by the U.K. government in the Rhodesia independence conflict.

Economies of scale. These exist when expansion of the scale of productive capacity of a firm or industry causes total production costs to increase less than proportionately with OUTPUT. As a result LONG-RUN average costs of production fall (⇨ AVERAGE COSTS). Economies of scale are generally classified as:

(a) *Internal economies*: These occur as a result of the expansion of the individual firm, independently of changes in size of the rest of the firms in the industry. The most important of the sources of economies of scale are:

(i) Indivisibilities: Many types of plant and machinery have, for engineering reasons, a single most efficient size. Either it will be technically impossible to make the equipment at a different size, or the production costs associated with other sizes are higher. Then, as scale of output increases up to this optimum, increasing productive efficiency is achieved. Similarly, there may be indivisibilities in production processes, as well as plant. Certain types of production processes may only be viable at certain rates of output. The word *indivisibilities* is used to categorize these sources of scale economies because they would not arise if the plant and processes were capable of being increased or decreased in scale

135

by small amounts without any change in their nature, i.e. if they were perfectly divisible.

(ii) Expansion in scale of activities permits greater specialization and DIVISION OF LABOUR among workers (cf. ADAM SMITH'S dictum that division of labour is limited by the extent of the MARKET). This, in effect, is also an 'indivisibility', in that it is the result of the fixed capacity of an individual worker and the fact that this is optimally utilized when devoted exclusively to a specific task.

(iii) There may be certain 'OVERHEAD processes' which must be undertaken if any output is to be produced, but which have the same scale regardless of the subsequent rate of output. Examples would be the process of designing an aeroplane, setting up the print for a newspaper or book or, indeed, writing a book. Clearly, the more units produced the lower the cost per unit of these overhead processes.

(iv) Area-volume relationships: As a physical fact, if the volume of some vessel or container is increased to the cube of itself (i.e. a volume x is increased to x^3), the area enclosing it is increased only to the square of itself (i.e. an area y is increased to y^2). If the output capacity therefore depends on the volume while cost depends on the area, then cost increases less than proportionately to output. Among others, this relationship is held to account at least in part for the trend towards very large bulk-cargo ships (oil tankers, ore carriers).

(v) If several interrelated processes are required to make a particular product, and each process has a different optimal scale of operation, then the overall combined optimum scale is the lowest common multiple of the individual process optima.

(vi) Where stocks of raw materials, components, GOODS or MONEY are held in anticipation of random fluctuations in output, expenditure or receipts, then in general the size of the stocks will vary less than proportionately with the scale of output, expenditure or receipts. ⟡ LAW OF LARGE NUMBERS.

Thus, the above are the main ways in which internal economies of scale arise. Some, especially (i) and (ii), apply just as much to organizational and managerial activities as to production activities. In terms of the conventional theory of the firm (⟡ FIRM, THEORY OF), the effect of internal economies of scale is to cause the long-run average COST CURVE of the firm to slope downwards; if such economies exist over a very large range of outputs, then it is likely that firms will be large in size, and OLIGOPOLY or MONOPOLY will tend to emerge.

(b) *External economies:* These exist if the expansion in scale of the whole industry or group of firms results in a fall in costs of each individual firm. Analogously to external DISECONOMIES of scale, external economies are generally classified as:

(i) Pecuniary economies, or savings in money outlays, technological conditions remaining unchanged. An example would be where expansion of the whole industry led to a significant increase in demand for a particular component, whose PRICE then fell because of internal economies of scale in its manufacture.

(ii) Technological economies, resulting from increased technological efficiency, improvement in quality of INPUTS, etc.

The effect of external economies of scale in the standard theory of the firm is to shift the whole long-run average cost curve of the firm downwards. That is, long-run average cost of each firm is less at every level of output, and this requires a new curve to be drawn.

Économistes, Les. ⟡ PHYSIOCRATS.

Edgeworth, Francis Ysidro (1845–1926). Edgeworth held the Chair of Political Economy at Oxford University from 1891 to 1922 and edited the *Economic Journal* from 1891 to 1926. His published work includes *Mathematical Psychics* (1881), *Theory of Monopoly* (1897), *Theory of Distribution* (1904) and *Papers Relating to Political Economy* (1925). The latter includes the two reports of 1887 and 1889 of the committee on the study of INDEX NUMBERS set up by the British Association for the Advancement of Science, for which Edgeworth acted as secretary. Apart from economics, Edgeworth made valuable contributions to statistics and statistical method. In showing the inadequacy of the VALUE theory of W. S. JEVONS, Edgeworth invented the analytical tools of INDIFFERENCE CURVES and CONTRACT CURVES. ⟡ V. F. D. PARETO.

Elasticity. Defined, in general terms, as a measure of degree of responsiveness of one VARIABLE to changes in another. Thus, the *price elasticity of demand* is the degree of responsiveness of the quantity demanded of a good to changes in its price; INCOME ELASTICITY OF DEMAND refers to the responsiveness of the quantity demanded of a GOOD to changes in INCOME of consumers; *price elasticity of supply* is the responsiveness of the quantity of a good supplied to change in its PRICE. Numerically, it is given by the proportionate change in the DEPENDENT VARIABLE, e.g. quantity demanded, quantity supplied, divided by the proportionate change in the INDEPENDENT VARIABLE, e.g. price, income, which brought it about. The resulting elasticity measure is thus a pure number, independent of units, and so its magnitude can be readily compared for things measured in different units. For example, the price elasticity of demand for cornflakes is greater than that for Rolls-Royce motor-cars, if the elasticity measure for the former is 2, i.e. a 10 per cent fall in price increases demand for cornflakes by 20 per cent, and that for the latter is 1, i.e. a 10 per cent fall in price causes an increase of 10 per cent in quantity. It obviously means more to say that the demand for cornflakes is more responsive to change in its price than is the demand for Rolls-Royce motor-cars on the basis of this measurement, than on the basis of absolute price and quantity changes. Since elasticity is a measure of responsiveness of one variable to changes in another, it is implicit in the shape of the DEMAND CURVES, SUPPLY CURVES and COST CURVES used by the economist. Elasticity can be measured in two ways:

(a) *Arc elasticity:* Let two variables, X and Y, be such that the values taken by Y depend on those taken by X. If X changes by a certain number of units, say, DX units; then Y will also change by a certain number of units, say DY units (where D is a symbol meaning 'a small, finite change in'). The proportionate change in X can be measured in three different ways, viz:

$$DX/X_1 \text{ or } DX/X_2 \text{ or } DX \bigg/ \frac{X_1 + X_2}{2}$$

where X_1 is the initial value and X_2 the final value; and similarly we may measure the proportionate change in Y as

$$DY/Y_1 \text{ or } DY/Y_2 \text{ or } DY \bigg/ \frac{Y_1 + Y_2}{2}$$

The elasticity of Y with respect to changes in X is then:

$$\frac{\text{proportionate change in } Y}{\text{proportionate change in } X}$$

This measure is called an *arc elasticity* measurement because it is taking finite changes in X and Y, and so, if we imagine the relationship between X and Y being portrayed as a curve between two axes, we are measuring the proportionate change in Y as a result of a change in X over an arc of this curve. The defects of this measure are that the value of the elasticity may depend on the size of the change in X taken (which is essentially arbitrary), and will certainly differ according to which of the three methods of measuring the proportionate change is chosen. These defects are avoided by the second measure:

(b) *Point elasticity:* Here, we take an infinitely small change in X, dX, and find the corresponding infinitely small change in Y, dY, and express these as proportions, respectively, of their initial values, X and Y (d is a symbol meaning 'an infinitely small change in'; those who know some calculus will recognize it as the differential operator). We then find the point elasticity of Y with respect to changes in X as:

$$\frac{\text{proportionate change in } Y}{\text{proportionate change in } X} = \frac{dY/Y}{dX/X} = \frac{dY}{dX} \cdot \frac{X}{Y}$$

This measure is called a '*point*' *elasticity* measurement because it effectively measures elasticity at a point on the curve relating Y to X, corresponding to the values of X and Y chosen, and this is a result of taking infinitely small changes in X and Y. The above expression for point elasticity included the term dY/dX, which readers with some knowledge of calculus will recognize as the first derivative of Y with respect to X. In fact, point elasticity is calculated by evaluating this derivative at a particular pair of values of X and Y and inserting this into the above formula. ⟡ ALFRED MARSHALL.

With reference to price elasticity of demand (defined above), if the measured elasticity is greater than 1, it is said that the good has 'elastic demand' (e.g. cornflakes in the above example); if the elasticity is equal to 1, the good is said to be of unit elasticity (e.g. Rolls-Royce cars in the above example); and if the elasticity is less than 1, the good is said to have 'inelastic demand'. The importance of the measure of price elasticity of demand is that it tells us what will happen to total expenditure on a good if its price should change.

Elasticity of substitution. The percentage change in the proportion in which two INPUTS are used, divided by the percentage change in the RATE OF TECHNICAL SUBSTITUTION. That is, as we move from point to point along an ISOQUANT, the rate of technical substitution between the inputs will change, as will the proportion in which inputs are used. The elasticity of substitution then measures the relationship between these changes as we move along an isoquant. The usefulness of the measure is that it summarizes the ease with which one input can be substituted for the other without changing OUTPUT. A value of zero would indicate that there is no change in the proportion in which inputs must be used, i.e. they have to be used in fixed proportions and hence are not SUBSTITUTES. A

139

value of infinity would indicate no change in the rate of substitution as factor proportions are varied, i.e. they are perfect substitutes.

Eligible paper. A first-class SECURITY. 'Eligible paper' is a TREASURY BILL, short-dated government BOND or BILL OF EXCHANGE, accepted by an ACCEPTING HOUSE or a British bank and which the BANK OF ENGLAND will rediscount or accept as COLLATERAL security for LOANS to the DISCOUNT HOUSES. Since the discount office of the Bank of England is the LENDER OF LAST RESORT for the MONEY MARKET, what it classifies as eligible paper has an important influence on the PORTFOLIOS held by the discount houses who do not wish to have too great a proportion of their ASSETS in a form which could not be turned into CASH in this way.

Empirical testing. The confrontation of theories with facts.

Employment, full. The economy is said to be at full employment when only FRICTIONAL UNEMPLOYMENT exists. That is, everyone who wishes to work at the going wage-rate for his type of labour is employed, but, because it takes time to switch from one job to another, there will at any one moment be a small amount of unemployment. Thus, the full employment level of GROSS DOMESTIC PRODUCT can be thought of as measuring full-capacity output, i.e. the largest OUTPUT of which the economy is capable when all RESOURCES are employed to their feasible limits. ⟡ LORD BEVERIDGE.

Endogeneous variable. A VARIABLE whose VALUE is to be determined by forces operating within the MODEL under consideration. For example, in a model of the MARKET for wheat, the price of wheat is an endogeneous variable because it is determined by the forces of SUPPLY and DEMAND, which are incorporated in the model. ⟡ EXOGENEOUS VARIABLE.

Engel, Ernst (1821–96). ⟡ ENGEL'S LAW.

Engel's law. A law of economics stating that, with given tastes or preferences, the proportion of INCOME spent on food diminishes as incomes increase. The law was formulated by Ernst Engel, the director of the Bureau of Statistics in Prussia, in a paper published by him in 1857.

Enterprise. One or more firms under common ownership or control as defined in the Companies Act 1948. A term used in the CENSUS OF PRODUCTION to distinguish the reporting unit (ESTABLISHMENT) from the firm or unit of control.

Entrepôt. A centre at which goods are received for subsequent distribution. An *entrepôt* port has facilities for the transhipment of imported goods or their storage prior to their RE-EXPORT, without the need to pass through customs control. The port of Rotterdam is an example of an *entrepôt*.

Entrepreneur. The name given in economic theory to the owner-manager of a firm. The functions of the entrepreneur are to: (a) supply the CAPITAL of the firm; (b) organize production by buying and combining INPUTS; (c) decide on the rate of OUTPUT, in the light of his expectations about DEMAND; and (d) bear the RISK involved in these activities, risks which inevitably arise out of the fact that RESOURCES must be committed to production before the output can be sold. PROFITS constitute the income of the entrepreneur. Like the firm itself in economic theory (▷ FIRM, THEORY OF), the entrepreneur is a theoretical abstraction, although he does have an empirical counterpart in the many small firms in the economy. In the large JOINT-STOCK limited liability companies which supply the great proportion of GOODS and SERVICES in the economy, however, the entrepreneurial functions are divided. Capital is supplied by individuals and institutions who make fixed-interest LOANS, buy BONDS and DEBENTURES or ORDINARY SHARES. The firm is actually owned by its ordinary shareholders, who receive profits from operations in the form of DIVIDENDS. Since dividends fluctuate with profits and business conditions, and may be zero, ordinary shareholders also bear the risks of the enterprise. The functions of decision-taking in the firm, and the actual taking of risks (as opposed to risk-bearing), are carried out by the board of directors and salaried executives of the company. Thus, in the most important companies of the present-day economy, there is no single entrepreneur. If it could be shown that the predictions that the standard economic theory makes about the behaviour of the firm corresponded reasonably closely to what happens in practice, then its simplified 'entrepreneur' would be a useful abstraction. Many economists currently working in this field, however, regard the separation of the entrepreneurial functions as having important implications for economic theory and for the behaviour of the firm. ▷ SEPARATION OF OWNERSHIP FROM CONTROL.

Entry. ▷ BARRIERS TO ENTRY; FREEDOM OF ENTRY.

Equation of international demand. The law of comparative cost (▷ D. RICARDO) sets out the limits of the TERMS OF TRADE within which one country will exchange commodities with another. JOHN STUART MILL realized that the point at which exchange actually took place within these limits set by costs would depend on the reciprocal DEMAND of each country for the other's commodities.

141

This 'equation of international demand' will determine the EQUILIBRIUM terms of trade. It will depend, *inter alia*, on the ELASTICITIES of demand and SUPPLY of the goods traded.

Equilibrium. A state in which forces making for change in opposing directions are perfectly in balance, so that there is no tendency to change. For example, a MARKET will be in equilibrium if the quantities of the product which buyers want to buy at the prevailing PRICE is exactly matched by the amount which sellers wish to sell. If this were not so, then the price would be changing, as buyers try to buy more of a GOOD than is in fact available, or sellers try to sell more of a good than buyers are prepared to accept at prevailing prices. In this case, price is the equilibriating mechanism. The concept of equilibrium is a very general one, which can be applied to any situation which is characterized by a set of interacting forces. ⟡ GENERAL EQUILIBRIUM.

Equilibrium price. The PRICE at which a MARKET is in EQUILIBRIUM. ⟡ MARKET ANALYSIS; PRICE SYSTEM.

Equilibrium quantity. The quantity of a good which is bought and sold when a MARKET is in EQUILIBRIUM.

Equities. ⟡ EQUITY.

Equity. The residual VALUE of a company's ASSETS after all outside LIABILITIES (other than to shareholders) have been allowed for. In a MORTGAGE, or HIRE PURCHASE contract, equity is the amount left for the borrower if the asset concerned is sold and the lender repaid. The equity in a company under LIQUIDATION is the property of holders of ORDINARY SHARES, hence these shares are popularly called *equities*. Because equity prices, although fluctuating, have risen as the VALUE of MONEY has fallen, they have proved better long-term INVESTMENTS than fixed-interest STOCKS in the period since the Second World War. Equity prices have risen because current earnings tend to rise as the value of money falls. The increased demand for equities by INSTITUTIONAL INVESTORS may underpin the equity market, but it has not prevented sharp fluctuations in prices.

Establishment. An operating unit of a business, to be distinguished from a firm or ENTERPRISE which is a controlling unit. In British censuses an establishment is a reporting unit; thus a large firm may have several factories, each of which will complete a census form but all of which will be owned or controlled by the firm itself.

Estate Duties Investment Trust (E.D.I.T.H.). An INVESTMENT TRUST formed in 1953 to acquire holdings in small companies.

The trust does not interfere in the management of the companies and its facilities are designed to be of service to executors and trustees of family companies who need to realize SHARES in companies in order to pay ESTATE DUTY, but do not wish to relinquish control.

Estate duty. A TAX payable on a person's property at his death and before it passes into the hands of others. Thus *estate duty* differs from an *inheritance tax*, which is payable by the recipient and which may vary according to the financial circumstances of the inheritor. In Britain estates not exceeding £12,500 are exempt from duty and on larger estates duty is charged at graduated rates from 25 to 85 per cent on successive slices of the estate with an overall maximum average rate of 80 per cent. Duty on real estate may be paid by instalments over a period of eight years, and there are special reliefs for agricultural property and companies controlled by five or fewer persons. Duty is payable on gifts made within seven years of death.

Estimates. An Estimate is the document which the U.K. government presents to Parliament by way of asking for a given sum for a particular service. It also shows in some detail how it is proposed to spend that sum. As such, it forms an important part of the control of government expenditure. ⟡ BUDGET; SELECT COMMITTEE ON ESTIMATES.

Euler, Leonhard (1707–83). Economists have found that certain propositions in theoretical mathematics developed by Leonhard Euler, a Swiss mathematician, can be usefully applied to problems in economic theory. The most notable application concerns a theory of distribution based on MARGINAL PRODUCTIVITY. This theory states that FACTORS OF PRODUCTION (i.e. LAND, LABOUR and CAPITAL) will each earn an INCOME corresponding to the VALUE of OUTPUT produced by the last unit of the factor employed. For instance, if a firm employs nineteen workers at an average wage of £20 per week, it will employ an additional worker as long as his output is greater than £20. Moreover, if the twentieth worker yields, say, £21 per week, it will be worthwhile to pay him more than £20 to attract him. The firm cannot, however, pay its workers different wages if they have the same skill, and therefore must pay all of them more than £20 per week. A similar argument is applied to other factors of production and for the total national output as well as for a single firm. However, total output must, by definition, equal total income (⟡ NATIONAL INCOME). National output is distributed among the three basic factors of production: land,

143

labour and capital. No arithmetical reasons, however, could be thought of as to how the different factor incomes, derived from marginal productivities, could necessarily add up to the same as total output. Euler's Theorem resolved the problem by showing what assumptions about the nature of the PRODUCTION FUNCTION (which describes how the factors of production are combined to produce outputs) had to be made in order for the equality between the sum of incomes and the sum of outputs to be achieved. ⟡ DISTRIBUTION, THEORY OF.

Euler's Theorem. ⟡ L. EULER.

Euro-currency. ⟡ EURO-DOLLARS.

Euro-dollars. Dollars held by individuals and institutions outside the United States. In its Annual Report in 1966, the BANK FOR INTERNATIONAL SETTLEMENTS described the Euro-dollar phenomenon as 'the acquisition of dollars by banks located outside the United States, mostly through the taking of DEPOSITS, but also to some extent through swapping other CURRENCIES into dollars, and the relending of these dollars, often after redepositing with other banks, to non-bank borrowers anywhere in the world'. It should be noted, therefore, that the market for Euro-dollars is not confined to Europe. In terms of a simple example, what happens is as follows. A London bank, as a result of a commercial transaction of one of its customers, has, say, a CREDIT balance with an American bank in New York. A Belgian businessman asks his bank for dollars to finance imports from the U.S. In order to meet this request, the Brussels bank accepts the dollar deposit transferred by the London bank from its account in New York. The essential point about this operation is that it creates credit. The London bank still has a claim, on Brussels instead of New York, whereas the Brussels bank now has a claim on New York, which its customer can use to finance his trade. The questions are naturally raised, why should London be willing to transfer its deposit, and why should Brussels finance its requirements in this way? The former can be answered broadly by the fact of the U.S. BALANCE OF PAYMENTS deficits supplying the means, and interest rate ARBITRAGE (New York *versus* Brussels) supplying the PROFIT. On the second question, again relative RATES OF INTEREST are a factor, but, in addition, the existence of national EXCHANGE CONTROLS and credit controls encourages the practice. The Brussels bank avoids the need to exchange francs for dollars. In practice, of course, there can be many relending transactions between banks in response to differentials in interest rates.

The size of the market has increased substantially in recent years, from about $10,000 million in 1965 to about $25,000 million in 1968 and $59,000 million in 1970. London has obtained the major share of the transactions in this business acting as a BROKER by borrowing dollars from a country with a dollar surplus, and lending it out to foreign banks or directly at favourable interest rates. Alternatively the London houses (⟡ ACCEPTING HOUSES) may convert the dollars into sterling and lend to U.K. institutions such as HIRE PURCHASE firms or local authorities. The U.S. deficit is not the only source of funds; the market also attracts U.S. funds directly. Early in 1969, the deflationary policy of the U.S. government (⟡ DEFLATION) induced the overseas branches of U.S. banks to repatriate to their parent banks dollars borrowed on the Euro-dollar market to such an extent as to cause European interest rates to rise sharply and European central bankers (⟡ CENTRAL BANKS) to express some concern at the volatile nature of such a large source of funds which can move outside the usual exchange control regulations. A recent innovation is the *dollar certificate of deposit* issued by the overseas branches of U.S. banks and which is fully transferable and negotiable. There are similar markets in other currencies – Euro-currencies – but these are relatively small compared with the Euro-dollar and mainly arise because of specific national restrictions. For instance, in order to discourage SPECULATION on the revaluation of the Deutsche Mark, the West German government imposed restrictions on the payment of interest on deposits held by foreigners in West German banks. Rather than let their balances remain idle, therefore, depositors were encouraged to transfer them on short-term loan to other banks.

European Coal and Steel Community (E.C.S.C.). The Schuman Plan (named after the French foreign minister) for the establishment of a common market in coal and steel was embodied in a treaty and ratified by the member countries, Germany, France, Italy and BENELUX, in 1952. In February 1953, all import duties and QUOTA restrictions on coal, iron ore and scrap iron were eliminated on intra-community trade, in May 1953 on ordinary steel and finally, in August 1954, on special steels. An exception was made for Italy, which was allowed to phase its internal TARIFF reductions on coke and metal products over a period ending in 1958. By February 1958, the community had adopted a common external tariff on these coal and steel industry products which was levied at two percentage points above the lowest tariff (Benelux). The treaty also provided

145

for the control of restrictive practices and MERGERS considered contrary to the maintenance of free competition. Overall executive responsibility is invested in the High Authority which has power to raise finance by means of a TAX on producers. This INCOME finances, *inter alia*, a readaptation fund which gives assistance to redundant or redeployed workers. The authority may make LOANS for capital INVESTMENT. It may also, at the request of the Council of Ministers, fix price levels and production and trade quotas. The Council of Ministers acts as a liaison between the member governments and the High Authority. A consultative committee of producers, workers and consumers acts in an advisory capacity to the High Authority. In addition, the treaty established a parliamentary common assembly and a court of justice, both of which were merged with the corresponding institutions of the EUROPEAN ECONOMIC COMMUNITY when the latter came into existence. In 1954, the U.K. entered into an agreement with the E.C.S.C. for continuous consultation on matters of common interest in the coal and steel industries and in 1971 applied for full membership. ⟐ CUSTOMS UNION.

European Common Market. ⟐ EUROPEAN ECONOMIC COMMUNITY.

European Economic Community (E.E.C.). Six countries of Western Europe – France, West Germany, Italy, Belgium, Netherlands and Luxembourg – signed the Treaty of Rome in 1957 for the creation between them of a CUSTOMS UNION or common market. By this treaty, the E.E.C. came into force on 1 January 1958. The primary aims of the treaty were the elimination of all obstacles to the free movement of GOODS, SERVICES, CAPITAL and LABOUR between the member countries, and the setting up of a common external commercial policy, a common agricultural policy and a common transport policy. The treaty foresaw the prohibition of most SUBSIDIES and DUMPING and the supranational control of public MONOPOLIES and the vetting of MERGERS. The executive management of the E.E.C. was vested in a commission which has nine members appointed for periods of four years. Problems of policy are the concern of the Council of Ministers, to which the commission's proposals are submitted. Each member country is represented by one minister in the council. The treaty also established a parliamentary assembly and a court of justice. Consultative institutions include an economic and social committee and a monetary committee. Under the treaty, the European Investment Bank was formed, with powers to lend money for the development of backward regions of the community, including associate members. In addition, a European Social Fund was set up to assist the redeployment of workers thrown out of work, particularly if caused by the creation of the community. The establishment of the Common Market was planned to take place over a transitional period. The treaty laid down a programme divided into three stages of four years each for the abolition of custom duties between the six and the erection of a common external TARIFF by 1970. However, this programme was accelerated, and all internal import duties were abolished and the common external tariff established by 1 July 1968. For agricultural products, all protectionist measures such as QUOTAS and import duties have been replaced by a levy which is determined by the difference between the world price and the internal (guaranteed) price; protection remains on only a few internal agricultural products. Some progress has been made in encouraging the free movement of LABOUR. Since 1969, workers and their families can move from one country to another without a permit and foreign workers from within the community have the same rights to social security and are subject to the same taxation as native workers. However, a lack of harmonization exists in, for instance, turnover and consumer taxes, and the common agricultural and transport policy yet remain to be fully achieved. Under a 'Treaty of Fusion', the E.E.C. institutions have been merged with those of the EUROPEAN COAL AND STEEL COMMUNITY and Euratom. The treaty recognized the possibility of an increase in the membership of the E.E.C., and the U.K. has applied for full membership together with two other countries of the EUROPEAN FREE TRADE ASSOCIATION (Norway and Denmark) as well as Eire. Negotiations were completed in 1971. ⟡ GENERAL AGREEMENT ON TARIFFS AND TRADE; KENNEDY ROUND OF TRADE NEGOTIATIONS.

European Free Trade Area. Pressure for the formation of a FREE TRADE AREA between the seventeen countries of the ORGANIZATION FOR EUROPEAN ECONOMIC COOPERATION gathered strength in the early 1950s. Impetus was given to this idea by the conferences in 1955 and 1956, which led to the signing of the Treaty of Rome in 1957 between the six countries which were to establish the EUROPEAN ECONOMIC COMMUNITY. The O.E.E.C. opened negotiations which, it was hoped, would lead to the formation of a free trade area between the E.E.C. and the other member countries of the O.E.E.C. These negotiations proved abortive, the E.E.C. fearing that the integrity of their own association might be prejudiced.

147

In the event, a free trade area was established in the EUROPEAN FREE TRADE ASSOCIATION, but was restricted to the three countries of Scandinavia, the U.K., Austria, Portugal and Switzerland, with the later additions of Finland and Iceland.

European Free Trade Association (E.F.T.A.). The text of the convention setting up the European Free Trade Association was approved at Stockholm in November 1959 by the U.K., Norway, Sweden, Denmark, Austria, Portugal and Switzerland. In April 1961, these seven concluded a trade agreement with Finland which, in effect, brought Finland within the association. In March 1970, Iceland was also admitted as a full member. The Stockholm Agreement established a FREE TRADE AREA between the member countries. While retaining their own individual TARIFFS on imports from non-members, they agreed to eliminate (over a transitional period) import duties on goods originating in any member country. In fact, import duties on virtually all manufactured goods had been eliminated by December 1966 (for Finland a year later). On agricultural goods, a proportion of trade flows duty free as a result of inter-member bilateral agreements. In addition, there are special exceptions for particular countries. As the group is a free trade area rather than a CUSTOMS UNION, rules are necessary to prevent products from non-members from being sold in a high tariff member country via a low tariff member. To qualify for free entry, at least 50 per cent of the value of the imported good must be accounted for by domestic manufacture. In addition, a specified list of commodities are treated as of E.F.T.A. origin, even though they may in fact originate outside the association. Certain processes of production are also accepted as alternative criteria to the 50 per cent rule. CERTIFICATES OF ORIGIN issued by the government-accredited institutions (generally chambers of commerce) must accompany the import documents. The chief executive organ is the council, composed of ministerial representatives from each member. Amendments to the Stockholm Convention may be achieved by a unanimous vote in the council. A consultative committee made up of employers, trade unions and other representatives of the various sectors of economic life was also set up under the convention. General administration is conducted by a secretariat at Geneva. An economic committee acts as a forum for the exchange of views on economic policy. ⟱ GENERAL AGREEMENT ON TARIFFS AND TRADE; KENNEDY ROUND OF TRADE NEGOTIATIONS.

European Fund. The EUROPEAN MONETARY AGREEMENT which

came into force at the end of 1958 established a European Fund with a capital of $600m., partly from the transfer of the CAPITAL residue of the defunct EUROPEAN PAYMENTS UNION and partly from fresh contributions. The fund is empowered to extend two-year loans to countries to finance short-run BALANCE OF PAYMENTS deficits.

European Investment Bank. ⟡ EUROPEAN ECONOMIC COMMUNITY.

European Monetary Agreement (E.M.A.). After the post-war recovery had been completed in Europe, the countries of Western Europe were able to restore the CONVERTIBILITY of their CURRENCIES. During the recovery period, a clearing system had been established for their international payments under the EUROPEAN PAYMENTS UNION. With the restoration of convertibility, the E.P.U. was replaced by the E.M.A., which came into operation in December 1958, although it had in fact been agreed in 1955. It continued the BANKING function of the E.P.U. in relation to the clearing of balances between members, the main difference being that all settlements had to be made in gold or convertible currencies and the granting of automatic credits was terminated. The agreement also established a EUROPEAN FUND for the finance of temporary BALANCE OF PAYMENTS deficits. ⟡ INTERNATIONAL LIQUIDITY; INTERNATIONAL MONETARY FUND.

European Payments Union (E.P.U.). The seventeen member countries of the ORGANIZATION OF EUROPEAN ECONOMIC COOPERATION established the European Payments Union between themselves in 1950. The E.P.U. replaced the INTRA-EUROPEAN PAYMENTS AGREEMENT set up under the EUROPEAN RECOVERY PROGRAMME. This was a clearing system for the multilateral international debits and credits which arose between the member countries. In addition, however, it afforded a mechanism for the extension of automatic lines of credit to any member with a BALANCE OF PAYMENT deficit with fellow members. A deficit with the union in any month was automatically covered by credits up to 20 per cent of the debtor's quota. Deficits beyond this were, in increasing proportion, payable in gold or dollars. Similarly, members with surplus balances extended credit up to 20 per cent of their quotas; beyond this they were permitted to draw 50 per cent of their surplus in gold or dollars. The quotas were based on the trade of the member countries with Western Europe. The BANK FOR INTERNATIONAL SETTLEMENTS acted as agent for the union. The union was replaced in 1958 by the EUROPEAN MONETARY AGREEMENT when the Western

European countries restored currency CONVERTIBILITY. The union was an important stimulus to European unification and prevented the growth of BILATERALISM in Europe.

European Recovery Programme. In June 1947, the U.S. Secretary of State, General G. C. Marshall, in a speech at Harvard made clear the willingness of the United States to extend economic assistance to countries whose productive ASSETS had been destroyed in the Second World War. This offer did not exclude the U.S.S.R. and the Eastern European countries, but was never accepted by them. The resultant European Recovery Programme became known as MARSHALL AID. Sixteen Western European countries attended a conference at Paris in 1947 which led to the establishment of the ORGANIZATION FOR EUROPEAN ECONOMIC COOPERATION in 1948 to coordinate the recovery programme in conjunction with the U.S. ECONOMIC COOPERATION ADMINISTRATION. Although some U.S. aid had been distributed in 1947, the recovery programme did not get fully under way until 1948. It was established on the basis of a four-year commitment to provide Western Europe with between $15,000m. and $17,000m.

European Social Fund. ⬦ EUROPEAN ECONOMIC COMMUNITY.

Ex ante. Intended, desired or expected before the event. Thus, ex-ante DEMAND is the quantity which buyers wish or intend to buy at the going price; ex-ante INVESTMENT is the amount which firms plan or intend to invest. It must be distinguished from the outcome which actually occurs – that is, the actual quantity bought, the actual volume of investment – since these need not be equal to the ex-ante values, and in fact in DISEQUILIBRIUM situations they may well not be. ⬦ EX POST.

Ex-dividend. Without DIVIDEND. The purchaser of a SECURITY quoted ex-dividend does not have the right to the next dividend when due. The term 'ex-', meaning excluding, is also used in a similar sense in relation to RIGHTS ISSUE, capitalization issue (⬦ BONUS ISSUE), etc.

Exempt companies. ⬦ PRIVATE COMPANY.

Ex post. The ex-post VALUE of some VARIABLE, e.g. supply, INVESTMENT, quantity bought, is the value which the variable actually takes in the event. Ex post is opposed to the EX-ANTE value, which is the expected or intended value. Thus, ex ante, a consumer might plan to buy ten units of a particular GOOD, but in the event might only buy eight units, because an insufficient quantity was on sale, or its PRICE turned out to be higher than at first expected.

Excess capacity. 1. In a narrow sense, refers to the proposition that, under MONOPOLISTIC COMPETITION, free entry of firms will result in only normal PROFIT being earned, but with too many firms, each producing at too low a rate of output to exploit ECON-OMIES OF SCALE to the full. The difference between actual output, and the output required to achieve full economies of scale, is known as excess capacity. The excess capacity prediction was regarded as one of the most novel insights of the theory when it first appeared. ⇨ E. H. CHAMBERLIN; J. V. ROBINSON. **2.** In general terms, excess capacity exists when actual output is below the rate at which all the INPUTS of a firm, industry or economy, are fully employed.

Excess demand. A situation in which the amount of a good or SERVICE which buyers wish to buy exceeds that which sellers are prepared to sell. The result is that the price is bid up, so inducing sellers to increase the quantity they are prepared to sell, and buyers to reduce the quantity they wish to buy. Price will continue to rise until excess demand is eliminated, i.e. until DEMAND and SUPPLY are equal. Excess demand is thus a DISEQUILIBRIUM situation. It may also relate to an economy-wide AGGREGATE DEMAND for goods and services which is greater than the capacity of the economy to meet it. This will then lead to a general price increase, i.e. to INFLATION.

Excess profit. ⇨ PROFIT.

Excess supply. A situation in which the quantity of a good or SERVICE which sellers wish to sell at the prevailing price is greater than the quantity which buyers wish to buy. This causes sellers to bid down prices, thus causing an increase in the quantity demanded and a decrease in the quantity offered for sale, until SUPPLY and DEMAND are equal. Excess supply like EXCESS DEMAND, is thus a DISEQUILI-BRIUM situation.

Exchange control. The control by the state through the BANKING system of dealings in gold and foreign CURRENCIES. Exchange control is concerned with controlling the purchase and sale of currencies by residents alone, since governments do not have complete powers to control the activities of non-residents. This must be done through the MARKET and is a matter of exchange management (⇨ EXCHANGE EQUALIZATION ACCOUNT). Exchange control is only required where a country wishes to influence the international value of its currency. It is not willing to leave the VALUE of its currency in terms of other currencies or gold to be determined in the FREE MARKET, as it would be under a system of floating exchange rates, or to allow the fixed external value of

151

its currency to be the determinant of the domestic price level as it was under the GOLD STANDARD. Almost all countries now exercise some form of exchange control, although in some instances this is only on CAPITAL and not current transactions. In Britain there has been continuous exchange control since the Second World War. The Exchange Control Act of 1947 restricted the purposes for which foreign currencies might be bought by residents and restricted the disposal and retention of foreign currency and gold that came into their possession. It also required all dealings in gold and foreign currencies to be made through the COMMERCIAL BANKS, who were appointed as 'authorized dealers'. Subsequent Acts and regulations have refined the exchange control system in Britain, e.g. until 1969 residents were allowed to purchase a maximum of £50-worth of foreign currency per annum for the purposes of foreign travel. Many of the regulations of the exchange control system apply only to residents of the STERLING AREA, since within this area payments can be made without restriction. The exchange control system restricts private and commercial capital movements ($\lozenge$ CAPITAL ISSUES COMMITTEE) as well as current payments.

While it has been relaxed since 1947, exchange control is still considered necessary in Britain because of the weakness of the BALANCE OF PAYMENTS. This means, basically, that there is an insufficient demand for sterling and an excessive demand for foreign currencies from residents at the present EXCHANGE RATE. In its most extreme form, a country facing a balance of payments deficit may use exchange control to restrict imports to the amount earned in FOREIGN EXCHANGE by its nationals. In Brazil, in the 1960s, foreign currency in the form of import licences were auctioned to the highest bidder. All forms of exchange control are discouraged by the ORGANIZATION FOR ECONOMIC COOPERATION AND DEVELOPMENT and other international organizations concerned with encouraging INTERNATIONAL TRADE, but they are the inevitable results of fixed exchange rates. It should be noted that a currency is not fully convertible ($\lozenge$ CONVERTIBILITY) when exchange control is operated.

Exchange economy. An economy in which specialization ($\lozenge$ DIVISION OF LABOUR) takes place, which then creates the need for exchange, either through BARTER, or through the operation of MARKETS. It is difficult to think of any economy today in which specialization has not proceeded far enough to make that economy an exchange economy.

Exchange equalization account. An account controlled by the TREAS-URY and managed by the BANK OF ENGLAND which buys and sells sterling for gold and foreign CURRENCIES with the object of off-setting major fluctuations in the exchange value of the pound and keeping the SPOT MARKET price for the pound around the 'fixed rate. The account was set up by the 1932 Finance Act after the abandonment of the GOLD STANDARD in the previous year. The ASSETS of the account include the GOLD AND FOREIGN EXCHANGE RESERVES and sterling, provided by the EXCHEQUER, invested in TREASURY BILLS. The account also operates in the FORWARD MARKET for sterling. Similar funds or stabilization accounts are operated by other countries, e.g. the U.S. and France. ⇨ EXCHANGE RATE; INTERNATIONAL MONETARY FUND.

Exchange equation. ⇨ I. FISHER.

Exchange of shares. A means of business combination which can take two forms. In form (a) the companies retain their separate identities, but exchange a quantity of SHARES so that each company holds shares in the other and normally some directors will sit on both boards (⇨ INTERLOCKING DIRECTORATES). In form (b) two com-panies will merge, shares of one company being exchanged with or without a cash adjustment, for the whole of the issued share CAPITAL of the other. ⇨ MERGER; REVERSE TAKE-OVER.

Exchange rate. The price (rate) at which one CURRENCY is exchanged for another currency or for gold. These transactions are carried out spot or forward (⇨ SPOT MARKET and FORWARD MARKET) in the FOREIGN EXCHANGE MARKETS. The actual rate at any one time is determined by SUPPLY and DEMAND conditions for the relevant currencies in the market. These in turn would depend on the BALANCE OF PAYMENTS deficits or surpluses of the relevant economies and the demand for the currencies to meet obligations and expectations about the future movements in the rate. If there were no government control over the exchange market (such as the U.K. exercises through the EXCHANGE EQUALIZATION AC-COUNT), there would be a *free* or *floating exchange rate* in operation. With a freely floating system, no GOLD AND FOREIGN EXCHANGE RESERVES would be required as the exchange rate would adjust itself until the supply and demand for the currencies were brought into balance (⇨ PURCHASING POWER PARITY THEORY). Under the rules of the INTERNATIONAL MONETARY FUND, established at the BRETTON WOODS Conference towards the end of the Second

World War, exchange rates have been fixed at a par value in relation to the dollar, and fluctuations around this value were confined within a $\pm$ 1 per cent band. The dollar itself was not subject to this restriction, because the U.S. government was committed to buying gold on demand at a fixed rate of $35·0875 per ounce. However, in August 1971 the United States suspended the CONVERTIBILITY of the dollar into gold and other currencies, imposed a 10 per cent surcharge on IMPORTS and took other measures aimed at eliminating its balance of payments deficit. There followed a period during which the major currencies were allowed to float but subject to exchange control regulations to keep the exchange rate movements within limits (a 'dirty float'). In December 1971, the 'Group of Ten' in the I.M.F. agreed to a realignment of exchange rates which left the dollar devalued by about 10 per cent against an average of all other currencies in exchange for a rise in the dollar price of gold to $38 per ounce and the removal of the surcharge. In addition, it was agreed that, as a temporary measure, the margin of permitted fluctuations should be ±25 per cent. Governments are technically not permitted to change the par value of their currencies unless the INTERNATIONAL MONETARY FUND can be persuaded that there exists a 'fundamental DISEQUILIBRIUM' in their balance of payments. However, the French government devalued by 12·4 per cent in August 1969 without any prior consultation whatever with any international organization.

There has been much discussion in the past of the relative merits of floating compared with fixed exchange rates, and indeed of many hybrid systems which lie between these extremes. The floating rate has apparent attractions comparable to the advantages obtained, in terms of efficient resource allocation ($\diamond$ RESOURCES), by a freely operating price mechanism ($\diamond$ PRICE SYSTEM). This comparison, however, is superficial, because exchange rates are not just a PRICE; changes in exchange rates are likely to alter substantially the INCOME levels of communities. Fluctuations in the rate are inconvenient for trading, and these fluctuations could be volatile if left to move freely. Moreover, because of the pressure of short-term CAPITAL movements or SPECULATION, the exchange rate could move in a direction different from what might be required by the domestic economy as reflected in its basic balance of payments. The Canadian dollar was left to float between 1950 and 1962, but its rate was kept high by an inflow of funds, although the domestic economy needed a fall in the rate to stimulate a rise in exports to take up surplus capacity. U.K. TREASURY and BANK OF ENG-LAND officials proposed a floating rate for the U.K. at the time of the sterling crisis of 1952 as part of a policy package called Robot, but the idea was abandoned. The Canadian dollar was again floated from May 1970. The Deutsche Mark and the guilder were also floated from May 1971, as were all other major currencies from August 1971. However, all currencies, with the exception of Canada, returned to fixed parities in December 1971. The current system of fixed rates has recently come under criticism on the grounds of its inflexibility and the fact that it places too much of the adjustment burden on the domestic economy. A middle course has been proposed in the 'moving-parity', 'sliding-parity', 'dynamic' or 'crawling peg' idea. In the *moving parity*, the par rate is automatically adjusted according to a moving average of past rates taken over a number of months. Professor J. E. Meade has put forward a refined version of this, called the *sliding-parity* or *crawling-peg*. In this, instead of the whole amount of a revaluation or devaluation taking place at once, it is spread in small percentages over a number of months. For instance, a 10 per cent devaluation may be achieved by means of a monthly $\frac{1}{5}$ per cent reduction for fifty months. This system has the advantage that it is known and certain, while the monthly adjustment is too small to cause excessive speculative flows. Hendrick Houthakker, in his capacity as a member of the U.S. President's Council of Economic Advisers, has put forward proposals for a crawling peg which are similar to Professor Meade's. He has suggested that gradual adjustments in the exchange rate should be allowed up to a maximum of 2 to 3 per cent per annum. These adjustments, however, should be linked to the level of a country's reserves rather than past exchange rates. However, U.S. proposals for more flexible exchange rates were rejected by the Group of Ten of the I.M.F. in July 1970. ⏃ INTERNATIONAL LIQUIDITY; MACMILLAN COMMITTEE; RADCLIFFE REPORT.

Exchequer. The account of the central government kept at the BANK OF ENGLAND. ⏃ CONSOLIDATED FUND.

Exclusive dealing. Restriction by a manufacturer of the sales of his products to particular sales outlets. Examples are 'tied garages' that sell only one brand of petrol, or pubs owned by particular breweries. Exclusive dealing has to be registered and approved under the RESTRICTIVE TRADE PRACTICES ACT. Exclusive dealing is usually defended on grounds of maintaining standards of service to customers, e.g. for motor-cars, although it might in certain

155

circumstances prevent a new manufacturer from selling his products or a new retailer from competing with existing retail outlets.

Exogenous variable. A VARIABLE which, although playing an important part in a MODEL, is determined by forces outside the model, and is unexplained by it. For example, in a model of the market for wheat, weather conditions may play an important part in determining the supply and hence the price of wheat. But the model itself does not try to explain what determines weather conditions. ⟡ ENDOGENOUS VARIABLE.

Expectations. Attitudes, beliefs or states of mind about the nature of future events. Expectations are often crucial in determining economic behaviour. A firm may select a PRICE, or a level of output, or make any other policy choice, in the light of its expectations about the future. Similarly, a consumer may base his current purchases on his expectations of what the price will be over the next month. The difficulty this presents for economics is that, though they may determine current behaviour, they cannot be directly observed, and this then makes it difficult to test the validity of hypotheses. For example, we may hypothesize that a rise in price causes a fall in quantity demanded. Yet we may observe a rise in price of, say, an ORDINARY SHARE to be followed by an increase in the quantity demanded. We may then argue that our theory of demand is not refuted, because the buyers' expectations were of a further rise in price, after which they could sell at a PROFIT. But unless we can find some way of finding out what buyers' expectations really are, we cannot firmly answer the question. One possible solution is to attempt to explain how expectations are formed, e.g. by hypothesizing that they are some function of the current and past values of the relevant variables. Another is to attempt to find, by questionnaire, what the expectations of a particular group of decision-takers are, and then to try to find what determines the changes in expectations over time. The subjective nature of expectations, however, still presents a problem to formal economics.

Export councils. ⟡ BRITISH NATIONAL EXPORT COUNCIL.

Export Credits Guarantee Department (E.C.G.D.). A U.K. government department set up in 1930 as an independent department, although it had operated in another form from 1919. It is responsible to the Secretary of State for Trade and Industry, and has the authority, under TREASURY control, to issue INSURANCE policies to cover risks met by exporters. The risks are, broadly, insolvency or default of debtor, refusal of goods on delivery and risks of a political nature such as the imposition of import licensing and EXCHANGE CONTROLS. The policies may be either 'comprehensive' or 'specific', the former being in respect of short-term cover up to six months, and the latter of longer term credit up to ten years or more. The department generally limits the extent of its cover to about 90 per cent of the potential loss. The department has been induced to grant better terms in the past to bring its rates into line with those of similar institutions in other countries who have used this type of insurance as a vehicle for concealed export subsidies (⟡ EXPORT INCENTIVES). However, the department is run on a profit-making basis and receives no grant or subsidy from the government. In February 1970, the authority which the department had prior to the setting up of the Ministry of Overseas Development to issue LOANS for economic aid was widened so that it can now make loans to countries for the purchase of U.K. exports (⟡ FACTORING).

Export-Import Bank. A U.S. government agency, established in 1934 for the purpose of encouraging U.S. trade by supplying CREDIT to overseas countries. It also gives U.S. exporters INSURANCE cover (⟡ EXPORT CREDITS GUARANTEE DEPARTMENT). In 1964, the U.K. began buying U.S. military aircraft and missiles, and in 1966 to draw on credit advanced by the Export-Import Bank for this purpose. Payments to the U.S. manufacturers were made during production and before delivery. These payments were settled by drawing on the sums advanced by the Export-Import Bank, which in turn required their repayment by instalments over seven years.

Export incentives. Preferential treatment for firms who sell their products abroad, compared with firms who sell to the home market. They may take the form of direct SUBSIDIES, special CREDIT facilities, grants, concessions in the field of DIRECT TAXATION, benefits arising from the administration of indirect taxation, and export credit INSURANCE on exceptionally favourable terms. Various international associations discourage the practice of artificially stimulating exports by any of these methods. The GENERAL AGREEMENT ON TARIFFS AND TRADE lays down special provisions relating to export subsidies, direct or indirect, in an attempt to limit them. The Stockholm Convention setting up the EUROPEAN FREE TRADE ASSOCIATION lists various forms of aid to exporters which member countries are required to avoid. The Treaty of Rome, which established the EUROPEAN ECONOMIC COMMUNITY, although less specific than the Stockholm Convention, neverthe-

157

less discourages the granting of privileged aid to any economic sectors.

Export multiplier. The ratio of the total increase in a country's NATIONAL INCOME to the increment in export revenue generating the increase. The size of the multiplier depends on the propensities to save (⮕ AVERAGE PROPENSITY TO SAVE; MARGINAL PROPENSITY TO SAVE) of the recipients of the increases in INCOMES derived from the increase in export revenue and the country's PROPENSITIES TO IMPORT. The export multiplier can be regarded as a special case of the general MULTIPLIER.

Export rebates. ⮕ CUSTOMS DRAWBACK; EXPORT INCENTIVES.

Export surplus. ⮕ BALANCE OF PAYMENTS.

Exports. The goods and SERVICES produced by one country which are sold to another in exchange for the second country's own goods and services, for gold and FOREIGN EXCHANGE, or in settlement of DEBT. Countries tend to specialize in the production of those goods and services in which they can be relatively most efficient, because of their indigenous factor endowments (⮕ FACTORS OF PRODUCTION). Countries devote home resources to exports because they can obtain more goods and services by international exchange than they would obtain from the same resources devoted to direct home production. About 20 per cent of the U.K. domestic production is exported, compared with about 13 per cent for the world as a whole. ⮕ BALANCE OF PAYMENTS; INTERNATIONAL TRADE; MERCANTILISM.

Exports, unrequited. ⮕ UNREQUITED EXPORTS.

External economies. ⮕ ECONOMIES OF SCALE.

External deficit. A synonym for BALANCE OF PAYMENTS deficit.

External diseconomies. ⮕ DISECONOMY.

External effects. ⮕ EXTERNALITIES.

External sterling. STERLING BALANCES held by non-residents of the STERLING AREA.

External surplus. A synonym for BALANCE OF PAYMENTS surplus.

Externalities. Externalities in CONSUMPTION exist when the level of consumption of some GOOD or SERVICE by one consumer has a direct effect on the welfare of another consumer, as opposed to an indirect effect through the price mechanism (note 'goods' are defined very broadly to include anything which yields UTILITY); production externalities exist when the production activities of one firm directly affect the production activities of another firm (external ECONOMIES OF SCALE and diseconomies of scale (⮕ DISECONOMY)

are therefore particular cases of externalities in production).
Examples of consumption externalities are:
(i) A, wanting privacy, builds a high fence, which reduces the amount of sunshine flooding in through B's window.
(ii) A, in making a right turn on a busy two-way road, causes a large traffic jam to build up behind him.
(iii) Miss A wears a miniskirt.
Examples of production externalities are:
(i) Firm A discharges effluent into a river, which greatly increases costs of Firm B downstream.
(ii) Firm A set up a training school for computer programmers, which increases the availability of programmers to Firm B.
There may also, of course, be mixed production/consumption externalities. For example:
(i) Night flights by jet airliners may cause residents in areas close to an airport to lose sleep, and hence adversely affect their work.
(ii) Holiday motorists may increase congestion on a road, and hence increase costs of road-haulage firms.
The essence of externalities, whether in production or consumption, is that their costs or benefits are not reflected in market prices, and so the decision of the consumer or firm creating the externalities on the scale of the externality-creating activity generally does not take its effect into account. Hence, since the time of A. C. PIGOU, economists have argued that SOCIAL WELFARE would be increased if the private consumption or production decision were modified so as to take the external effect into account. The means of doing this were traditionally held to be the imposition of taxes on activities which created losses in welfare or increases in costs, and payment of SUBSIDIES on activities which increased welfare or lowered costs. In practice, tax-subsidy schemes are rarely adopted. More frequently, externalities are uncorrected, or absolutely prohibited – right turns in certain streets, smoking in certain railway compartments – or property rights are created and redress is possible through the courts, e.g. the common law 'right to lights'. For certain types of externalities (proximity to an abattoir, or to an airport), compensation might be paid, either directly, or through reductions in rates.

F

Face value. Nominal as distinct from MARKET value. The face value of a SECURITY is the price at which it will be redeemed; of an ORDINARY SHARE its PAR VALUE or issued price; of a coin the amount stamped on it, which might for a silver or gold coin be less than its market value.

Factor. 1. ⇨ FACTORS OF PRODUCTION. **2.** ⇨ FACTORING. **3.** An agent who buys and sells goods on behalf of others for a COMMISSION called *factorage*.

Factor markets. MARKETS on which FACTORS OF PRODUCTION are bought and sold. In aggregate terms, for instance, 'the LABOUR MARKET' or 'the CAPITAL MARKET', and in specific terms the market for a particular type of factor of production, e.g. the market for carpenters, the market for short-term capital.

Factor payments. Payments made to FACTORS OF PRODUCTION in return for the SERVICES they render.

Factor price equalization theorem. ⇨ P. A. SAMUELSON.

Factorage. ⇨ FACTOR.

Factoring. The business activity in which a company takes over the responsibility for the collecting of the DEBTS of another. It is a service primarily intended to meet the needs of small and medium-size firms. It has developed comparatively slowly in the U.K. compared with the U.S. in spite of the fact that the banks have taken important interests in the leading factoring companies. Typically, the client debits all his sales to the factor and can draw cash up to about 80 per cent of their value, thus increasing his cash flow considerably. The factor takes over the entire responsibility for retrieving the debts due from the client's customers and protects the client from bad debts. The factor, however, has some control over sales either by imposing a maximum CREDIT limit which he is willing to meet or by vetting specific prospective clients. Through international factoring companies, the factor can offer a service to exporters by protecting his customers from bad debts overseas and by giving, for instance, expert advice on FOREIGN EXCHANGE transactions (⇨ EXPORT CREDITS GUARANTEE DEPARTMENT).

Factors of production. According to MARSHALL, these are 'the things required for making a commodity'. In modern terminology, they

160

would be referred to as 'INPUTS'. Typically, they are grouped into LAND, LABOUR and CAPITAL, for broad purposes of analysis, but it is always recognized that these are not hard-and-fast groupings, since a given input may seem to be classifiable into more than one. Similarly, within each broad category there will be a wide diversity of types. ⟡ NATURAL RESOURCES; J. B. SAY.

Fair trade policy. ⟡ RECIPRICOCITY.

Farm price review. The U.K. has a system of agricultural SUBSIDY which is based on the fixing of guaranteed prices of products to farmers. The price to the consumer is allowed to find its MARKET level and the government reimburses the farmer to the extent that the market price falls below the guaranteed price. These deficiency payments may be related to 'standard quantities' in such a way that an expansion of farm output beyond the required level does not attract commensurate INCOME. The levels of the guaranteed prices are published every year in a White Paper, *Annual Review and Determination of Guarantees*, in accordance with the Agriculture Acts of 1947 and 1957. In addition, the review fixes the level of the direct subsidies and grants on such items as fertilizers, calves and cows, hill sheep, drainage, INVESTMENT incentives and general farm improvements. The 1971 review estimated that the total cost of agriculture support would be £343 million in 1971/2, of which £164 million would be the cost of the implementation of the price guarantees, £60 million in livestock production grants and £33 million for fertilizer grants. The principle behind this system of price guarantees is that the consumer should benefit directly from low-cost imports. It contrasts with the method of subsidy established in the EUROPEAN ECONOMIC COMMUNITY which the U.K. will adopt on entry. In the latter case, a target price is fixed at a level considered to yield the necessary income to efficient farms within the community. An import levy is applied, which is calculated on the difference between the import price and the target price in order to maintain prices at the required level on the home market. If surpluses appearing from domestic production should drive the market prices down below about 90 per cent of the target price, the E.E.C. commission is empowered to buy, using the import levy funds. It may also grant export subsidies from this source. The U.K. has moved slightly towards this system in the case, for instance, of wheat and barley. In agreement with the main exporting countries, minimum and maximum import prices are agreed and an import levy imposed to bring import prices in line with 'target' indicator prices. Deficiency payments are calculated on the difference between the latter and the guaranteed price. However, the U.K. White Paper for 1971 stated that, 'The government's declared aim is to adapt the present system of agricultural support to one relying increasingly on import levy arrangements, under which the farmer will get his return increasingly from the market.' The government announced in October 1970 that it would introduce as soon a possible interim levy schemes for beef and veal, mutton and lamb and some milk products.

Farm subsidies. ⟡ FARM PRICE REVIEW.

Federal reserve bank. ⟡ FEDERAL RESERVE SYSTEM.

Federal reserve board. ⟡ FEDERAL RESERVE SYSTEM.

Federal Reserve System. The central banking system of the United States. It differs from that of most other countries' CENTRAL BANKS in that it consists not of one bank but of twelve regional banks and some twenty-four branches under the control of the Federal Reserve Board in Washington. The capital of the reserve banks is owned by the 6,000 member banks, i.e. COMMERCIAL BANKS, who receive a fixed DIVIDEND. The considerable surpluse that the reserve system earns go to the U.S. internal revenue. The regional reserve banks act as central banks for their members, an act as LENDERS OF LAST RESORT by rediscounting bills (⟡ DISCOUNTING), hold their CASH requirements and provide clearing facilities. The U.S. commercial BANKING system is a unit rather than a BRANCH BANKING system; three quarters of the 14,000 banks in the U.S. have no branches. In many states, branches are not allowed by law, although through the development of amalgamations and holding companies the U.S. commercial banking system is not as fragmented as it appears. Considerably less than half of the commercial banks are members of the Federal Reserve System, but these members hold about 85 per cent of the total DEPOSITS of all commercial banks. Some of the commercial banks, i.e. 'national banks' are required to join the reserve system by law, and others may apply for membership if they wish to do so. The Federal Reserve Board consists of governors appointed for long periods by the President of the United States, with Senate approval. The board acts, in effect as the central bank and approves the discount and other RATE OF INTEREST of the system, sets CASH RATIO requirements, supervises foreign business and generally regulates the operation of the banking system. The Federal Open Market Committee, a sub committee of the board, through controlling the purchases of government SECURITIES by the reserve banks, effectively gives the board power to conduct open market operations.

Fertility rate. ⬦ BIRTH RATE.

Fiduciary issue. Paper MONEY (⬦ BANK-NOTE) not backed by gold or silver. The term has its origins in the Bank Charter Act of 1844, which fixed the fiduciary issue limit at £14 million. Any notes issued in excess of this amount had to be fully backed by gold. The fiduciary limit has been successively raised and the monetary authorities are now free to alter the note issue as they wish; effectively the note issue is now entirely fiduciary. ⬦ BANKING AND CURRENCY SCHOOLS.

Final products. GOODS used by consumers in CONSUMPTION, rather than by firms as INPUTS into processes of production, i.e. INTERMEDIATE PRODUCTS. A good may, of course, be both.

Finance. The provision of MONEY when and where required. Finance may be short term (usually up to one year), medium term (usually over one year and up to five to seven years) and long term. Finance may be required for CONSUMPTION or for INVESTMENT. For the latter when provided it becomes CAPITAL. ⬦ BUSINESS FINANCE; CONSUMER CREDIT; PUBLIC FINANCE.

Finance company. An imprecise term covering a wide range of FINANCIAL INTERMEDIARIES, most commonly a synonym for FINANCE HOUSE.

Finance house. A financial institution engaged in the provision of HIRE PURCHASE. Also called finance companies, hire-purchase finance companies and INDUSTRIAL BANKS. There are some 1,500 finance houses in the U.K., which account for some 60 per cent of INSTALMENT CREDIT debt, the remainder being owed to retailers. The bulk of hire-purchase business is accounted for by the seventeen members of the FINANCE HOUSES ASSOCIATION. The finance houses' sources of funds consist of their own CAPITAL (about 20 per cent of the total), DEPOSITS from the public (50 per cent) and LOANS from the BANKING system, including bills discounted (⬦ DISCOUNTING). The finance houses usually receive deposits at RATES OF INTEREST varying from BANK RATE to about $1\frac{1}{2}$ per cent over bank rate, depending on the length of notice required, with a minimum of $4\frac{1}{2}$ per cent. Of the hire-purchase CREDIT advanced, some 60 per cent is for passenger cars, commercial vehicles and buses, 10 per cent for industrial plant and equipment and the remainder for household furnishings and equipment. Hire purchase is not the sole, although it is the main, activity of the finance houses; they also make loans for other purposes, including bridging finance, FACTOR-ING and house purchase. Since 1958 the COMMERCIAL BANKS and other institutions, e.g. the motor manufacturers, have acquired control in, or set up, new finance houses.

Finance Houses Association (F.H.A.). One of the two associations of FINANCE HOUSES in the U.K. mainly concerned with HIRE PUR-CHASE. At the time of the RADCLIFFE REPORT (1959), the F.H.A. had seventeen members who accounted for 80 per cent of the total hire-purchase DEBT to finance houses. The association represents the industry to the government, especially on MONETARY POLICY, maintains a code of practice and a creditworthiness register of clients. ⇨ INDUSTRIAL BANKERS ASSOCIATION.

Financial intermediaries. Institutions which hold MONEY balances of, or which borrow from, individuals and other institutions, in order to make LOANS or other INVESTMENTS. Hence, they serve the purpose of channelling funds from lenders to borrowers. It is usual to distinguish between banks in the BANKING sector and so-called non-bank financial intermediaries. The importance of this distinction arises from the fact that the LIABILITIES of banks form part of the MONEY SUPPLY, and this is not true of the non-bank financial intermediaries (whose liabilities may nevertheless be regarded as 'NEAR' MONEY). The most important of the non-bank financial intermediaries are the BUILDING SOCIETIES, HIRE-PURCHASE companies, INSURANCE companies, SAVINGS BANKS, PENSION FUNDS and INVESTMENT TRUSTS among others.

Financial ratios. 1. Specifically, measures of creditworthiness. The principal measures are the CURRENT RATIO, the DEBT or NET WORTH ratio (long-term debt to net worth), DIVIDEND COVER, INTEREST COVER and the net tangible ASSETS ratio (total tangible assets less current LIABILITIES and minority interests to long-term debt). All these ratios are measures of the asset or income cover available to the suppliers of CAPITAL to the business. **2.** Generally, calculations based on company accounts and other sources, such as STOCK EXCHANGE share prices, designed to indicate the profitability or other financial aspects of a business, e.g. return on net assets, PRICE-EARNINGS RATIO and stock-sales ratio (⇨ INVENTORY TURNOVER). ⇨ RATE OF RETURN.

Financial Times Actuaries Share Indices. A detailed series of PRICE indices, EARNINGS and YIELD averages for British SECURITIES on the London STOCK EXCHANGE published daily, with some history, in the *Financial Times* newspaper. The indices are produced in cooperation with the London and Edinburgh Actuary Institutes, and are of particular value to PENSION FUND managers and others who wish to follow movements in the values of share PORT-FOLIOS. Unlike the FINANCIAL TIMES STOCK INDICES, the actuaries' share indices are base-weighted chain-link indices, 10 April 1962 = 100. Over fifty price indices and averages are published in the series, based on 700 individual securities, of which some 650 are EQUITIES and the remainder fixed-interest STOCKS. The equities included mainly have a market CAPITALIZATION of over £4 million and account for 60 per cent of the value of all quoted equities and about 90 per cent of those of a capitalization of over £1 million. In addition to price indices, average earnings and divi-dend yields are provided for equities, while for fixed-interest securities prices and yields are given. The 500 share index consists of equities broken down into CAPITAL goods, CONSUMER goods, and further into industry, e.g. aircraft, household goods; the financial group of equities is broken down into sectors, e.g. banks, DISCOUNT HOUSES; an all-share index consists of equities only; a COMMODITY share index is broken down into commodities, e.g. rubbers, coppers; and a fixed-interest index is broken down into types of security, e.g. 20 per cent GOVERNMENT STOCKS. ⟡ INDEX NUMBER; SHARE INDICES.

Financial Times Industrial Ordinary Index. ⟡ FINANCIAL TIMES STOCK INDICES.

Financial Times Stock Indices. A series of price indices published daily in the *Financial Times* newspaper for GOVERNMENT SECURITIES (1926 = 100), fixed-interest SECURITIES (1928 = 100), gold-mine shares (1955 = 100) and industrial ORDINARY SHARES (1935 = 100). For ordinary shares, EARNINGS, YIELD and PRICE-EARNINGS RATIO averages are also given. There is also an index of STOCK EXCHANGE activity which measures changes in the number of daily dealings (1942 = 100). The Financial Times Industrial Ordinary Index is probably the best-known barometer for the stock MARKET: like the time or cricket scores, it is available to telephone subscribers by dialling a number, and there was considerable publicity on 23 August 1968 when the index passed 500. The index is an arith-metic average for thirty BLUE CHIPS. ⟡ INDEX NUMBER; SHARE INDICES.

Financial trusts. ⟡ TRUST.

Financial year. Years of account for financial purposes often do not coincide with calendar years, and are hence referred to as financial years. A financial year 1968–9, for example, might run from 31 August 1968 to 1 September 1969, or from 31 May 1968 to 1 June 1969. The British government fiscal or tax year runs from 6 April of one year to 5 April in the following year. In the United States, the fiscal year runs from 1 July to 30 June.

Firm, Theory of. That part of MICROECONOMICS which is concerned to explain and predict decisions of the firm, particularly in respect of rate of output, PRICE, level of utilization of INPUTS, and changes in these. The traditional theory of the firm deals with the firm at a very high level of abstraction. It assumes away many of the characteristics of modern firms – divorce of ownership from management as represented in the JOINT-STOCK COMPANY, large, complex organizational structures, imperfections of information about the external environment the firm faces, etc. – and considers the firm as attempting to maximize PROFITS, subject to given known DEMAND and COST conditions. The nature of these demand conditions, and therefore the levels of output and/or PRICE, and inputs selected by the firm, may differ according to whether the firms sell in a perfect or imperfect market (⟡ PERFECT COMPETITION). Nevertheless, the underlying theory of the firm is the same in each case: the firm maximizes profits with full information and complete certainty, with no problems of an organizational character.

The theory is obviously unrealistic in a descriptive sense. Nevertheless, it is still a cornerstone of the accepted body of microeconomics. This is not, as some would argue, because economists are so obsessed with theoretical elegance and neat abstractions that they ignore the 'real world'. Rather, it is because the theory is so simple yet so powerful: it permits a wide range of predictions to be made about the behaviour of firms, which are reasonably accurate and which might not be obtained so easily and unambiguously from more complicated theories. In addition, it is the essential first step in the process of building up a theory of MARKETS, and from that, a theory of the process of RESOURCE allocation in the economy as a whole, and these have given considerable insight into the workings of FREE MARKET ECONOMIES.

Nevertheless, there has been a great deal of dissatisfaction with the traditional theory of the firm. Partly, this arises from a desire for realism for its own sake. Partly, it stems from the fact that certain predictions of the theory seem to have been refuted, e.g. that firms will not change price in response to a change in a fixed cost. Finally, the importance of oligopolistic markets (⟡ OLIGOPOLY) has created a need for revision of the theory of the firm, for two reasons: (a) the indeterminancy of the standard theory of the firm in situations of oligopoly suggests that if definite predictions are to be made, more attention must be paid to the actual behaviour of firms in such situations; and (b) the fact that oligopolistic firms are to some extent shielded from competitive pressures means that they have discretion to pursue goals other than profits.

Since the early 1950s, there has been a steady development of theories which attempt to improve upon the traditional theory. The most significant developments have concentrated on the objectives of the firm, i.e. the assumption of profit maximization. It was observed that shareholders, the recipients of profits and the owners of the firm, tend not to participate actively in running their firms, but instead just expect a reasonable level of dividend to be maintained, while managers actually control the decision-making of the firm. This then led to a series of theories based on the hypothesis that decisions would be taken to further the objectives of the top executives, subject always to the constraint that shareholders were paid satisfactory levels of DIVIDENDS. Thus, a theory put forward by W. J. Baumol in *Business Behaviour, Value, and Growth* suggested that firms would try to maximize their size, as measured by sales revenue, since managerial satisfaction and rewards depended more on size than profits. This led to certain predictions of behaviour which differ from those which would be made by profit maximization, e.g. firms would produce larger outputs and advertise more than under profit maximization, and would respond to an increase in fixed costs by raising prices.

A MODEL on similar lines was developed by Oliver E. Williamson in *The Economics of Discretionary Behaviour*. He suggested that the satisfaction of managers depended on the sizes of their departments (as measured by administrative expenditure), the amount of declared profits they could retain rather than distribute to shareholders (since this then gave them discretion to make INVESTMENTS which do not have to meet with the approval of shareholders), and finally the size of expense accounts and amount of other perquisites (company cars, etc.) which managers are able to get for themselves. Again, the theory gives a wide range of predictions which differ both from the classical model and the theory of Baumol just described.

A third model somewhat in this vein is that developed by R. Marris in *The Economic Theory of Managerial Capitalism*, which took the maximization of the rate of growth of the firm as being the manager-

167

ial objective. The notable feature of this model is that it drops the static framework of the conventional theory (maintained in the two models discussed above) and attempts explicitly to construct a dynamic analysis of the firm (◊ ECONOMIC DYNAMICS).

The common feature of these 'modern' theories of the firm is that they concentrate on the objectives of the firm, tending still to ignore problems of organization, and imperfections in information. They also assume that the firm attempts to maximize something, i.e. seek the greatest value possible, rather than achieve certain satisfactory levels of sales, profits, etc. In these respects, they are still very close to the traditional approach. The most significant departure from this has been made by the BEHAVIOURAL THEORY OF THE FIRM, which drops the assumption that firms maximize something, and instead concentrates on the decision processes of the firm, and the way in which these are affected by the organizational environment. This last theory probably comes closer than any other to being a realistic description of real-world firms. ◊◊ J. K. GALBRAITH

Fiscal policy. That part of government policy which is concerned with raising revenue through TAXATION and other means and deciding on the level and pattern of expenditure. It is through the level and pattern of budgetary surpluses and their means of financing that the government can control the level of DEMAND in the economy. There has been a recent revival of criticism of the U.K. government that it has placed too much reliance on budgetary measures for regulating the level of activity in the economy, and has given insufficient recognition to the importance of the QUANTITY THEORY OF MONEY. ◊◊ BUDGET; M. FRIEDMAN; J. M. KEYNES; MONETARY POLICY.

Fiscal year. ◊ FINANCIAL YEAR.

Fisher, Irving (1867–1947). A mathematician by professional training, Fisher was Professor of Political Economy at Yale University from 1898 to 1935. His main works on economics were *Mathematical Investigations in the Theory of Value and Prices* (1892), *Nature of Capital and Income* (1906), *Rate of Interest* (1907), *Purchasing Power of Money* (1911), *The Making of Index Numbers* (1922) and *Theory of Interest* (1930). *The Rate of Interest*, which was substantially revised in 1930, progressed the theory of INTEREST onwards from BÖHM-BAWERK towards the modern theory of INVESTMENT APPRAISAL. The RATE OF INTEREST is governed by the interaction of two forces: (a) the 'willingness or impatience' of individuals with respect to the giving up of INCOME now compared with income in the future (Fisher invented the term TIME-PREFERENCE); and (b) the 'investment opportunity principle', the technological ability to convert income now into income in the future. He called the latter the 'rate of return over cost', which KEYNES said was the same as his 'marginal efficiency of capital' ($\diamond$ INTERNAL RATE OF RETURN). He defined this 'rate of return over cost' as that DISCOUNT RATE which equalized the PRESENT VALUE of the possible alternative investment choices open. He showed how the ranking of investment choices depended on the rate of interest used. He clarified economists' ideas on the nature of CAPITAL, distinguishing between a stock and a flow of WEALTH. A house is capital stock, but its use is a flow of income. He was the author of the 'quantity of money' (exchange) equation $MV = PT$, in which M = the stock of money, V = the velocity of circulation, P = the PRICE level and T = the output of GOODS and SERVICES ($\diamond$ QUANTITY THEORY OF MONEY). Fisher developed the theory of INDEX NUMBERS and established a set of conditions which an index should satisfy.

Fisher Equation. $\diamond$ IRVING FISHER; QUANTITY THEORY OF MONEY.

Fixed asset. $\diamond$ ASSET.

Fixed capital. $\diamond$ BUSINESS FINANCE; CAPITAL.

Fixed charge. $\diamond$ FLOATING CHARGE.

Fixed costs. COSTS which in the short-run do not vary with output. These costs are borne even if no output is produced and are consequently also called OVERHEADS, e.g. payment of RENT on buildings, and interest payments on past borrowing. In the LONG-RUN, by definition, there are no fixed costs; that is, all the costs are variable.

Fixed debenture. $\diamond$ FLOATING DEBENTURES.

Fixed exchange rate. $\diamond$ EXCHANGE RATE.

Fixed trust. A form of UNIT TRUST in which the investment PORTFOLIO is fixed in the trust deed and the proportions of different SECURITIES in which the trust funds are invested is not varied during the life of the trust. The unit share certificates in the trust represent a specific number of each of the SHARES in the trust portfolio. The advantage of the fixed trust as opposed to other types of unit trust are that the small investor can buy into a known and wide cross-section of shares and that there is no risk of loss through inefficient management. On the other hand, fixed trusts are clearly less satisfactory than a well-managed FLEXIBLE TRUST, which can weed out poor INVESTMENTS and switch funds into better securities. For these reasons, new fixed trusts are now relatively less common than they were in the early days of the unit trust movement.

Flags of convenience. An expression relating to the practice of many shipowners, especially since the Second World War, to register their vessels with countries other than that of their own home port in order to avoid taxes or stringent safety regulations. The extent of the movement can be seen from the growth of the merchant fleets of such small countries as Panama and Liberia.

Flat yield. A YIELD on a fixed-interest SECURITY calculated by expressing the annual INTEREST payable as a proportion of the purchase price of the security. It omits any allowance for the difference between the purchase price and the redemption price. ⇨ REDEEMABLE SECURITIES.

Flexible budget. ⇨ BUDGET.

Flexible exchange rate. ⇨ EXCHANGE RATE.

Flexible trust. The most common form of UNIT TRUST, in which the PORTFOLIO of SECURITIES purchased by the trust can be varied at the discretion of the managers. Also called a 'managed' trust. Flexible trusts were developed in the 1930s to overcome the problems raised by the inflexibility of FIXED TRUSTS.

Floating asset. ⇨ FLOATING CAPITAL.

Floating capital. CAPITAL which is not invested in fixed ASSETS, such as machinery, but in work in progress, wages paid, etc. Synonomous with WORKING CAPITAL. ⇨ CURRENT RATIO.

Floating charge. An assignment of the total ASSETS of a company or individual as COLLATERAL for a DEBT, as opposed to particular assets, when such an assignment is called a *fixed charge*.

Floating debentures. A type of DEBENTURE where the LOAN is secured by a charge on the assets of a firm generally. Where specific assets secure a debenture LOAN, it is known as a *fixed debenture*.

Floating debt. 1. Generally, any short-term DEBT as opposed to FUNDED DEBT. **2.** Specifically, that part of the NATIONAL DEBT that consists of short-term borrowing, i.e. TREASURY BILLS, TREASURY DEPOSIT RECEIPTS, and to a minor extent, WAYS AND MEANS ADVANCES from the BANK OF ENGLAND. Treasury bills form an important part of the LIQUID assets of the money market, so that the size of the floating debt, now about one sixth of the national debt, has considerable influence over the total MONEY SUPPLY.

Floating exchange rate. ⇨ EXCHANGE RATE.

Floating pound. ⇨ EXCHANGE RATE.

Flotation. Raising new CAPITAL by public subscription, usually for a new company. A private company issuing SHARES to the public for the first time is said to be 'going public'.

F.o.b. (free on board). A term applied to the valuation of goods up to the point of embarkation. It compares with c.i.f. (charged in full or cost-insurance-freight), which is the valuation including all transport costs and INSURANCE to destination. U.K. imports are entered by Customs in the overseas trade accounts as c.i.f., and exports as f.o.b. For the BALANCE OF PAYMENTS accounts, the IMPORT figures are adjusted to an f.o.b. basis to make them comparable with exports, the revenues or costs represented by the difference between c.i.f. and f.o.b. being included in INVISIBLES.

Food and Agricultural Organization (F.A.O.). An organization set up in 1945 within the framework of the United Nations, which has its headquarters in Rome. It conducts research and offers technical assistance with the aim of improving the standards of living of agricultural areas. It is concerned with the improvement of PRODUCTIVITY and distribution networks for the agricultural, forestry and fishing industries. It conducts surveys, issues statistics, produces forecasts of the world food situation and sets minimum nutritional standards.

Forced saving. SAVING which takes place because goods are not available for CONSUMPTION, rather than because consumers actually wish to save. In a FREE MARKET ECONOMY, it can only exist in a DISEQUILIBRIUM situation, and normally changes would be taking place which would tend to eliminate it. Thus, in response to the existence of unsatisfied DEMAND for goods, firms will be attempting to increase output. If they are successful, the desired expenditure will be made and forced saving will disappear. If, because of FULL EMPLOYMENT, they cannot increase output, PRICES will rise until the excess consumption demand is 'choked off'. Only in a command economy (◊ PLANNED ECONOMY), where MARKETS do not operate freely, is there the possibility of continuously creating forced saving. Certainly, governments regard TAXATION as an alternative to voluntary saving in their attempts to restrain consumption expenditure and control INFLATION.

Forces of the market. ◊ MARKET FORCES.

Foreign balance. ◊ BALANCE OF PAYMENTS.

Foreign bill of exchange. A commercial BILL OF EXCHANGE which is not an INLAND BILL OF EXCHANGE. The Bills of Exchange Act states: 'An inland bill is a bill which is or on the face of it purports to be (a) both drawn and payable within the British Isles or (b) drawn within the British Isles upon some person resident therein. Any other bill is a foreign bill.'

Foreign exchange. Claims on another country held in the form of the currency of that country or interest-bearing BONDS. ⟷ GOLD AND FOREIGN EXCHANGE RESERVES.

Foreign exchange market. The MARKET in which transactions are conducted to effect the transfer of the CURRENCY of one country into that of another. The market is not located at a single centre, but is international, with transactions conducted by telephone and cable. The need to settle accounts with foreigners gave rise to the FOREIGN BILL OF EXCHANGE which was accepted by banks or other institutions of international standing (⟷ ACCEPTANCE HOUSE). These bills were traded at discount, and in this way the foreign exchange market was established, the bills reflecting actual international trade flows. However, the market has developed in modern times and is now dominated by financial institutions which buy and sell foreign currencies, making their PROFIT from the divergencies between the EXCHANGE RATES and RATES OF INTEREST between the various financial centres. ⟷ CONVERTIBILITY; FORWARD EXCHANGE MARKET.

Foreign investment. The acquisition by institutions or individuals in one country of ASSETS of firms in another. Foreign investment is defined to cover both DIRECT INVESTMENT and PORTFOLIO investment and includes both public authorities and private firms and individuals. For a country in which SAVINGS are insufficient relative to the potential demand for INVESTMENT, foreign capital can be a fruitful means of stimulating rapid growth. Australia in particular has in recent years benefited in this way, with foreign investment reaching over 20 per cent of the total CAPITAL FORMATION in that country. In addition, direct investment may be a means of easing the strain on the BALANCE OF PAYMENTS which might otherwise occur in response to an increase of home demand. Direct investment often involves the setting up of subsidiary companies for the domestic production of COMMODITIES which previously were imported from the parent company. There is some controversy as to whether the export of private capital from the U.K. has in recent years been of net benefit to the balance of payments, after taking into account the inflow of funds derived from the profits earned by the CAPITAL invested. In fact, the U.K. Chancellor in 1967 did impose restrictions on private capital exports by requiring proof that these would, over a period of years, yield net benefits to the balance of payments. The U.S. has, in recent years, suffered a considerable widening in her deficit on the capital account of her balance of payments because of the increase in her direct investment overseas (particularly in Western Europe) and her overseas economic aid.

Foreign Operations Administration. ⇨ ECONOMIC COOPERATION ADMINISTRATION.

Forward exchange market. A MARKET in which contracts are made to supply CURRENCIES at fixed dates in the future at fixed PRICES. Currencies may be bought and sold in the FOREIGN EXCHANGE MARKET either 'spot' or 'forward' (⇨ SPOT MARKET and FORWARD MARKET). In the former case, the transaction takes place immediately and it is in this market that EXCHANGE RATES are kept at agreed (PAR VALUE) levels in relation to the dollar, and the dollar itself to gold, under the rules of the INTERNATIONAL MONETARY FUND. In the forward exchange market, currencies are bought and sold for transacting at some future date, i.e. in three months' or six months' time. The I.M.F. rules in respect of the limits within which rates of exchange can move do not apply to the forward market. The difference between the 'spot' rate of exchange and the 'forward' rate is determined by the RATE OF INTEREST and the exchange risk; that is, the possibility of revaluation or DEVALUATION of the currencies transacted. Therefore, the size of the PREMIUM or DISCOUNT of forward sterling compared with spot sterling indicates the strength of the market's expectation of a revaluation or devaluation of sterling and its extent. The BANK OF ENGLAND intervened substantially in the forward exchange market for sterling during the 1964/5 BALANCE OF PAYMENTS crisis. By supporting the forward rate, the bank attracted sales of sterling away from the spot market and thereby eased the immediate pressure on the reserves. It is also possible that, by narrowing the difference between the spot rate and the forward rate, it helped to restore confidence in the authorities' intention to maintain the parity.

Forward market. Any MARKET in FUTURES; that is to say, a market in which promises to buy or to sell SECURITIES or COMMODITIES at some future date at fixed PRICES are bought and sold. An example of a forward market is the FORWARD EXCHANGE MARKET.

Franked investment income. INCOME on which company TAXATION has already been paid at source, i.e. income received as a DIVIDEND by one company from another is not chargeable to profits tax a second time (⇨ CORPORATION TAX).

Free depreciation. ⇨ CAPITAL ALLOWANCES.

Free enterprise economy. ⇨ CAPITALISM.

Free exchange rates. ⇨ EXCHANGE RATE.

Free goods. Goods which are not relatively scarce, and therefore which do not have a PRICE, e.g. fresh air, sea water.

Free market. A MARKET in which the forces of SUPPLY and DEMAND are allowed to operate unhampered by government regulation or other interference. The word 'free' does not have the connotation of 'virtuous' in economics.

Free market economy. An economy in which RESOURCES are allowed to be allocated by the operation of FREE MARKETS. ⇨ PRICE SYSTEM.

Free-on-board. ⇨ F.O.B.

Free port. A port which will accept cargo without the imposition of any TARIFF or tax (⇨ ENTREPÔT).

Free reserves. ⇨ COMPANY RESERVES; NET WORTH.

Free trade. The condition in which the free flow of GOODS and SERVICES in international exchange is neither restricted nor encouraged by direct government intervention. Now virtually an archaism, since all governments are heavily involved today in regulating overseas trade. The most common means of affecting the distribution and level of international trade are import TARIFFS, import QUOTAS and export subsidies (⇨ EXPORT INCENTIVES). It has been broadly accepted among economists that an international free-trade policy is desirable to optimize world output and INCOME levels in the long run. The ORGANIZATION FOR EUROPEAN COOPERATION AND DEVELOPMENT and the United Nations are both committed to freeing world trade, but most economists would agree that under present conditions complete freedom of trade would not be desirable. In any case, it is clear that individual countries could gain from protectionism (⇨ CUSTOMS UNION; INFANT INDUSTRY ARGUMENT; PROTECTION). Towards the end of the eighteenth century, there was a reaction against MERCANTILISM, which had advocated government intervention to obtain surpluses on VISIBLE TRADE. This reaction gathered strength in a new economic liberalism and the doctrine of LAISSEZ-FAIRE. The CLASSICAL ECONOMISTS' support of a free-trade policy was not so much based on specific economic analyses of international trade as simply part of their general belief in what ADAM SMITH called the 'hidden hand': the greatest good is achieved if each individual is left to seek his own PROFIT. The free-trade era lasted in England for almost a century. After the First World War, economic nationalism reached its peak and free trade was abandoned for protectionism. However,

since the end of the Second World War there has been a general acceptance internationally of the dangers of protectionism and some reduction in INTERNATIONAL TRADE barriers, especially for manufactured goods. Progress has been slow, and has paradoxically been associated with the growth of regional CUSTOMS UNIONS.
⇨ GENERAL AGREEMENT ON TARIFFS AND TRADE; EUROPEAN ECONOMIC COMMUNITY; EUROPEAN FREE TRADE ASSOCIATION.

Free-trade area. An association of a number of countries between whom all import TARIFFS and QUOTAS and export subsidies and other similar government measures to influence trade (⇨ EXPORT INCENTIVES) have been removed. Each country, however, continues to retain its own international trade measures *vis-à-vis* countries outside the association. ⇨ CUSTOMS UNION; EUROPEAN FREE TRADE ASSOCIATION.

Freedom of entry. Ability of a new supplier to enter the MARKET for a GOOD. Entry is free when BARRIERS TO ENTRY do not exist. ⇨ PERFECT COMPETITION.

Frequency distribution. A table or graph which shows how a group of items is distributed according to their values of some particular measurable attribute. It is prepared by dividing the range of values of the attribute up into classes, and by counting the number of items having values in each class. For example, suppose that the heights (the attribute) of fifty people (the items), range from 5 ft 3 in. to 6 ft 5 in. We could define five classes of 3 in. each (where 3 in. would be called the 'class interval'). The classes are shown in the table below. By assigning each height to the appropriate class, the number of people falling in each class can be entered alongside the classes. The table illustrates, then, a frequency distribution of a group of people by height.

Height	Frequency
5′ 3″ and under 5′ 6″	4
5′ 6″ and under 5′ 9″	15
5′ 9″ and under 6′ 0″	25
6′ 0″ and under 6′ 3″	5
6′ 3″ and under 6′ 6″	1
Total	50

The 'frequency' is the number of items falling in each class. The table shows then how these frequencies are distributed over the classes of the VARIABLE.

Frequency distributions are used extensively in presenting numerical

175

information in the social sciences. For example, the distribution of firms (the items) by some measure of size (the attribute); distribution of households by INCOME (the 'INCOME DISTRIBUTION'); distribution of cities by population; distribution of people by age, height, weight, number of years spent in full-time education; and so on. The usefulness of the frequency distribution lies in the fact that it is a reasonably concise way of presenting a great deal of information, while at the same time showing clearly the underlying characteristics of the data, especially the 'central tendency' of the data (⇨ AVERAGE) and the extent and evenness of dispersion about the central values (⇨ VARIANCE).

Frictional unemployment. UNEMPLOYMENT resulting from the time lags involved in the redeployment of LABOUR. Even if the number of vacancies for each type of labour was exactly equal to the number seeking employment, so that in principle there should be no unemployment, in practice it takes time for the unemployed to find vacancies, be interviewed and taken on. At any one time, therefore, there will be a small pool of unemployment owing to these 'frictions' in the working of the LABOUR MARKET. Frictional unemployment has probably been reduced by improving the mechanism by which employers and unemployed are brought together – that is, by setting up employment exchanges – but it cannot be eliminated altogether.

Friedman, Milton (1912–   ). Professor of Economics at the University of Chicago, and leading member of the 'Chicago School'. After a short period with the Natural Resources Commission in Washington, Professor Friedman joined the research staff of the National Bureau of Economic Research in 1937 and, apart from a short period, he has maintained a close association with this important research organisation. During the Second World War, he served in the Tax Research Division of the U.S. Treasury. In 1946, he was appointed associate professor of Economics and Statistics at the University of Chicago, becoming Professor of Economics there in 1948. His main published works in economics include *Taxing to Prevent Inflation* (1943), *Essays in Positive Economics* (1953), *A Theory of the Consumption Function* (1957), *A Programme for Monetary Stability* (1960), *Price Theory* (1962), *A Monetary History of the United States 1867–1960* (1963), *Inflation Causes and Consequences* (1963) and *The Great Contraction* (1965).

Friedman has made contributions to the theory of DISTRIBUTION arguing for an approach in which high incomes are regarded as a reward for taking risks. He has also been a leading defender of the

Marshallian tradition in MICROECONOMICS ($\Diamond$ MARSHALL), and made a methodological defence of classical economics which stimulated controversy for a decade. His 'permanent income hypothesis' was also an important contribution to the theory of the CONSUMPTION FUNCTION. His main work however, has been on the development of the QUANTITY THEORY OF MONEY and its empirical testing. He has extended the FISHER equation to include other VARIABLES such as WEALTH and RATES OF INTEREST, and made statistical tests to attempt to measure the factors determining the demand for money to hold (LIQUIDITY PREFERENCE).

Fringe benefits. Rewards for employment over and above the WAGES and salaries paid. They may include pension arrangements, subsidized meals, the provision of housing or goods at a discount. The term is sometimes taken to include statutory requirements, such as holidays with pay, social security contributions and the like. Some fringe benefits, such as the provision of a car, may be assessed as INCOME by the tax authorities. In a series of Truck Acts from 1831 onwards, it was made illegal to pay workers wholly in kind instead of in MONEY. These Acts became necessary because of a growing practice of paying workers in food or other goods, or in vouchers encashable for goods at certain shops.

'Front door'. $\Diamond$ 'BACK DOOR'.

Full employment level. $\Diamond$ EMPLOYMENT.

Full-line forcing. The practice whereby a seller forces a buyer to take several products, rather than just some of them, and hence forces him to take a 'full line'. It can be used most effectively when the seller has a MONOPOLY in some of the products, but has competitors in the others. The full-line force can then be used to extend the monopoly power of the firm, at the expense of competing firms. A recent example of a full-line force is given by the practice of Kodak Ltd of selling colour film 'process paid'; that is, on purchase of the film, the buyer paid also a charge for developing the negative. Thus, the buyer did not have the option of buying the film from Kodak and the processing from someone else. Kodak had virtually a monopoly of colour film sales, but quite a large number of independent processors existed, who were quite capable of providing the processing service. The MONOPOLIES COMMISSION ($\Diamond$ *Colour Film: a Report on the Supply and Processing of Colour Film*, 1966), considered that the PROFITS made by Kodak on colour film were such as to suggest that the practice of selling film process paid was not in the public interest, and should be discontinued.

Funded debt. Generally, short-term DEBT that has been converted into long-term debt (▷ FUNDING). Specifically, the funded debt was originally that consisting of CONSOLS, the INTEREST on which was paid out of the CONSOLIDATED FUND. Then it came to mean all government perpetual LOANS, such as consols $3\frac{1}{2}$ per cent war loan, but now is taken to include all government SECURITIES quoted on the STOCK EXCHANGE.

Funding. The process of converting short-term to long-term DEBT by the sale of long-term SECURITIES and using the funds raised to pay off short-term debt. Funding may be carried out by a company because its CAPITAL STRUCTURE is inappropriate, i.e. to take advantage of the fact that long-term CAPITAL is normally cheaper and less likely to be withdrawn than short-term capital. Companies or governments may also take advantage of a period of low RATES OF INTEREST to repay long-term STOCKS at the earliest possible date and replace them with new stocks at lower rates of interest. Funding has also been used as an instrument of MONETARY POLICY by the government as well as for NATIONAL DEBT management. By selling long-dated securities and purchasing TREASURY BILLS (which are treated as part of the CASH reserves of the COMMERCIAL BANKS), the LIQUIDITY of the BANKING system is reduced.

Funding operations. The conversion of short-term fixed-interest DEBT (FLOATING DEBT) to long-term fixed interest debt (FUNDED DEBT). It is normally used in relation to the work of the NATIONAL DEBT commissioners, but the BANK OF ENGLAND's operations in TREASURY BILLS and government BONDS approaching maturity are also covered by the term. Private companies with bank OVERDRAFTS or other short-term sources of CAPITAL may also decide to convert them to long-term debt by funding operations.

Futures. Contracts made in a 'future MARKET' for the purchase or sale of COMMODITIES on a specified future date. Many commodity exchanges, e.g. wool, cotton and wheat, have established futures markets which permit manufacturers and traders to HEDGE against changes in PRICE of the raw materials they use or deal in. ▷▷ FORWARD EXCHANGE MARKET; SPECULATION.

G

Galbraith, John Kenneth (1908–   ). A leading American political economist, he was born in Canada, and after graduating at Toronto in agriculture he took a PH.D. at the University of California. In 1949 he became Professor of Economics at Harvard University, and was, from 1961 to 1963, U.S. Ambassador to India. His major books include *A Theory of Price Control* (1952), *American Capitalism* (1952), *The Great Crash 1929* (1955), *The Affluent Society* (1958), *The Economic Discipline* (1967) and *The New Industrial State* (1967). He has been a sharp critic of current economic theory because of its preoccupation with growth (▷ GROWTH THEORY). He has accused advanced societies of producing waste simply to satisfy the need for growth for its own sake. He has argued that in modern advanced economies the problems of the DISTRIBUTION of the total product to the different sectors of society should be given more attention. At the same time, he believes that academic theoretical economics is too bound by its old tradition of the efficacy of competition to the extent of losing touch with the real world. In *American Capitalism* he showed how modern society breeds monopolistic power systems. MONOPOLY in industry induces a countervailing monopoly or MONOPSONY in distribution, in LABOUR and even in government purchasing agencies.

In the *The New Industrial State*, he argued that the 'technostructure' (managers) of the largest corporations in modern industrial society are motivated primarily by a desire to remain secure and to expand their corporation rather than to maximize PROFITS. The highly capitalized nature of the industrial system has required a considerable extension of planning and control, notably of the CAPITAL supply, through SELF-FINANCING, and of DEMAND, through advertising and distribution techniques. Under these conditions, the assumption of CONSUMER SOVEREIGNTY that underlies modern micro-economic theory (▷ MICROECONOMICS) is invalid and the theory no longer relevant to much of the economic system. Galbraith's views have been challenged by many economists as an overstatement of monopolistic power, but are none the less sometimes accepted as an accurate statement of tendency in the modern economy. ⬦ CONSUMPTION; CORPORATE PLANNING; FIRM, THEORY OF THE; J. S. MILL; OLIGOPOLY.

Galiani, Ferdinando (1728–87). A Neapolitan priest, who wrote a number of treatises on economic subjects, in particular *Della Moneta* (1751) on MONEY and exchange, and *Dialogues sur le commerce des blès* (1770) on FREE TRADE in cereals. He resolved the so-called *paradox of value*, e.g. water is useful but cheap, whereas diamonds are useless but expensive, by analysing the PRICE of a COMMODITY in terms of its SCARCITY on the one hand and its UTILITY on the other; utility being not only a reflection of a commodity's usefulness, but also its pleasure-giving potential. He explained how price both influences and is influenced by DEMAND. Much of his work in VALUE theory was original, though part of a long tradition of ecclesiastical thought. However, he was not familiar to English economists of the early nineteenth century, and much of the ground covered by Galiani was gone over again by them. ⬦ MARGINAL UTILITY.

Galloping inflation. Picturesque term given to very rapid INFLATION, such as that which characterized Germany and several other European countries just after the First World War. PRICES rose so rapidly that MONEY quickly lost its VALUE, people lost confidence in the monetary system, and ultimately the system broke down and people resorted to BARTER. These consequences do not inevitably follow, however. In Latin American countries since the Second World War, inflation has been very rapid, with prices rising at a rate of 20–50 per cent per annum. Yet the economies in question appear to have adjusted to this, the monetary system continues to function and there does not seem to be a tendency for inflation to get out of control.

Games, theory of. A theoretical analysis of two basic types of situation: (a) the situation of pure conflict, where the gains made by one 'player' are the losses of the other or others; and (b) the situation of mixed conflict and cooperation, where 'players' may cooperate to increase their joint pay-off, but conflict arises over its division. The theory attempts to abstract the essential elements of a wide range of economic, political and social situations. For example, the nuclear arms race, the behaviour of oligopolists (⬦ OLIGOPOLY) and voting behaviour in committees can be shown to have important similarities which permit general analysis. Game theory is essentially concerned with the question of whether in the various situations of conflict and cooperation, self-seeking behaviour by the players will lead to a determinate EQUILIBRIUM. Its originators were J. von Neumann and O. Morgenstern.

Gearing. The ratio of fixed-interest DEBT to shareholders' interest plus the debt. (⇨ NET WORTH). A corporation may borrow CAPITAL at fixed interest, and if it can earn more on that capital than it has to pay for it in interest, then the additional earnings accrue to the EQUITY shareholders. A firm with high gearing will be able to pay higher DIVIDENDS per SHARE than a firm with lower gearing earning exactly the same return on its total capital, provided that return is higher than the rate it pays for LOAN CAPITAL. However, the contrary is also true, so that the higher the gearing, the greater the risk to the equity shareholder. Roughly speaking, if a firm's initial capital consists of £7,000 subscribed by ordinary shareholders, and £3,000 borrowed at fixed interest, for example through DEBENTURES, it would be said to have a gearing of 30 per cent. Gearing is also called the *debt ratio*, and in the U.S., *leverage*.

General Agreement on Tariffs and Trade (G.A.T.T.). An international organization with a secretariat in Geneva which came into operation in January 1948 as a result of an agreement made at an international conference the previous year, which also included plans for an INTERNATIONAL TRADE ORGANIZATION. Nothing came of the latter, but G.A.T.T. has proved a useful body for international TARIFF bargaining. Its articles of Agreement pledge its member countries, which now number seventy-six, to the expansion of multilateral trade (⇨ MULTILATERALISM) with the minimum of barriers to trade, reduction in import tariffs and QUOTAS and the abolition of preferential trade agreements. There have been successive negotiations between the contracting parties, aimed at reducing the levels of tariffs, from the first meeting in Geneva in 1947, up to the sixth, the so-called KENNEDY ROUND which began in 1964 and was concluded in July 1967. The first major revision of G.A.T.T. was ratified in March 1955. The provisions regarding the treatment of SUBSIDIES designed to reduce IMPORTS or increase exports were strengthened (⇨ EXPORT INCENTIVES). Members are required to give details of any subsidies, and if these are liable to prejudice the interests of any other member they are required to discuss the possibility of reduction or elimination. On export subsidies, in particular, member governments 'should seek to avoid' the use of subsidies on the export of primary products. For exports of other products, subsidies, whether direct or indirect, should cease 'as soon as practicable' if they result in export prices lower than the home prices of the product. In 1965, a revision came into force of the section of the agreement dealing with trade and development which laid emphasis on the special problems of the DEVELOPING NATIONS and a committee on trade and development was given the responsibility of progressing the elimination of barriers on the trade in products of particular interest to the developing nations. This new approach enables the MOST FAVOURED NATION principle to be waived in relation to agreements entered into with developing countries. Since the completion of the Kennedy Round, there has been a growing tendency for countries to become more protectionist (▷ PROTECTION) through the imposition of non-tariff barriers and for economic blocs to make preferential trade agreements with other countries. Examples of the latter are the EUROPEAN ECONO-MIC COMMUNITY in respect of countries in the Mediterranean, and the U.S. in respect to Latin America. Examples of non-tariff barriers are government agencies which direct purchases in favour of particular countries and the American selling-price system by which the U.S. tariff on imports of some chemicals is calculated not on the value of the imports but on the home-produced alternative. The U.S. promised to abolish the practice as part of the Kennedy Round agreement. It has been suggested that the next 'round' of negotiations should be concerned with these aspects of trade.

General agreements to borrow. ▷ INTERNATIONAL MONETARY FUND.

General equilibrium. The existence of EQUILIBRIUM on all the MAR-KETS in an economy. Economists see the economy as being composed of a system of interrelated markets for FINAL PRODUCTS, INTER-MEDIATE PRODUCTS and FACTORS OF PRODUCTION. HOUSE-HOLDS sell their SERVICES in FACTOR MARKETS, in return for INCOME, which they spend in product markets. Firms sell in final or intermediate product markets, receiving revenue, which is then paid out to factors of production. Equilibrium exists in any one market when SUPPLY equals DEMAND. In a general equilibrium system, however, all markets are interdependent, and so general equilibrium exists only when supply equals demand in all markets in the economy. ▷ GENERAL EQUILIBRIUM ANALYSIS; M. E. L. WALRAS.

General equilibrium analysis. The analysis of the conditions which are necessary for the economy to be in GENERAL EQUILIBRIUM, and of the consequences throughout the economy of changes in a particular MARKET or group of markets. General equilibrium analysis might be used, for example, to examine the effects of the discovery of natural gas. This would involve examining the interrelations between the market for gas and other markets – electricity, coal, oil, domestic appliances, gas engineers – and the interrelations between these and still other markets – coal miners, electricity generating equipment, oil tankers – and so on, until the ramifications of the initial change have been traced throughout the economy. This type of analysis is to be contrasted with PARTIAL EQUILIBRIUM ANALYSIS, which considers only the effects of the change on the initial market or small group of related markets. Clearly, general equilibrium analysis is more complicated than partial equilibrium analysis, particularly as it must take the possibility of feedback into account, i.e. the possibility that induced changes in other markets react back on to the market in which the initial change occurred. The choice of methods of analysis, therefore, involves weighing up the relative complexities of the methods against the scope and accuracy of their conclusions. ⟲ W. W. LEONTIEF; M. E. WALRAS.

Geneva Conference (1947). ⟲ GENERAL AGREEMENT ON TARIFFS AND TRADE.

Genoa Conference (1922). ⟲ BRUSSELS CONFERENCE (1920).

Geometric mean. ⟲ AVERAGE.

Geometric progression. A series of numbers in which each value is a constant multiple of the preceding value: viz., $x, ax, a^2x, a^3x \ldots a^n x$. ⟲ ARITHMETIC PROGRESSION.

George, Henry (1839–97) An American economist and politician who stood for election as Mayor of New York for the 'single tax' party. His major publication was *Progress and Poverty* (1879). He was considerably influenced by the English Classical economists, ADAM SMITH, DAVID RICARDO and J. S. MILL (⟲ CLASSICAL ECONOMICS). Ricardo's analysis had drawn attention to the way in which agricultural production could yield an INCOME to landowners in the form of RENT which was surplus to all costs, including normal PROFIT. J. S. Mill had suggested that all future additions to rental income should be taxed away. This would have the merit, George claimed, of enabling the exchequer to be financed by one TAX only and of avoiding the distortions caused by multiple taxation of different economic activities. This idea has some affinity with '*l'impôt unique*' of the PHYSIOCRATS. Some similarity with these ideas appears in the Central Land Board, set up in Britain by the Town and Country Planning Act 1947 which taxed development rental profits by 100 per cent, and also with the Land Commission of 1967–71.

Giffen, Sir Robert (1837–1910). ⟡ GIFFEN GOODS; GIFFEN PARADOX.
Giffen goods. Goods which do not obey the 'law of DEMAND', viz.
that less is bought as PRICE rises. Rather, the quantity demanded
of a Giffen good falls, as its price falls, and it therefore has a positively
sloped DEMAND CURVE. The expression is named after Sir Robert
Giffen, to whom is attributed the observation that, among the
labouring classes, when the price of bread (the main item of their
diet) rose, their consumption rose, and when its price fell, their
consumption also fell (⟡ GIFFEN PARADOX). This he saw as a
refutation of the 'law of demand'. However, Giffen goods are nowadays seen as special cases of standard demand analysis, rather than
refutations of it. If the total expenditure on a particular good by a
consumer constitutes a large proportion of his INCOME, then changes
in price of that good have a significant effect on his REAL INCOME.
If a good is an INFERIOR GOOD (a rise in consumer's income causes
a fall in demand, a fall in income causes a rise in demand), it is then
possible that a rise in price could cause an increase in demand, and
a fall in price could cause a fall in demand, via this INCOME EFFECT.
For quantity demanded actually to change in the same direction as
price, it is not enough that the income effect work in the way just
described; it must also be strong enough to outweigh the SUB-
STITUTION EFFECT. Given a change in the price of a good, if the
consumer's real income is held constant (by a compensating change
in money income), the quantity of the good demanded will always
change in the opposite direction to the price change: if the price rises,
substitute goods whose prices have stayed the same, are now relatively cheaper than the good in question, and so will be substituted
for the latter; if price falls, substitute goods will now be relatively
more expensive, and the good in question will be substituted for
them. The overall change in quantity of the good demanded, following a change in its price, is the resultant of these two effects – the
income effect and the substitution effect. If the income effect works
so as to change demand in the same direction as the price change
(i.e. good is an inferior good), while the substitution effect works
so as to change demand in the opposite direction to the price change
(always the case), and if the former effect outweighs the latter, the
net effect is that the quantity demanded changes in the same direction
as price. It was this special case which was observed by Giffen.
Giffen paradox. Refers to the observation by Giffen that a rise in the
PRICE of bread caused more of it to be bought, contrary to the
general idea that DEMAND varies inversely with price. However,

this possibility is seen as an extreme case in the theory of demand, rather than as a sign of a refutation of it. ⟡ GIFFEN GOODS.

Gift tax (U.S.). A levy on the VALUE of certain property given away to others and paid by the donor. In Britain, neither the recipient nor the donor pay any taxes on gifts as such, although they are added back into the estate of the donor for duty purposes if made within seven years of the donor's death. In certain instances, a gift is counted as a realization of an asset by the donor, who is liable to CAPITAL GAINS tax on any increase in its value since it was originally acquired by him. ⟡ ESTATE DUTY.

Gilt-edged securities. Fixed-interest British GOVERNMENT SECURITIES traded on the London STOCK EXCHANGE. They are called gilt-edged because it is certain that INTEREST will be paid and that they will be redeemed (where appropriate) on the due date. Gilt-edged securities are not, of course, a risk-free investment because of fluctuations in their market value. Gilt-edged securities do not include TREASURY BILLS. ⟡ YIELD.

Giro system. ⟡ CREDIT TRANSFER.

Gold and foreign exchange reserves. The stock of gold and foreign CURRENCIES held by a country to finance any calls that may be made from its creditors for the settlement of DEBT. The extent of these requests for settlement are dependent, firstly, on the size of the outstanding LIABILITIES, which, in turn, is related to the BALANCE OF PAYMENTS surplus or DEFICIT; and secondly, on the willingness of creditors to hold the debt (currency) in question. Pressure on the reserves, therefore, may be either a reflection of the underlying trading problems of the country, or the expectation of a fall in the EXCHANGE RATE of the country's currency. Britain's exchange reserves, which in recent years have fluctuated around £1,000 million, are low, both in relation to her share of world trade, and to the wide use of sterling itself as a RESERVE CURRENCY by other countries. The official published figures of reserves, however, do not necessarily reflect the total amount of gold and foreign currency which could be used to meet obligations, any more than an individual's CURRENT ACCOUNT at the bank. The reserves exclude, for instance, the CREDIT facilities available through the INTERNATIONAL MONETARY FUND and PORTFOLIO foreign investments.

Gold exchange standard. A special form of the GOLD STANDARD. In this system the CENTRAL BANK will not exchange its CURRENCY for gold on demand (as is the case under the gold standard), but will exchange it for a currency which is itself on the gold standard. The Central Bank holds the parent country's currency in its reserves along with gold itself. The Scandinavian countries adopted this system in respect of sterling up until 1931, when the U.K. came off the gold standard.

Gold market. There are five member firms in the gold MARKET in London, in which dealings in gold BULLION take place. Each day the members meet to fix the price of gold for that day in relation to the pressure of demand (⇨ INTERNATIONAL LIQUIDITY).

Gold points. ⇨ SPECIE POINTS.

Gold standard. A country is said to be on the gold standard when its CENTRAL BANK is obliged to give gold in exchange for any of its CURRENCY presented to it. When the U.K. was on the gold standard before 1919, anybody could go to the BANK OF ENGLAND and demand gold in exchange for BANK NOTES. The gold standard was central to the CLASSICAL ECONOMIC view of the equilibrating processes in INTERNATIONAL TRADE. The fact that each currency was freely convertible into gold, fixed the EXCHANGE RATES between currencies (⇨ SPECIE POINTS), and all international debts were settled in gold. A BALANCE OF PAYMENTS surplus caused an inflow of gold into the central bank's reserves. This enabled the central bank to expand the money supply without fear of having insufficient gold to meet its LIABILITIES. The increase in the quantity of money (⇨ MONEY SUPPLY) raised prices, resulting in a fall in the demand for EXPORTS and therefore a reduction in the balance of payments surplus. The reverse happened in the event of a DEFICIT. The U.K. came off the gold standard in 1914, partly returned to it in 1925, but was forced to abandon gold finally in 1931. ⇨ BANKING AND CURRENCY SCHOOLS; GOLD EXCHANGE STANDARD.

Gossen, Hermann Heinrich (1810–58). Born in Düren, near Aachen, in Germany, Gossen studied law and went into government service in deference to his father's wishes. It was not until after his father's death, in 1847, that he dedicated himself to the study of economics. His major economic work is *Entwicklung der gesetze des menschlichen verkehrs und der daraus fliessenden regeln fur menschliches Handeln* (1854). In this book, Gossen set out a theory of consumer behaviour based on theories which were subsequently to be independently rediscovered and enshrined in the theory of MARGINAL UTILITY by JEVONS, MENGER and WALRAS. The first edition of his book was completely ignored, and Gossen's recognition had to wait until after his death. It was Jevons who, in the preface to his own *Theory of Political Economy* (1891), drew attention to the significance of Gossen's achievement, admitting that Gossen had 'completely anticipated him as regards the general principles and methods of economics'. Gossen's first law states that the pleasure obtained from each additional amount consumed of the same COMMODITY diminishes until satiety is reached. Gossen's second law states that once a person had spent his entire INCOME, he would have maximized his total pleasure from it only if the satisfaction gained from the last item of each commodity bought was the same for each commodity. Gossen's third law, derived from the first two, states that a commodity has a subjective VALUE, and the subjective value of each additional unit owned diminishes and eventually reaches zero. ⟡ BERNOULLI'S HYPOTHESIS.

Government expenditure. ⟡ BUDGET.

Government securities. All government fixed-interest paper, including FUNDED DEBT and TREASURY BILLS. The government does not, of course, issue EQUITY capital.

Government stocks. Fixed-interest SECURITIES issued by the government, often known as 'GILT-EDGED'. ⟡ FUNDED DEBT.

Graduated Pension Scheme. ⟡ NATIONAL INSURANCE.

Gresham's Law. If two coins are in circulation whose relative FACE VALUES differ from their relative BULLION content, the 'dearer' coin will be extracted from circulation for melting down. 'BAD MONEY DRIVES OUT GOOD'. The law is named after Sir Thomas Gresham (1519–79), a leading Elizabethan businessman and financial adviser to Queen Elizabeth I.

Grey area. ⟡ HUNT COMMITTEE.

Gross cash flow. ⟡ CASH FLOW.

Gross domestic product (G.D.P.). A measure of the total flow of goods and SERVICES produced by the economy over a particular time period, normally a year. It is obtained by valuing outputs of goods and services at MARKET prices, and then aggregating. Note that all INTERMEDIATE PRODUCTS are excluded, and only goods used for final CONSUMPTION or investment goods (⟡ CAPITAL) are included. This is because the VALUES of intermediate goods are already implicitly included in the PRICES of the final goods. The word 'gross' means that no deduction for the value of expenditure on capital goods for replacement purposes is made. Because the INCOME arising from INVESTMENTS and possessions owned abroad is not included, only the value of the flow of goods and services produced in the country is estimated; hence the word 'domestic' to distinguish it from the GROSS NATIONAL PRODUCT. Since no adjustment is made for indirect taxes (⟡ DIRECT TAXATION) and SUBSIDIES, the measure here defined is often referred to as 'Gross domestic product at market prices'. ⟡ GROSS DOMESTIC PRODUCT AT FACTOR COST.

Gross domestic product at factor cost. In measuring GROSS DOMESTIC PRODUCT, MARKET prices are used to value outputs so that they can be aggregated. This implies that, to the extent that market prices include indirect taxes, i.e. PURCHASE TAX, and SUBSIDIES, the VALUE of output will not equal the value of INCOMES paid out to FACTORS OF PRODUCTION. This is because it is the revenue received by firms after indirect taxes (⟡ DIRECT TAXATION) which is distributed as factor incomes. Thus, by substracting the total of indirect taxes (and, since subsidies have the opposite effect of taxes, by adding in subsidies) from the G.D.P. we arrive at the estimate of the G.D.P. at factor cost, which is consistent with the value of incomes paid to factors of production.

Gross fixed capital formation (G.F.C.F.). ⟡ CAPITAL FORMATION.

Gross investment. INVESTMENT expenditure inclusive of replacement of worn out and obsolescent equipment, i.e. inclusive of DEPRECIATION. ⟡ NET INVESTMENT.

Gross margin. In a retail business, the margin on a sale which is the difference between the purchase PRICE of a GOOD and the price paid by the retailer, i.e. it makes no allowance for OVERHEADS, stock appreciation or TAX. The gross margin is sometimes loosely referred to as *gross profit*, but this term has a different, strictly defined, meaning in accounting (⟡ PROFIT).

Gross national product (G.N.P.). GROSS DOMESTIC PRODUCT plus the INCOME accruing to domestic residents arising from INVESTMENT abroad less income earned in the domestic market accruing to foreigners abroad.

Gross national product at factor cost. GROSS NATIONAL PRODUCT at MARKET prices minus all indirect taxes (⟡ DIRECT TAXATION) and SUBSIDIES. ⟡ GROSS DOMESTIC PRODUCT AT FACTOR COST.

Gross national product at market prices. GROSS NATIONAL PRODUCT with all flows valued at MARKET prices. Since market prices include indirect taxes (⟡ DIRECT TAXATION) and SUBSIDIES, and since taxes and subsidies are regarded simply as TRANSFER PAYMENTS, it is often preferable to measure national output excluding these. This gives the measure of national output, net of TAXATION and subsidies, known as GROSS NATIONAL PRODUCT AT FACTOR COST.

Gross national product deflator. A price INDEX NUMBER used to correct MONEY values of GROSS NATIONAL PRODUCT for PRICE changes, so as to isolate the changes which have taken place in the physical output of GOODS and SERVICES.

Gross profit. ⇨ PROFIT.

Gross trading profit. Gross PROFIT before allowing for DEPRECIATION, INTEREST and stock APPRECIATION.

Group of Ten. ⇨ INTERNATIONAL MONETARY FUND.

Growth theory. That part of economics which is concerned with analysing the determinants of the rate at which an economy will grow over time. By the growth of an economy, we mean, of course, the growth in its major economic aggregates: NATIONAL INCOME, CONSUMPTION, total employment, CAPITAL, etc. Growth theory is a highly abstract branch of economics which, though it has yielded some insight into the workings of the economy, is probably more notable for its mathematical than for its economic content. It should not be confused with the economics of growth of DEVELOPING COUNTRIES, which is a far more pragmatic subject. ⇨ HARROD-DOMAR MODEL.

H

Halesbury Committee. ⟡ DECIMAL COINAGE.

Hammered, hammering. Terms used in the situation of a member of the STOCK EXCHANGE who cannot meet his obligations, when a formal announcement to that effect is made by the council.

Hard currency. A CURRENCY traded in a FOREIGN EXCHANGE MARKET for which DEMAND is persistently high relative to the SUPPLY. ⟡ SOFT CURRENCY.

Harrod, Sir Roy Forbes (1900–). Educated at New College, Oxford, he began his career in 1922 as lecturer at Christ Church, Oxford, and continued teaching there until 1952. From 1940 until 1942, Professor Harrod served under Lord Charwell and in the prime minister's office and then held the post of Statistical Adviser to the Admiralty until 1945. In 1952, he was appointed Nuffield Reader of International Economics. His publications include *The Trade Cycle, an Essay* (1936), *Towards a Dynamic Economics* (1948), *The Life of John Maynard Keynes* (1951), *Policy Against Inflation* (1958), *The British Economy* (1963), *Reforming the World's Money* (1965), *Towards a New Economic Policy* (1967), *Dollar-Sterling Collaboration* (1968) and *Money* (1969).

His *Essay in Dynamic Theory* (1939) brought together in a mathematical framework the accelerator and the MULTIPLIER (⟡ ACCELERATOR-MULTIPLIER MODEL). The essay shifted economic theory away from its preoccupation with the conditions of stationary EQUILIBRIUM towards the analysis of the problems of growth (⟡ GROWTH THEORY). Harrod investigated the implications for growth of the interactions of the ACCELERATION PRINCIPLE and the multiplier (⟡ HARROD-DOMAR MODEL).

In the debate concerning the appropriate economic policy to pursue in the U.K.'s post-war economy, which has been dominated by 'STOP-GO', he has come out against PAISH's argument for the need to maintain a level of spare capacity in the economy, represented by a margin of about $2\frac{1}{2}$ per cent UNEMPLOYMENT. Harrod has argued that it can be shown that PRICES have not risen as fast in the upturn as in the periods of low growth, which is contrary to what one would expect in a situation of EXCESS DEMAND. He is also doubtful of the value of DEVALUATION. Devaluation yields benefit too late, and moreover induces INFLATION. Harrod's solution lies in an incomes policy. ($\diamond$ PRICES AND INCOMES POLICY).

Harrod-Domar model. A MODEL which, as a synthesis of the independent work of two economists (Sir ROY HARROD and Evsey D. Domar), was one of the earliest analyses of the process of growth of the economy. In its simplest form, it can be regarded as an attempt to make the simple KEYNESIAN theory of INCOME DETERMINATION dynamic, by taking into account the effects of changes in certain VARIABLES over time. The model shows, in a simple world consisting only of: (a) firms which produce and sell GOODS, spend on new INVESTMENT, and pay INCOMES to households for productive SERVICES; and (b) households which spend part of the income they receive on CONSUMPTION goods, and save the rest; that if the amount saved is equal to the amount invested at every period, then the economy will tend to grow at a rate which is determined by the MARGINAL PROPENSITY TO SAVE and the incremental CAPITAL-OUTPUT RATIO (the so-called 'warranted growth rate'). Though obviously highly simplified, this model clarified certain issues, raised certain new problems and suggested the areas to which attention should subsequently be directed.

Hawtrey, Sir Ralph George (1879–   ). After a long career in the TREASURY, which lasted from 1904 to 1945, Sir Ralph Hawtrey was appointed Professor at the Royal Institute of International Affairs. He held this post until his retirement in 1952. Hawtrey's publications include *Currency and Credit* (1919), *The Gold Standard in Theory and Practice* (1927), *The Art of Central Banking* (1937), *Capital and Employment* (1937), *A Century of Bank Rate* (1938), *The Balance of Payments and the Standard of Living* (1950) *Cross-Purposes in Wages Policy* (1955) *The Pound at Home and Abroad* (1961) and *Incomes and Money* (1967).

His theory of the TRADE CYCLE emphasizes monetary factors. The amount which consumers and investors were willing to save or spend depended on the level of RATES OF INTEREST. Fluctuations in economic activity arose through variations in the quantity of money ($\diamond$ MONEY SUPPLY), especially bank CREDIT, because these variations alter the level of the rate of interest ($\diamond$ L. E. VON MISES). He criticized the Radcliffe Committee ($\diamond$ RADCLIFFE REPORT) because he felt that it had not given sufficient attention to the possibility that the rate of interest had a significant influence on a firm's willingness to hold stocks of commodities ($\diamond$ INVENTORIES).

Hayek, Friedrich August von (1899–). Born in Vienna, Hayek was director of the Austrian Institute for Economic Research from 1927 to 1931 and lectured at Vienna University. In 1931, he was appointed Tooke Professor of Economics Science and Statistics at the London School of Economics, a post he held until 1950. From 1950 until 1962 he was Professor of Social and Moral Science at Chicago University. He is Professor of Economics at the University of Freiburg. His published works include *Monetary Theory and the Trade Cycle* (1929), *Prices and Production* (1931), *Profits, Interest, Investment* (1939), *The Pure Theory of Capital* (1941), *Individualism and Economic Order* (1948), *The Constitution of Liberty* (1961) and *Studies in Philosophy, Politics and Economics* (1967).

A member of the AUSTRIAN SCHOOL, Hayek elaborated the TRADE CYCLE theory of L. E. VON MISES by integrating it with BÖHM-BAWERK'S theory of CAPITAL. In a boom, REAL WAGES fall because of the rise in prices, and firms therefore switch to less 'roundabout' (CAPITAL-INTENSIVE) methods of production. In consequence, INVESTMENT in total is reduced. In recession (⇨ DEPRESSION), the reverse situation induces 'roundabout' production methods and investment is stimulated. ⇨ ACCELERATION PRINCIPLE; J. M. KEYNES; RICARDO EFFECT.

Heckscher-Ohlin principle. The law of comparative advantage (⇨ D. RICARDO) had been established by economists as an explanation for the existence and pattern of international trade based on the relative COST advantages of producing different commodities as between different countries. The law says nothing about why or how a comparative advantage exists. The Heckscher-Ohlin principle states that advantage arises from the different relative FACTOR endowments of the countries trading. A country will export those commodities which are intensive (⇨ CAPITAL-INTENSIVE and LABOUR-INTENSIVE) in the factor in which it is most well endowed. The principle was first put forward by Eli F. Heckscher (1879–1952) in an article published in 1919 and reprinted in *Readings in the Theory of International Trade* (1949). It was refined by Bertil Ohlin in his *Interregional and International Trade* (1933). The principle has been developed further by Professor P. A. SAMUELSON in his factor price equalization theorem.

Hedge. Action taken by a buyer or seller to protect his business or assets against a change in PRICES. A flour miller who has a contract to supply flour at a fixed price in two months' time can hedge against the possibility of a rise in the price of wheat in two months' time by buying the necessary wheat now and selling a two months FUTURE in wheat for the same quantity. If the price of wheat should fall, then the loss he will have sustained by buying it now will be offset by the gain he can make by buying in the wheat at the future price and supplying the futures contract at higher than this price and, *vice versa*. In practice, perfect hedging may not be possible because spot (◊ SPOT MARKETS) and future prices will not balance one another out after the event, but a significant reduction in risk is normally possible. Hedging in this form is, in effect, shifting risk on to specialized futures operators. The purchase of EQUITIES, or other things for which prices are expected to move at least in line with the general price level, is often referred to as a 'hedge' against INFLATION.

Hedonism. The interpretation of the motivation of all human action in terms of pleasure and pain. ◊ UTILITARIANISM.

Herfindahl Index. ◊ CONCENTRATION RATIO.

Hicks, Sir John Richard (1904–　). Educated at Balliol College, Oxford, Hicks lectured at the London School of Economics from 1926 until 1935, when he became a fellow of Gonville and Caius College, Cambridge. In 1938, he was appointed to the Chair of Political Economy at the University of Manchester. In 1946, he was made Official Fellow of Nuffield College, Oxford, and in 1952, Drummond Professor of Political Economy at Oxford, a post he held until 1965. His major published works include *The Theory of Wages* (1932), *Value and Capital* (1939), *The Social Framework* (1942), *A Contribution to the Theory of the Trade Cycle* (1950), *A Revision of Demand Theory* (1956), *Capital and Growth* (1965), *Critical Essays in Monetary Theory* (1967) and *A Theory of Economic History* (1969).

In an article in *Economica* in 1934, Hicks and Professor R. G. D. ALLEN showed how the INDIFFERENCE CURVE could be used to analyse consumer behaviour on the basis of ORDINAL UTILITY. Their exposition, although not entirely original, did give an important impetus to the development of this tool of analysis in economic theory. ◊ E. SLUTSKY. In his work on the TRADE CYCLE, Hicks demonstrated by means of mathematical MODELS how the *accelerator* could induce several types of fluctuation in total output. ◊ R. F. HARROD.

'Hidden hand'. ◊ 'INVISIBLE HAND'; ADAM SMITH.

Hire purchase (H.P.). A form of CONSUMER CREDIT in which the purchaser pays a DEPOSIT on an article and pays the balance of the purchase price plus INTEREST in regular instalments over periods of six months to two years or more; hence the U.S. name, 'INSTALMENT CREDIT'. In a hire purchase contract, unlike a credit sale, ownership of the goods does not pass from the seller to the buyer until the final payment is made, i.e. the goods are SECURITY for the LOAN. Until that time the seller is entitled to repossess the goods under law. Abuse of the right, extortionate RATES OF INTEREST and the practices of certain salesmen, who persuaded customers to buy more than they could afford, led to a series of Hire Purchase Acts from 1938 onwards to give protection to the buyer. Because interest charges are calculated on the total loan and not the amount outstanding, hire purchase is a more expensive form of CREDIT than it often seems to be. The total amount of H.P. credit outstanding in Britain in 1970 was over £1,300 million, but about the same as in 1964 and much lower per head than in other countries with higher incomes, such as the U.S. and Australia. Approximately half of furniture and television-set sales are made on H.P. Motor vehicles account for about half of the outstanding debt, one fifth of all new motor-cars being bought on H.P. Private purchases account for the bulk of H.P. sales, but it is also an important source of credit for certain types of machinery and equipment (⋄ FINANCE HOUSE). Hire purchase originated with retailers in the U.S. during the nineteenth century, and the development of PERSONAL LOANS and other forms of credit do not appear to have affected H.P. business very much. Now no more than 40 per cent of instalment credit is provided directly by retailers, the majority by specialized finance houses or INDUSTRIAL BANKS.

The control of the volume of hire purchase activity has been an important object of monetary policy in recent years, and for this reason H.P. credit grew little during the second half of the 1960s. Initial attempts at control were directed at limiting the supply of bank credit for H.P. companies and restricting CAPITAL issues by the finance houses. These measures were unsuccessful and H.P. terms, i.e. the percentage minimum deposit and maximum repayment periods, are controlled directly. While fairly effective in restricting consumer expenditure, 'H.P. measures' do bear heavily on particular industries, e.g. the motor industry. ⋄ CROWTHER COMMITTEE.

Historical costs. ⋄ COSTS, HISTORICAL.

Hoarding. The withdrawal of MONEY from active circulation by an individual or group, by accumulating it rather than spending it on

CONSUMPTION, or on buying ASSETS. It can be thought of as a withdrawal of money from the MARKET for borrowing and lending, in order to hold it in idle balances (⟡ INACTIVE MONEY). It represents, therefore, the net change in stocks of idle balances.

'Hog-cycle' phenomenon. ⟡ COBWEB THEOREM.

Holding company. A company that controls one or more other companies, normally by holding a majority of the SHARES of these SUBSIDIARIES. A holding company is concerned with control, and not with INVESTMENT, and may be economically justifiable where one holding company can perform financial, managerial or marketing functions for a number of subsidiaries; I.C.I. are a very good example of this, and, indeed, most large companies in Britain are holding companies exercising a greater or lesser degree of control over their subsidiaries. The holding-company form of organization also has a number of practical advantages, e.g. it is a simpler and less expensive way of acquiring control of another company than by purchasing its ASSETS, and the original company can retain its name and goodwill. It is possible for a holding company to control a large number of companies with a combined CAPITAL very much greater than its own, since it needs to hold only half or even less of the shares of its subsidiaries. Abuse of this possibility of 'pyramiding', as it is sometimes called, is now limited by company legislation (⟡ COMPANY LAW).

Homogeneous product. When the outputs of different firms producing a given product are undifferentiated and identical in the eyes of consumers, then the product is said to be homogeneous. ⟡ PERFECT COMPETITION.

Horizontal integration. ⟡ MERGER.

Hot money. Funds which flow into a country to take advantage of favourable RATES OF INTEREST in that country. They improve the BALANCE OF PAYMENTS and strengthen the EXCHANGE RATE of the recipient country. However, these funds are highly volatile and will be shifted to another FOREIGN EXCHANGE MARKET when relative interest rates favour the move. ⟡ ARBITRAGE; BANK FOR INTERNATIONAL SETTLEMENTS.

Hotelling, Harold (1895–). Associate Professor of Mathematics at Stanford University from 1927, Hotelling became Professor of Economics at Columbia University in 1931. He held this post until 1946, when he was appointed Professor of Mathematical Statistics of the University of North Carolina. His article *The General Welfare in Relation to Problems of Taxation and of Railway and Utility Rates*

195

published in *Econometrica* in 1938, put forward the case for MARGI-NAL COST PRICING by public utilities. He argued that even if, by so doing, such industries ran at a loss which had to be financed by lump sum payments by the state, total economic welfare would be increased by such a pricing policy (⇨ WELFARE ECONOMICS).

Household. An economic unit which is defined for the purpose of the CENSUS of population as a single person living alone or a group voluntarily living together, having meals prepared together and benefiting from housekeeping shared in common. Because of the fact of shared use, which is a household's characteristic, it is an important economic statistic when considering the MARKET potential for certain consumer products. The percentage of households owning certain consumer durables, such as washing machines, television sets, vacuum cleaners and refrigerators, is critical to the growth of the future sales of these products. In the initial introductory period sales grow fast, as households buy for the first time, but they slow down rapidly when a high proportion of the households own the product (⇨ LOGISTIC CURVE). Thereafter, sales can only be for replacement. It has been estimated that the number of households in the U.K. at the end of 1968 was about 18·4 million, with the number increasing by about 1 per cent per annum.

Housing and Home Finance Agency (H.H.F.A.) (U.S.). A U.S. government agency which supervises a number of other agencies concerned with providing housing MORTGAGES, federal assistance for low-rent public housing, technical assistance for urban planning, etc.

Human capital. The skills, capacities, abilities possessed by an individual, which permit him to earn INCOME. We can thus regard income he derives from supplying personal SERVICES (as opposed to lending MONEY, letting property), as the return on the human capital he possesses. We can regard a period of formal or informal training and acquisition of these skills as a process of creating human capital, just as the construction of machinery, buildings, etc., creates physical CAPITAL.

Hume, David (1711–76). Scottish philosopher, whose systematic treatment of economics is contained in several chapters of his *Political Discourses* (1752). He exposed as unwarranted the mercantilist fear (⇨ MERCANTILISM) of a chronic imbalance of trade and loss of gold. He argued that the international movement of BULLION and specie responded to the rise and fall of prices, and in so doing kept national price differences within limits and prevented permanent BALANCE OF PAYMENTS surpluses or deficits. He also foresaw how this mechanism could be distorted by the growth of domestic BANKING and of paper money ($\Rightarrow$ BANK-NOTES). He accepted a QUANTITY THEORY OF MONEY, but distinguished between SHORT-RUN and LONG-RUN effects. By tracing the course of the effects of a rise in the quantity of money, he came to the conclusion that MONEY was not neutral but could affect employment. His belief that the level of the RATE OF INTEREST depended on the rate of business profits became the basis of ADAM SMITH's interest rate theory ($\Rightarrow$ INTEREST, CLASSICAL THEORY OF.)

Hunt Committee. A committee set up in 1967 under the chairmanship of Sir Joseph Hunt to study the regions of the U.K. which were 'intermediate' between those classified as DEVELOPMENT AREAS and those which enjoyed a high level of employment and economic activity. The committee made its report in April 1969. The committee considered that the north-west and the Yorkshire and Humberside regions were the two areas most in need of government assistance outside the Development Areas. In order to attract industry, these regions should be given, *inter alia*, training grants, industrial building grants and CAPITAL grants of 85 per cent. The government did not accept the committee's recommendations in their entirety, but did recognize the need for some additional assistance for these 'Grey Areas'.

Hutcheson, Francis (1694–1746). The teacher of ADAM SMITH at Glasgow University. Smith succeeded him to the Chair of Moral Philosophy.

Hypothesis. A statement about any set of phenomena, which is capable of being refuted by confrontation with facts. A hypothesis is therefore a theoretical proposition, which may be right or wrong, as opposed to a *tautology*, which is always true by definition. Examples of hypotheses in economics are: (a) the quantity of a GOOD demanded depends on its PRICE; (b) consumers' expenditure is positively related to total DISPOSABLE INCOME; (c) firms attempt to maximize PROFITS; (d) the quantity of MONEY which individuals in the economy wish to hold depends on the level of NATIONAL INCOME, the general price level and the RATE OF INTEREST. Examples of tautologies in economics, on the other hand, are: (a) national income is equal to the sum of consumers' expenditure, INVESTMENT expenditure, government expenditure, and exports minus IMPORTS; (b) the amount of a good bought is equal to the amount sold. Any field of study which adopts a scientific method proceeds by formulating hypotheses, testing them against facts, rejecting those which appear to be refuted, or reformulating and amending as the feedback of information from the testing deems appropriate. The procedure of formulating and testing hypotheses is the essence of scientific activity, whatever the classification of the field of study in terms of the conventional distinction between 'arts' and 'sciences'.

I

Idle money. ⟡ INACTIVE MONEY.

Illiquidity. Opposite of LIQUIDITY.

Impact effect. The immediate effect of some change or policy measure, in contrast to longer-term effects. The ultimate effect of the change will differ from the impact effect if certain forces are set in motion which take time to work themselves out, but which gradually modify the initial changes. Thus, the impact effect of a rise in DEMAND in a particular MARKET might be a sharp rise in PRICE. However, if this creates excess PROFITS, and if there are no BARRIERS TO ENTRY, new entrants will be attracted into the industry. The effect of this is to increase SUPPLY and reduce price as compared to the level resulting from the impact effect, and the ultimate effect might be a very small price rise. There is a close similarity here with the analysis of the SHORT-RUN and LONG-RUN in economics: the impact effect may be looked upon as the effect in the shortest of all runs.

Imperial Preference. ⟡ COMMONWEALTH PREFERENCE.

Imperfect competition. ⟡ MONOPOLISTIC COMPETITION.

Imperfect market. A MARKET in which the theoretical assumptions of PERFECT COMPETITION are not fulfilled. This may be because there are few buyers, few sellers, a non-HOMOGENEOUS PRODUCT, restrictions on the flow of information or BARRIERS TO ENTRY. There are three types of imperfect market which are separately analysed, viz. MONOPOLY, OLIGOPOLY and MONOPOLISTIC COMPETITION.

Import deposits. A system of IMPORT RESTRICTION under which importers are required to deposit with a government institution a percentage of the VALUE of their IMPORTS. This DEPOSIT is held by the government for a period of time, after which it is then repaid to the importer. The system restricts imports because it reduces the LIQUIDITY of importers and also imposes an extra charge on them, in as much as they are, in effect, forced to give an interest-free loan to the government. However, the impact of import deposits may be weakened if there is sufficient liquidity generally in the economy to enable importers to obtain loans at favourable RATES OF INTEREST against the COLLATERAL SECURITY of their import-deposit receipts. Again, foreign exporting companies may be willing to finance the deposits themselves, rather than lose their market position, especially if it is expected that the scheme is only a temporary one. The U.K. imposed such a scheme in November 1968. Fifty per cent of the value of imports was required as a deposit on all goods except food and raw materials. This was reduced to 40 per cent in December 1969, to 30 per cent in May 1970, to 20 per cent in September 1970 and finally abolished at the beginning of December 1970. U.K. Customs received the deposits and retained them for six months before repaying them, without interest. About £600 million of deposits were paid during the first six months of the scheme. ⇨ GENERAL AGREEMENT ON TARIFFS AND TRADE.

Import duties. ⇨ TARIFFS.

Import Duties Act 1932. An Act which marked the final abandonment of the FREE TRADE policy which dominated the U.K.'s foreign trade in the nineteenth century and to which she had clung with increasing difficulty after the First World War. The Act imposed a 10 per cent duty on all IMPORTS, except foodstuffs and raw materials and some other items, originating from non-Commonwealth countries (⇨ COMMONWEALTH PREFERENCE).

Import licence. A document which gives the importer authority to import the commodity to which the licence applies. It is a device to enable the government to regulate and supervise the flow of IMPORTS; for instance, under its import QUOTA regulations.

Import quotas. ⇨ QUOTAS.

Import restrictions. Restrictions on the importation of products into a country may be effected by means of TARIFFS, QUOTAS or IMPORT DEPOSITS, and are generally imposed to correct a BALANCE OF PAYMENTS deficit. Their purpose, as with DEVALUATION, is to divert expenditure away from foreign-produced goods in favour of goods produced at home. The magnitude of this diversionary effect will depend on the ELASTICITY of demand for the IMPORTS in question; that is to say, the degree to which acceptable SUBSTITUTES are available on the home market. In addition, import restrictions could be used to increase a country's economic welfare (⇨ WELFARE ECONOMICS) at the expense of foreign countries to the extent it has power to exploit its foreign suppliers, e.g. as a monopolist (⇨ MONOPOLY), without fear of retaliation. Finally, import duties may be applied to protect the market of domestic industry while it is being established (⇨ FREE TRADE; INFANT INDUSTRY ARGUMENT; PROTECTION). Non-tariff BARRIERS TO TRADE include revenue duties, such as British PURCHASE

TAX, which, being imposed as a percentage on landed, i.e. duty-paid, VALUE, increase the cost of imported goods more than locally produced goods and thus discriminate in favour of the latter. Other examples are domestic taxes applied according to the technical characteristics of goods, e.g. on engine capacity, which may subtly discriminate against imports. ⇨ GENERAL AGREEMENT ON TARIFFS AND TRADE.

Import specie point. ⇨ SPECIE POINTS.

Import surcharge. As a part of the measures to correct the trade deficit of £540 million generated by aggregate EXCESS DEMAND in 1964, the U.K. government increased import TARIFFS on a range of commodities by 15 per cent, subsequently reduced to 10 per cent. This surcharge was applied to manufactured and semi-manufactured goods and covered about 20 per cent of all IMPORTS. The government gave assurances that the surcharge would be temporary, and in the BUDGET proposals of May 1966 announced its removal with effect from the following November. In August 1971, the U.S. government imposed a 10 per cent surcharge on about 50 per cent of imports. It was lifted in December 1971.

Import tariffs. ⇨ TARIFFS.

Imports. The flow of goods and SERVICES which enter for consumption into one country and which are the products of another country. In the U.K., IMPORTS of goods currently account for about 74 per cent of the total, compared with about 86 per cent just before the Second World War. The U.K. has relatively few indigenous natural resources, and must therefore obtain its requirements from overseas in exchange for EXPORTS. About 20 per cent of total domestic expenditure in the U.K. is spent on imports compared with, for instance, the U.S., where the proportion is about 5 per cent. As is to be expected, therefore, a high proportion of U.K. imports is accounted for by food and raw materials which the U.K. is not able to supply from its own resources. About 60 per cent of the value of total visible imports is made up of items in these categories. However, one of the features of U.K. trade in recent years has been the acceleration in imports of goods which compete with domestic production. Ten years ago, only about 30 per cent of the value of imports were accounted for by manufactured goods, compared with the current level of about 40 per cent. This is partly a reflection of a change in world trade generally. With the growth of DEVELOPING COUNTRIES, the traditional raw materials, such as cotton, are no longer coming to the industrialized countries in that form, but as semi-manufactured goods. At the same time, the growth in technology and the advantage of specialization (⇨ DIVISION OF LABOUR) have stimulated trade in manufactures between the advanced nations. However, there is no doubt that the growth in the share of manufactures in U.K. imports is also a reflection of the loss of competitive edge in world MARKETS arising from the relatively fast rise in U.K. PRICES. This was a contributory factor which led to DEVALUATION in November 1967. ⇨ BALANCE OF PAYMENTS; INTERNATIONAL TRADE.

Imputed cost. The OPPORTUNITY COST of INPUTS owned by a firm, which it 'supplies' to itself, and which have alternative uses. The owner of a firm may supply certain FACTORS OF PRODUCTION – the use of a site he owns, FINANCE for INVESTMENT, managerial SERVICES, etc. In practice, he may not be paid the 'PRICE' of each of these inputs, but rather will take the residual of revenues after all cost payments have been made to factors of production 'bought in'. However, any input supplied by the owner may have an alternative use, with a corresponding price, and this represents the effective cost of using that input in the firm in question. Hence, we could attribute a price or cost to each input supplied by the owner of the firm, even if no explicit price is in fact paid. Such a price is called the 'imputed cost' of the input. Thus, if the firm owns the land it uses, and pays no explicit RENT, we can impute a rent for that land, equal to what the firm could obtain for it in some alternative use. A similar interpretation could be given to imputed INTEREST (finance supplied by the owner) and imputed salary (managerial services supplied by the owner). The important corollory to the doctrine of imputed costs is the idea that if sales revenues are insufficient to cover actual outlays and imputed costs, then, in the long-run, the firm should not stay in business. If it does stay in business, it must mean that the FACTORS owned by the firm are receiving less than their imputed costs, and hence could be more profitably employed elsewhere. On the other hand, if the revenues remaining after payment of all actual outlays exceeds the imputed costs, then the firm is earning excess or super-normal PROFIT.

Imputed income. IMPUTED COSTS to the firm represent imputed income to the FACTORS OF PRODUCTION being supplied.

'In the bank'. When DISCOUNT HOUSES need to borrow MONEY from the BANK OF ENGLAND, the MONEY MARKET is said to be 'in the bank'. ⇨ LENDER OF LAST RESORT.

Inactive money. That portion of the total stock of MONEY or MONEY

SUPPLY (CURRENCY plus BANK DEPOSITS) in existence at any one time, which is not being used to finance current transactions, or being lent out on the MONEY MARKET. It may also be referred to as *idle money*. It need not remain constant in amount over time, since part of it is meeting the demand for money arising out of the SPECU-LATIVE MOTIVE, and so will vary with changes in RATES OF INTEREST and prices of other financial ASSETS – BONDS, STOCKS, SHARES, etc. Inactive money can be represented as resulting from what KEYNES called LIQUIDITY PREFERENCE, i.e. the desire to hold money rather than INTEREST-earning assets, and real goods.

Income. In general terms, income is the flow of MONEY or goods accruing to an individual, group of individuals, a firm or the economy over some time period. It may originate from the sale of productive services (as wages, INTEREST, PROFITS, RENT, NATIONAL INCOME), or it may simply represent a gift, e.g. a legacy from a will or income of a TRUST fund, or TRANSFER PAYMENTS, e.g. old age pension. Similarly, it may be in money or 'in kind', e.g. use of company car by a business executive. Its essential feature is that it is a flow of wealth accruing to a particular economic unit. Income is an extremely important concept in economics. On the one hand, the analysis of the behaviour of FACTORS OF PRODUCTION and firms is carried out on the assumption that they choose between alternatives in such a way as to maximize income (where the income to the owners of the firm is, of course, profit). On the other hand, income appears in the theory of consumer choice as the factor which constrains the consumer in his choice of consumption pattern, since he cannot spend more on consumption than his total income, unless he dis-saves (⟡ DISSAVING), and therefore must allocate his fixed income among goods in a way which maximizes his UTILITY. Finally, the question of what determines the aggregate flow of income in the economy as a whole forms an important part of the subject-matter of MACROECONOMICS, the implication being that national income is an important determinant of SOCIAL WELFARE. For the accounting definition ⟡ NET INCOME.

Income and earned surplus statement (U.S.). ⟡ DOUBLE-ENTRY BOOKKEEPING.

Income, circular flow of. INCOME, in the form of FACTOR payments, is paid out by firms to HOUSEHOLDS which supply INPUTS. Households in turn spend part of their income on goods and SERVICES, this expenditure then accruing to firms as revenue, and being again paid out by them to FACTORS OF PRODUCTION, and so on. It is this process of a flow of income from firms to households and a flow of expenditure from households to firms which is known as the circular flow of income. It is, in fact, a very simplified MODEL of the working of the economy. Viewed in one way, it shows the interrelationship between product and factor MARKETS, with firms alternately in the roles of sellers and buyers, and households alternately in the roles of buyers and sellers. Viewed in another way, it is the basic prototype of the MACROECONOMIC model of INCOME DETERMINATION. since it shows that NATIONAL INCOME will remain at the same level as long as households' 'withdrawals' from the circular flow, in the form of SAVING (non-expenditure), TAXATION or expenditure on IMPORTS are counteracted by 'injections' into the flow, such as government expenditure (⟡ BUDGET), INVESTMENT expenditure, and export demand. If this is the case, the payments by firms to households, which become consumption, saving and taxes will be equal to the receipts of firms, which consist of consumers' expenditure, investment expenditure, government expenditure, and exports, and so firms will have no reason to vary their production levels. ⟡ MULTIPLIER; TABLEAU ÉCONOMIQUE.

Income determination, theory of. The theory which attempts to explain the determinants of the level of NATIONAL INCOME at a particular point in time, and of the changes in national income over time. In its modern form, the theory was first developed by J. M. KEYNES in his *General Theory of Employment, Interest, and Money*, but this drew on much earlier work, and has been considerably added to and amended since then. Briefly, the rate of production of goods and SERVICES, and hence the level of national income, depends on the level of AGGREGATE DEMAND. The level of aggregate demand itself depends partly on income (*via* CONSUMPTION, and possibly INVESTMENT and government expenditure (⟡ BUDGET) components), and partly on the RATE OF INTEREST (*via* consumption and investment). The rate of interest in turn is determined partly by the flows of SAVINGS and investment (since interest is the price which borrowers have to pay lenders), and partly by conditions on the MARKET for existing SECURITIES, especially the extent to which individuals wish to hold ASSETS in each of the various forms of MONEY, BONDS (short and long term), ORDINARY SHARES, etc. The total MONEY SUPPLY which the government and BANKING system make available is held by HOUSEHOLDS and firms partly to finance normal transactions, and partly as an asset (that is, as a way of storing WEALTH), and the total demand for money to hold in each of these forms must be consistent with the total supply available. EQUILIBRIUM in the level of national income can then occur only if the levels of INCOME and interest rates are such that there is simultaneous equilibrium on the markets for goods and services, for new borrowing and lending, and for existing assets. Keynes emphasized that an equilibrium level of income could occur at a level of employment which was below the FULL EMPLOYMENT level, and therefore that persistent unemployment, such as that which characterized most industrial economies during the 1930s, could be generated by the 'normal' workings of the economy.

Much academic debate centred on this last proposition, but in fact not a great deal hangs upon it. It is possible to show that the economy would in fact tend to return to full employment equilibrium, if it were ever out of it. But this process could take so long, as to make this irrelevant for policy purposes, and so the Keynesian policy prescriptions retain their validity. The major advantage of the theory of income determination is that it is a considerable simplification of the complex reality which at the same time retains most of the important causal relationships. It therefore provides a useful and usable MODEL of the economy, of particular usefulness to government policy in management of the economy (⟡ DEMAND MANAGEMENT).

Income distribution. The way in which total NATIONAL INCOME is divided among HOUSEHOLDS in the economy. It is measured statistically, first by dividing annual household income into size classes, e.g.:

less than   £500 p.a.

£500 – £999 p.a.

£1,000 – £1,499 p.a.

and so on. Then, on the basis of a SAMPLE survey, the numbers of households whose annual incomes fall within each size class are found. The resulting tabulation of numbers of households against income classes gives the distribution of income by households. A characteristic of the income distribution of virtually all economies is that a high proportion of households have incomes falling within the lower-size classes, while a very small proportion of households fall within the high-income classes. This feature remains remarkably stable over time, the main changes being a general upward shift in the whole distribution, rather than a greater compression of it. ⟡ V. F. D. PARETO.

Income effect. The effect which a change in PRICE of a good has on the REAL INCOME of the consumer, and, through that, on his DEMAND for the good. Suppose a consumer has a given money income, which he spends on a range of products, one of which, product X, costs 50p per unit. Assume the consumer initially buys 10 units of X. If now its price fell to 30p, the real income of the consumer has increased, since with his money income unchanged, he can consume the same quantities of goods as before, and have 10(20p) = £2 left over to spend on more goods. This change in real income will have the effect of increasing the consumer's demand for certain goods. If X is one of them, then the change in real income has contributed to the overall increase in quantity demanded of X resulting from its price fall. If no more of X is bought as a result of the real income change alone, then the change in the quantity of X is due entirely to the fact that, because X is now cheaper relative to its substitutes than it was previously, it will tend to be substituted for them (hence this is called the SUBSTITUTION EFFECT of the price change). Finally, if the increase in real income would actually tend, other things being equal, to decrease the quantity of X bought, (i.e. X is an INFERIOR GOOD), then the income effect will tend to offset the substitution effect, and we may observe only a small increase in the quantity of X, or even a decrease, where the income effect outweighs the substitution effect. This latter case, of a good being so strongly inferior that its income effect outweighs its substitution effect and causes a fall in quantity demanded of a good whose price has fallen, is the theoretical explanation of the famous 'GIFFEN GOOD' case.

Income elasticity of demand. The responsiveness of the DEMAND for a good to changes in the buyer's INCOME. It is measured as the proportionate change in quantity demanded, divided by the proportionate change in income which brought it about. As with other ELASTICITY concepts, e.g. price elasticity of demand, income elasticity of demand may be measured by the point elasticity formula or the arc elasticity formula. Normally, we would expect the income elasticity of demand for a good to be positive (increase in income causes increase in demand), or zero (increase in income causes no change in demand). However, in some cases, the elasticity may be negative, at least for some levels of income, and in such cases the goods are termed INFERIOR GOODS.

Income tax. A TAX on INCOME. In the U.K. individuals are taxed on the full amount of their income from employment or INVEST-

MENT in the FISCAL YEAR. (Not including gifts (⇨ ESTATE DUTY), CAPITAL GAINS are taxed separately.) Deductions, such as personal and earned income allowances, dependant's allowance, certain life assurance premiums and building society interest are allowed by the Tax Act in arriving at taxable income. Persons with an income of £416 per annum, or less, are not subject to tax (£504 if over 65 years old). Income tax is progressive in its effect; the principal rate is called the 'standard rate' (38·75 per cent), and there is an additional tax on higher incomes called SURTAX. The combined average rate of income and surtax for a single person, with personal and earned income reliefs only, having an income of £1,000 is 17½ per cent; for £5,000 it is 28 per cent; and for £100,000 it is 71 per cent. Tax rates and allowances are often announced in the BUDGET (the figures given here apply to 1971–2). In 1971, the government announced that income tax and surtax would be replaced by a single tax in 1973, and that other measures would be taken to simplify the tax system. Persons in employment are normally taxed under the PAY-AS-YOU-EARN system under the so-called Schedule E. The self-employed, including those in PARTNERSHIPS, are taxed under the so-called Schedule D, Cases I and II. Under this schedule, the assessment is made on the PROFITS of a continuing trade or profession for the year preceding the year of assessment, which is called the *basis year*. Other schedules deal with investment income (where tax is not deducted at source), income from abroad and other sources of income. Company income is taxed under a different system (⇨ CORPORATION TAX).

Income velocity of circulation. The rate at which MONEY circulates through the economy in order to finance transactions. It is measured as: $v = \dfrac{Y}{M}$, where M is the MONEY SUPPLY available in the economy for a specified period (generally a year), Y is the money value of NATIONAL INCOME over that period, and v is the income velocity of circulation. In general, v is greater than 1, indicating that the quantity of money circulates more than once through the economy to finance the total volume of transactions. v was at one time regarded as an 'institutional constant', determined by factors such as the intervals at which wages and salaries are paid (weekly, monthly, etc.), the extent to which payments and receipts of income earners, firms, etc., are synchronized, and so on. As such, it played an important role in both classical and KEYNESIAN theories of the demand for money (⇨ QUANTITY THEORY OF MONEY). However, more recently, it has been suggested that v may in fact be influenced by the RATE OF INTEREST. When interest rates are high, people will try to economize on the CASH balances they hold (since the interest rate is the opportunity COST of holding money) and hence a given volume of transactions can be financed with a smaller stock of money, i.e. v increases. The converse applies when interest rates are low. ⟡ RADCLIFFE REPORT.

Incomes policy. ⟡ PRICES AND INCOMES POLICY.

Incorporation. The action of forming a company by carrying out the necessary legal formalities. ⟡ COMPANY LAW.

Increasing returns, law of. ⟡ ECONOMIES OF SCALE.

Incremental capital-output ratio. ⟡ CAPITAL-OUTPUT RATIO, INCREMENTAL.

Independent variable. A VARIABLE whose VALUE we are free to choose, within some permitted range, and whose value then determines the value taken by another variable. ⟡ DEPENDENT VARIABLE.

Index number. A single number which gives the AVERAGE value of a set of related items, expressed as a percentage of their average value at some BASE PERIOD. The statement: 'The Wholesale Price Index is currently 140', means that the average VALUE of current wholesale prices is 140 per cent of the average value in, say, 1958, i.e. that they have on average increased by 40 per cent between 1958 (or whenever the base period is) and now. A whole series of index numbers thus attempts to give a concise summary of the broad movement in the values of a set of items over time. Index numbers can be classified into three groups on the basis of the types of items they are calculated for: (a) *Price index numbers*, e.g. the Retail Price Index; the Wholesale Price Index; Index of Share Prices; Index of Wages and Salaries; etc. (b) *Volume index numbers*, e.g. index of Industrial Production; Indices of Imports and Exports at constant prices; Index of Consumers' Expenditure at constant prices; etc. (c) *Value index numbers*.

A *price index number* finds the price of a given physical quantity of each item in the current period, expresses this as a percentage of the price of the same quantity in the base period, and then takes a WEIGHTED AVERAGE of these percentages (or 'price relatives') to give the overall price index.

A *volume index* finds the average of the percentage changes in the physical volumes of the items, abstracting from price changes. In general, the basic data may not initially be available in volume terms, but only in value (price times quantity) terms. This could be because of the way in which the data is collected, or, more importantly, because a particular item, e.g. chemicals, may in fact be an aggregation of several sub-items, e.g. plastics, pharmaceuticals, organic chemicals, inorganic chemicals, etc., which may be measured in different physical units, e.g. tons, gallons, cubic feet, and so cannot be summed. The money values of outputs must be found and aggregated. These money values will however be influenced by PRICE changes, and so to isolate the change in values due purely to volume changes, it is necessary to 'deflate' the money values, i.e. remove the influence of price changes by, in effect, valuing the physical quantities in each year at the prices which prevailed at one particular year. Hence, there is obtained a series of money values of the items 'at constant prices', and these values reflect only the changes in physical volumes of the items. By expressing the value of each item as a percentage of the value at the base period, a set of 'quantity relatives' is obtained, and these are then averaged to give the overall volume index number for the whole set of items.

A *value index* takes the money value of each item at a particular period, expresses each money value as a percentage of the money value of the item at the base period, and averages these percentages. A value index thus shows the (net) effects of price and quantity changes.

When the price, volume or value percentages for the items are averaged to obtain the overall index number, a weighted average is normally taken. The weights may relate to the base period, in which case we have a 'base-weighted index', or to the current period, in which case we have a 'current-weighted index'. A current-weighted index still has a 'base-period', in the sense that all values are expressed as percentages of their values in some past year; however, the weights used in calculating the average percentage change will be chosen on the basis of information in the current year. For a further discussion of the weighting procedure, ⟡ RETAIL PRICE INDEX.

Index numbers are a very concise and efficient way of providing information. They have the usual property of averages in summarizing the values of a large number of items. Also, by the device of relating all values to a single base period, they make comparison of values at different periods very easy – the relation between 140 and 120 is much more quickly seen than the relation between £17,650 million and £15,320 million. Finally, they highlight the aspects of TIME SERIES which we are most often interested in, viz. the proportionate rate of change through time. The fact that index numbers are averages necessarily means that all the information about the underlying items is not presented – particular components will necessarily move in ways different from the average. Similarly, the fact that they are generally *weighted* averages means that there is a difficult problem of choice of appropriate weights, and that there may be an element of distortion as weights become inappropriate (⟡ INDEX NUMBER PROBLEM). Despite these limitations, however, index numbers remain very useful summary statistics. ⟡ F. Y. EDGEWORTH; LASPEYRES INDEX; PAASCHE INDEX.

Index number problem. In general terms, this is the problem of obtaining a satisfactory measure of the changes in some attribute of a group of items by using a single summary measure or INDEX NUMBER. Specifically, however, it is used in economics to denote the difficulty in measuring differences in the 'standard of living' or well-being of communities at different times or at different places. Consider the problem of measuring the change over time in the standard of living of a group of people. A reasonable approach might be to take some standard set of commodities purchased, in fixed quantities, and then to find how the cost of these changes over time, i.e. we could construct a LASPEYRES INDEX of prices. Naturally, the actual quantities of commodities purchased over time will change in response to relative PRICE changes (more of goods which became cheaper, and less of goods which became dearer, will be bought). However, if we find that the cost of the actual purchases which were made exceeds the cost of the BASE-YEAR quantities, when both sets are valued at current prices, we can conclude that the standard of living must have risen. This is so because, since they cost less, the base-year quantities could have been bought, but instead people preferred another set of quantities which previously were not available to them, and so they must be better off. In addition, we might take the current year quantities purchased, value them at base-year prices, and thus see how the cost of the current consumption has changed over time, i.e. we would construct a PAASCHE INDEX of prices. If we find that the current quantities would have cost less in the base year than they do in the current year, we can conclude that the standard of living has gone down. This is because, since they cost less at base-year prices, the current quantities could have been bought then, but were not, and hence the previous set of quantities must have been preferred. However, if we find that the cost of base-year purchases at current prices is greater than the value of current purchases at current prices; while the cost of current purchases at base-year prices is also greater than the cost of base-year purchases at base-year prices; then we are unable to say whether the standard of living has increased or not, since the current quantities were not available in the base year, and the base-year quantities are not available now. This is the index number problem. The problem becomes even more intractable if we wish to make comparisons over time periods long enough for tastes to have changed significantly, since the above discussion assumed constancy of tastes.

Indicative planning. ⇨ STATE PLANNING.

Indifference analysis. The analysis of consumer demand based on the notion of ORDINAL UTILITY. The consumer is thought of as having a given amount of money available to him to spend, and as being faced with given PRICES of all the goods he might consume. He will then decide on some set of quantities of the goods to buy, given his tastes, the money available and their prices. The basic problem of consumer demand analysis is then (a) to clarify how these factors interrelate to determine the consumer's pattern of purchases; (b) to see what can be said about the nature of the EQUILIBRIUM position; and (c) to predict the effects on his purchases of various kinds of changes in prices, INCOMES and tastes. In doing this, indifference analysis rejects the idea that the consumer's tastes can be represented by measurements of the amounts of utility various quantities of the different goods yield him. Indeed, it shows that such measurements are unnecessary for the purpose. It assumes instead that, faced with a set of alternative 'bundles' of goods (where one 'bundle' differs from another in having different amounts of the same collection of goods), the individual is able to rank them all in order of preference. That is, given any two bundles, he is able to tell us whether he prefers one to the other, or whether he is indifferent between them, i.e. regards them as equally desirable, or equivalent. On the basis of this very mild assumption, a model of the consumer is constructed, which is then used to analyse the problems described above. ⇨ DEMAND, THEORY OF; INDIFFER-ENCE CURVE; INDIFFERENCE MAP; MARGINAL UTILITY.

Indifference curve. A curve showing a set of combinations of quantities of two things, such that an individual is indifferent between any combinations in the set. Thus, suppose the two things in question were consumption goods, say sugar and potatoes. We have confronted an individual with a large number of different 'bundles' of sugar and potatoes, each bundle consisting of a certain amount of sugar and a certain amount of potatoes. We have asked the individual to rank the bundles in order of preference or indifference, and he has done so. He has, for example, told us that he prefers the bundle consisting of 2 lb. of sugar and 4½ lb. of potatoes, to the bundle consiting of 5 lb. of sugar and 2 lb. of potatoes; but that he is indifferent between the latter and the bundle consisting of 2 lb. of sugar and 3¾ lb. of potatoes. We could, from the individual's own information, similarly find all other bundles, such that he is indifferent between each of these and the bundle consisting of 5 lb. of sugar and 2 lb. of potatoes. We could then represent all these bundles on a graph as follows:

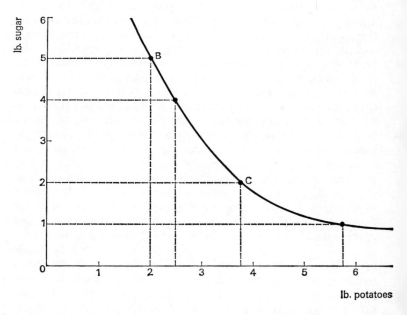

Each point on the curve represents a particular sugar/potatoes bundle, e.g. point *B* represents 5 lb. of sugar and 2 lb. of potatoes, and so on. Note that the particular indifference curve which is drawn will reflect the preferences of the individual and so will probably be different for different individuals. However, as drawn, the indifference curve has two properties which are expected to hold for all individuals:

(a) It is drawn sloping downwards from left to right. This simply expresses the idea that if we subtract some quantity of one of the goods from his bundle, we would have to increase the quantity of the other, to 'compensate', and so leave him with a new bundle equivalent to the first. This obviously rests on the assumption that both goods yield positive satisfaction. If this is so, a person will always prefer to have a combination containing more of at least one good and no less of the other. This then rules out indifference curves which are horizontal, vertical or sloping upwards from left to right. If, on the other hand, one of the goods actually yielded dissatisfaction (garbage, aircraft noise, work), then we would expect the indifference curve to slope upwards from left to right.

(b) It is drawn convex to the origin, i.e. it bulges outward when looked at from below. This particular curvature of the indifference curve simply gives expression to the idea that as one good becomes more plentiful relative to the others, its subjective worth becomes smaller in terms of the others. This can be illustrated as follows:

Beginning at point B in the above diagram, we could imagine 'moving' the individual along his indifference curve by reducing the amount of sugar in the bundle, and increasing the amount of potatoes. That is, we substitute potatoes for sugar in such a way as to leave him always with bundles which he regards as equivalent to B. Now, at B, the individual has a lot of sugar and not many potatoes. If we subtract 1 lb. of sugar from his bundle, we have to 'compensate' by giving roughly $\frac{1}{2}$ lb. of potatoes, leaving him with a new bundle which is equivalent to B. At C, on the other hand, the individual has a lot of potatoes and little sugar. If we now subtract 1 lb. of sugar from his bundle, we find we have to give him more than 1 lb. of potatoes in order to give him a bundle which is equivalent to C.

Thus, the quantity of potatoes which are required to compensate the individual for the loss of 1 lb. of sugar gets steadily greater as potatoes become plentiful and sugar scarce, and this is reflected in the shape of the curve.

The concept of the indifference curve is used extensively in the theory of consumer DEMAND, in WELFARE ECONOMICS and indeed in any area of economics concerned with problems of choice between alternative combinations of things. It is a way of representing the preferences of a decision-taker, on the basis of information on rankings alone, and no assumption of the measurability of utility is involved. ⟡ R. G. D. ALLEN; F. Y. EDGEWORTH; INDIFFER-ENCE ANALYSIS; MARGINAL RATE OF SUBSTITUTION; ORDINAL UTILITY; F. V. D. PARETO.

Indifference map. A set of INDIFFERENCE CURVES which describe an individual's preferences concerning the alternatives in some particular problem of choice.

Indirect taxation. ⟡ DIRECT TAXATION.

Indivisibilities. ⟡ ECONOMIES OF SCALE.

Induced investment. That part of total INVESTMENT which occurs in response to changes in output. ⟡ ACCELERATION PRINCIPLE.

Industrial and Commercial Finance Corporation (I.C.F.C.). ⟡ MAC-MILLAN COMMITTEE; RISK CAPITAL

Industrial bank. Another name for a FINANCE HOUSE, i.e. an institution providing HIRE PURCHASE credit; mainly applied to the smaller institutions, of which there are large numbers outside London. Although receiving DEPOSITS and making LOANS and other financial activities ancillary to their hire-purchase business for consumer and capital goods, the industrial banks do not offer a full range of BANKING services like the COMMERCIAL BANKS.

Industrial Bankers Association (I.B.A.). An association of the smaller INDUSTRIAL BANKS set up in 1956. The I.B.A. requires that at least 75 per cent of its members' ASSETS should consist of HIRE PURCHASE contracts and imposes other conditions on LIQUIDITY, NET WORTH and bank practice generally. ⟡ FINANCE HOUSE.

Industrial organization, economics of. A general term for that branch of applied economics which deals with the factors affecting the structure of industry and the way it is owned and managed. It can therefore be regarded as an area of applied MICROECONOMICS. ⟡ MARKET STRUCTURE.

Industrial Reorganization Corporation (I.R.C.). An independent organization set up by the British government at the end of 1966, and dissolved in 1971, to promote industrial efficiency and assist the U.K. economy, mainly by promoting concentration and rationalization, but also, if necessary, by establishing and developing industrial enterprise. The I.R.C. had a small total staff of about thirty people under a chairman, board and managing director. Under the terms of the I.R.C. Act of 1966, the corporation could draw up to £150 million of public funds which it could lend on any terms, although the corporation was expected to earn an overall commercial return on its operations. The I.R.C. operated rather like a MERCHANT BANK – making LOANS either at fixed INTEREST or in return for

EQUITY, arranging MERGERS and other business relationships where it considered that the structure or development of an industry would benefit in the national interest. The I.R.C. was principally concerned with promoting rationalization where this increased industrial efficiency and competitive power, promoted technological development and affected the BALANCE OF PAYMENTS favourably, e.g. by import saving schemes. In the field of reorganization, the corporation played a notable and controversial role in the A.E.I.-G.E.C.-English Electric mergers and that between Leyland and British Motor Holdings, to which it had loaned money for the purchase of machine tools from U.K. companies. In the development field the I.R.C. loaned the Reed Paper Group £1·5 million for the establishment of two plants for de-inking waste paper. Similar organizations exist in France and Japan.

Infant industry argument. An argument in support of the retention of a protective import TARIFF. An industry does not operate at an optimum least-cost output until it has reached a sufficient size to obtain significant ECONOMIES OF SCALE. A new industry, therefore, in, say, a DEVELOPING COUNTRY, will always be in a competitively vulnerable position *vis-à-vis* an established industry in an advanced country. It follows that the stage of growth at which the industry (or country) can 'take off' (↪ W. W. ROSTOW) industrially will be postponed indefinitely. The argument concludes that protection is necessary until the industry has reached its optimum size.

Inferior good. A good the DEMAND for which falls when its consumers' INCOMES rise. For example, as people become richer, they may substitute more cars for bicycles, and bicycles would be regarded as an inferior good. It follows that an inferior good has a negative INCOME ELASTICITY OF DEMAND. ↪ INCOME EFFECT.

Inflation. A process of steadily rising prices, resulting in diminishing purchasing power of a given nominal sum of MONEY. Inflation has been a marked characteristic of most economies since the Second World War, and has received considerable attention from economists. Theories of its causes can be divided into COST-PUSH theories and DEMAND-PULL theories, the latter of which would include the issue of the influence of the MONEY SUPPLY on the price level (↪ QUANTITY THEORY OF MONEY). Solutions to the problem of inflation most often suggested include: (a) to use MONETARY POLICIES and FISCAL POLICIES to restrain AGGREGATE DEMAND; (b) to increase UNEMPLOYMENT and hence reduce inflationary pressure; and (c) to make a direct intervention in the MARKETS for goods and FACTORS OF PRODUCTION to restrain price and wage increases (⟡ PRICES AND INCOME POLICY). There have even been proposals that taxes, related to the size of wage increases granted, should be imposed on firms, to 'stiffen employers' resistance' to wage claims. However, apart from distorting the operation of the price mechanism (⟡ PRICE SYSTEM) in its allocative role, it is unlikely that measures of administrative intervention would restrain inflation completely in the absence of controls on aggregate demand, since the administrative task of preventing implicit wage and price increases would be enormous (see, e.g., WAGE DRIFT). The real difficulty is to balance the costs of inflation against the costs of avoiding it, in terms of higher unemployment, lower output of real goods and services, etc. A low rate of inflation (perhaps about 2 to 3 per cent per annum), would not in general be considered objectionable, and, indeed, might be considered an inevitable consequence of an expanding economy. The 'evils' of inflation, however, are generally held to result from:

(a) The possibility that a slow rate of inflation may accelerate and become GALLOPING INFLATION, the consequences of which could be serious.

(b) The fact that there may be undesirable redistributions of real INCOME, since those whose money incomes rise at a slower rate than the rate of inflation clearly lose, while the real incomes of those whose money incomes rise faster than the rate of inflation increase. At the extreme, those whose money incomes change infrequently, e.g. old-age pensioners, may become very badly off.

(c) Inflation may discourage SAVING, since the real value of the sum saved falls through time. However, RATES OF INTEREST will tend to rise to offset this, and also many forms of saving exist which provide a 'HEDGE' against inflation, because their money values rise accordingly, e.g. ORDINARY SHARES. Thus, inflation tends to affect the direction rather than the amount of saving.

(d) Probably the most important effect, to an economy which engages extensively in INTERNATIONAL TRADE, is that the PRICES of its goods may rise relative to those of other countries, thus causing IMPORTS to increase, exports to fall, NATIONAL INCOME to be lower than it otherwise would be, and BALANCE OF PAYMENTS difficulties to develop. However, note that the relevant thing here is the rate of that country's inflation relative to that of other countries. If all countries were inflating at the same rate, relativities would remain unchanged – and, indeed, debtor countries, such as the U.K. currently is, would gain, since the real value of their external debts is then falling.

These drawbacks of inflation are such as to cause anti-inflationary policies to be adopted in most countries. However, until recently it did not seem to be the case that they were considered so serious as to stimulate the creation of large-scale unemployment to restrain inflation.

Inflationary gap. A situation in which AGGREGATE DEMAND in the economy is greater than the AGGREGATE SUPPLY of resources coming forward to meet the demand. The consequences are persistently rising PRICES and costs and DISEQUILIBRIUM in the BALANCE OF PAYMENTS. ⟡ INFLATION.

Inflationary spiral. ⟡ GALLOPING INFLATION; INFLATION.

Infrastructure. The underlying CAPITAL of a society embodied in roads and other transportation and communications systems, as well as water supplies, electric power and other public services. Sometimes called *social overhead capital*, the term is also often widened to include the health, skills, education and other qualities of the population.

Inheritance tax. ⟡ ESTATE DUTY.

Initial allowances. ⟡ CAPITAL ALLOWANCES.

Inland bill of exchange. A BILL OF EXCHANGE drawn and payable in one country. Sometimes called *domestic bill of exchange*.

Innovation. The introduction of new products or production processes. Innovation is therefore the last stage in the important process of (a) *invention:* the discovery or devising of new products and processes; and (b) *development:* the process by which the ideas and principles thrown up at the stage of invention are embodied in concrete products and techniques of production leading to innovation. In a sense, innovation is economically the most important of these stages, since it is only when this stage is completed that the fruits of invention and development are gained.

Input-output analysis. A branch of economics concerned with the structure of the production relationships in an economy, and in particular with the relation between a given set of demands for final goods and SERVICES, and the implied amounts of manufactured INPUTS, raw materials and LABOUR this requires. The first step is to draw up a list of basic commodity groups, and then to find, from empirical data, the amount of the output of any one group which is required to produce one unit of output of each other group, including itself. These latter are referred to as the 'input-output' coefficients. Given these coefficients, it is then possible to trace through the effects on the whole production pattern of the economy of some initial set of output requirements. Input-output analysis has been very widely applied in economics. Its originator was the economist W. W. LEONTIEF.

Input-output matrix. ⇨ INPUT-OUTPUT ANALYSIS; W. W. LEONTIEF; MATRIX.

Inputs. Goods and SERVICES used in production. ⇨ FACTORS OF PRODUCTION.

Insolvency. A firm is insolvent if its LIABILITIES, excluding EQUITY capital, exceed its total ASSETS.

Instalment credit (U.S.). Term for HIRE PURCHASE, though sometimes used generally to refer to a credit sale when payment is made in instalments (⇨ CONSUMER CREDIT).

Institutional investor. An organization, as opposed to an individual, which invests funds arising from its receipts from the sale of SECURITIES, from DEPOSITS and other sources, i.e. INSURANCE companies, INVESTMENT TRUSTS, UNIT TRUSTS, PENSION FUNDS and trustees. Institutional investors probably own half of all quoted securities and are now investing over £1,000 million a year on the STOCK EXCHANGE – roughly 1 per cent of the present CAPITALIZED VALUE of all securities quoted and more, in a number of recent years, than the value of new issues. The pressure of institutional investment has undoubtedly been a major factor in the overall increase in EQUITY prices in recent years, changes in trustee law as well as investment policy having led to some switch of new funds to equities from fixed-interest securities.

Insurance. A contract to pay a PREMIUM in return for which the insurer will pay compensation in certain eventualities, e.g. fire, theft, motor accident. The premiums are so calculated that, on average in total, they are sufficient to pay compensation for the policyholders who will make a claim together with a margin to cover administration costs and profit (⇨ ACTUARY; UNDERWRITING). In effect, insurance spreads risk, so that loss by an individual is compensated for at the expense of all those who insure against it, and as such it has an important economic function.

The traditional forms of insurance are *general insurance*, i.e. marine, fire, and accident, and *life insurance*, the last named strictly being ASSURANCE, because the cover is given against the occurrence of an event which is inevitable. There are also many other kinds of insurance, including sickness and unemployment insurance, some of which, like NATIONAL INSURANCE and the B.U.P.A. insurance for private medical treatment, are not carried out by the traditional insurance companies. Traditional insurance is carried out, in Britain, by over 400 companies grouped into tariff and non-tariff. The former adhere to agreed premiums and policy coverage and conditions in respect to general insurance. The bulk of their ASSETS consist of INVESTMENTS made out of premium income against their LIABILITIES to 'pay out' on life policies; only about 10 per cent of their assets are in respect of general funds. Of the life funds in 1957, 14 per cent were MORTGAGES on houses, factories and other buildings, 28 per cent were GOVERNMENT SECURITIES, 17 per cent in ORDINARY SHARES, 10 per cent in property and most of the remainder in other fixed-interest SECURITIES. The flow of life funds for new investment was well over £300 million in 1957, i.e. about one fifth of total fixed CAPITAL FORMATION in that year (⇨ INSTITUTIONAL INVESTORS). By 1970, insurance companies held equity valued at £2,800 million or 16 per cent of the total equity available. There are important INCOME TAX concessions on life-insurance premiums, and life insurance is a popular way of providing for old age and purchasing a house or even EQUITY shares, as well as protecting the financial position of dependants. ⇨ PENSION; UNIT TRUST.

Insurance broker. An intermediary who brings together persons or organizations requiring INSURANCE with insurance companies who provide it. He obtains a COMMISSION from the insurance companies, but, being independent from them, he is in a position to advise his clients on which companies offer the most favourable terms. Insurance brokers handle claims, queries and loans against insurance policies as well as arranging insurance in the first instance.

Intangible assets. ⇨ ASSETS.

Integration. ⇨ MERGER; VERTICAL INTEGRATION.

Integration, lateral. ⇨ MERGER.

Intensive. ⇨ CAPITAL-INTENSIVE; LABOUR-INTENSIVE.

Interest, abstinence theory of. An explanation of RATES OF INTEREST in terms of a reward for choosing to abstain from consumption. ⇨ INTEREST, CLASSICAL THEORY OF; N. W. SENIOR; TIME PREFERENCE.

Interest, classical theory of. In the early tradition of classical theory, e.g. ADAM SMITH, DAVID RICARDO, the RATE OF INTEREST was regarded as simply the RATE OF RETURN on CAPITAL invested.

219

It was treated as an INCOME to capital rather like RENT to land. With the subsequent development of the classical system, the nature of and the determinants of the rate of interest came to be regarded in terms of a more complex pattern. The rate was arrived at by the interaction of two forces operating on the supply of, and the demand for, funds. On the one hand, the strength of demand was related to businessmen's expectations regarding PROFITS. This was connected with the marginal productivity of INVESTMENT. On the other hand, the supply was dependent upon the willingness to save. This willingness was in turn related to the marginal rate of TIME PREFERENCE. People judge how much a pound is worth to them today compared with a pound in the future. They make their decision whether to save by comparing this 'rate of exchange' between now and the future with the current rate of interest. In the classical system, therefore, it was the rate of interest which brought SAVINGS into balance with investment. J. M. KEYNES attacked this assumption in his *General Theory of Employment, Interest and Money*. The balance was brought about, he argued, by means of changes in INCOME and output. The rate of interest was itself more closely related to monetary factors. ⟫ LIQUIDITY PREFERENCE; LOAN-ABLE FUNDS; D. HUME.

Interest cover. The number of times the fixed interest payments made by a company to service its LOAN CAPITAL are exceeded by EARN-INGS. This ratio shows the decline in earnings that could take place before interest payments could not be met out of current income and is therefore a useful guide for the prospective fixed interest investor.

Interest, natural rate of. One of the conditions put forward by K. WICKSELL for monetary EQUILIBRIUM – i.e. a situation in which there are no forces tending to make PRICES in general go on rising – was that the money RATE OF INTEREST should be equal to the 'natural rate'. The owner of a forest has a choice between two alternatives in any one year. He can either cut down his trees and lend out the money obtained from them, or he can let the trees grow another year. The RATE OF RETURN he gets from lending is the 'money rate'; the return he gets from growing his trees heavier is the 'natural rate'. Wicksell thought of the natural rate, therefore, in terms of a physical investment. However, Myrdal in developing this theme, pointed out that the natural rate should also take into account the price at which the timber was expected to sell. ⟫ I. FISHER; J. M. KEYNES.

Interest, productivity theories of. Theories which place the emphasis of the explanation for the existence of a RATE OF INTEREST on the YIELD from INVESTMENT. BÖHM-BAWERK, in particular, developed this theory as one of his reasons for the existence of a positive interest rate. It was built upon his theory of 'roundabout' production methods. A direct method of obtaining drinking water, for example, is to go to a stream and drink. A more roundabout method is to manufacture a bucket and use it to fetch water. An even more roundabout method is to build a water-pipe, pump and tap. Each stage involves more CAPITAL, and also more time, but nevertheless yields increased product. Goods available today, therefore, have more value than goods available tomorrow, for two reasons. First, goods today can be used in a time-consuming roundabout process to yield benefits tomorrow which are greater than could be obtained by the same goods applied to direct production tomorrow. Secondly, they also yield greater benefits over the same goods applied to roundabout production tomorrow. This is because there are DIMINISHING RETURNS to the extension of roundabout methods. Present goods are, therefore, always technically superior to future goods, and it follows that there must exist a positive rate of interest by which future goods are equated to present goods. ⇨ INTEREST, NATURAL RATE OF; INTEREST, CLASSICAL THEORY OF; J. M. KEYNES.

Interest rate. ⇨ RATE OF INTEREST.

Interest, time preference theory of. A psychological theory of the existence of RATES OF INTEREST. An individual prefers consumption now to consumption in the future for two reasons. First, he is aware of the possibility that he may be dead before he can derive the benefits from postponing consumption. Secondly, and less rationally there exists a tendency for people to undervalue future benefits – a 'deficiency of the telescopic faculty'. ⇨ BÖHM-BAWERK; I FISHER; INTEREST, CLASSICAL THEORY OF; INTEREST, NATURAL RATE OF; INTEREST, PRODUCTIVITY THEORY OF; TIME PREFERENCE.

Interim dividend. ⇨ DIVIDEND.

Interlocking directorate. The holding by an individual of directorships in two or more separate companies.

Intermediate areas. ⇨ HUNT COMMITTEE.

Intermediate products. Goods which are used in the production of other goods, rather than for final consumption, e.g. steel. Some goods may, of course, be both, e.g. milk, which is directly consumed, but also used to make products such as chocolate, cheese and tinned rice pudding.

Internal economies. ⟡ ECONOMIES OF SCALE.

Internal rate of return. That RATE OF INTEREST which, when used to discount the CASH FLOWS associated with an INVESTMENT project, reduces its net PRESENT VALUE to zero. Hence, it gives a measure of the 'break-even' RATE OF RETURN of an INVESTMENT, since it shows the highest rate of interest at which the project makes neither a PROFIT nor a loss. If the internal rate of return is greater than the rate of interest which has to be paid, this would suggest that a project is profitable and should be undertaken; and conversely if it is smaller. However, as a measure of investment profitability it suffers from two important defects: (a) a given project may have more than one interest rate which discounts its cash flows to zero, and so the method may not give a clear-cut answer. This can happen when cash inflows (profits) within the lifetime of the project are followed by cash outflows. And (b) the method may give incorrect rankings of alternative projects, in that the actual profitability of one project may be greater than that of another, even though its internal rate of return is lower. The internal rate of return is also known as the *marginal efficiency of capital*, the *investor's yield* and the *d.c.f. yield* (⟡ DISCOUNTED CASH FLOW).

International Bank for Reconstruction and Development (I.B.R.D.). Also known as the World Bank, the establishment of the I.B.R.D., like the INTERNATIONAL MONETARY FUND, was agreed upon by the representatives of forty-four countries at the U.N. Monetary and Financial Conference at BRETTON WOODS in July 1944. It began operations in June 1946. The purpose of the bank is to encourage CAPITAL investment for the reconstruction and development of its member countries, either by channelling the necessary private funds or by making LOANS from its own resources. Two per cent of each member's subscription is paid into the bank's funds in gold or dollars, 18 per cent in the country's own CURRENCY and the remainder is retained but available for call to meet any of the bank's LIABILITIES if required. The bank also raises MONEY by selling BONDS on the world market. Generally speaking, the bank makes loans either direct to governments or with governments as the guarantor. The bank operates through its affiliates, the INTERNATIONAL FINANCE CORPORATION and the INTERNATIONAL DEVELOPMENT ASSOCIATION. ⟡ DEVELOPING COUNTRIES.

International Clearing Union. ⟡ KEYNES PLAN.

International commodity agreements. A number of international commodity agreements have been signed since the Second World War. They include coffee, olive oil, sultanas, sugar, wheat, tin. It has been a feature of the MARKETS in primary commodities that imbalance between SUPPLY and DEMAND give rise to wide fluctuations in PRICES. Primary commodities often have long production cycles which are difficult to adjust to bring into EQUILIBRIUM with relatively short-run fluctuations in demand. At the same time, the development of the economies of the primary producing countries depend heavily on the export earnings of these commodities, with the result that, in response to a fall in demand, there is a tendency to increase supply to maintain total earnings in the face of intensified competition, thereby forcing prices down even further. There are two features, therefore, of commodity agreements. They may (a) be concluded for the stabilization of prices, or (b) for the raising or maintenance of prices. The Coffee Agreement signed in 1962, and covering the five years to 1968, was designed to halt the long decline in prices by fixing export QUOTAS for each producing country. The agreement was renewed for a further five years in 1968. The International Tin Agreement is an example of a 'price stabilization' agreement. The first operated for five years from July 1956, the second for the following ten years and the third agreement was for the five years ended in June 1971. The fourth agreement came into force on 1 July 1971. A 'buffer' stock of tin was created and a manager appointed who had the responsibility of buying and selling tin such as to keep the PRICE within a 'ceiling', at which point he sold, and a 'floor', when he bought tin. There has been some debate that 'price supporting' agreements could be used to raise DEVELOPING COUNTRIES' incomes to offset the deterioration in their TERMS OF TRADE. ⟐ UNITED NATIONS CONFERENCE ON TRADE AND DEVELOPMENT.

International company. ⟐ MULTINATIONAL CORPORATION.

International Cooperation Administration. ⟐ ECONOMIC COOPERATION ADMINISTRATION.

International corporation. ⟐ MULTINATIONAL CORPORATION.

International Development Association (I.D.A.). An institution affiliated to the INTERNATIONAL BANK FOR RECONSTRUCTION AND DEVELOPMENT and established in 1960. It gives long-term LOANS at little or no INTEREST for projects in the DEVELOPING COUNTRIES. It is intended for INVESTMENTS for which finance cannot be obtained through other channels without bearing uneconomically

223

high interest charges, and is mainly for items of INFRASTRUCTURE, e.g. roads, power supply. The repayment period for the loan may be up to fifty years. In July 1970 the I.B.R.D. agreed to double the contributions to I.D.A. to $800 million per annum for the three years ending 1974. Of this total, the U.S. contributes $320 million, the U.K. $104 million, Western Germany $78 million, France and Canada $50 million each and Japan $48 million. Smaller contributions are made by twelve other member countries.

International Finance Corporation (I.F.C.). An affiliate of the INTERNATIONAL BANK FOR RECONSTRUCTION AND DEVELOPMENT. In the early 1950s it was recognized that the requirement that I.B.R.D. loans should have a government guarantee was a significant handicap to the attraction of private INVESTMENT to DEVELOPING COUNTRIES. The I.F.C. was created in 1956 so that greater advantage could be taken of private initiative in the launching of new CAPITAL projects. Until 1961, when its charter was amended, its activities were restricted because it had little resources and could not participate itself in EQUITY holdings. Since that time its activities have been able to develop rapidly. The corporation can invest directly and give LOANS and guarantees for private investors. It can hold equity interests in private companies, although its interest in any one company is generally restricted to 25 per cent. The I.F.C. is empowered to borrow from the I.B.R.D. to relend to private investors without government guarantee. It is financed by subscriptions from the eighty or so countries which make up its membership.

International Standard Industrial Classification. ⟡ STANDARD INDUSTRIAL CLASSIFICATION.

International investment. ⟡ FOREIGN INVESTMENT.

International Labour Organization (I.L.O.). An organization established in 1919 under the Treaty of Versailles which became affiliated to the U.N. in 1946. Its aims are the improvement of working conditions throughout the world, the spread of social security and the maintenance of standards of social justice. It has drawn up a labour code based on these aims. The I.L.O. offers technical assistance to DEVELOPING COUNTRIES, especially in the field of training. Its membership has grown from fifty to over eighty countries.

International liquidity. The amount of gold, RESERVE CURRENCIES and SPECIAL DRAWING RIGHTS available for the finance of international trade. Since 1958, when sterling became convertible (⟡ CONVERTIBILITY), the leading reserve currencies have been the dollar and sterling. Therefore, apart from *ad hoc* LOANS made by the INTERNATIONAL MONETARY FUND, the growth in LIQUIDITY needed to finance the expansion of world trade for the past almost fifteen years has had to be found in the expansion of the output of gold and the supply of dollars and sterling. The physical supply of gold is virtually limited to the output of the mines in South Africa, and its total value is limited because the official price of gold in terms of dollars has been fixed firstly until the end of 1971 at its 1934 level of $35 an ounce, and then at $38 an ounce. With the decline in the U.K.'s position in world trade, sterling's acceptability as a reserve currency has become suspect (⟡ STERLING AREA). The needed growth of liquidity, therefore, has been found in the outflow of dollars from the U.S. arising from the fact that the U.S. BALANCE OF PAYMENTS has for many years run into deficit. Pressures eventually built up for the elimination of this deficit, and consequently concern developed as to whether there would be adequate liquidity in future to finance trade. Broadly, if sufficient reserves are not available, a fall in prices and world trade could follow (⟡ QUANTITY THEORY OF MONEY). A crisis of confidence finally erupted: in November 1967 sterling was devalued (⟡ DEVALUATION), and early in 1968 control over the GOLD MARKET broke down. The old fixed price survived, but only for gold in international finance. A separate price now exists for FREE MARKET gold. Again, in August 1971, the U.S. government, troubled by an increasing balance of payments deficit, imposed a 10 per cent surcharge, suspended the convertibility of the dollar and introduced other measures to correct the balance. In December 1971, the 'Group of Ten' countries in the I.M.F. agreed to revalue their currencies to give the U.S. dollar an effective devaluation of 10 per cent, and the surcharge was lifted. Having taken measures to reverse the U.S. deficit, it was agreed that it was essential to hold discussions to consider the reform of the international monetary system over the long term. There are two types of solution to the problem: (a) a system of flexible EXCHANGE RATES which would at the extreme make international liquidity held in the form of gold and FOREIGN EXCHANGE reserves unnecessary; and (b) an increase in liquidity by raising the price of gold or by inventing a new CURRENCY. The former alternative was dismissed as unrealistic in 1968, and the 'Group of Ten', meeting in December 1971, reaffirmed that discussions take place against the need for stable exchange rates. J M. KEYNES had already put forward a scheme for a CENTRAL BANK for central banks at the BRETTON WOODS Conference, which would issue its own currency called BANCOR. Keynes argued, 'We need a quantum of international currency, which is neither determined in an unpredictable and irrelevant manner as, for example, by the technical progress of the gold industry, nor subject to large variations depending on the gold reserve policies of individual countries, but is governed by the actual current requirements of world commerce'. In 1969, the I.M.F.'s articles of agreement were revised so that it could set up and distribute to member countries SPECIAL DRAWING RIGHTS which have a strong affinity with Keynes's bancor. The first distribution of S.D.R.s, valued at $3,500 million, was made at the beginning of 1970. ⇨ CREDITOR NATIONS; UNITED NATIONS CONFERENCE ON TRADE AND DEVELOPMENT.

International Monetary Fund (I.M.F.). The I.M.F. was set up by the BRETTON WOODS Agreement of 1944 and came into operation in March 1947. The fund was established to encourage international cooperation in the monetary field and the removal of FOREIGN EXCHANGE restrictions, to stabilize exchange rates and to facilitate a multilateral (⇨ MULTILATERALISM) payments system between member countries. Under the I.M.F.'s articles of agreement, member countries are required to observe an EXCHANGE RATE, fluctuations in which should be confined to ± 1 per cent around its PAR VALUE. This par value is quoted in terms of the U.S. dollar, which is in turn linked to gold. In December 1971, the 'Group of Ten' (see below) agreed on new 'central values' of currencies in order to achieve a dollar devaluation of 10 per cent with a permissible margin of $\pm 2 \cdot 25$ per cent. This was, however, regarded as unofficial, and it was agreed that discussions would be held to review the whole problem of INTERNATIONAL LIQUIDITY. A member is required to consult with the I.M.F. before devaluing or revaluing its CURRENCY. Each member country of the I.M.F. is also required to subscribe to the fund a quota which is paid 25 per cent in gold and 75 per cent in the member's own currency. Quotas have been raised three times, the last being in 1970 when the total was increased to $28,900 million. This fund is used to tide members over temporary BALANCE OF PAYMENTS difficulties and thus to help stabilize exchange rates. Borrowing ability and voting rights are determined by this quota. Under the present system, the U.S. holds about 23 per cent of the voting strength and the EUROPEAN ECONOMIC COMMUNITY about 19 per cent; and so since an 85 per cent majority is required to make a major change in I.M.F. procedure, both the U.S. and the E.E.C. have the power of veto. A member in temporary balance of payments deficit obtains foreign exchange from the fund in exchange for its own currency, which it is required to repurchase within three to five years. Members in deficit with the fund are obliged by the terms of the agreement to consult with the I.M.F. on the procedures being taken to improve their balance of payments. The U.K. has benefited considerably from the I.M.F. arrangements particularly in the 1964 sterling crisis, when up to $2,400 million was borrowed, and again after DEVALUATION in November 1967. At the beginning of 1969 about $3,000 million was due to be repaid by the U.K. to the I.M.F. by between 1971 and 1974.

During the early 1960s it became evident that there was a strong case for increasing the size of the fund, and in 1962 the General Agreement to Borrow was signed by ten countries, viz. U.S., U.K., W. Germany, France, Belgium, the Netherlands, Italy, Sweden, Canada and Japan, called the 'Group of Ten' or the 'Paris Club', under which $6,000 million credit was made available to the I.M.F. should it be required. In addition, Switzerland, which is not a member of the I.M.F., made available $200 million. Countries in difficulty can also negotiate stand-by credit on which they can draw as necessary. The I.M.F. cannot, however, make use of any of the currency in this scheme without prior consent of the lending country. The agreement was not made use of until the U.K. requested assistance to prevent the devaluation of sterling in 1964. In September 1967, at the I.M.F. meeting in Rio de Janeiro, the creation of an international paper money was agreed in principle, and proposals for the amendment of the I.M.F.'s articles were put to members in 1968. The scheme was ratified in July 1969. The system proposed is that annual increases in international credit would be distributed to I.M.F. members by means of SPECIAL DRAWING RIGHTS (S.D.R.s). These credits would be distributed among member countries in proportion to their quotas, and could be included in their official reserves; $3,500 million was distributed in this way on 1 January 1970, $3,000 million in 1971 and a further $3,000 million in 1972. There is a limit on the acceptability for payment in S.D.R.s in that no country need hold more than twice its S.D.R. quota. (◊ KEYNES PLAN). The argument for the creation of new money is the fear that since international liquidity is growing much less rapidly than world trade, a contraction in world trade will eventually be inevitable (◊ EUROPEAN FUND).

International Settlements, Bank for. ◊ BANK FOR INTERNATIONAL SETTLEMENTS.

International Standard Industrial Classification (I.S.I.C.). ⧫ STANDARD INDUSTRIAL CLASSIFICATION.

International trade. The exchange of goods and SERVICES between one country and another. This exchange takes place because of differences in costs of production between countries, and because it increases the economic welfare of each country by widening the range of goods and services available for CONSUMPTION. RICARDO showed by the law of comparative advantage that it was not necessary for one country to have an absolute cost advantage in the production of a commodity for it to find a partner willing to trade. Even if a country produced all commodities more expensively than any other, trade to the benefit of all could take place, provided only that the relative costs of production of the different commodities were favourable. Differences in costs of production exist because countries are differently endowed with the resources required. Countries differ as to the type and quantity of raw materials within their borders, their climate, the skill and size of their LABOUR FORCE and their stock of physical CAPITAL. Countries will tend to export (⧫ EXPORTS) those commodities whose production requires relatively more than other commodities of those resources (⧫ FACTORS OF PRODUCTION) which it has most of (⧫ HECKSCHER-OHLIN PRINCIPLE). By increasing the scope for the specialization of labour (⧫ DIVISION OF LABOUR) and for achieving ECONOMIES OF SCALE by the enlargement of MARKETS, there is a presumption that international trade should be free from restrictions (⧫ FREE TRADE). The classical economists (⧫ CLASSICAL ECONOMICS) condemned MERCANTILISM for its advocacy of government control over trade in order to achieve export surpluses, and the nineteenth and early twentieth century was a period of free trade in the U.K. This philosophy gave place to the economic protectionism (⧫ PROTECTION) of the inter-war years, but was revived again in the GENERAL AGREEMENT ON TARIFFS AND TRADE in 1948. The latter has had some success in reducing TARIFFS on IMPORTS, culminating in the KENNEDY ROUND in 1967. However, many non-tariff IMPORT RESTRICTIONS still remain. At the same time, there has been an increase in the number of CUSTOMS UNIONS, such as the EUROPEAN ECONOMIC COMMUNITY, EUROPEAN FREE TRADE ASSOCIATION, LATIN AMERICAN FREE TRADE ASSOCIATION and CENTRAL AMERICAN COMMON MARKET. While these unions do establish free trade between member countries, they discriminate against outsiders. International trade since the end of the Second World War has grown rapidly, and many changes in the pattern of goods and SERVICES traded have taken and are taking place. The DEVELOPING COUNTRIES, in their attempt to achieve faster ECONOMIC GROWTH, are changing from being simply raw-material exporters to exporters of finished or semi-finished goods. At the same time, the developed nations are taking advantage of technological specialization, so that trade in high-value finished manufactures is increasing between them.

International Trade Organization (I.T.O.). At the U.N. conference held at Geneva in 1947 at which the GENERAL AGREEMENT ON TARIFFS AND TRADE was signed, a charter was put forward for the setting up, within the U.N. Organization, of a new agency to be called the International Trade Organization. Fifty nations signed the charter in Havana the following year, but it was never subsequently ratified by the required number of countries. The aim of the proposed organization was to work out principles for the general conduct of international trade and to draw up proposals for the implementation of policies based on these principles. Its terms of reference covered TARIFFS, QUOTAS, taxes, INTERNATIONAL COMMODITY AGREEMENTS and whatever was considered to have a bearing on the development of international trade and was based on policies of non-discrimination and tariff reductions. In practice, the G.A.T.T. has carried out most of the functions envisaged for the I.T.O.

Intervention. Any form of government interference with MARKET FORCES to achieve economic ends. The EXCHANGE EQUALIZATION ACCOUNT, for example, buys or sells pounds sterling or foreign CURRENCIES in order to influence the EXCHANGE RATE of the pound.

Intra-European Payments Agreement. A payments system established between the member countries of the ORGANIZATION FOR EURO-PEAN ECONOMIC COOPERATION in 1948 to facilitate the distribution of U.S. aid under the EUROPEAN RECOVERY PROGRAMME and to encourage intra-European trade by facilitating the settlement of intra-European BALANCE OF PAYMENTS deficits. Based on a set of intra-European bilateral trade forecasts, a country for which a surplus balance of payments was expected received U.S. aid above a certain minimum only on condition that it extended drawing rights to its European partners in its own CURRENCY. A deficit country, therefore, received aid both from the U.S. and from the European countries in surplus. The surplus country, on the other hand, to obtain similar levels of U.S. aid, was required itself to extend aid to its partners. This system, based on what was known as 'compensation agreements', was very ungainly and the forecasts often proved hopelessly inaccurate. It was completely replaced by the EUROPEAN PAYMENTS UNION in 1950.

Inventories (U.S.). Stocks or stores of raw materials, components, work in progress or finished goods. Inventories are held for one or more of the following reasons:

(a) Deliveries of raw materials, components, etc., take place at discrete intervals in time, whereas production takes place continuously. Hence inventories provide a pool from which the needed INPUTS can be continuously taken.

(b) Similarly, shipments of the finished product take place at discrete intervals, whereas production yields output continuously and so inventories permit the accumulation of output before shipment.

(c) There may be economies in having production runs at a constant rate of output (say 100 units per week), while sales, and hence shipments, may fluctuate (fifty units one week, 150 the next), and inventories reconcile these by taking the excess production in one time period and supplying the excess demand in another.

(d) It may be impossible to forecast demand with complete certainty. Hence, inventories may be held in case demand exceeds the expected level.

Inventory analysis. A body of techniques which attempts to determine the optimum level of INVENTORIES to hold in any given situation. The problem is essentially to determine the relevant set of COSTS, to find the way in which these vary with certain key VARIABLES, to set up a MODEL of the situation using the cost relationships, and then to find the values of variables which minimize the costs of holding inventories. To take a simplified example: suppose we are considering a retailer of a single good, X, which he sells at a known, constant rate per week. Given this rate of sales, he has to decide how large an inventory to hold, which in effect involves two decisions: how often a delivery of X should be made; and how much should be delivered each time. In fact, if we assume that deliveries will be timed for when inventories should have run down to a certain minimum level, the only variable whose size has to be determined is the size of the order quantity. The relevant costs are:

(a) Ordering costs: these consist of the administrative OVERHEADS of making the order (which do not depend on the quantity ordered), and the delivery costs (which may well not increase in proportion to the size of the order).

(b) Inventory costs: these consist of storage and warehousing costs, INSURANCE and deterioration costs and, most important, the INTEREST cost of money 'tied up' in inventories (◊ R. G. HAWTREY). All these costs tend to vary directly, and possibly more than proportionately, with size of inventories.

Since the size of inventories can easily be written in terms of the order quantity, an equation can be written which shows how total costs (ordering *plus* inventory) depend on the order quantity. Using standard techniques, the level of the order quantity can be found which makes total costs a minimum. One of the interesting implications of this calculation is that if sales should increase, the optimal inventory level increases by the square root of the sales increase, i.e. the inventory level increases less than proportionately with the sales increase, and so there are ECONOMIES OF SCALE in inventory holding. ◊ CYCLE; INVENTORY INVESTMENT.

Inventory investment. The building up or running down of INVENTORIES, by permitting production to exceed or fall short of sales. The situation in which stocks are run down is known as DISINVESTMENT or negative investment. Unanticipated inventory investment or disinvestment is often the first indication to a firm that production is not appropriately matched with sales.

Inventory investment cycle. Fluctuations in economic activity caused by changes in INVENTORY INVESTMENT. The levels of production of firms, and therefore the levels of NATIONAL INCOME and employment, are determined not only by sales, but also by the extent to which firms wish to add to or run down INVENTORIES. If firms aim to maintain some fixed relationship between inventories and sales, then a change in the level of sales causes a firm to adjust its level of inventories. For instance, a firm is selling 100 units per annum and has found from experience that a ratio of 50 per cent of stock to sales is the optimum. With sales constant, it will produce 100 units per annum. If sales rise by, say, 10 per cent to 110 units, the firm must increase its stocks from fifty units to fifty-five units. In that year it must therefore increase its output by 15 per cent: ten units to meet the increase in sales and five units to go into stock. In the following year, if sales were constant, output would fall to 110 as no additions to stock would be necessary. It can be seen, therefore, that the existence of stocks 'accelerates' the growth in sales in terms of output, and also generates greater fluctuations in output.

Inventory turnover. The rate at which INVENTORIES are turned into sales. It can be found by dividing the average rate of sales over a given time period by the average level of inventories in the same time period. Also known as *stock turnover*.

Investment. Strictly defined, investment is expenditure on real CAPITAL goods. However, in everyday language, it is also taken to mean purchase of any ASSET, or indeed the undertaking of any commitment, which involves an initial sacrifice followed by subsequent benefits. For example, one may speak of the purchase of an ORDINARY SHARE as an investment, or the decision to go to university as an investment. However, in the theory of INCOME DETERMINATION, investment means strictly expenditure on capital goods. In this sense, investment is the amount by which the stock of capital of a firm or economy changes, once we have allowed for replacement of capital which is scrapped. ⟷ GROSS INVESTMENT; NET INVESTMENT.

Investment allowances. ⟷ CAPITAL ALLOWANCES.

Investment appraisal. 1. The analysis of the prospective costs and benefits of possible new INVESTMENTS, and the evaluation of the desirability of committing resources to them. **2.** A branch of business economics which deals mainly with the formulation of rules, techniques and criteria designed to help practical decision-takers in their problem of choosing investments. ⟷ DISCOUNTED CASH FLOW; INTERNAL RATES OF RETURN; PRESENT VALUE.

Investment bank (U.S.). A financial intermediary which purchases new issues and places them in smaller parcels among investors. In Britain, a MERCHANT BANK or ISSUING HOUSE.

Investment demand curve. A curve showing the total amount of MONEY which firms wish to borrow for INVESTMENT expenditure at each possible RATE OF INTEREST. Since the rate of interest is the PRICE which has to be paid on borrowed funds, the investment demand curve is analogous to the consumer demand curve, in that it shows the quantity demanded at each price.

Investment expenditure. ⟷ INVESTMENT.

Investment function. The relationship between INVESTMENT and its major determinants; viz. the rate of change of output, the CAPACITY UTILIZATION RATE and the RATE OF INTEREST. ⟷ ACCELERATION PRINCIPLE.

Investment goods. ⟷ CAPITAL.

Investment grants. ⟷ INVESTMENT INCENTIVES.

Investment incentives. Government assistance designed to encourage firms to invest in physical ASSETS in total, in particular industries or in particular locations. Investment grants were abolished by the new Conservative government as from the end of October 1970, and replaced by a system of tax allowances and tax reductions. It was considered that the system of grants discriminated against the service industries, and could give support to firms which were losing money. A new system of DEPRECIATION allowances was introduced which enabled 60 per cent of the CAPITAL expenditure on plant and machinery to be written off against tax in the first year of its life. In addition, 25 per cent of the reducing balance of the expenditure could be written off against tax in succeeding years. These benefits apply to service as well as manufacturing industries. In the DEVELOPMENT AREAS, the investment grant payable was previously 40 per cent (double that which was applicable elsewhere). This was also abolished in favour of free depreciation for plant and machinery for industrial use. An initial allowance of 40 per cent for industrial buildings in the development areas compared with a current level of 30 per cent, probably falling in 1972 to 15 per cent elsewhere, will continue. Special incentives for the Development Areas are also available through the Local Employment Acts. In October 1970, the building grant of 35 per cent was increased to 45 per cent. Grants and LOANS are also payable, for instance, for clearing derelict land. Investment grants payable on ships were also terminated in October 1970 in favour of free depreciation, which is applicable whether or not the capital expenditure is in a development area. This also applies to the free depreciation granted to capital expenditure for scientific research. ⇨ CAPITAL ALLOWANCES; TAXATION.

Investment, negative. ⇨ DISINVESTMENT.

Investment opportunity curve. A curve showing the relationship between increasing amounts of MONEY currently devoted to INVESTMENT expenditure, and the future income which will result. The curve was extensively used in the classic work by IRVING FISHER on the theory of CAPITAL and INTEREST

Investment trust. A company whose sole object is to invest its CAPITAL in a wide range of other companies. An investment trust issues SHARES and uses its capital to buy shares in other companies. A UNIT TRUST, on the other hand, issues units that represent holdings of shares. Unit holders thus do not share in the PROFITS of the company managing the trust. Although sharing the advantages of widespread investment with unit trusts, investment trusts pay their manage-

233

ment expenses out of taxed INCOME and not out of shareholders' incomes. The total funds managed by investment trusts are almost four times greater than those of unit trusts. Investment trusts can also raise part of their capital by fixed-interest SECURITIES, and the YIELD on ORDINARY SHARES can thus benefit from GEARING. There are some 300 investment trust companies in Britain, and like most INSTITUTIONAL INVESTORS they have been investing an increasing proportion of their funds in EQUITIES. Some investment trusts underwrite new issues (▷ NEW ISSUE MARKET).

Investor's yield. ▷ INTERNAL RATE OF RETURN.

Invisible balance. ▷ BALANCE OF PAYMENTS.

'Invisible hand'. ADAM SMITH believed that society was such that, although individuals pursued their own advantage, the greatest benefit to society as a whole was achieved by their being free to do so. Each individual was 'led by an invisible hand to promote an end which was no part of his intention'. ▷ B. DE MANDEVILLE; PRICE MECHANISM; RESOURCES.

Invisible. Those 'invisible' items, such as financial services, included in the current BALANCE OF PAYMENTS accounts, as distinct from physically visible IMPORTS, EXPORTS and RE-EXPORTS of goods. In the U.K. balance of payments accounts, they include government grants to overseas countries and subscriptions to international organizations, net payments for shipping services, travel, royalties, commissions for banking and other services, transfers to or from overseas residents, INTEREST, PROFITS and DIVIDENDS received by or from overseas residents. The pattern of U.K. invisible earnings has changed in the post-Second World War period. The shipping account deteriorated into deficit as a result of a steady rise in the payments made to foreign shipowners; the fact that the profits and interest earned by the U.K. did not keep pace with the increase in these payments made to foreigners together with the growth of U.K. government aid to other countries all contributed to a fall in the surplus on invisible account. The result has been that this surplus became insufficient to give long-run support to the traditional deficit on visible account, and was a contributing factor to sterling DEVALUATION in November 1967. However, there has been a recovery in the invisible balance since devaluation.

Involuntary saving. ▷ FORCED SAVING.

Irredeemable security. A SECURITY which does not bear a date at which the CAPITAL sum will be paid off or redeemed, e.g. $2\frac{1}{2}$ per cent CONSOLS or certain DEBENTURES. Sometimes called UN-

DATED SECURITIES. Possession of an irredeemable security entitles the owner to INTEREST payments but not to repayment of face-value capital. This affects the price at which the security is marketable. For example, $2\frac{1}{2}$ per cent consols which are irredeemable £100 stock bearing $2\frac{1}{2}$ per cent interest, might, depending on prevailing interest rates, fetch only about £50, i.e. the price at which they will give a 5 per cent yield. If this stock were redeemable in one year's time, their price would obviously be very much higher.

Iso-cost lines. Lines which show those combinations of the amounts of two goods or FACTORS OF PRODUCTION which can be bought for a constant total expenditure.

Iso-product curve. ⇨ ISOQUANT.

Isoquant (or iso-product curve). A curve which shows the combinations of two INPUTS required to produce a given quantity of a particular product. For example, in the diagram, we measure units of LABOUR input along the horizontal axis, and units of CAPITAL along the vertical. The isoquant $Q = 100$ shows the quantities of capital and labour which can be used together to make 100 units of output, e.g. K_1 of capital, L_1 of labour, or K_2 of capital, L_2 of labour, or any other combination represented by a point on the curve. Similarly,

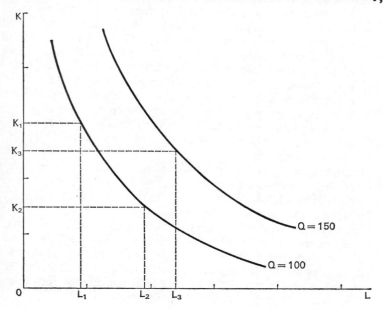

the curve $Q = 150$ shows combinations of capital and labour required to make a given quantity – in this case 150 units – of output. We can note several features of these isoquants, and the assumptions which give rise to them:

(a) The curves are smooth and continuous. This implies that both inputs are infinitely divisible, i.e. they do not come in discrete lumps, but rather we can choose any fractional value we wish, e.g. 3·7526 units of capital, and 7·0004 units of labour. It also implies that they are physically substitutable, i.e. we are not forced to use labour and capital in fixed proportions, e.g. one man to one machine.

(b) They slope downwards from left to right, i.e. they have negative slopes. This implies that if we reduce the quantity of one input (say labour), we must increase the quantity of the other in order to leave output unchanged. The amount by which we have to increase the capital input, divided by the amount by which we reduced the labour input, is referred to as the rate of technical substitution of capital for labour, and is identical to the mathematical definition of the slope of the isoquant (i.e. dK/dL).

(c) They are convex, that is, they are relatively flat at small amounts of capital and large amounts of labour, but get steadily steeper as capital increases and labour diminishes. When there is little capital and much labour, a reduction in labour can be compensated for by a relatively small increase in capital; but at a lower level of labour input, the same size reduction in labour requires a larger increase in capital to maintain output at the same level. An explanation for this is given by the law of DIMINISHING MARGINAL PRODUCTIVITY: briefly, when the quantity of a factor is small, the increase in output which results from increasing the quantity of factor by one unit is larger than when a lot of the factor is being used.

There is a strong similarity between isoquants and INDIFFERENCE CURVES. The crucial point of difference is, however, that output is measurable while UTILITY is not, so that quantities can be attached to isoquants but not to indifference curves.

Isoquants are used in the theory of the firm ($\diamond$ FIRM, THEORY OF), to derive the COST CURVES which the firm faces in making its output decision, and to derive the DEMAND CURVES of the firm for the FACTORS OF PRODUCTION. The purpose of isoquants in this analysis is to summarize the technological possibilities open to the firm, in combining inputs to produce outputs.

Some of the assumptions underlying isoquants, particularly (a) above, are patently unrealistic, and unlikely to hold in practice, although this does not detract from their theoretical usefulness. Nevertheless, economists have recognized the importance of cases where the assumptions do not hold, and, together with mathematicians and engineers, have developed techniques to deal with cases in which they do not hold. (⋄ LINEAR PROGRAMMING).

The use of only two inputs in the above discussion, incidentally, is not restrictive, since the concept can quite easily be generalized to many inputs: although it cannot then be illustrated by two-dimensional geometry (⋄ PRODUCTION FUNCTION).

Issued capital. That part of a company's CAPITAL that has been subscribed to by shareholders. It may or may not be paid up (⋄ PAID-UP CAPITAL).

Issuing broker. A BROKER acting as an agent for a new issue of SECURITIES.

Issuing house. An institution, usually a MERCHANT BANK, that organizes the raising of CAPITAL by new issues of SECURITIES on behalf of clients. The issuing house will advise the client on the timing and form of the issue in conjunction with the ISSUING BROKER, and in return for a commission will underwrite all or part of the issue. The sponsorship of an issue by an established issuing house greatly affects the confidence of the investor and success of the issue. For this reason, issuing houses are extremely selective in the new issues they will sponsor. According to the RADCLIFFE REPORT, some 60 per cent of new issues by PUBLIC COMPANIES are sponsored by issuing houses. ⋄ NEW ISSUE MARKET; UNDERWRITING.

Issuing Houses Association (I.H.A.). An association of institutions acting as ISSUING HOUSES, set up in 1945 to represent the interests of its members to maintain standards and to liaise with the council of the STOCK EXCHANGE, the CAPITAL ISSUES COMMITTEE, the BANK OF ENGLAND and other official bodies. It has some sixty members.

J

Jenkins Committee. ⟡ COMPANY LAW.

Jevons, William Stanley (1835–82). He studied natural science and worked as an assayer to the Australian Mint, from 1853 to 1859. He became Professor of Logic at Owens College, Manchester in 1866 and in 1876 at University College, London. His main theoretical economic work is *Theory of Political Economy* (1871). Other aspects of his work are collected together in *Investigations in Currency and Finance* (1884). He was one of the three economists to put forward a MARGINAL UTILITY theory in the 1870s. He argued that one COMMODITY will exchange for another, such that the ratio of the PRICES of the two commodities traded equals the ratio of their marginal utilities. EDGEWORTH criticized the way Jevons developed these ideas, and in so doing invented the INDIFFERENCE CURVE. Jevons also made an important contribution to the theory of CAPITAL, many aspects of which were, in fact, taken over by the AUSTRIAN SCHOOL. He superimposed on the CLASSICAL ECONOMIC theory the idea that capital should be measured in terms of time as well as quantity. An increase in the amount invested is the same as an increase in the time period in which it is being employed. Output can be increased by extending the period in which the investment is available by, for instance, reinvesting the output instead of consuming it at the end of the production period. With given levels of LABOUR and capital, output becomes a function of time only. He derived from this a definition of the RATE OF INTEREST as the ratio of the output gained by an increase in the time capital remains invested divided by the amount invested (⟡ BÖHM-BAWERK; MARGINAL PRODUCTIVITY OF CAPITAL). Jevons was also one of the founders of ECONOMETRICS: he invented MOVING AVERAGES. He also propounded a theory of the TRADE CYCLE based on sun-spots, but this is of little importance except for the stimulus it gave to the study of statistics for economic empirical work. ⟡ H. H. GOSSEN; C. MENGER; M. E. L. WALRAS.

Jobber. A dealer in stock exchange SECURITIES. One of the two distinct classes of member of the STOCK EXCHANGE, jobbers may only deal with BROKERS and not with the general public. Jobbers actually set the prices on the exchange. A broker who wishes to buy or sell a particular SHARE will ask the jobber to quote a dealing PRICE. Like any other dealer, a jobber makes his profit out of the difference between the price at which he buys and the price at which he sells and he will quote two prices: a buying and a selling price. He may not, at the time, know at what price he can obtain the shares, so that the 'turn' or difference between his buying and selling prices does not necessarily indicate his PROFIT. If his quote is accepted for a purchase, he must then 'even up his position' by bidding for the security to other brokers or jobbers unless he already has the stock in question on his books. Dealings are regulated by many rules and conventions, e.g. as to the amount of stock that the jobber is obliged to deal in at his quoted price. Jobbers are normally members of jobbing firms and specialize in particular types of security, e.g. oil shares or GILT-EDGED SECURITIES.

Joint costs. COSTS which are incurred in production of two or more products, and which cannot be attributed to any one of them.

Joint demand. The DEMAND for two goods which, for reasons of their complementarity in use, have to be bought together, e.g. left and right shoes.

Joint products. Two or more products which are necessarily produced by a given process. For example, production of mutton also gives wool. It is possible, however, to have alternative processes which yield differing qualities and quantities of the two products.

Joint-stock banks. ⇨ COMMERCIAL BANKS.

Joint-stock company. A now virtually obsolete term for a business enterprise in which the CAPITAL is divided into small units permitting a number of investors to contribute varying amounts to the total, PROFITS being divided between stockholders in proportion to the number of SHARES they own. The joint-stock company developed from the seventeenth century onwards because of the need for increasingly large amounts of capital by certain types of enterprise, such as overseas trading companies. By 1720, abuse of the joint-stock system (culminating in the South Sea Bubble crisis) made it necessary to control business more closely, and the statutory company has its origins in the Act of that date. ⇨ COMPANY LAW.

Joint supply. ⇨ JOINT PRODUCTS.

K

Kaldor, Nicholas (1908–   ). Born in Budapest, Kaldor graduated at the London School of Economics in 1930, and lectured there until 1947. Between 1943 and 1945, he was a Research Associate at the National Institute of Economic and Social Research, and in 1947 was appointed Director of the Research and Planning Division of the Economic Commission for Europe, a post he held for two years. He was a member of the Royal Commission on Taxation of Profits and Incomes from 1951 to 1955. In 1952 he moved to Cambridge University as Reader, and in 1966 was appointed Professor of Economics. From 1964 to 1968, he was special adviser to the Chancellor of the EXCHEQUER on economic and social aspects of TAXATION policy. His published works include 'The Quantitative Aspects of the Full Employment Problem in Britain', Appendix to *Full Employment in a Free Society* by W. H. BEVERIDGE (1944), reprinted in *Essays in Economic Policy* (1964), *An Expenditure Tax* (1955), *Essays on Economic Stability and Growth, Essays on Value and Distribution* (1960), *Capital Accumulation and Economic Growth* (1961) and *Causes of the Slow Rate of Growth of the U.K.* (1966). In his capacity as goverment adviser, Professor Kaldor was an advocate of the long-term CAPITAL GAINS tax and the SELECTIVE EMPLOYMENT TAX. ✧ DISTRIBUTION, THEORIES OF.

Kennedy Round of Trade Negotiations. There has been a series of rounds of negotiations between the signatories of the GENERAL AGREE-MENT ON TARIFFS AND TRADE designed to reduce TRADE BARRIERS on a multilateral basis. The first round took place in 1947, and the Kennedy Round was the sixth. It commenced in 1964, and was concluded in July 1967. This round was distinguished from its predecessors by the fact that its aim was straight percentage tariff reductions right across the board rather than item-by-item agree-ments. This approach was made possible by the fact that in 1962, President Kennedy obtained the authority of the U.S. Congress to negotiate reductions in tariffs of up to 50 per cent under the Trade Expansion Act. Forty-nine countries took part in the Kennedy Round, including all the principal industrial and trading nations of the world except the U.S.S.R. and China. In the event, agreements for the reduction of industrial tariffs by up to 50 per cent, with an overall average of 30 per cent, were achieved. Two timetables were agreed. The first, being followed by the U.S., provided for reductions in five annual stages and commenced in January 1968. The second, being followed by the EUROPEAN ECONOMIC COMMUNITY, EUROPEAN FREE TRADE ASSOCIATION, and Japan, laid down that two fifths of the reduction should be made in July 1968, so coinciding with the final tariff adjustments of the E.E.C. Subsequent reduction took place in January 1970, 1971 and 1972. ⬦ DUMPING.

Keynes, John Maynard (1883–1946). Educated at Eton, Keynes won prizes there in mathematics as well as in English and Classics before going up to King's College, Cambridge. At university, he graduated with a first in mathematics. During his stay at Cambridge he studied philosophy under Alfred Whitehead and economics under ALFRED MARSHALL and A. C. PIGOU. After a period in the Civil Service, he accepted a lectureship in economics at King's College, Cambridge. In 1911, he became editor of the *Economic Journal*. During the First World War he held a post in the TREASURY, but resigned because he believed that the figure for German war reparations was set too high (*The Economic Consequences of the Peace* (1919)). He was also a severe critic of the decision of the government to return to the GOLD STANDARD and at the pre-war EXCHANGE RATE (*The Economic Consequences of Mr Churchill*). In 1930 he published *A Treatise on Money*, and in the same year was appointed a member of the MACMILLAN COMMITTEE on Finance and Industry. His major work, *The General Theory of Employment, Interest and Money*, appeared in 1936. He served a second spell in the Treasury during the Second World War, and was responsible for negotiating with the U.S. on Lend-Lease. He took a leading part in the discussions at BRETTON WOODS in 1944 which established the INTERNATIONAL MONETARY FUND.

UNEMPLOYMENT during the inter-war period persisted in the U.K. at very high levels, never falling below 5 per cent, and at its worst reaching as much as 20 per cent of the total LABOUR force. The failure of the economy to recover from such a long depression was unprecedented in the economic history of industrial society. Fluctuations in activity were well known, and had received much attention from theorists on the TRADE CYCLE in the past. The classical economists (⬦ CLASSICAL ECONOMICS) held that in the downturn of the trade cycle both wage rates (⬦ EARNINGS) and the RATE OF INTEREST fell. Eventually, they reached levels low enough for businessmen to see a significant improvement in the profitability of new INVESTMENTS. The investment, so induced, generated employment and new INCOMES and the economy expanded again until rising prices in the boom brought the next phase in the cycle. The classical economists therefore concluded that the failure of the economy to expand was because wages were inflexible. Their policy recommendations were that the unions should be persuaded to accept a wage-cut. Keynes argued that, although this policy might make sense for a particular industry, a general cut would lower CONSUMPTION, income and AGGREGATE DEMAND, and this would offset the encouragement to employment by the lowering of the 'PRICE' of labour relative to the price of CAPITAL, e.g. plant and machinery. A. C. Pigou countered Keynes's argument by pointing out that, by lowering wages, the general price level would be lowered; therefore, liquid balances which people owned would have a higher spending value (⟡ PIGOU EFFECT). The upturn, it was agreed, was stimulated by businessmen responding to lower wages with increased investment expenditure. Why, said Keynes, should not the government take over the businessman's function and spend money on public works? Current opinion upheld the belief that government budget deficit financing would bring more hardship than already existed. The BALANCED BUDGET was regarded as equally the correct accounting practice for the government as it was for a private household. Most economists of the period accepted that public-works expenditure would reduce unemployment, even given the need to keep the budget in balance. A. C. Pigou showed the mechanism by which this could be brought about. However, the Treasury view was that public works would merely divert SAVINGS and labour from the private sector, and as the former was less productive, the net effect would be a worsening of the situation. It was not until after Keynes had written his *General Theory* and crystallized his arguments into a coherent theoretical framework that his views were accepted.

Keynes did not deny the classical theory. He agreed that a reduction in wage rates could, in theory, be beneficial, but it would operate only through the LIQUIDITY PREFERENCE schedule. A fall in prices would increase the value of the stock of money in people's hands in real terms. This would make available an increase in the amount that people were willing to lend, with a consequent drop in the rate of interest to the benefit of investment. However, if this is so, why not operate directly on the rate of interest or the quantity of money in the economy? Moreover, Keynes argued that there exists a level of interest rate below which further increases in MONEY SUPPLY are simply added to idle balances (⟡ INACTIVE MONEY) rather than being used to finance investment. Wage cuts or not, the economy would stick at this point with chronic unemployment. In the classical system, the national product (⟡ NATIONAL INCOME) was determined by the level of employment and the latter by the level of REAL WAGES. The quantity of money determined the level of prices. Savings and investment were brought into balance by means of the rate of interest. In Keynes's system, the equality of savings and investment was achieved by adjustments in the level of national income or output working through the MULTIPLIER. The rate of interest was determined by the quantity of money people desired to hold in relation to the money supply. The level of output at which savings equals investment does not necessarily correspond to full employment. The innovation in the Keynesian system was that the quantity of money determined the rate of interest, and not the level of output, as in the classical system. In the Keynesian model if you increased the propensity to invest or consume, you did not simply raise the rate of interest, you raised output and employment (⟡ CONSUMPTION FUNCTION). Keynes's study of monetary aggregates of investment, savings, etc., led to the development of national accounts. Keynes's general theory of employment is now criticized for its reliance on special cases (wage rigidity; the insensitivity of investment to the rate of interest, and the idea of a minimum rate of interest at which the demand for money became infinitely elastic); its preoccupation with EQUILIBRIUM; and the fact that, despite its presentation as a radical new departure, it nevertheless embodied many of the analytical limitations of the 'CAMBRIDGE SCHOOL' of economics. However, the transformation which Keynes brought about, in both theory and policy, was considerable. In effect, he laid the foundations for what is now MACROECONOMICS.

Keynes Plan. The U.K. TREASURY submitted proposals for the establishment of an International Clearing Union for discussion at the BRETTON WOODS Conference in 1944. These proposals were primarily the work of J. M. KEYNES, and became known as the Keynes Plan. The International Clearing Union would have basically the same functions as a domestic BANK and CLEARING HOUSE. International DEBTS would be cleared on a multilateral basis between its members. It would give OVERDRAFT facilities to a member running a temporary BALANCE OF PAYMENTS deficit and would create its own unit of

CURRENCY, called BANCOR, in which the overdraft facility would be made available. Bancor would have a gold EXCHANGE RATE in the initial phases of the scheme, though it was expected that it would eventually break its gold connection and replace gold in international finance. Each member would have a quota which determined the limits of its credit facilities with the International Clearing Union. There was a set of suggested safeguards and penalties to encourage the elimination not only of deficits but also of persistent surpluses. The plan did not win approval at Bretton Woods and the less radical INTERNATIONAL MONETARY FUND was established, which was more in line with the ideas put forward by the U.S.

Knight, Frank Hyneman (1885–   ). Appointed Associate Professor of Economics at the University of Iowa in 1919 and Professor in 1922, after studying at Cornell and Chicago Universities, in 1928, Knight returned to Chicago as Professor of Economics. His major published works include *The Economic Organization* (1933), *The Ethics of Competition and Other Essays* (1935), *The Economic Order and Religion* (1945), *Freedom and Reform* (1947), *Essays on the History and Method of Economics* (1956) and *Intelligence and Democratic Action* (1960). His most influential work has been *Risk, Uncertainty and Profit*, published in 1921. In this work, he made a clear distinction between insurable RISK and uninsurable uncertainty. It was the latter which gave rise to PROFIT. A businessman must guess future demand and selling prices and pay in advance his FACTORS OF PRODUCTION amounts based on his guesses. The accuracy of his guesses is reflected in the profit he makes. It follows that profits are related to uncertainty, the speed of economic change and business ability.

Kondratieff cycle. A TRADE CYCLE of very long duration – SCHUMPETER applied the term to a cycle of fifty-six years in duration. Named after the Russian economist N. D. Kondratieff, who made important contributions in the 1920s to the study of long-term fluctuations.

L

Labour. One of the primary FACTORS OF PRODUCTION, 'labour' is the collective name given to the productive services embodied in human physical effort, skill, intellectual powers, etc. As such, there are of course a large number of types of labour INPUT, varying in effort and skill content, and in particular types of skill content. It is often a useful theoretical simplification, however, to talk of the quantity of labour as if it were homogeneous.

Labour, division of. ⟡ DIVISION OF LABOUR.

Labour-intensive. A process or product is called labour-intensive if it uses proportionately more LABOUR in its production than the other FACTORS OF PRODUCTION. Hand-made goods with a low material content are produced by a labour-intensive process. The service industries are generally labour-intensive (⟡ SELECTIVE EMPLOYMENT TAX).

Labour force. That part of the population which is employed or available for work. The fact that the BIRTH RATE fluctuates and changes over time means that the labour force is not a constant proportion of the total population. In the U.K., for instance, the size of the labour force has remained constant over the past few years while the population has grown steadily. These movements therefore have an important effect on the growth of NATIONAL INCOME per head.

Labour, marginal productivity of. ⟡ MARGINAL PRODUCTIVITY OF LABOUR.

Labour market. The MARKET in which WAGES and conditions of employment are determined.

Labour, mobility of. The mobility of LABOUR has two aspects: (a) The spatial or geographical mobility of labour. This relates to the rate at which labour moves between geographical areas and regions in response to differences in WAGES or job availability. And (b) the occupational mobility of labour. This relates to the extent to which workers change occupations or skills in response to differences in wages or job availability.

The importance of labour mobility is that it determines the rate at which LABOUR MARKETS adjust to EQUILIBRIUM from DISEQUILIBRIUM situations. Assume the country consists of two regions, *A* and *B*, and that, initially, there is full EMPLOYMENT in each region, and wages for a given type of labour are equal. Suppose there is an increase in DEMAND for some products in A which causes an increase in the demand for some types of labour, and the reverse happens in B. The result would be that wages are higher in A than in B, with an excess of job vacancies over available workers in A, and UNEMPLOYMENT in B. If the particular types of skill now in increased demand in A match those in reduced demand in B, then the length of time for which the 'regional unemployment problem' persists depends on the geographical mobility of labour. If the skills do not match, however, then the occupational mobility of labour would also be important. Thus one could take the persistence of the 'regional unemployment problem' in the U.K., virtually since the end of the First World War, as evidence of a very low geographical and occupational mobility of labour. This would be an oversimplification, however, since factors such as the continued rate of decline of demand, the rate of growth of population, and the extent to which CAPITAL as well as labour is geographically mobile are also important.

There are, however, many factors – economic, social and psychological – which tend to lead to low geographical and occupational mobility. Costs of moving, housing difficulties (e.g. council house waiting-lists), reluctance to cut family and social ties, preference for a known rather than new environment, unemployment benefits, are all well-known reasons for geographical immobility. Similarly, costs of retraining, the slow learning processes of older workers, trade union restrictions, are sources of occupational and skill immobility. The importance of increasing labour mobility of all types is reflected in various government grants to assist in the costs of movement, disseminating of information through employment exchanges and setting up retraining centres, for example, but, in fact, most effort is devoted to offsetting labour immobilities by increasing the flow of 'work to the workers', i.e. by stimulating new firms to move to areas of high unemployment.

Labour, specialization of. ⋄ DIVISION OF LABOUR.

Labour theory of value. ⋄ VALUE, THEORIES OF.

Labour turnover. The rate at which workers leave a firm. Clearly, the greater this is the higher will tend to be the LABOUR costs of the firm, due to the administrative costs of hiring new workers, costs of training, etc. Labour turnover is normally expressed as the ratio of the number of workers who leave in a year to the firm's total work force.

'**Laissez-faire**'. '*Laissez-faire, laissez-passer*' was the term originally taken up by the PHYSIOCRATS. They condemned any interference with industry by government agencies as being inappropriate and harmful (because only agriculture produced a surplus), except in so far as it was necessary to break up private MONOPOLY. The principle of the non-intervention of government in economic affairs was given full support by the classical economists (⟡ CLASSICAL ECONOMISTS), who took up the theme from ADAM SMITH: 'The Statesman, who should attempt to direct private people in what manner they ought to employ their capitals, would not only load himself with a most unnecessary attention, but assume an authority which could safely be trusted, not only to no single person, but to no council or senate whatever, and which would nowhere be so dangerous as in the hands of a man who had folly and presumption enough to fancy himself fit to exercise it' – *Wealth of Nations*, Book IV, Chapter 2. ⟢ MANCHESTER SCHOOL; B. DE MANDEVILLE; J. C. L. S. DE SISMONDI.

Land. Land in economics is taken to mean not simply that part of the earth's surface not covered by water, but also all the 'free gifts of nature', such as minerals, soil fertility, etc. Land provides both space and specific resources. Much semantic argument has taken place on the extent to which land as a FACTOR OF PRODUCTION is 'really distinct' from CAPITAL. Many of the services of land in fact require expenditure of RESOURCES to obtain or maintain them, and hence they are often 'produced means of production'. However, although at the edges the distinction may often become blurred, it has been retained as a useful analytical convenience. Land is also meant to include the resources of the sea, so that, once again, we have a difference between the economic and everyday usage of a word.

Large numbers, law of. ⟡ LAW OF LARGE NUMBERS.

Laspeyres index. An INDEX NUMBER which measures the change in some aspect of a group of items over time, using weights based on values in some base-year. For example, a Laspeyres price index measures the percentage change in prices of a group of commodities, between now and some base-year, by dividing the total cost of the quantities of the commodities bought by consumers in the base-year, valued at today's prices, by the total cost of those same quantities valued at the base-year prices. Similarly, a Laspeyres quantity index finds the percentage change in quantities of COMMODITIES bought, by dividing the total COST of current quantities purchased, valued at the prices prevailing in the base-year, by the total cost of the quantities purchased in the base-year, again valued at base-year prices. Unlike the PAASCHE INDEX, the Laspeyres index has the advantage that, since the weights are constant from year to year, a whole run of index numbers can be compared with each other. It also requires less information, since the weights have only to be calculated at intervals, rather than every year. ⇪ INDEX NUMBER PROBLEM.

Lateral integration. ⇕ MERGER.

Latin American Free Trade Association (L.A.F.T.A.). The treaty setting up the Latin American Free Trade Association was agreed at Montevideo in 1960, under which the seven participating countries, viz. Argentina, Brazil, Chile, Mexico, Paraguay, Peru and Uruguay, agreed to establish a FREE TRADE AREA. Ecuador and Colombia joined in 1961, and Venezuela in 1966. Significant reductions in internal import TARIFFS have been achieved, though little progress has been made for the harmonization of a common external tariff. However, in 1968, the heads of state of the Latin American countries agreed in principle to the establishment of a common market for Latin America by 1985. This would include the CENTRAL AMERICAN COMMON MARKET.

Lausanne School. The Chair of Economics in the Faculty of Law at Lausanne was founded in 1870 with LÉON WALRAS as the first incumbent. He retired in 1892, and was succeeded by V. PARETO. The school was noted for the emphasis given to mathematics and the development of a general EQUILIBRIUM theory.

Law, John (1671–1729). A Scottish financier who put his monetary theories into practice in France through such institutions as the Banque Royale and the Compagnie des Indes. His most significant publication appeared in 1705 under the title *Money and Trade considered, with a proposal for supplying the nation with money.* He was in favour of the replacement of specie coin by paper money (⇕ BANK-NOTE). Not only would this save expensive precious metals, but it would enable the state to manage the CURRENCY more effectively, by making it independent of the MARKET for precious metals. Moreover, it would facilitate increasing the quantity of money in circulation and therefore the stimulation of economic activity. ⇪ DAVID HUME; QUANTITY THEORY OF MONEY.

'Law of demand'. ⇕ DEMAND CURVE.

Law of large numbers. The tendency for peculiarities of individual members of a group to cancel out, which becomes stronger the larger the size of the group. This means that the group as a whole shows much more uniformity than any one individual member. For example, a single EQUITY share might fluctuate in price quite unpredictably over time, but if we take a large collection of SHARES, i.e. a PORTFOLIO, individual shares in this portfolio may fluctuate in opposite directions, and hence the overall value of the portfolio may be far more stable and predictable than that of any one share. This is, in fact, the principle underlying UNIT TRUSTS, or DIVERSIFICATION generally.

'Leads and lags'. The differences in timing in the settlement of DEBTS in INTERNATIONAL TRADE. These differences could cause a deficit or surplus for a short period in the BALANCE OF PAYMENTS, even though the underlying trade was in balance. The effect may be particularly acute when there is an expectation of a change in the EXCHANGE RATE. Importing countries will delay payment to their supplying country if it is expected that the latter will devalue (▷ DEVALUATION).

Lease. An agreement between the owner of property (lessor) to grant use of it to another party (lessee) for a specified period at a specified RENT payable annually, quarterly or monthly. The rental may be subject to review, say, every seven years. It is possible to lease cars, machinery, etc., as well as buildings or LAND, and a recent development has been the rapid growth of leasing arrangements in which the title of the property passes to the lessee at the end of the lease for a nominal charge. In effect, this is a form of HIRE PURCHASE without a down payment, and is subject to differences in tax treatment which may be advantageous.

Lease-back. An agreement in which the owner of property sells that property to a person or institution and then leases it back again for an agreed period and rental. Lease-back is often used by companies that want to free for other uses CAPITAL tied up in buildings.

Least squares regression. A particular method by which the average relationship between two or more VARIABLES is quantified. Let us take, e.g., the problem of quantifying the relationship between consumers' expenditure, C, on the one hand, and their disposable INCOME, Y, on the other. Economic theory leads us to expect them to be closely related, and we may wish to test this; we may also be interested in making quantitative predictions of the consequences of certain types of change in components of AGGREGATE DEMAND (▷ CONSUMPTION FUNCTION; INCOME DETERMINATION, THEORY OF; MULTIPLIER). We begin by measuring, at successive points in time (generally each year) the observed values of C and Y. We make the linear HYPOTHESIS that $C = a + bY$; i.e. consumers' expenditure depends linearly on income ($\diamond$ LINEAR RELATION-SHIP). This is not strictly necessary: some other form of relationship between C and Y could be assumed, provided always that, by suitable transformation of variables, we would end up with a linear relationship: $C^1 = a + bY^1$. The basic problem in regression analysis is to find, in some sense, the 'best' values for a and b, and then to try to decide whether we can really believe that this relationship in fact holds (using techniques of STATISTICAL INFERENCE). If we plot, on a 'scatter diagram', the pairs of income and CONSUMPTION values we observed over the years, it may look like that shown below:

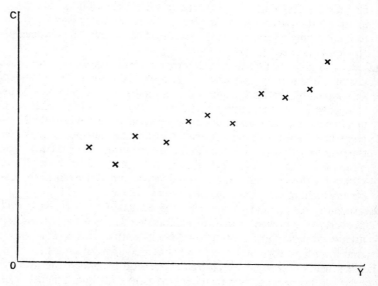

If all the data lay along a straight line, there would be no need for regression analysis. The fact that this will almost never be so in the case of any economic data is rationalized by arguing that, although the true underlying relationship is as written above, there is a 'random error term', which we denote by e, and which influences the actual observed value of C, in an unsystematic way, from year to year. Thus, *actual C*, denoted by $\hat{C}$, is really determined by the relationship: $\hat{C} = a + bY + e$, and so the problem is to find a and b, i.e. fit a line to the scatter of points in the above diagram, in the best way possible.

Least squares regression is a particular method for doing this. It proceeds as follows. Any line drawn through the scatter of points implies a particular average relationship between C and Y, and also implies a particular set of differences between $\hat{C}$, the actual consumption, and C, the consumption 'predicted' from the fitted line. These differences, $\hat{C}-C$, are clearly estimates of e, the error terms. The following diagram illustrates:

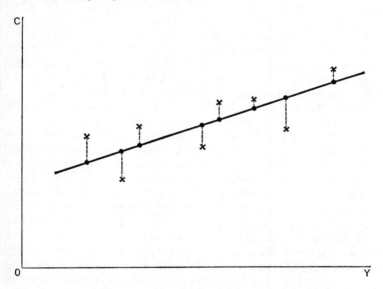

Then, the least-squares method suggests that the *best* line to draw, in the sense of having certain very desirable statistical properties, is the line which makes the sum of the squares of the differences between $\hat{C}$ and C as small as possible, i.e. which involves the 'least sum of squares'. Out of all the possible lines which could be drawn, one and only one has this property, and there are standard procedures for finding which it is, and which values of a and b it implies.

Legal tender. That which must be accepted in legal settlement of a money DEBT. Although, in Britain, BANK OF ENGLAND notes are legal tender up to any amount, silver (actually cupro-nickel) coins are only legal tender up to the value of £2.

Lender of last resort. An essential function of a CENTRAL BANK is to be willing to lend to the BANKING system at all times, although it does so on its own terms. In practice, this permits the bank to in-

251

fluence the level of RATES OF INTEREST and the MONEY SUPPLY as well as providing a basis of confidence for the banking system (⍄ BANK RATE). In Britain, the BANK OF ENGLAND acts as a lender of last resort only to the DISCOUNT HOUSES, and will not lend to the COMMERCIAL BANKS. When the discount houses (strictly speaking, members of the Discount Houses Association only) have insufficient CASH to balance their books, they can obtain cash from the discount office at the Bank of England. This assistance cannot be refused, although the bank can decide whether to grant a LOAN secured by BONDS or to rediscount SECURITIES (ELIGIBLE PAPER). The minimum rate at which it will do either of these things is the bank rate, and this rate is deliberately set at a 'penal' level, i.e. 1–2 per cent above MONEY MARKET rates. In other countries, the central bank lends directly to the commercial banks.

Leontief, Wassily W. (1906–   ). Born in Leningrad, Leontief obtained a post in the University of Kiel in Germany in 1927. In 1931, he moved to Harvard and was appointed Professor of Economics there in 1946. Apart from the works mentioned below, his publications include *Studies in the Structure of the American Economy* (1953), *Input-Output Economics* and *Collected Essays* (1966). The interdependence of the various sectors of a country's economy has long been appreciated by economists. The theme can be traced from CANTILLON and QUESNAY and the 'TABLEAU ÉCONOMIQUE' through MARX and WALRAS.

The sheer complexity of the interactions and interrelationships between the different sectors of a modern economy was a Gordian knot which had to be cut before the theoretical structure could be translated into a practical reflection of an actual economy and serve as the basis for policy recommendations. Leontief's achievement was to see the solution of this problem in MATRIX ALGEBRA, and modern computers have made INPUT-OUTPUT ANALYSIS a practical proposition. His book *The Structure of the American Economy, 1919–1929*, was first published in 1941, and a second edition, *1919–1939*, appeared in 1951. In these studies, he attempted, with the limited statistical facts available to him, to establish a 'Tableau Économique' of the U.S. The economy was described as an integrated system of flows or transfers from each activity of production, CONSUMPTION or DISTRIBUTION to each other activity. Each sector absorbs the outputs from other sectors and itself produces COMMODITIES or SERVICES which are in turn used up by other sectors, either for further processing or for final consumption.

All these flows or transfers were set out in a rectangular table – an input/output MATRIX. The way in which the outputs of any industry spread out through the rest of the economy could be seen from the elements making up the rows. Similarly, the origins of its INPUTS could be seen directly from the elements of the appropriate column. Given such a structure, the implications of a specific change in one part of the economy could be traced through to all the elements in the system. ⟡ SOCIAL ACCOUNTING.

Lerner, Abba Ptachya. ⟡ MARSHALL-LERNER CRITERION.

Letter of credit. An order from a bank to a bank abroad authorizing payment to a person named in the letter of a particular sum of MONEY or up to a limit of a certain sum. Letters of CREDIT are often required by exporters who wish to have proof that they will be paid before they ship goods, or who wish to minimize delay in payment for the goods. Letters of credit, unlike BILLS OF EXCHANGE, are not negotiable, but being cashable at a known bank, are immediately acceptable to the seller in the exporting country. A confirmed letter of credit is one that has been recognized by the paying bank. Letters of credit may be irredeemable or revocable, depending on whether or not they can be cancelled at any time.

Leverage. ⟡ GEARING.

Liabilities. Sums of MONEY for which account has to be made. The liabilities of a company include its BANK LOANS and OVERDRAFT short-term DEBTS for goods and SERVICES received (*current liabilities*) and its LOAN capital and the CAPITAL subscribed by shareholders. ⟡ BALANCE SHEET.

Limited liability. The restriction of an owner's loss in a business to the amount of CAPITAL that he has invested in it. If a limited public company is put into LIQUIDATION because it is unable to pay its DEBTS, for example, the individual shareholders are liable only for the nominal VALUE of the SHARES they hold. Before the principle of limited liability was recognized, investors could be made liable for the whole of their personal possessions in the event of INSOLVENCY. The extension of limited liability to private as well as public companies that wished to register for it in the second half of the nineteenth century greatly increased the flow of capital, and today the limited liability company is the predominant form of business organization. ⟡ COMPANY LAW; JOINT STOCK COMPANY.

Linear programming. A mathematical technique for finding numerical solutions to a special class of problems. These problems involve the search for the best values of certain VARIABLES, where the 'best' generally means that set of values which maximizes PROFIT or minimizes COST. An essential part of the problem will be the existence of constraints or limitations on the values of the variables which may be selected. The problem is then to choose the best possible values out of those permitted by the constraints. Examples might be:

(a) The problem of deciding how much of six different products to produce and sell, when each product requires a particular amount of LABOUR, machine time and warehouse space for every unit produced, and where there are fixed limits on the amounts of labour, machine time and warehouse space available. Thus, the most profitable output mix must be found within the constraint of availability of resources.

(b) The problem of deciding how much of twelve different nutrients to include in an animal feedstuff, given the cost of each, and the particular combination of vitamins each contains. The object would be to minimize the cost of the feedstuff, subject to its containing at least some minimum amount of each vitamin.

(c) The problem of deciding how much crude oil to ship from each of a number of oilfields at different locations to each of a number of refineries at different locations in such a way as to minimize transport costs. The constraints here arise out of the fact that more cannot be shipped from an origin than exists there, and more cannot be shipped to a destination than is required there.

A further important feature of linear programming is that, as its name suggests, all the relationships involved must be linear ($\diamond$ LINEAR RELATIONSHIP).

Linear regression model. $\diamond$ LEAST SQUARES REGRESSION.

Linear relationship. A mathematical relationship which, in its simplest form, gives a straight line when drawn in two dimensions. Thus the equation $y = a + bx$ would describe a straight line once we assign particular values to a and b. The essential feature of the linear relationship is that, no matter how large x is, a change in it of one unit always leads to a change in y of b units. The linear relationship can be generalized to make y depend on two or more variables, e.g. $y = a + bx + cz + dw$.

Liquid. 1. In economics, an ASSET is liquid if it is CASH or can be quickly converted into cash at little loss. Assets are said to possess degrees of LIQUIDITY which are their nearness to cash. Highly liquid assets other than cash and bank deposits are post office SAVINGS, TREASURY BILLS, MONEY at call, etc. $\diamond$ LIQUIDITY

PREFERENCE. **2.** INTERNATIONAL LIQUIDITY consists of the total of GOLD AND FOREIGN EXCHANGE RESERVES and SPECIAL DRAWING RIGHTS of all countries.

Liquidation. The termination, dissolution or winding up of a limited company (◊ LIMITED LIABILITY). Liquidation of a company may be initiated by the shareholders, the directors (voluntary liquidation) or by its creditors, or by a court order if the company is insolvent (◊ INSOLVENCY). Where initiated by the creditors, a liquidator is appointed to realize the company's ASSETS and to pay the creditors. In case of insolvency, these functions are performed, initially at least, by the Official Receiver. If the company is solvent, the ordinary shareholders will receive any surplus after the company's liabilities have been met. ◊ BANKRUPTCY.

Liquidity. The ease with which an ASSET can be exchanged for MONEY. The liquidity of an asset is determined by the nature of the MARKET on which it is traded. For example, an ORDINARY SHARE of a British company is liquid because there is a well-organized market on which SHARES can be bought and sold, and hence, within quite a short time, a share can be exchanged for CASH. A house, on the other hand, tends to be rather illiquid, since it can take some time, and effort, to sell, even when DEMAND for houses may be fairly strong. The term may also be applied to an institution or individual; a firm is said to be liquid if a high proportion of its assets are held in the form of money or very liquid assets. The extent of the firm's liquidity in this sense then gives an indication of its ability to meet its expenditures quickly enough to satisfy creditors and avoid BANKRUPTCY.

Liquidity preference. The desire to hold MONEY rather than other forms of WEALTH, e.g. STOCKS and BONDS. It can be thought of as stemming from the TRANSACTIONS MOTIVE, SPECULATIVE MOTIVE and PRECAUTIONARY MOTIVE for holding money, and so it will be influenced by the level of INCOME, RATES OF INTEREST and bond prices, EXPECTATIONS and the institutional features of the economy which determine the INCOME VELOCITY OF CIRCULATION. ◊ J. M. KEYNES.

Liquidity ratio. 1. The proportion of the total ASSETS of a bank which are held in the form of CASH and LIQUID assets. These latter consist in general of MONEY lent out to the DISCOUNT HOUSES at CALL and short notice, and short-term BONDS issued by the government and other borrowers. By convention, in the U.K., CLEARING BANKS should not let this ratio fall below 28 per cent. Historically, the importance of the liquidity ratio is as an indicator of the banks' ability to meet the public's demands for cash. However, for several decades this consideration has ceased to have real significance as the determinant of its level and stability, and its main significance stems from its use by the monetary authorities in control of the MONEY SUPPLY. ⟡ CASH RATIO. **2.** The ratio of liquid assets to the current LIABILITIES of a business. Also called the CASH RATIO, it is a very crude test of SOLVENCY.

'Little Neddies'. The colloquialism for the economic development committees of the NATIONAL ECONOMIC DEVELOPMENT COUNCIL.

Lloyd Jacob Report. A report by the Committee on Resale Price Maintenance published in 1949. The committee's main recommendation was that collective RESALE PRICE MAINTENANCE should be abolished, but any single manufacturer should be allowed 'to prescribe and enforce resale prices for goods bearing his brand' subject to certain safeguards. The Labour government in 1951 published a White Paper which rejected the findings of the committee in favour of the general abolition of resale price maintenance. However, the MONOPOLIES COMMISSION's Report in 1955, on *Collective Discrimination – A Report on Exclusive Dealing, Collective Boycotts, Aggregated Rebates and Other Discriminatory Trade Practices* (coming out generally in favour of the line taken by the Lloyd Jacob Committee), served as the basis for the RESTRICTIVE TRADE PRACTICES ACTS 1956.

Loan. The borrowing of a sum of MONEY by one person, company, government or other organization from another. Loans may be secured or unsecured (⟡ SECURITIES), INTEREST bearing or interest free, long term or short term, redeemable or irredeemable. Loans may be made by individuals and companies, banks, INSURANCE and HIRE PURCHASE companies, BUILDING SOCIETIES and other FINANCIAL INTERMEDIARIES, PAWNBROKERS, or by the issue of SECURITIES. ⟡ FINANCE; TERM LOANS.

Loan capital. Fixed-interest borrowed funds. Alternative term for DEBENTURES.

Loan stock. Synonym for DEBENTURE.

Loanable funds. MONEY which is available for lending to individuals and institutions. The main sources of these funds are: SAVINGS of individuals and firms, e.g. as RETAINED EARNINGS, DEPRECIATION allowances, etc.; DISHOARDING; and an increase in the MONEY SUPPLY made available by government and banks. Thus, loanable funds represent a flow of money on to the MARKET for LOANS of all kinds.

Location theory. A body of theory which attempts to explain and predict the locational decisions of firms, and the spatial patterns of industry and agriculture which result from aggregates of the individual decisions. The main aim of locational theorists has been to integrate the space dimension into conventional economic theory.

Location theory originated in the work of VON THÜNEN and Weber, who developed MODELS of location for firms in an environment of PERFECT COMPETITION. Both assumed that ENTREPRENEURS attempted to maximize PROFITS in the face of a given PRICE fixed by the MARKET and outside their control, with perfect knowledge of the COST characteristics of all locations. As a result of these assumptions, locational decisions were explained solely in terms of differences in production and transport costs between sites. The main difference between the two was that von Thünen began with an agricultural producer in a fixed location, and attempted to explain his choice of product; whereas Weber took the case of a manufacturer with a given product, and tried to explain his choice of location.

Until relatively recently, most work on location theory followed Weber and von Thünen in assuming perfect competition, and concentrating on cost minimization models, taking sales revenue as constant over all locations. The simplest of such models assume that producers have a market at one location and a raw-material source at another, with the problem being to predict the choice of location of the firm. If the assumption is made that production costs are constant over all locations, then the problem is simply that of finding the location which minimizes TRANSFER COSTS. Although the assumptions clearly create a highly simplified model, several definite predictions can be made which tend to be consistent with the behaviour of firms for which TRANSFER COSTS are a high proportion of total costs. Briefly, some of these predictions are:

(a) If a production process involves loss of weight (e.g. ore refining), loss of bulk (cotton ginning) or decrease in perishability (fruit canning), the firm will locate to the raw-material source.

(b) If the process involves gains in weight, bulk or perishability, the firm will locate to the market.

(c) Location between the market and raw-material source will not in general occur, for two reasons: first, freight rates per ton-mile diminish as the distance carried increases, which makes one

257

long haul cheaper than two hauls with the same total distance; and secondly, a central location would mean loading and unloading charges for both raw material and finished product, rather than just one of them. Major exceptions to this generalization are: if there is a transhipment point between raw-material source and market, it may pay to locate there; if the freight carrier grants a fabrication in transit privilege, the disadvantages of a central location fall in fact on the carrier rather than the firm, and so such a location may be chosen.

Obvious generalizations of this model have been made by introducing several markets and raw-material sources, and by removing the assumption of equal production costs over all locations. However, as long as the assumptions of profit maximization and given product price were retained, the emphasis lay on determination of least-cost locations, their characteristics and the patterns of industrial location to which they give rise. As a price of greater realism, the models not only become more complex, but also much less definite in their predictions.

In the past twenty years or so, emphasis has shifted to the relation between location and demand, while the assumption of perfect competition has tended to be replaced by an assumption of IMPERFECT COMPETITION. The idea of profit maximization as the basic motivation of the firm has, however, remained. The leading theorists in this line of development are the late August Losch and Walter Isard ($\diamond$ A. Losch, *The Economics of Location*, and W. Isard, *Location and the Space Economy*).

Location theory can be viewed as an extension of the theory of the firm ($\diamond$ FIRM, THEORY OF) to analysis of location decisions, whereas in conventional MICROECONOMICS, only decisions on PRICE, output, INVESTMENT and selling expenditures are normally considered. It is not surprising, therefore, in view of the long history of criticism of the profit-maximization assumption in the theory of the firm, and the development of models based on alternative assumptions ($\diamond$ BEHAVIOURAL THEORY OF THE FIRM), that criticisms of, and modifications to, the assumption of profit maximization are being made in location analysis. This is reinforced by the empirical studies on actual location decisions which have been carried out, and which tend to suggest that traditional location theory does not accurately describe the behaviour and decision processes of firms when they make location decisions.

Logistic curve. A curve which is often used to represent the growth process of some VARIABLE. Its shape is shown in the following diagram. Its mathematical equation is:

$$y = \frac{a}{1 + be^{-cx}}$$

where y and x are the variables, a, b, c are PARAMETERS; and e is the well-known mathematical constant, equal approximately to 2·71828, and which plays an important role in growth processes of all kinds.

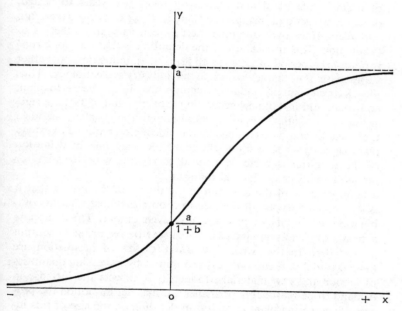

If we think of y as the total sales of a new product, for example, and x as time, the above curve would imply that sales of the new product grow rather slowly at first, but then the product 'takes off', and there is a period of rapid growth, followed by a levelling off as a product reaches its SATURATION POINT. ⇨ HOUSEHOLD.

Lombard Street. A term sometimes used as a synonym for MONEY MARKET as many of the institutions of this market are located in or near this street in the City of London.

Long-dated securities. ⇨ DATED SECURITIES.

Long-end of the market. That part of the market for BONDS which is concerned with dealings in long-term issues.

Long rate. The RATE OF INTEREST on long-term BONDS.

Long-run. In PRICE THEORY, the long-run is strictly defined as the time period long enough for the firm to be able to vary the quantities of all of its FACTORS OF PRODUCTION, rather than just some of them. For example, suppose that a firm uses LABOUR, raw materials and machinery to make a particular product. Labour is hired on a weekly contract; raw materials take one month to arrive, from date of order, while plant and machinery takes two years to design, order, construct and install. The 'long run' for this firm is therefore two years, since over this time the firm can vary all its factors of production. The implication of the definition is that the 'long run' is not a fixed period of time for all firms in all industries, but rather varies with the characteristics of an industry's technology. Thus the electricity supply industry requires five to six years to plan, construct, and install new generating capacity, and so its 'long run' is five to six years. Note also that although it is normally assumed that the long run is determined by the time period required to extend plant capacity, this need not always be the case, and the definition of the long-run is perfectly neutral as regards which INPUT (or inputs) actually determines the long-run.

The importance of the long run in the theory of the firm is that it is long enough to permit the firm to choose the most efficient combination of inputs to produce any given output. Thus, suppose a firm experiences an increase in DEMAND, requiring an output greater than that at which AVERAGE COSTS of production are lowest. Initially, it can only expand output by increasing quantities of labour and raw materials, though if it expects the increase in demand to be reasonably permanent, it may set in motion the process of increasing plant capacity. In deciding on the size of this increase, it can aim at the best combination of plant, labour and raw materials to produce the given rate of output. In the meantime, however, it must work within the limitations of its existing amount of plant, and this will generally involve it in using too little plant, and too much labour (and possible other inputs) relative to that which it can achieve in the long run Hence it will tend to incur higher average costs of production than it will in the long run, due to the fact that it is not able to use the most efficient input combination.

More generally, the long-run is often loosely taken as the period long enough for underlying economic factors causing tendencies to change to work themselves out fully. It was in this sense that KEYNES was using the term in his famous dictum: 'In the long run we are all dead.' ⟡ A. MARSHALL.

Long-term capital. ⟡ BUSINESS FINANCE.

Longfield, Samuel Mountifort (1802–84). An Irish lawyer who became the first incumbent of the Chair of Political Economy at Trinity College, Dublin. His most important work in economics was *Lectures on Political Economy*, which was published in 1834. He argued convincingly against the labour theory of value (⟡ VALUE, THEORIES OF) and developed a marginal revenue productivity theory (⟡ MARGINAL REVENUE PRODUCT) of LABOUR and CAPITAL. Moreover, some of his ideas on capital and INTEREST foreshadowed the work of the AUSTRIAN SCHOOL.

Lorenz curve. A curve which shows the relation between the cumulative percentage of some group of items (firms, HOUSEHOLDS) and the cumulative percentage of the total amount of some VARIABLE (employment, INCOME) which they hold. For example, from information on the SIZE DISTRIBUTION OF FIRMS, we might construct the following table:

Percentage of firms	Percentage of total employment which they account for
%	%
10	2
20	8
30	15
40	23
50	32
60	42
70	53
80	64
90	80
100	100

We would then draw the Lorenz curve as shown in the diagram on the following page.

The purpose of the Lorenz curve is to show the degree of inequality in the relevant distribution it is taken from. If there was perfect equality, each successive equal step up in the cumulative percentage of firms, in the above table, would be accompanied by a similar increase in the cumulative percentage of employment. Hence,

261

Lorenz curve

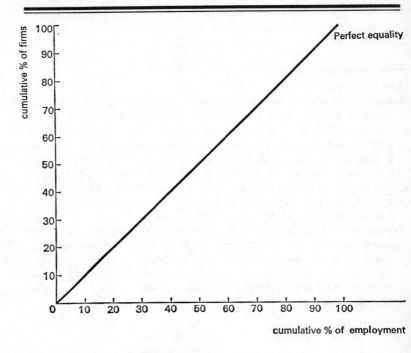

the curve, when graphed, would show a straight line, as shown in the diagram. The greater the curvature of the Lorenz curve, the greater the degree of inequality. The Lorenz curve is often used to show the inequality in the INCOME DISTRIBUTION.

M

Macmillan Committee. The Committee on Finance and Industry, set up in 1929, which published its report in 1931. It was under the chairmanship of Lord Macmillan, and J. M. KEYNES was a member. The committee carried out its task against an economic background in which the GROSS DOMESTIC PRODUCT had reached, after sixteen years, a level only 5 per cent above pre-war. Unemployment was 10 per cent in 1929, and was to rise to over 20 per cent by the time the committee published its report. The committee took the evidence from many leading economists of the day, such as A. C. PIGOU, D. H. ROBERTSON and L. C. ROBBINS on the subject of UNEMPLOYMENT policy (⟡ CLASSICAL SCHOOL). It decided in favour of the so-called TREASURY view that expenditure on public works was not the answer, in spite of the signing of Addendum I by some of its leading members. This addendum, which was signed by J. M. Keynes, A. A. G. Tullock, J. Frater Taylor, Sir T. Allen, Ernest Bevin and R. McKenna, advocated a programme of public works and IMPORT restrictions. However, the committee insisted that monetary policy should be concerned with 'the maintenance of the parity of the foreign exchanges before the avoidance of the credit cycle and the stability of the price level'. The maintenance of the EXCHANGE RATE was agreed to be the first priority by all, including the signatories of Addendum I. (Two months after the report was published, the U.K. came off the GOLD STANDARD and the exchange rate depreciated immediately by 2 per cent and continued downwards for twelve months.) The committee expressed concern that small companies found it difficult to raise long-term capital (⟡ BUSINESS FINANCE) by the usual means of placing issues through the ISSUING HOUSES; this has become known as the 'MACMILLAN GAP'. It recommended the setting up of an institution which would 'provide adequate machinery for raising long-dated capital in amounts not sufficiently large for a public issue, i.e. amounts ranging from small sums up to say £200,000 or more'. This recommendation was eventually met by the creation of the Industrial and Commercial Finance Corporation in 1946. In 1945, the CLEARING BANKS and Scottish banks with the support of the BANK OF ENGLAND combined to finance the creation of the I.C.F.C.

with initial resources of £45 million and a remit to make long-term loans and to subscribe to private placings of share capital between £5,000 and £200,000. The I.C.F.C., which has since regularly supplemented its resources by raising LOAN CAPITAL, has continued to expand. It now has some eighteen branches throughout Britain, and its financing commitment to individual companies has risen as high as £500,000. ⟡ BOLTON COMMITTEE; RADCLIFFE REPORT.

Macmillan Gap. The report of the Committee on Finance and Industry in 1931 (MACMILLAN COMMITTEE) highlighted the difficulties which small and medium-sized firms experienced in raising long-term capital (⟡ BUSINESS FINANCE). The report made proposals for dealing with this 'gap' arising from the lack of facilities for public issues in small amounts. Facilities for coping with small issues were later developed, especially through ISSUING HOUSES, placing small amounts privately with INSTITUTIONAL INVESTORS, such as INSURANCE companies. In addition, new institutions have been set up, such as the Industrial and Commercial Finance Corporation. ⟡ BOLTON COMMITTEE.

Macroeconomics. That part of economics which is primarily concerned with the study of relationships between broad economic aggregates, the most important of which are NATIONAL INCOME, aggregate SAVING and consumers' expenditure, INVESTMENT, aggregate employment, the quantity of money (⟡ MONEY SUPPLY), the average PRICE LEVEL, and the BALANCE OF PAYMENTS. It is largely concerned with explaining the determinants of the magnitudes of these aggregates, and of their rates of change through time. A major preoccupation is also the role of government expenditure (⟡ BUDGET), TAXATION, and MONETARY POLICY in determining the general level of economic activity, i.e. the levels of national income, UNEMPLOYMENT, etc. Macroeconomics proceeds by defining and analysing, in some depth, relationships between the aggregates, finding the conditions under which the system is in static or dynamic EQUILIBRIUM and noting the characteristics of the equilibrium state. This then enables predictions to be made about the consequences of changes in certain key magnitudes, e.g. the level of investment or government expenditure. Modern macroeconomics largely dates from the publication of KEYNES's *The General Theory of Employment, Interest, and Money* in 1936. ⟡ FISCAL POLICY; INCOME DETERMINATION, THEORY OF; TRADE CYCLE.

Maintaining capital intact. Making good the stock of CAPITAL consumed in production. This is a concept used in economic theory and national accounting in which 'true' DEPRECIATION is used to restore the INCOME-producing capacity of capital, so that, e.g., a measure of NET DOMESTIC PRODUCT or NET INVESTMENT can be made, i.e. the GROSS DOMESTIC PRODUCT or GROSS INVESTMENT less an estimate of CAPITAL CONSUMPTION. Net domestic product would thus measure total output while maintaining the nation's capital intact, while net investment would measure the net addition to the nation's stock of capital over the period.

Malthus, Thomas Robert (1766–1834). He was educated at St John's College, Cambridge, and became a fellow there, after studying mathematics and philosophy. He entered the Church of England and became a country parson. He was subsequently Professor of History and Political Economy at the East India Company's Haileybury College. His *Essay on the Principle of Population as it Affects the Future Improvement of Society* was published in 1789, and a revised edition in 1803. His other works include: *An Inquiry into the Nature and Progress of Rent* (1815), *The Poor Law* (1817), *Principles of Political Economy* (1820) and *Definitions of Political Economy* (1827). Malthus is remembered for his essays on POPULATION. Population had a natural growth rate described by a GEOMETRIC PROGRESSION, whereas the natural resources necessary to support the population grew at a rate similar to an ARITHMETIC PROGRESSION. Without restraints, therefore, there would be a continued pressure on living standards, both in terms of room and of output. He advocated moral restraint on the size of families. Malthus also carried on a long argument with RICARDO against Say's law (⇨ J.-B. SAY). Briefly Say's law stated that there could be no general overproduction or under production of COMMODITIES on the grounds that whatever was bought by somebody must have been sold by somebody else. (J. M. KEYNES found some affinity between Malthus's conclusions and his own in his *General Theory*.) Malthus, however, was arguing strictly within the basic assumption of the equality of planned SAVINGS and INVESTMENT in CLASSICAL ECONOMICS, and was a long way away from Keynes's revolutionary assumption that they are made equal only by movements in total INCOME. Saving to Malthus was investment. His argument for underconsumption was simply that an increase in savings necessarily diminished consumption on the one hand, and on the other increased the output of consumer's goods through increased investment. At the same time, because the LABOUR supply was inelastic (⟡ ELASTICITY), WAGES rose and therefore so did costs. ⟡⟡ J. C. L. S. DE SISMONDI.

Malynes, Gerald (1586–1641). An English merchant and government official and a leading exponent of MERCANTILISM. His publications include *A Treatise of the Canker of England's Commonwealth* (1601), *Saint George for England, Allegorically Described* (1601), *England's View in the Unmasking of two Paradoxes* (1603), *The Maintenance of Free Trade* (1622) and *The Center of the Circle of Commerce* (1623). He showed how an outflow of precious metals could lead to a fall in PRICES at home and a rise in prices abroad. This was an important clarification of the economic thought of the time. He suggested that higher import TARIFFS should be levied and EXPORTS of BULLION prohibited, because he believed that a country's growth was related to the accumulation of precious metals. He thought that exchange control should be used to improve the U.K. TERMS OF TRADE, supporting his policy on the belief that the U.K.'s exports were price inelastic (⟡ ELASTICITY). ⟡⟡ QUANTITY THEORY OF MONEY.

Managed currency. A CURRENCY is said to be managed if the EXCHANGE RATE is not fixed by FREE MARKET forces, i.e. if the government influences the rate by buying and selling its own MONEY or other means. Most currencies are managed in some sense today, even when they are allowed to float. ⟡⟡ EXCHANGE CONTROL; INTERNATIONAL MONETARY FUND.

Management accountancy. Business accounting practice concerned with the provision of information to management for policy-making purposes as opposed to that required for the preparation of BALANCE SHEETS and other information required by law. In so far as the two sets of information overlap, the phrase is imprecise, but it usefully emphasizes the recent aspects of the development of accounting, notably in cost control (⟡ COST ACCOUNTING) and INVESTMENT APPRAISAL.

Manchester School. 'Manchesterism' was an epithet applied in Germany to those who subscribed to a political-economic philosophy of 'LAISSEZ-FAIRE'. It was applied, in particular, to the movement in England from 1820 to 1850 which was inspired by the propaganda of the Anti-Corn Law League. This was headed by Cobden and Bright, and supported by the economics of DAVID RICARDO. The 'school' believed in FREE TRADE and political and economic freedom with the minimum of government restraint.

Mandeville, Bernard de (1670–1733). Born at Dort in Holland, Mandeville obtained an M.D. at Leyden and established himself in London as a general practitioner. In 1705 he published a poem called *The Grumbling Hive*, which was reissued in 1714 and 1729 under the title of *The Fable of the Bees or Private Vices, Public Benefits*. In this pamphlet he showed how although individuals indulge in unholy vices in their private behaviour nevertheless in the aggregate they contributed to the public good and therefore could be excused. ADAM SMITH was severely critical of the satirical nature of the work (⟡ HIDDEN HAND).

Marginal analysis. An idea underlying most of MICROECONOMICS and much of MACROECONOMICS is that of the marginal change in something, or the ratio of the marginal change in one thing to a marginal change in another. For example ⟡ MARGINAL UTILITY, MARGINAL COST, MARGINAL REVENUE, MARGINAL PRODUCT, MARGINAL RATE OF SUBSTITUTION, in microeconomics; and MARGINAL PROPENSITY TO CONSUME, MARGINAL PROPENSITY TO SAVE, in macroeconomics. A marginal change is a very small increment or decrement to the total quantity of some VARIABLE; and marginal analysis is the analysis of the relations between such changes in related economic variables. The importance of marginal analysis arises in two somewhat different ways, one of which is associated more with its use in microeconomics, the other relating more to its macroeconomic applications. Much of microeconomics is concerned with the analysis of optimizing behaviour, i.e. the search for OPTIMUM values of particular variables. The consumer is assumed to maximize UTILITY; the firm is assumed to maximize PROFIT, and, in doing so, to minimize COSTS for every level of output; the policy-maker is assumed to maximize SOCIAL WELFARE. Now the maximum of a variable is found by finding a value of the variable such that a small increase and decrease from that value both cause the value of the MAXIMAND to fall. Similarly, a minimum is found by finding a value of the variable such that a small increase and decrease from that value both cause the value of the MINIMAND to rise. The search for optimum values necessarily involves us in the definition and analysis of marginal concepts, and this is how virtually all the marginal concepts in microeconomics arise. The mathematician will, of course, recognize 'marginal analysis' as a straightforward application of the differential calculus, with the various marginal concepts being special names given to first derivatives of particular functions; and he will also appreciate how they arise in the search

for maxima and minima, constrained and unconstrained, of functions such as profits as a function of output; utility as a function of
quantities of goods consumed; output as a function of quantities
of INPUTS used.

Marginal analysis arises in macroeconomics not so much because
we are trying to find optimum solutions, but because we are directly
concerned with the effects of changes in certain variables – e.g.
INVESTMENT, EXPORTS, government expenditure – on certain other
variables, e.g. EMPLOYMENT and NATIONAL INCOME (this sort
of consideration also occurs in microeconomics, of course). The
analysis of the relationship between small changes in variables is
therefore of direct interest. ⇨ H. H. GOSSEN; W. S. JEVONS; C.
MENGER; J. H. VON THÜNEN; M. E. L. WALRAS.

Marginal cost. The change in total COSTS of production which results
when output is varied by one unit or the AVOIDABLE COSTS of
producing an additional unit of output. A distinction is generally
made between (a) *short-run marginal costs* – the increase in costs which
results from an increase in production when not all the INPUTS
used by the firm can be varied; and (b) *long-run marginal costs* – a
change in costs resulting from a change in output when all inputs,
and in particular CAPITAL, can be varied. ⇨ LONG-RUN;
MARGINAL ANALYSIS; SHORT-RUN.

Marginal cost pricing. A method of setting prices in which PRICE
is made equal to MARGINAL COST. Since price must always be
set in such a way that all output is sold, and since marginal cost
varies with output, marginal cost pricing implies setting price at the
point at which the DEMAND curve cuts the marginal cost curve.
Marginal cost pricing is recommended as an appropriate policy for
NATIONALIZED INDUSTRIES on the grounds that it maximizes
economic welfare (⇨ WELFARE ECONOMICS). Marginal cost pricing
may imply equality of price with LONG-RUN or SHORT-RUN
marginal cost. ⇨ H. HOTELLING; MARGINAL ANALYSIS.

Marginal efficiency of capital. ⇨ INTERNAL RATE OF RETURN.

Marginal efficiency of investment. ⇨ INTERNAL RATE OF RETURN.

Marginal physical product. ⇨ MARGINAL REVENUE PRODUCT.

Marginal product. The increase in output which results from increasing
the quantity of an INPUT by one unit, the quantities of all other
inputs remaining constant. ⇨ DIMINISHING RETURNS, LAW OF;
MARGINAL ANALYSIS.

Marginal productivity of capital. ⇨ INTERNAL RATE OF RETURN.

Marginal productivity of labour. The change in output which results from changing the labour INPUT by one unit. ⇨ MARGINAL PRODUCTIVITY THEORY OF WAGES.

Marginal productivity theory of wages. A theory based on the idea that the DEMAND for LABOUR is determined by its marginal productivity (⇨ DISTRIBUTION, THEORY OF), and indeed, that the WAGE of labour will be equal to the value of its MARGINAL PRODUCT. This stems from the idea that it pays a firm to increase the amount of labour it employs, until the extra revenue gained by employing one more unit of labour is just equal to its price. Thus, just as the inter-action of SUPPLY and DEMAND determine the value of a good, so the relationship between the marginal productivity and the supply of labour interact to determine wages. ⇨ BARGAINING THEORY OF WAGES; DISTRIBUTION, THEORY OF.

Marginal propensity to consume (M.P.C.). The proportion of a small increase in INCOME which will be devoted to increased CONSUMP-TION expenditure. The value of the M.P.C. is derived from the slope of the CONSUMPTION FUNCTION. Typically, it is expected to be less than one. That is, an increase in income leads to a smaller increase in consumption expenditure, the difference being saved. The M.P.C. was first defined by J. M. KEYNES, and forms an important part of his theory of the MULTIPLIER. Keynes in fact asserted, as a 'funda-mental psychological law', that as NATIONAL INCOME rose the M.P.C. would fall. That is, the richer people are, the greater the proportion of an increase in income which would be saved. ⇨ INCOME DETERMINATION, THEORY OF; MARGINAL PROPENSITY TO SAVE.

Marginal propensity to save (M.P.S.). The proportion of an increase in INCOME which will be saved. Since an increase in income will be partly saved and partly consumed, the M.P.S. is equal to one minus the MARGINAL PROPENSITY TO CONSUME. The M.P.S. plays an important part in J. M. KEYNES's theory of the MULTIPLIER. In fact, in its simplest form, the multiplier is calculated as 1/M.P.S. The corollary of Keynes's 'fundamental psychological law', that the M.P.C. falls as income rises, is that the M.P.S. rises as income rises. ⇨ CONSUMPTION FUNCTION; INCOME DETERMINATION, THEORY OF.

Marginal rate of substitution (M.R.S.). The rate at which one good must be substituted for another as a consumer moves along his INDIFFERENCE CURVE. Thus, consider the indifference curve in the diagram on p. 270. If the individual is initially at point A, representing a particular quantity of x and a particular quantity of y, we can 'move him along' his indifference curve by subtracting a small amount of x, and substituting for it the appropriate amount of y. What is 'appropriate' depends on the shape of the indifference curve, and varies along it. Thus in moving from A to B, a relatively small increment in y is quite enough to compensate for the reduction

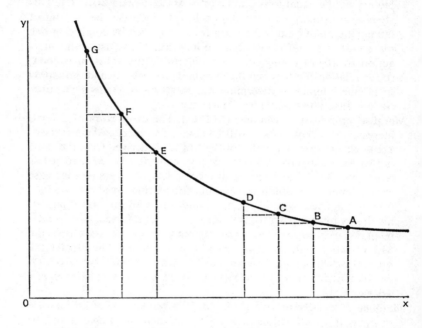

in x. At E, however, the same reduction in x requires a much larger increment in y to compensate. Let us denote the (supposedly very small) change in x by dx; and the appropriate change in y – required to 'get back on to' the indifference curve - by dy. The marginal rate of substitution of y for x is then defined as dy/dx, i.e. the ratio of the required change in y to the change in x. Alternatively, if we were thinking in terms of increasing x and reducing y, we could define the M.R.S. of x for y, as dx/dy. Clearly, the two expressions are reciprocal. Mathematically, the M.R.S. measures the slope of the indifference curve, and the type of curvature normally assumed implies a decreasing M.R.S., i.e. a slope which increases in absolute value, but decreases in numerical value, as we move from right to left.

Marginal revenue. The change in total REVENUE which results from changing output sold by one unit. Marginal revenue to a firm will either be equal to or below PRICE. If the price of the good is the same for whatever quantity the firm sells, i.e. if the firm is in PERFECT COMPETITION, then the increase in revenue from selling one more unit is equal to price. If, however, the attempt to sell an additional unit of output forces the firm to reduce price on *all* the output it sells, then marginal revenue will equal the new price, less the fall in revenue on the units which would have been sold at the higher price. The concept of marginal revenue plays an important role in theories of imperfect competiton (◊ MONOPOLISTIC COMPETITION), since equality of marginal revenue and MARGINAL COST determines the profit-maximizing EQUILIBRIUM of the firm. ◊ MARGINAL ANALYSIS.

Marginal revenue product. The marginal revenue product of an INPUT is derived by multiplying the MARGINAL PRODUCT of the input by the MARGINAL REVENUE of the good when it is sold. The marginal product of an input is defined in terms of physical units of output – hence it is often called the *marginal physical product*. Suppose the marginal product of an input, X, is 1·2 units, while the marginal revenue of the good is £3. Then the marginal revenue product of X is simply £3 × 1·2 = £3·6 per unit of X. That is, we are simply finding the extra revenue which is brought in by increasing the quantity of X by one unit. ◊ MARGINAL PRODUCTIVITY THEORY OF WAGES; MARGINAL VALUE PRODUCT.

Marginal social product. The effect on SOCIAL WELFARE of a small change in the quantity of an INPUT used. The definitions of MARGINAL PRODUCT, MARGINAL REVENUE PRODUCT and MARGINAL PRODUCT itself are framed implicitly in terms of the private returns which can be gained through sales of the output on a MARKET and which accrue to the individual. However, there may be certain effects on social welfare resulting from an increase in quantity of an input used, which differ from the direct gains to the individual, and so the marginal social product of the input may differ from its marginal 'private' product. (For a further discussion of the reasons for divergence between private and social costs and returns, with examples, ◊ EXTERNALITIES.) Where the subject of concern, in analysis or policy, is social welfare, then the appropriate concept is the marginal social product of an input rather than its private product.

Marginal utility. The increase in total UTILITY of CONSUMPTION of a good which results from increasing the quantity of the good consumed by one unit. This concept played an extremely important part in Marshallian demand theory ($\diamond$ ALFRED MARSHALL) but has been less important since the introduction of INDIFFERENCE ANALYSIS. It is important to appreciate the distinction between marginal and total utility. A good may have a very low marginal utility, but a very high total utility, e.g. water; and since it is the marginal utility which (in conjunction with supply) determines PRICE, this explains the old *paradox of value* of why goods which are essential for life, i.e. have high total utility, sell at low prices, whereas inessential goods, such as diamonds, sell at a high price. $\diamond$ CONSUMER SURPLUS; VALUE, THEORIES OF; M. E. L. WALRAS.

Marginal utility, law of diminishing. A law stating that, after some point, successive equal increments in the quantity of a good yield smaller and smaller increases in UTILITY, i.e. MARGINAL UTILITY is diminishing. As a broad proposition, this hypothesis has some plausibility: even the most ice-cream addicted child will begin to experience diminishing marginal utility after his fifth ice-cream in a short space of time. However, economists' main objection to the 'law' was directed at its implication that utility is a quantity capable of being measured in terms of fixed units, so that n units of a good can be said to yield 'x units of utility'. Comparison of differences in total utility requires utility to be measurable. But it has proved impossible to find an objective yardstick with which to measure utility. As a result, Marshallian demand theory ($\diamond$ A. MARSHALL), which is based on the law of diminishing marginal utility, was superseded by INDIFFERENCE ANALYSIS. $\diamond$ F. Y. EDGEWORTH.

Marginal utility of money. The increase in total UTILITY which results from increasing the quantity of MONEY an individual has by one unit. Since, typically, money is only valued because of the power it gives to buy goods (now or in the future), the MARGINAL UTILITY of money must ultimately derive from the marginal utilities of the goods (and SAVING) on which it is spent. Consistent with the law of diminishing marginal utility ($\diamond$ DIMINISHING MARGINAL UTILITY, LAW OF), it is generally held that the marginal utility of money diminishes as the quantity of money possessed by an individual increases. $\diamond$ ALFRED MARSHALL.

Marginal value product. Analogous to the MARGINAL REVENUE PRODUCT of an INPUT, the marginal value product is a measure of the extra revenue which results from increasing the quantity of an input used by one unit, all other input quantities remaining constant. The marginal value product is found by multiplying the MARGINAL PRODUCT of the input by the PRICE of the product. Where the price at which a firm sells its output is the same whatever the quantity sold, i.e. where the market is in PERFECT COMPETITION, then MARGINAL REVENUE is equal to price, since the revenue brought in by the sale of an extra unit of output is always equal to the price. Hence, in this case, MARGINAL REVENUE PRODUCT and marginal value product are equal, and the latter correctly measures the extra revenue brought in by increasing the quantity of an input used by one unit. If the marginal product of an input is, say, 1·1 units, while its price is £2 per unit, then its marginal value product is £2 × 1·1 = £2·2. If, however, the firm must reduce price in order to sell a greater quantity, i.e. if it is in imperfect competition (⟡ MONOPOLISTIC COMPETITION), then marginal revenue will generally be less than price, and so marginal value product will overstate the extra revenue actually brought in by increasing the quantity of an input used by one unit. This extra revenue will be accurately measured by the marginal revenue product. ⟡ MARGINAL PRODUCTIVITY THEORY OF WAGES.

Maritime Industrial Development Areas (M.I.D.A.S.). The description given originally by the National Ports Council in 1964 to an industrial estate situated adjacent to deep water. It has been recognized that significant economic benefits could be obtained by encouraging primary industries to locate at sites adjacent to a port which has sufficient depth of water for the raw materials required by the industry to be imported in large bulk carriers (for oil, 250,000 dwt tankers and larger; for iron ore, 100,000 dwt bulk carriers). Land and INFRASTRUCTURE would also be made available for secondary industries dependent on the primary industries and also perhaps benefiting from the port as an IMPORT and EXPORT point for other supplies and products. The development is, therefore, an integrated one, with each industry being interrelated with the others and/or with the port and enjoying common infrastructure benefits. Examples of developments of this nature are at Fos, near Marseille, and at Rotterdam.

Market. A market exists when buyers wishing to exchange MONEY for a good or SERVICE are in contact with sellers wishing to exchange goods or services for money. Thus, a market is defined in terms of the fundamental forces of SUPPLY and DEMAND, and is not necessarily confined to any particular geographical location. The concept of the market is basic to most of contemporary economics, since, in a FREE MARKET ECONOMY, this is the mechanism by which RESOURCES are allocated. ⟡ PRICE SYSTEM.

Market capitalization. ⟡ CAPITALIZATION.

Market demand curve. ⟡ DEMAND CURVE.

Market economy. ⟡ FREE MARKET ECONOMY.

Market forces. The forces of SUPPLY and DEMAND, which together determine the PRICE at which a product is sold and the quantity which will be traded. The economic behaviour of government agencies or very large firms in the private sector is sometimes described as being insulated from market forces, i.e. it can ignore or influence these forces.

Market share. This can refer to (a) the sales of the product or products of a firm as a proportion of the sales of the product or products of the industry as a whole, e.g. sales of Ford motor-cars compared with total U.K. motor-car sales. Or (b) to the sales of a particular COMMODITY compared with the total sales for the class of commodity of which the particular commodity is a member, e.g. sales of twin-tub washing machines compared with sales of all washing machines. The presumption is that the firm's product in (a) and the particular commodity in (b) are faced with competitive SUBSTITUTES in their respective MARKETS.

Market shares may also be calculated in terms of the proportion of the product in the total existing stock of that class of products, as opposed to its share of the flow of new sales. ⟡ SATURATION.

Market structure. The underlying characteristics of a MARKET which determine the competitive relations between sellers. The most important of these characteristics are: (a) the SIZE DISTRIBUTION OF FIRMS; (b) the size distribution of buyers; (c) the BARRIERS TO ENTRY of new buyers and sellers; (d) the degree of product DIFFERENTIATION; and (e) the degree of VERTICAL INTEGRATION. Other characteristics which may be important are the capital intensity (⟡ CAPITAL-INTENSIVE) of production, the stability of DEMAND for the product on the market and the spatial distribution of buyers and sellers.

Market supply. The SUPPLY of a good or SERVICE forthcoming from all sellers in a MARKET.

Market supply curve. ⟡ SUPPLY CURVE.

Marketable securities. SECURITIES dealt in on the STOCK EXCHANGE.

Marketing. Broadly, the functions of sales, distribution, ADVERTISING and sales promotion, product planning and market research. That is, those functions in a business that directly involve contact with the consumer and assessment of his needs, and the translation of this information into outputs for sale consistent with the firm's objectives.

Marshall Aid. At the end of the Second World War, the U.S. found that only it had the necessary productive capacity to make good the losses experienced by other countries. European countries had heavy BALANCE OF PAYMENTS deficits *vis-à-vis* the U.S. In 1946, in order to alleviate the resultant shortage of dollars, the U.S. and Canada made substantial LOANS, including £1,000 million to the U.K. It was expected that these loans would be sufficient to cover requirements over the short period which was all that was expected necessary for the world economies to recover. However, in 1948 a general LIQUIDITY crisis was only avoided by further loans made under the EUROPEAN RECOVERY PROGRAMME, through which the U.K. received loans amounting to £1,500 million between 1948 and 1950. This programme was called Marshall Aid, after the then U.S. Secretary of State, General G. C. Marshall. The loans were allocated under the direction of the ORGANIZATION FOR EURO-PEAN ECONOMIC COOPERATION set up for this purpose.

Marshall, Alfred (1842–1924). He was educated at Merchant Taylor's School and graduated in mathematics at St John's College, Cambridge. In 1868, he was appointed to a lectureship in Moral Science at Cambridge, and it was during this period that he began to study economics. In 1882, he moved to the Chair of Political Economy at Bristol. In 1885, he returned to Cambridge as Professor of Political Economy, a post he retained until his retirement in 1908. His most important works include *The Pure Theory of Foreign Trade* (1879), *The Principles of Economics* (1890), *Industry and Trade* (1919) and *Money, Credit and Commerce* (1923). Marshall was in the long tradition of the English CLASSICAL SCHOOL which was founded by ADAM SMITH and DAVID RICARDO, and his influence on succeeding generations of economists has been very great. His achievement was to refine and develop MICROECONOMIC theory to such a degree that much of what he wrote is still familiar to readers of the elementary economic textbooks today. His theory of VALUE brought together the diverse elements of previous theories. On the one hand, he showed how the demand for a COMMODITY is dependent on a consumer's UTILITY or welfare. The more of a commodity a consumer has, the less extra utility or benefit accrues to him from an additional purchase (⟡ H. GOSSEN). He will not go on buying a commodity until this extra benefit falls to zero. Rather, he will stop buying

275

extra when he finds that the MONEY he has to pay for it is worth more to him than the gain from having an extra unit of the commodity. At this point of EQUILIBRIUM a fall in the PRICE, therefore, will mean that it becomes worthwhile to him to exchange his money for more of the commodity. In general, therefore, a fall in price will increase the quantity of the commodity demanded, and in theory, a schedule could be drawn up which shows how much would be demanded at each price. The resultant graph would show a downward sloping DEMAND CURVE. Marshall invented the expression ELASTICITY to describe his measure of the response of demand to small changes in price. Similarly, on the supply side, higher prices are necessary to bring forward increased outputs and a supply schedule with its corresponding supply curve can be drawn up. The price of the commodity is determined at the point where the two curves intersect. These worked like a pair of scissors, neither blade of which cuts without the presence of the other.

Marshall recognized that his consumer utility theory was in some ways an oversimplification. It does not take account of complementary or competitive goods (⬦ COMPLEMENTARY DEMAND), and assumes that the MARGINAL UTILITY of money is constant. However, he argued that his analysis applied to small price changes and to goods upon which only an insignificant proportion of income was spent. It was within this framework that Marshall discussed the idea of CONSUMER SURPLUS (⬦ DUPUIT). For a given quantity of a commodity purchased on a competitive market, the price will be the same for each unit of the commodity sold. However, for any individual purchaser the price is equal to the utility to him of the last unit of the total quantity purchased; the last but one being worth more, the last but two worth more again, and so on. These utilities can be added up and the extra, over the price and quantity paid out, is the consumers' surplus. He was aware of the shortcomings of the 'Stationary State' of the typical classical analysis and emphasized the importance of the production period. 'The element of time which is centre of chief difficulty of almost every economic problem.' He considered (a) a market period in which supplies are all fixed, (b) a short period in which supplies can be increased, but only to the extent possible by better use of current capacity, and (c) a long period in which capacity itself can be increased. The classical economists had shown how RENT is received by landowners as a surplus. As land was a FACTOR OF PRODUCTION in fixed supply, it differed from other factors of production in that its returns were not related to work done. Marshall extended the concept by pointing out that, in the short run, man-made CAPITAL was in fixed supply also, and during the period which it took to manufacture, it earned a QUASI-RENT. ⟡ A. A. COURNOT; MARSHALL-LERNER CRITERION; J. S. MILL.

Marshall-Lerner criterion. A rule which states the ELASTICITY conditions under which a change in a country's EXCHANGE RATE would improve its BALANCE OF TRADE. A. P. Lerner set out the appropriate formulae in his book *Economics of Control* on the basis of the elasticity concepts developed by A. MARSHALL. In its simplest form, the rule states that the price elasticities of demand for IMPORTS and EXPORTS must sum to greater than unity for an improvement to be effected. The volume of exports increases and the volume of imports decreases in response to a fall in the PRICE of the former and a rise in the price of the latter when a CURRENCY is devalued (assuming, for the sake of the argument, that there are no other factors influencing the MARKET, such as SUPPLY restrictions). There would, therefore, be an improvement in the balance of trade in volume terms, i.e. in terms of the prices ruling prior to DEVALUA-TION. However, what is important for the BALANCE OF PAY-MENTS is the impact of devaluation on the value of trade. If the price elasticity of exports plus the price elasticity of imports is less than unity, it means that the increased cost of imports in terms of the domestic CURRENCY outweighs the value of the growth in exports. Putting it another way, the improvement in the volume of the balance of trade is not sufficient to offset the fall in the value of the balance of trade occasioned by the devaluation. ⟡ TERMS OF TRADE.

Marshall Plan. ⟡ MARSHALL AID.

Marx, Karl (1818–83). Born in Coblenz, he studied philosophy at the Hegelian Centre at Berlin University, and took a doctorate at Jena. For a time, he was editor of *Rheinische Zeitung*, but the paper was suppressed, and in 1843 he fled to Paris. There he met Friedrich Engels who encouraged in him an interest in political economy. After a brief return to Germany he was banished, and in 1849 he settled in London where he remained until his death in 1883. The *Communist Manifesto*, written jointly by Marx and Engels, was published in 1848. In 1859, the first fruits of his long painstaking research at the British Museum appeared: the *Critique of Political Economy*. The first volume of *Das Kapital* came out in 1867. The remaining volumes, edited by Engels, were published posthumously in 1885 and 1894.

Marx's economics was essentially that of the CLASSICAL SCHOOL, especially of DAVID RICARDO, to whom he owed a great debt. However, he lifted economics out of its preoccupation with agriculture and stationary states. For Marx, CAPITALISM was a stage in the process of evolution removed from the primitive agricultural economy, and moving towards the inevitable elimination of private property and the class structure. Marx attempted a synoptic view of the development of the whole structure of human society. His economics was only a part, though a fundamental part, of his all-embracing sociological and political theories. Marx postulated that the class structures of societies, their political systems and, indeed, their culture, were determined by the way in which societies produced their goods and SERVICES. Moreover, the whole structure was evolutionary. The class structure of a capitalist state was a reflection of the split between owners and non-owners of CAPITAL, which division characterized the manner in which production was carried out, and which already had within it the necessary ingredients of change.

Marx developed from ADAM SMITH and David Ricardo their labour theory of value ($\diamondsuit$ VALUE, THEORIES OF), which held the central place in his economic theory. For Ricardo, the amount of LABOUR used in the production of COMMODITIES was a rough determinant of relative prices in the long run. For Marx, however, the quantity of labour used up in the manufacture of a product determined value, and this value was fundamental and immutable. He did not satisfactorily explain any connection with relative prices. Labour consumption determined exchange value, which differed from use value. The distinction between the two in the case of labour, regarded in itself as a commodity, was a vital one in Marx's analysis. The capitalist pays WAGES which are determined by the exchange value of workers. This exchange value is, in turn, determined by the socially necessary labour time required to 'produce' the worker. That is the labour inputs required to rear, feed, clothe and educate him. However, in return the capitalist gets the labourer's use value. The value of the labourer to the capitalist who uses him is greater than the value the capitalist paid in exchange for his services. This difference Marx called 'surplus value'(s). Only labour yields surplus value. Other FACTORS OF PRODUCTION, such as plant and machinery and raw materials, only reproduce themselves in the productive process. (These ideas have some affinity with the PHYSIOCRATS' '*produit net*', although in their case it was LAND which was the only factor which produced a surplus). The amount of capital required to pay wages Marx called variable (v) ($\diamond$ WAGES FUND), and the remainder he called constant (c). GROSS NATIONAL PRODUCT in the Marxian system therefore is given by $c + v + s$. The ratio of constant capital in total capital $c/c + v$ he called the organic composition of capital. The 'exploitation rate' was s/v. The rate of profit was $s/c + v$. The desire for further wealth, coupled with competition and technical change, induced capitalists to invest from the surplus (which they expropriated from the workers) and in labour-saving machinery. The organic composition of capital therefore rose over time as more was spent on plant and machinery (c) compared with wages (v), with the result that, as only variable capital produced a surplus (and assuming that the exploitation rate remained constant), the rate of profit tended downwards ($\diamond$ PROFIT, FALLING RATE OF). On the one hand, diminishing profits and stronger competition would lead to MONOPOLY and the concentration of WEALTH in a few hands, and on the other hand, there would be an increasing squeeze on the REAL INCOMES of workers by the capitalists in their attempt to maintain PROFITS and the emergence of a large 'reserve army of unemployed' arising from mechanization ($\diamond$ under RICARDO). The class conflict would become increasingly acute until the environment was such that the change inherent in the economic structure would be made manifest by the overthrow of capitalism.

Matrix. An array of numbers set out in rows and columns. For example:

$$\begin{bmatrix} 1 & 2 \\ 3 & 4 \end{bmatrix}, \quad \begin{bmatrix} 5 & 2 \\ 7 & 6 \\ 0 & -3 \end{bmatrix}$$

are matrices. The individual numbers are called the elements of the matrix. It is usual to denote the elements of a matrix by some letter, say 'a', so we would write the matrix as:

$$A = \begin{bmatrix} a_{11} & a_{12} \ldots a_{1h} \\ a_{21} & a_{22} \ldots a_{2n} \\ \cdots \cdots \cdots \cdots \\ a_{m1} & a_{m2} \ldots a_{mn} \end{bmatrix}$$

where each element is now defined by two subscripts, the first of which gives the row in which the element appears, the second the column. For example a_{21} would denote the element in the second row and first column. Since the matrix A above has m rows and n columns, it is said to be of 'order $m \times n$'. Matrices are of considerable importance in modern economics, since many economic MODELS have a mathematical structure which permits representation by matrices. ⬦ INPUT-OUTPUT ANALYSIS; MATRIX ALGEBRA.

Matrix algebra. A branch of mathematics which defines rules by which matrices (⬦ MATRIX) may be added, subtracted, multiplied and divided. It is also concerned with analysing the properties of particular types of matrices, and of particular types of expression involving matrices. Though initially a purely abstract branch of mathematics, it has found considerable application in economics and ECONOMETRICS, because many of the models which they use have a mathematical structure which permits representation by matrices. Indeed, such is the power and relative simplicity of matrix algebra, that matrix-based models are often applied to a problem, even though it is known that they are not strictly appropriate, it being argued that the degree of insight achieved more than makes up for the fact that answers will only be approximate. ⬦ INPUT-OUTPUT ANALYSIS.

Maximand. That which it is desired to maximize. For example, it may be desired to find the level of output which maximizes (makes as large as possible) the profits of a firm. In that case, PROFIT is the maximand.

Maximin strategy. A type of STRATEGY which is suggested by the theory of GAMES as being a rational strategy to adopt in game theoretic situations. It assumes that the player will first of all identify the worst possible outcome which might result from the choice of each of his possible strategies. That is, he finds the minimum outcome for each strategy. He then finds the strategy whose worst possible outcome is better than the worst possible outcome of any other strategy. This is then his maximum strategy.

Mean. ⬦ AVERAGE.

Meade, James Edward (1907–). ⬦ EXCHANGE RATE.

Means test. During the DEPRESSION of the 1930s, benefits in Britain were distributed to those not covered by national unemployment insurance. The level of benefits was decided according to the results of an investigation into the INCOME and WEALTH of the potential recipient and his relations. Today, in Britain, National Assistance is only given to those who can demonstrate that their lack of means justifies assistance. ⬦ UNEMPLOYMENT.

Median. ⟡ AVERAGE.

Medium of exchange. ⟡ MONEY.

Member banks (U.S.). ⟡ COMMERCIAL BANKS.

Memorandum of Association. The document which forms the basis of registration of a company. As required by the Companies Acts, the Memorandum of Association must list the subscribers to the CAPITAL of the company and the number of SHARES they have agreed to take, the name and address of the company, and where appropriate, the powers and objects of the company and that the LIABILITY of its members is limited (⟡ COMPANY LAW). The *Articles of Association* set out the rules by which the company will be administered, e.g. the voting of directors, the calling of meetings.

Menger, Carl (1840–1921). Professor of Economics in the Faculty of Law at Vienna University from 1873–1903. His major work, in which he develops his marginal utility theory, *Grundsatze der Volkswirtschaftslehre*, was published in 1871. He was one of the three economists in the 1870s who independently put forward the theory of VALUE based on MARGINAL UTILITY and whose work had a profound influence on the subsequent evolution of economic thought (⟡ H. H. GOSSEN; W. S. JEVONS; M. E. L. WALRAS). Exchange takes place, he argued, because individuals have different subjective valuations of the same COMMODITY. Menger saw commodities in terms of their reverse order in the productive process, i.e. bread is prior to flour and flour prior to wheat. The PRICE of the first order commodities, which is determined by their exchange for CONSUMPTION, is imputed back through to the higher ordered commodities. The theory of diminishing UTILITY was the catalyst which eventually unified the theories of production and consumption. Menger himself, however, overemphasized consumption demand in the theory of value, just as the CLASSICAL ECONOMISTS had overemphasized production supply (⟡ A. MARSHALL).

Mercantilism. The growth in INTERNATIONAL TRADE and the establishment of the power of the merchant after the medieval era led to the emergence of a body of thought, between the mid sixteenth and late seventeenth century, which was primarily concerned with the relationship between a nation's wealth and its balance of foreign trade. The mercantilists recognized the growing power of the national economy and were in favour of the intervention of the state in economic activity to maximize national WEALTH. Partly because the monetary system was very primitive in relation to the growing needs of economic expansion, mercantilist writing was often overburdened with the identification of national wealth with precious metals. However, its leading writers did make important progress in developing economic thought and made significant contributions to the analysis of international trade problems. ⟡ G. MALYNES; E. MISSELDEN; T. MUN; A. SERRA.

Merchant banks. Institutions that carry out a variety of financial services, including the acceptance of BILLS OF EXCHANGE, the issue and placing of LOANS and SECURITIES, PORTFOLIO management and some BANKING services. Several houses also provide RISK CAPITAL for small firms, deal in gold BULLION, insurance banking and HIRE PURCHASE. Historically, the merchant bankers were merchants dealing in overseas trade who used their knowledge of traders to accept bills of exchange and who developed other banking services connected with foreign trade, e.g. dealing in gold and foreign CURRENCY. Today, their most prominent function is that of advising firms on MERGERS and TAKE-OVERS and other financial matters, and many merchant banks are well known, e.g. Rothschilds, Barings, Hambros, Lazards and Schroders. Merchant banks are also referred to as ISSUING HOUSES, ACCEPTANCE HOUSES or INVESTMENT TRUSTS in exercising particular functions. The merchant banks' deposits amount to only about 10 per cent of those of the COMMERCIAL BANKS and they are in fact relatively small institutions which pride themselves on their personal, flexible management.

Merger. The fusion of two or more separate companies into one. In current usage, merger is a special case of COMBINATION, where both the merging companies wish to join together and do so on roughly equal terms, as distinct from a TAKE-OVER, which occurs against the wishes of one company. However, merger, take-over, amalgamation, absorption and fusion are sometimes all used as synonyms. Where two firms in the same business, i.e. competitors, merge, this is known as horizontal or lateral integration. Where two firms that are suppliers or customers of one another merge, this is known as VERTICAL INTEGRATION. ⟡ CONGLOMERATE; REVERSE TAKE-OVER

Microeconomics. Economic theory is conventionally divided into two parts: (a) microeconomics and (b) MACROECONOMICS. As the names suggest, the difference lies in the level of aggregation at which economic phenomena are studied. Microeconomics is concerned with the study of the individual 'decision units' – the consumer, HOUSEHOLDS, and firms, the way in which their decisions interrelate

to determine relative PRICES of goods and FACTORS OF PRODUC-
TION, and the quantities of these which will be bought and sold.
Its ultimate aim is to understand the mechanism by which the total
amount of RESOURCES possessed by society is allocated among
alternative uses. The central concept in microeconomics is the
MARKET. ⟳ FREE MARKET ECONOMY; PRICE SYSTEM.

Mill, John Stuart (1806–1873). John Stuart Mill's childhood was subjected to a régime of severe educational discipline by his father,
James Mill. He was acquainted with the major works of economics
of the day by the age of twelve, and was correcting the proofs of
his father's book, *Elements of Political Economy*, when he was
thirteen. He learnt Ricardian economics and Benthamite UTILITAR-
IANISM from his father. In 1823, he joined the East India Company,
where he remained for thirty-five years. For three years, before
moving to France to spend his retirement, he was a Member of
Parliament. He was an extraordinarily prolific writer, especially
when it is remembered that he had a full-time job to hold down.
His reputation was made by his *A System of Logic, Ratiocinative and
Inductive, being a connected view of the Principles of Evidence and the
Methods of Scientific Investigation*, which was published in 1843.
His essay *On Liberty* appeared in 1859, and *Examination of Sir
William Hamilton's Philosophy* in 1865. His two most important
works on economics are *Essays on Some Unsettled Questions of
Political Economy* (which came out in 1844, though he actually wrote
it in 1829 when he was only twenty-three) and *Principles of Political
Economy with some of their Applications to Social Philosophy* (1848).
The latter was intended to be a comprehensive review of the field
of economic theory at the time, and was, in fact, an up-to-date
version of ADAM SMITH's *Wealth of Nations*. It succeeded so well
that it remained the basic textbook for students of economics until
the end of the century. The work is regarded as the apogee of the
CLASSICAL SCHOOL of Adam Smith, DAVID RICARDO, T. R.
MALTHUS and J.-B. SAY. Mill himself said the book had nothing
in it that was original, and indeed basically it is an eclectic work,
intended simply to bring together the works of others. However,
it is not true to say that Mill lacked originality altogether. He
analysed the forces which lead to increasing RETURNS TO SCALE,
arguing that as a result there will be a tendency for industries to
become more and more concentrated in a few firms. The advantages
this gave should be set against the disadvantages that will accrue
in the form of higher prices from the loss of competition. Recogni-

tion of this tendency lead him to support strike action by trade unions. Trade unions were a necessary counterweight to the powerful employer (◊ J. K. GALBRAITH). In his exposition of the theory of VALUE, Mill showed how PRICE is determined by the equality of DEMAND and SUPPLY, although he did not demonstrate the relationship by means of graphs or schedules. Mill recognized as a distinct problem the case of COMMODITIES with JOINT COSTS. He showed also how reciprocal demand for each others' products affected countries' TERMS OF TRADE. Mill brought in the idea of ELASTICITY of demand (though the actual expression was invented later by A. MARSHALL) to analyse various alternative trading possibilities. His father had suggested that RENT, being a surplus according to Ricardian theory, was ideally suited to TAXATION. John Stuart took this idea up, and it became quite popular with the public. Mill proposed that all future increases in unearned rents should be taxed (◊ H. GEORGE).

Minimand. That which it is desired to minimize. For example, it may be desired to find the quantities of various INPUTS which minimize (make as small as possible) the COST of producing a particular output level. In that case, cost is the minimand.

Minimum list headings. ◊ STANDARD INDUSTRIAL CLASSIFICATION.

Minorities, Minority interest. Elements shown in the consolidated accounts of groups of companies where one or more of the SUBSIDIARIES is not wholly owned by the parent. Where a company owns 95 per cent of the ordinary CAPITAL of a subsidiary, for example, and its accounts are consolidated, then the whole of the assets and income of the subsidiary will be included in the consolidated accounts. In showing net assets attributable to shareholders of the parent company, 5 per cent in this case (the minority) belongs to the minority shareholders and must be deducted. Similarly, in calculating NET INCOME attributable to the same shareholders, earnings will be shown after minority interest.

Mintage. ◊ BRASSAGE.

Mises, Ludwig Edler von (1881–). Professor at Vienna University from 1913 until he joined the Graduate Institute of International Studies at Geneva in 1934. In 1940, he left Europe for the U.S. and was appointed five years later to a professorial chair at New York University, where he stayed until 1969. His published works include *The Theory of Money and Credit* (1912), *The Free and Prosperous Commonwealth* (1927), *Geldwertstabilisierung und Konjunkturpolitik* (1928), *Bureaucracy* (1944), *Omnipotent Government* (1944), *Human*

Action (1949), *Theory and History: An Interpretation of Social and Economic Evaluation* (1957) and *The Ultimate Foundation of Economic Science* (1962). Von Mises argued in favour of the PRICE SYSTEM as the most efficient basis of RESOURCE ALLOCATION. A PLANNED ECONOMY must be wasteful, because it lacks a price system and cannot institute such a system without destroying its political principles. He applied the MARGINAL UTILITY theory of the AUSTRIAN SCHOOL to develop a new theory of MONEY, and pointed out that UTILITY could be measured ordinally only and not cardinally (⟡ J. R. HICKS). He also outlined a PURCHASING POWER PARITY theory comparable to that of Gustav Cassel. His TRADE CYCLE theory explained fluctuations in terms of an expansion of bank credit in the up-turn which caused a fall in the RATE OF INTEREST and surplus INVESTMENT with a consequent reversal when the MONEY SUPPLY was reduced. ⟲ R. G. HAWTREY; F. A. VON HAYEK.

Misselden, Edward (1608–54). A leading member of the merchant adventurers and a member of the group of writers referred to as MERCANTILISTS. He argued that international movements of specie and fluctuations in the EXCHANGE RATE depended on international trade flows and not the manipulations of bankers, which was the popular view. He suggested that trading returns should be established for purposes of statistical analysis, so that the state could regulate trade with a view to obtaining EXPORT surpluses.

Mixed economy. An economy which contains elements of both private and state enterprise. The U.K. economy is a classic example of this, having both a large PRIVATE SECTOR, and a group of large NATIONALIZED INDUSTRIES. In fact, virtually all economies are to some extent 'mixed', in that no Socialist economy is without some degree of PRIVATE ENTERPRISE, while capitalist economies (⟡ CAPITALISM) invariably have some state-regulated industries. ⟲ NATURAL MONOPOLIES; PUBLIC SECTOR.

Mode. ⟡ AVERAGE.

Model. A theoretical system of relationships which tries to capture the essential elements in a real-world situation. Any real-world problem will, in general, consist of a large number of VARIABLES, and a large number of often quite complex relationships between them. If any headway is to be made in the analysis of such situations, it is necessary to try to isolate the most important elements and to disregard the rest. Although this may mean that a model is 'unrealistic' in the sense that it does not completely describe the real-world situation, it may still give us far more insight into a problem, and far greater predictive ability, than would a less abstract approach which tried to take everything into account (⇩ D. RICARDO).

Monetary policy. That part of economic policy which regulates the level of MONEY or LIQUIDITY in the economy in order to achieve some desired policy objective, such as the control of INFLATION, an improvement in the BALANCE OF PAYMENTS, a certain level of employment, or growth in the GROSS NATIONAL PRODUCT. It contrasts with more direct measures of control, such as TAXATION. ⇩ FISCAL POLICY; QUANTITY THEORY OF MONEY; RADCLIFFE REPORT.

Money. Anything which is generally acceptable as a means of settling DEBT. In present-day economies, money normally consists of LIABILITIES of the government (notes and coin) and of the banks (bank accounts), i.e. money consists of claims held by individuals on banks and the government, these claims being generally acceptable as a means of payment. This use of claims as money is a feature of relatively sophisticated systems of finance and CREDIT. In less well developed systems, articles which possessed intrinsic VALUE (pieces of gold, cows, cigarettes) were used as a means of payment. This difference reflects the importance of economic stability and well-developed financial institutions, since the use of money which has no intrinsic value of its own depends on confidence that it will be universally acceptable in exchange for goods. ⇩ GALLOPING INFLATION; INFLATION; MONEY, FUNCTIONS OF; MONEY SUPPLY.

Money at call and short notice. In Britain, MONEY loaned to the DIS-COUNT HOUSES, i.e. to the MONEY MARKET, on a short-term basis by the COMMERCIAL BANKS. These LOANS are regarded as part of the LIQUID assets of the banks because they can be withdrawn immediately, or at periods of notice of up to fourteen days. They also include overnight loans. The terms of the loans vary, and in practice the money may not be called in for long periods. The discount houses use the money to purchase TREASURY BILLS and other short-term paper, so that the call-money rate is normally always below the treasury bills rate. If the banks do call on their loans, then the discount houses may be forced to borrow from the BANK OF ENGLAND. The commercial banks are willing to loan their liquid funds to the money market in this way, because they know that the Bank of England will act as a LENDER OF LAST RESORT. In most other countries the major commercial banks invest directly in short-term paper and have direct access to the CENTRAL BANK for loans (e.g. ⟡ FEDERAL RESERVE SYSTEM).

Money, functions of. MONEY is generally regarded as fulfilling three functions:

   (a) As a medium of exchange: since a BARTER system may be very cumbersome and inefficient, it is generally found useful to have some good or token which is widely accepted as payment in settlement of DEBTS. Goods can be exchanged for money, which can then be exchanged for other goods, and hence money serves as the medium through which exchange is facilitated. Its ability to perform this function is, in fact, the defining characteristic of money.

   (b) As a unit of account: the units in which money is measured (pounds and pence, dollars and cents, etc.) are generally used as the units in which ACCOUNTS, debts, financial ASSETS, etc., are measured. This is a natural consequence of the use of money as a medium of exchange, although no exchange need be involved in the use of money as a unit of account.

   (c) As a store of value: part of an individual's INCOME may be set aside from immediate CONSUMPTION, and held in some form in order to yield future consumption. Money is one form in which this may be held. Since receipts and payments are never perfectly synchronized, the medium of exchange function of money will, in any case, lead to money being held over time as a store of VALUE or purchasing power. ⟡ TRANSACTIONS MOTIVE.

Money illusion. The propensity to respond to changes in MONEY magnitudes, as if they represented changes in real magnitudes. For example, suppose that we doubled your money INCOME, and the prices of all goods which you could buy. Any set of purchases you previously could afford you can still afford; any set you could not afford still cannot be bought. If the set of purchases you previously made was the one you most preferred out of all those available to you, there is absolutely no reason for you to change it now. On the other hand, if, because your money income has gone up, you feel richer and now buy more of the luxury goods and less of the necessities, you would be said to be 'suffering from' (that is the usual term) money illusion, since you have not realized that your REAL INCOME has remained the same.

Money, inactive. ⟡ INACTIVE MONEY.

Money in circulation. MONEY which is being used to finance transactions, as opposed to idle money (⟡ INACTIVE MONEY).

Money market. The financial institutions that deal in short-term

SECURITIES and LOANS, gold and FOREIGN EXCHANGE. MONEY has a 'time value', and therefore the use of it is bought and sold against payment of INTEREST. Short-term money is bought and sold on the MONEY MARKET, and long-term money on the CAPITAL MARKET. In Britain, the money market sometimes refers only to the DISCOUNT HOUSES and the COMMERCIAL BANKS dealing in TREASURY BILLS, BILLS OF EXCHANGE and MONEY AT CALL, with the BANK OF ENGLAND acting as LENDER OF LAST RESORT. In a wider context, the money market also includes the ACCEPTING HOUSES, the FOREIGN EXCHANGE MARKET and the BULLION market.

Money supply. The amount of MONEY which exists in an economy at a given time. There is not a single definition of exactly what constitutes the money supply. The essence of money is that it be generally acceptable as a means of payment, but this characteristic does not permit a unique definition of the actual money supply. Since notes and coin (nominally, claims against the government, but in fact simply tokens) are an accepted means of payment, they are clearly part of the money supply. In addition, CURRENT ACCOUNTS at banks are through the use of CHEQUES also used to settle DEBTS, and so are also part of the money supply. These two taken together give what can be thought of as the most narrow definition of the money supply. DEPOSIT ACCOUNTS are, strictly speaking, not capable of being used as money – one cannot draw a cheque on a deposit account and use it to settle a debt. Nevertheless, despite the formal rules, it is possible to meet a cheque drawn on one's current account by transferring the appropriate sum from a deposit account virtually at will, and hence a broader definition of the supply of money would also include deposit accounts. It could be argued that other types of LIABILITIES, e.g. the deposits held by a BUILDING SOCIETY, are so LIQUID that they could be included in the money supply, but in general they are excluded. ⇨ DOMESTIC CREDIT EXPANSION; NEAR MONEY; QUANTITY THEORY OF MONEY.

Money terms. ⇨ REAL TERMS.

Monopolist. ⇨ MONOPOLY.

Monopolies Commission. A commission set up by the Monopolies and Restrictive Practices (Inquiry and Control) Act of 1948. Under this Act, the commission was given the necessary powers to obtain any information it needed to investigate monopolies referred to it by the Board of Trade. MONOPOLY was defined in a broad way to include any firm which controlled more than one third of the MARKET, and the commission was required to judge them in the light of the public interest. The commission's report in 1955, *Collective Discrimination – A Report on Exclusive Dealing, Aggregated Rebates and other Discriminatory Trade Practices*, was the basis for the RESTRICTIVE TRADE PRACTICES ACT of 1956, which set up a register for collective agreements and a Restrictive Practices Court. The commission's powers were widened by the Monopolies and Mergers Act of 1965. MERGERS between firms in a monopoly situation or involving ASSETS exceeding £5 million could in future be referred to the commission by the Board of Trade (later the Department of Trade and Industry) and also firms in the service industries which had previously been exempt. In 1970 it was announced that legislation would be introduced to give the commission power to act on its own initiative, to recommend to the Department of Trade and Industry cases for investigation and to give it authority for the first time to study the NATIONALIZED INDUSTRIES. It was also stated that the commission is being 'encouraged to become the expert and authoritative source of information to the government on situations of imperfect competition' (⟡ MONOPOLISTIC COMPETITION).

Monopolistic competition. The market situation in which there is a large number of firms whose outputs are close but not perfect substitutes, either because of product differentiation (⟡ DIFFERENTIATION, PRODUCT), or geographical fragmentation of the MARKET. The fact that the products are not homogeneous means that any one firm may raise its PRICE relative to the prices of its competitors without losing all its sales, so that its DEMAND CURVE is downward-sloping rather than a horizontal straight line (as in PERFECT COMPETITION). The combination of a large number of firms, as in perfect competition, with downward-sloping demand curves, as in MONOPOLY, is responsible for the term 'monopolistic competition'. The theory was developed in the 1930s virtually simultaneously by E. H. CHAMBERLIN in the U.S. and J. V. ROBINSON in the U.K. ⟡ EXCESS CAPACITY.

Monopoly. Strictly speaking, a monopoly exists when a firm or individual produces and sells the entire output of some COMMODITY. The firm is then said to have a monopoly in that commodity, or to be a MONOPOLIST. In practice, however, less stringent definitions are often adopted, e.g. a firm can be referred to the MONOPOLIES COMMISSION as a monopolist if it accounts for more than 33 per cent of MARKET sales. It would be more appropriate in this situation perhaps, to call the Monopolies Commission the 'Oligopolie Commission' (◊ OLIGOPOLY).

Monopoly, discriminating. A MONOPOLY which practices PRIC DISCRIMINATION.

Monopsony. The situation in which there is only a single buyer in MARKET. ◊ MONOPOLY.

Monte Carlo method. An approach to the problem of finding th PROBABILITIES with which the possible outcomes of a give activity, process, experiment, etc., may occur, based on experimenta tion and SIMULATION. This is in contrast to an 'analytical' approach which would use techniques of mathematical statistics to attempt t find a mathematical expression for these probabilities. In man real problems, the complexity of the situation may be such that a analytical solution would be difficult or impossible. The procedur of repeating a large number of times the operation of the activity i the form of a MODEL, and using the results to build up the probabilit values of the outcomes, may then be a cheap and accurate approach This technique has received widespread use in OPERATION RESEARCH.

Mortgage. A legal agreement conveying conditional ownership o ASSETS as SECURITY for a LOAN and becoming void when th DEBT is repaid. BUILDING SOCIETIES and INSURANCE companie (*Mortgagees*) loan a proportion of the purchase PRICE of house: to individuals or companies (*mortgagors*), the property being mort gaged to the lender until the loan is repaid.

Mortgage debenture. ◊ DEBENTURE.

Most favoured nation clause. The clause in an international trade treaty under which the signatories promise to extend to each othe any favourable trading terms offered in subsequent agreements to third parties. ◊ GENERAL AGREEMENT ON TARIFFS AND TRADE.

Moving average. A series of AVERAGES which are calculated from groups of numbers which are in a series. Each group is obtained by adding the next number in the series and omitting the earliest, e.g. consider the series:

$$2 \quad 4 \quad 6 \quad 20 \quad 10$$

and

$$\frac{2+4}{2} = 3; \qquad \frac{4+6}{2} = 5; \qquad \frac{6+20}{2} = 13; \qquad \frac{20+10}{2} = 15$$

so that a new series is generated (3, 5, 13, 15) which is a moving average of the first series. The groups need not be of only two numbers, but could be of three or more depending on the length of the original series. Note that the derived series has reduced the relative size of the jump in the fourth place of the original series. Moving averages are used to smooth out TIME SERIES so that trends can be more easily picked out. ⟡ W. S. JEVONS; E. SLUTSKY.

Multicollinearity. The presence of significant CORRELATION between the INDEPENDENT VARIABLES in a regression model (⟡ REGRESSION ANALYSIS). Its effect is to invalidate some of the assumptions on which LEAST SQUARES REGRESSION is based, and hence to render inappropriate the use of that method, unless modified. The problem of multicollinearity occurs very frequently in econometric studies, and has been extensively studied in the theory of ECONOMETRICS.

Multilateralism. INTERNATIONAL TRADE and exchange between more than two countries without discrimination between those involved. In contrast to BILATERALISM. ⟡ GENERAL AGREEMENT ON TARIFFS AND TRADE; MOST FAVOURED NATION CLAUSE.

Multinational corporation. A company, or, more correctly, an ENTERPRISE, operating in a number of countries and having production or service facilities outside the country of its origin. The multinational corporation takes its principal decisions in a global context and thus often outside the countries in which it has particular operations. The rapid growth of these corporations and the possibility that conflicts might arise between their interests and those of the individual countries in which they operate has provoked much discussion among economists in recent years. Also called *international companies*.

Multiple correlation. The measurement of the degree of association between one VARIABLE on the one hand, and two or more variables on the other. It is thus an extension of simple CORRELATION which considers only the association between two variables. Thus, we may be interested in discovering how strongly expenditure on CONSUMPTION is related to INCOME, family size and WEALTH for a group of families. We would then compute the multiple correlation coefficient, a number lying between zero and one, which expresses how closely expenditure varies with income, family size and wealth over the group. A VALUE close to one would denote very strong association; close to zero, a very weak association. Note that the remarks made about the interpretation of the ordinary correlation coefficient apply equally here, and, in particular, that no CAUSAL relationship can be inferred from a high multiple correlation coefficient. ⟫ PARTIAL CORRELATION; REGRESSION ANALYSIS.

Multiple exchange rates. ♢ EXCHANGE RATE.

Multiplier. A measure of the effect on total NATIONAL INCOME of a unit change in some component of AGGREGATE DEMAND. Suppose that an economy is initially at less than full EMPLOYMENT, with given levels of aggregate INVESTMENT, CONSUMPTION, national income, etc. Then suppose that, for some reason, firms increase the rate of investment expenditure, i.e. they increase their expenditure on plant, machinery and buildings. We then expect national income to increase by the amount of this increase in expenditure. This investment expenditure is paid out as WAGES, salaries, PROFITS, etc., to suppliers of FACTOR services to the investment goods industries. The recipients of this income will save a portion of it, and will spend the rest on buying goods and services, which creates INCOME for the suppliers of those goods and services. At this stage, the total increase in national income is equal to the initial increase in investment expenditure, plus the portion of that increase which is respent, since this respending has in turn generated new income and output. The income generated by the respending will, again, be partly saved and partly spent, in turn generating new income, which is partly saved and partly spent, and so on, *ad infinitum*. The result of this is that the total increase in national income resulting from the initial increase in investment will, in the end, be several times larger than the increase in investment, i.e. it will be some multiple of the increase in investment. The expression which gives the value of this multiple is called the *multiplier*, and the overall effect of the investment increase is called the *multiplier effect*.

To show how the multiplier is determined, suppose that, throughout the economy, a proportion (b) of any increase in income is respent, while the remainder ($1-b$) is saved. If investment increased by, say, 10, then the amount which is respent at the first 'round' is given by $b \times 10$, and so the total income generated by the increase in investment is $10 + 10b$. The amount of income respent, $10b$, has become someone else's income, and this sum will in turn be partly respent. In fact, the proportion respent is $b \times (10b) = 10b^2$. This in turn becomes someone's income, a proportion of which is respent, to give a new increase in income of $b \times (10b^2) = 10b^3$.

And so on. Total new income generated is the sum of the income generated at each stage, i.e. it is: $10 + 10b + 10b^2 + 10b^3 + \ldots$; and it can be shown by elementary algebra that this sum is equal to $10\left(\dfrac{1}{1-b}\right)$. That is, if we know the value of b, and the amount of the increase in investment, then we can find the amount by which income will increase. Now, b is, in fact, the MARGINAL PROPENSITY TO CONSUME, which is generally held to be less than one; so $\dfrac{1}{1-b}$ must be greater than one, e.g. if $b = 0.8$, then $\dfrac{1}{1-b} = 5$. Thus, the increase in income will be some multiple of the increase in investment, the value of this multiple being given by $\dfrac{1}{1-b}$, which is accordingly called 'the multiplier'.

The multiplier has played an important role in MACROECONOMIC analysis since its use by KEYNES as a central element in his MODEL of the economy. When the word 'multiplier' is qualified by the word 'investment', the concept is used to refer only to the multiplier effects of an increase in investment. However, the multiplier concept is of general application, and can be shown to apply just as well to changes in export demand, government expenditure (◊ BUDGET) and TAXATION. Note, however, that if there is full employment in the economy, the simple multiplier described here is unlikely to provide an adequate prediction of the consequences of an increase in investment. This is because the increase in demand for investment goods will cause rising prices and RATES OF INTEREST rather than an increase in REAL INCOME, and although MONEY INCOME may increase, the precise extent to which it does so depends on the way the increases in prices and interest rates affect consumers' expenditure and investment itself.

Multi-product firm. A firm which produces more than one product. Though the standard economic analysis normally considers the single-product firm, it is not difficult to generalize it to the multi-product case. Empirically, of course, the multi-product firm is in the overwhelming majority.

Mun, Sir Thomas (1571–1641). An English mercantilist (◊ MERCANTILISM) and a director of the East India Company. His publications include *Discourse of Trade from England unto the East Indies* (1621) and *England's Treasure by Forraign Trade* (1664). He attacked the idea that EXPORTS of BULLION should be completely prohibited and other restrictions put on trade, pointing out that restrictions on trade invited retaliation in foreign MARKETS and raised domestic PRICES. He did emphasize, however, that an export surplus should be sought in the BALANCE OF TRADE of the country as a whole, although it was unnecessary to seek to achieve this with each trading partner.

Mutual company. A company without issued CAPITAL STOCK owned by those members that do business with it. The PROFITS of a mutual company, after deductions for reserves, are shared out among members. Some SAVINGS banks and INSURANCE companies, e.g. Standard Life, are mutual companies. In the U.S. the term 'mutual' is also used to refer to open-ended INVESTMENT TRUSTS or mutual funds.

Mutual Security Agency. ⟡ ECONOMIC COOPERATION ADMINIS-TRATION.

Myrdal, Gunnar Karl (1898–   ). ⟡ INTEREST, NATURAL RATE OF.

N

National accounts. ◇ SOCIAL ACCOUNTING.

National Board for Prices and Incomes (N.B.P.I.). An independent body set up by the British government in 1965, and abolished in 1971, to examine and report on PRICES and INCOMES with the object of exerting pressure on employers and employees to restrain increases in prices and incomes. The government alone could refer matters to the board for investigation, but the board had no statutory powers. The 1966 Prices and Incomes Act empowered the government to defer price or pay increases until they had been examined by the board. The board had an independent chairman, two deputy chairmen and seven other members including economists, businessmen and a trade unionist, and a secretary. Its secretariat was divided into two divisions: the Prices Review Division and the Incomes Review Division. The Prices and Incomes Board published a series of reports on the results of its investigations.

National debt. The DEBT of the central government EXCHEQUER. In the U.K., this debt is transacted through the CONSOLIDATED FUND, from which LOANS are made to the NATIONALIZED INDUSTRIES, etc. Some definitions may in fact include the debt of the whole of the public sector, i.e. that of the nationalized industries, local authorities, etc. The net national debt excludes the LIABILITIES held by government departments themselves. Claims on the Consolidated Fund are held in a wide range of paper SECURITIES which are divided into three groups:

(a) Non-marketable securities. These include National Savings Certificates, DEFENCE BONDS and PREMIUM SAVINGS BONDS. They totalled £8,023 million in 1970.

(b) The 'FLOATING DEBT', which includes TREASURY BILLS (◇ BANKING), which have a life of three months, and 'WAYS AND MEANS ADVANCES', which are advances to the fund made by the BANK OF ENGLAND. This group totalled £3,847 million in 1970/71.

(c) The third, and largest, group includes all the marketable securities, and covers the whole range of LIQUIDITY from the irredeemable bonds (FUNDED DEBT) such as 2½ per cent CONSOLS (consolidated stock), to the short-dated stocks, such as $6\frac{1}{4}$ per cent Exchequer loan 1972.

Between 1958 and 1970, the net national debt increased from £27,200 million to £39,000 million. Although it fell from about 1·4 times the NATIONAL INCOME to 0·9 times national income, the proportion of debt to national income is higher in the U.K. than other developed countries. (In West Germany, for instance, it is only about 30 per cent.) The bigger the debt the more difficult it is to manage in a way consistent with the needs for controlling the economy. By buying and selling on the MARKET, the central government can regulate the degree of liquidity in the economy. ⇨ BALANCED BUDGET; QUANTITY THEORY OF MONEY; RADCLIFFE COMMITTEE.

National development bond. A five-year government BOND introduced in 1964 and reissued from time to time at different RATES OF INTEREST. The maximum holding for any one issue is £2,500.

National Economic Development Council (N.E.D.C.). An economic development council, known as 'Neddy', set up by the U.K. government in 1962. It has the Chancellor of the EXCHEQUER as chairman and consists of leading figures from industry and the trade unions. It has a secretariat office (N.E.D.O.). In 1964, the first of over twenty economic development committees ('Little Neddies') was set up. These committees were each to study the problems preventing the growth of specific industries or services, and to make recommendations.

National Economic Development Office (N.E.D.O.). ⇨ NATIONAL ECONOMIC DEVELOPMENT COUNCIL.

National income. A measure of the MONEY value of the total flow of goods and services produced in an economy over a specified period of time. It can be calculated in three ways:

(a) As the value of the outputs of all goods and services in the economy, net of indirect taxes (⇨ DIRECT TAXATION) and SUBSIDIES, and corrected for inter-industry sales so as to avoid double-counting (⇨ VALUE ADDED).

(b) As the total flow of INCOMES paid out to HOUSEHOLDS in return for the supply of productive services, plus PROFITS retained by firms as reserves.

(c) As the sum of expenditure on consumers' goods and INVESTMENT goods, government expenditure (⇨ BUDGET), and expenditure by foreigners on our EXPORTS less domestic expenditure on IMPORTS.

In principle, each of these methods of measurement should give the same result, since the flow of expenditure on goods and services must equal the sales value of those goods and services, which in turn must equal the incomes paid out by firms as WAGES, salaries, INTEREST, DIVIDENDS, RENT, etc., plus undistributed profits. However, in practice, because of measurement problems, the three separate estimates of national income usually diverge, and the value finally adopted is a 'compromise estimate' of the three.

Since national income measures the flow of goods and services produced, its level can be taken as an indicator of the well-being of the economy, though, clearly, it can never be a perfect indicator of this. The latter depends not only on the size of the flow of goods and services, but also on the way in which this is distributed among households ($\Leftrightarrow$ INCOME DISTRIBUTION), the quality of the goods themselves, the state of the environment, etc., which need by no means improve with a rising national income.

National income is defined to include not only the incomes which arise from production within the economy, but also income which accrues to domestic residents from activities carried on abroad. Given also that it is calculated net of indirect taxes, it is identical to GROSS NATIONAL PRODUCT AT FACTOR COST. If we deducted an amount equal to DEPRECIATION, it would then be identical to NET NATIONAL PRODUCT AT FACTOR COST.

National Insurance. A social security scheme in the U.K. which provides UNEMPLOYMENT benefit, sickness benefit, flat-rate pensions, maternity benefits, childrens' allowances and other grants or benefits on widowhood, incapacity or death in return for regular weekly flat-rate contributions. These contributions are shared by employees and employers and paid by affixing stamps on an insurance card. The stamps also cover the National Health Service contribution and the SELECTIVE EMPLOYMENT TAX. Unless contracted out as members of an approved pension scheme, employees and employers also contribute to a Graduated Pension Scheme which provides an earning-related supplement to the flat-rate pension. Graduated contributions are collected through the PAY-AS-YOU-EARN system. A new scheme of occupational pensions related to earnings will come into effect in 1975.

National plan. The U.K. National Plan was prepared by the DEPARTMENT OF ECONOMIC AFFAIRS and published in September 1965. The plan was 'designed to achieve a 25 per cent increase in national output between 1964 and 1970'. It was severely criticized for being

297

over-optimistic, and these criticisms were proved justified in the light of the subsequent actual rates of growth of between 2 and 3 per cent per annum in national output instead of the expected 4 per cent. In February 1969, the D.E.A. published a much more limited planning document entitled *The Task Ahead*, which they described as being merely 'an economic assessment to 1972' in which various growth rates were considered, ranging from $2\frac{1}{2}$ to $3\frac{1}{2}$ per cent per annum between 1968 and 1972. ⟡ PLANNED ECONOMY.

National product. ⟡ NATIONAL INCOME.

National Research and Development Corporation (N.R.D.C.). A body set up in the U.K. by the Development of Inventions Act 1948 to stimulate innovation, provide funds for private inventors and to hold or dispose of the rights of inventions resulting from public research.

Nationalized industries. Industries owned and controlled by the state. In the U.K., the Labour government of 1945–50 carried out a programme for the nationalization of the major industries. The electricity, gas, coal and iron and steel industries were nationalized, as were also civil aviation, inland transport and the BANK OF ENGLAND. Subsequent Conservative governments denationalized most of road transport and the iron and steel industries. The Labour government of 1964–1970 restored the latter to state ownership, and changed the status of the Post Office from that of a civil service department to that of a nationalized industry. Control over these industries is exercised by the appropriate Minister working through his Department; by the Minister's exercise of his right to appoint chairmen; by the select committees of the House of Commons, which can call the management to account; and through questions in Parliament. Government White Papers have been published which lay down the financial obligations of these industries and the principles upon which they should operate. Some kind of target, such as a specified RATE OF RETURN on CAPITAL employed, is set for each to achieve over a certain time period, such as five years. In addition, they are required to set their PRICES on the basis of MARGINAL COSTS as far as possible. Government SUBSIDIES are available only for those operations which, although they cannot be run profitably, nevertheless should not be closed down for social reasons (⟡ BEECHING PLAN).

Natural monopolies. Monopolies with ECONOMIES OF SCALE over a large range of outputs, so that one firm can produce at lower AVERAGE COSTS than could more than one. Examples of natural monopolies are the electricity and gas industries. Having several companies supplying a given area would result in multiplication of cables, transformers, pipelines, etc., and a granting of MONOPOLY rights would seem the most efficient thing to do. The recognition of the inevitable trend towards monopolization in such industries has meant that, from their early history, and in most countries, there has been state regulation of these monopolies, and, in fact, in the U.K. virtually all natural monopolies are owned by the state or municipal authorities.

'Near' money. An expression applied to an ASSET which is transferable and which therefore can be passed in settlement of DEBT, but has not achieved the monetary status of BANK-NOTES, coins and CHEQUES, e.g. a BILL OF EXCHANGE. ⬧ QUANTITY THEORY OF MONEY.

'Neddy'. ⬧ NATIONAL ECONOMIC DEVELOPMENT COUNCIL.

Net assets. The CAPITAL employed in a business. It is calculated from the BALANCE SHEET by taking fixed ASSETS plus current assets less current LIABILITIES. Often used as a basis for calculating RATE OF RETURN on CAPITAL.

Net Book Agreement. The Net Book Agreement between publishers and booksellers came into force in 1900. The agreement laid down that books designated by publishers as net books should be subject to the terms of the agreement. Under this agreement, net books are not supplied to a bookseller unless he agrees to sell them at not less than their published PRICE. Any default by a bookseller could lead to him being stop-listed collectively by the publishers, and his source of supply of books on trade terms cut off. In 1933, an amendment allowed booksellers to grant a 10 per cent discount to recognized public libraries. In a judgement delivered in 1962 under the RESTRICTIVE TRADE PRACTICES ACT of 1956, it was deemed to be in the public interest that RESALE PRICE MAINTENANCE should be continued on books.

Net capital employed. ⬧ CAPITAL EMPLOYED.

Net capital formation. ⬧ CAPITAL FORMATION.

Net cash flow. ⬧ CASH FLOW.

Net domestic product. GROSS DOMESTIC PRODUCT less DEPRECIATION.

Net income. Net PROFIT on earnings after tax and, where appropriate, after MINORITY INTEREST.

Net investment. Gross expenditure on CAPITAL FORMATION, minus the amount required to replace worn-out and obsolete plant and equipment. This therefore gives a measure of the change in CAPITAL STOCK. It may in fact be negative, if not enough expenditure is made to replace DEPRECIATION fully.

Net national product. GROSS NATIONAL PRODUCT less DEPRECIATION.

Net output. ⬦ VALUE ADDED.

Net profit. ⬦ PROFIT.

Net tangible asset ratio. ⬦ FINANCIAL RATIOS.

Net worth. The worth of a business to its owners according to the BALANCE SHEET, i.e. the EQUITY of its proprietor or shareholders at BOOK VALUE. It is calculated from the balance sheet by taking the total share CAPITAL (the NOMINAL VALUE of ORDINARY SHARES and PREFERENCE SHARES) and adding to it the free reserves (retained PROFITS, including CAPITAL GAINS). Alternatively, net worth is arrived at by subtracting third-party claims on a business's ASSETS from its total assets, i.e. total assets minus long-term DEBT, MINORITY INTEREST, future TAX and CURRENT LIABILITIES. A synonym for *shareholders' interest*.

Net worth ratio. ⬦ FINANCIAL RATIOS.

New Deal. The U.S. Federal government, under President Roosevelt, began, in 1933, a number of projects designed to give financial assistance and work to the large number of people thrown out of employment by the great DEPRESSION, which followed the stock market collapse on Wall Street in 1929. This change of policy was called the New Deal. It met with a certain amount of opposition, because it lead to budget deficits. (⬦ BALANCED BUDGET). ⬦⬦ J. M. KEYNES.

New issue market. That part of the CAPITAL MARKET serving as the market for new long-term CAPITAL. Those institutions needing capital (industrial, commercial and financial companies and public authorities) offer SHARES and SECURITIES, usually through FINANCIAL INTERMEDIARIES, which are then purchased by each other and the general public. Although internally generated funds provide the bulk of the capital required by business, the new issue market is not only absolutely large, but of considerable importance, especially for larger businesses. The new issue market does not include certain other sources of new long-term external finance, such as MORTGAGES and other LOANS from financial institutions. Borrowers in the new issue market may be raising capital for new INVESTMENT, or they may be converting private capital into public capital; this is known as 'going public' (⬦ PUBLIC COMPANY).

In the U.K. gross issues by quoted public companies, local authorities and overseas borrowers amounted to £1,328 million in 1968. However, redemptions totalled £335 million so that net new issues were £993 million in 1968. In addition, the central government made gross cash issues of marketable securities of £681 million, although its cash redemptions were considerably in excess of this figure, so that net government issues were negative in that particular year. Of net new issues by quoted companies and local authorities the most important class of new issues are those for LOAN CAPITAL, which accounted for £608 million in 1968, or nearly 60 per cent of the total. The whole of the remainder is accounted for by ORDINARY SHARES; PREFERENCE SHARES have declined in importance for some years now, and in 1968 redemptions exceeded new issues by £10 million.

The largest concerns are able to issue stocks and shares direct to the public. These stocks and shares will normally be quoted on the STOCK EXCHANGE. Other concerns will raise their new capital through an ISSUING HOUSE that will either underwrite the issue or first purchase the securities and then offer them for sale to the public. In all cases the issues will actually be handled by an ISSUING BROKER. A full prospectus describing the company and its prospects as well as public advertising are necessary, and, for smaller issues, say under £250,000, costs can be reduced by private placing, that is by selling the shares to INSURANCE companies or other investors. Quoted companies may issue unquoted shares in this way, although the volume of business is relatively small (less than 5 per cent of new issues by quoted companies in recent years). Rather larger amounts are raised by private placing by other PUBLIC COMPANIES which have no quoted securities, but PRIVATE COMPANIES have no access to the new issue markets, since they cannot achieve quotations while retaining their private status. Well-established companies can greatly reduce the cost of raising new capital by offering shares to their existing shareholders by what are known as 'RIGHTS ISSUES'. Rights issues save the cost of advertising, issuing brokers and underwriting commissions, although the shares will normally have to be offered at well below market price to ensure the issue is fully taken up. The difficulty that smaller quoted and unquoted companies experience in raising new long-term capital was noted in the 1931 Macmillan Report (▷ MACMILLAN COMMITTEE), although a number of new institutions have since emerged to meet this need outside the new issue market. ▷▷ BOLTON COMMITTEE.

The new issue market, like the rest of the capital market, is increasingly becoming an international one. Foreign and Commonwealth public authorities still raise significant sums on the London market, and public companies, especially the so-called MULTINATIONAL CORPORATIONS, are increasingly doing so. British companies also raise money in overseas capital markets.

Nominal value. The FACE VALUE of a SHARE or BOND, which may be more or less than its market price. ⟡ PAR VALUE.

Nominal yield. The return or YIELD on a SECURITY in which DIVIDEND or INTEREST is expressed as a percentage of the NOMINAL VALUE of the security as opposed to its market price.

Non-linear programming. A mathematical technique for solving certain classes of problem. Just like LINEAR PROGRAMMING, the problem is to find the best values of some set of VARIABLES, given the existence of constraints. The main difference, as the name suggests, is that at least one of the relationships in the problem will not be linear. It is true to say that non-linear problems occur in practice more often than linear problems. However, because of its special nature, the linear version is much easier to solve, and so a linear form will always be substituted for a non-linear form, whenever it is thought to be a close enough approximation.

Non-price competition. Policies which a seller may use to attract customers away from rival sellers, but which do not involve PRICE reduction. The most common of such policies are ADVERTISING, use of 'free-gift' schemes, exclusive contracts with distributors, style, quality and design changes, etc.

Normal competitive return. ⟡ PROFIT.

Normal profit. ⟡ PROFIT.

Normative. Concerned with values, ethics, opinions of what *ought* to be rather than what is. Thus, normative propositions would be: sin is bad; UNEMPLOYMENT is too high; the faster the rate of growth of NATIONAL INCOME, the better for the country; INFLATION ought to be stopped.

O

Obsolescence. A reduction in the useful life of a CAPITAL good or consumer DURABLE GOOD through economic or technological change or any other external changes, as distinct from physical deterioration in use (DEPRECIATION). For example, a new process or machine may be developed, which renders existing equipment uneconomic, because a firm could significantly reduce its costs by scrapping its existing machinery, even though it might still have many years of physical life. Then the old equipment has become obsolescent. 'Planned obsolescence' is a term used to describe the way certain consumer durables, e.g. motor-cars, are altered in appearance or performance so that users will wish to buy new ones earlier than they would otherwise have done. In this instance, a consumer's UTILITY or satisfaction is said to be reduced subjectively by the knowledge that his car is not the latest model, even though its performance has not deteriorated in any way.

Ohlin, Bertil (1899–). ⟡ HECKSCHER-OHLIN PRINCIPLE.

Oligopolistic markets. ⟡ OLIGOPOLY.

On cost. The contribution of the COST of OVERHEADS added to the direct costs of production.

Oligopoly. A type of MARKET in which there is a relatively high degree of CONCENTRATION; that is, a small number of firms account for a large proportion of output, employment, etc. The essential feature of this market form is the high degree of interdependence among the decisions of the firms, which will generally be recognized by them. The result of this is that each seller must predict the reactions of his competitors before he can determine the consequences of any decision he might take. This obviously creates considerable RISK and UNCERTAINTY in the industry, and partly because of this, and partly because their PROFITS will be higher thereby, it is generally argued that oligopolists will adopt some kind of policy of COLLUSION. The most usual form will be an agreement to avoid price competition, although the firms may well compete through PRODUCT DIFFERENTIATION, particularly in consumer good industries. Because of the tendency for prices to be well above costs, and for expenditure on product differentiation to be excessive, collusive oligopolies have received a good deal of criticism from economists both in the U.K. and the U.S. (⟡ ANTI-TRUST; MONOPOLIES COMMISSION). It appears that oligopolies are becoming an increasingly important feature of the modern economy. ⟡⟡ GAMES, THEORY OF; MONOPOLY.

Open market operation. ⟡ BANK OF ENGLAND.

Open pricing. A form of restrictive practice (⟡ RESTRICTIVE TRADE PRACTICES ACT) in which firms in an industry circulate details of their prices and PRICE changes among themselves or through a trade association, in the expectation that this will encourage price conformity. Price conformity may, of course, occur even in the absence of open pricing through price leadership. ⟡⟡ OLIGOPOLY.

Opening prices. The PRICES at which dealings start at the commencement of business in a MARKET. In the STOCK EXCHANGE, for example, at the time of official opening dealers must begin by quoting prices before they have a full appreciation of the relative strength of SUPPLY and DEMAND. If they have reason to think that demand will be heavy where favourable news has been released overnight, then they will mark up their opening prices, compared with the closing prices of the previous day.

Operating cost (U.S.). A term for prime VARIABLE COST.

Operating profit. The difference between total revenue and total operating costs (or VARIABLE COSTS) and before deduction of FIXED COSTS. ⟡⟡ PROFIT

Operating ratios. Various measures of the efficiency of a business, e.g. the operating rate or CAPACITY UTILIZATION RATE, the stock–sales ratio, LABOUR turnover ratio, the creditor-debtor ratio and other FINANCIAL RATIOS.

Operations research. An interdisciplinary field of activity which attempts to develop procedures for finding OPTIMUM solutions to management problems. To do this, it has to identify the problems, construct MODELS of them and then use solution techniques to obtain from the models solutions which can be applied to the real problem. It draws heavily on mathematics, engineering and economics for both its personnel and its methods. At the same time, its concern with practical problems has provided considerable stimulus to these disciplines to extend the analysis of problems of optimization in general. Among the most useful techniques in operations research are CRITICAL-PATH ANALYSIS, DISCOUNTED CASH FLOW, INVENTORY ANALYSIS and LINEAR PROGRAMMING.

Opportunity cost. ⟡ COST.

Optimal resource allocation. ⟡ ECONOMIC EFFICIENCY.

Optimum. A word which occurs frequently in economics, and which means simply the best value which some VARIABLE can take, with reference to some particular objective. For instance, if a firm's objective is to maximize PROFITS, its optimum or best output is that at which profits are a maximum; alternatively, this output might simply be referred to as the optimum.

Option. An agreement with a seller or buyer permitting the holder to buy or sell, if he chooses to do so, at a given PRICE within a given period. In the STOCK EXCHANGE, an option may be purchased from a dealer, giving the right to purchase a certain number of SHARES at a certain price within a certain time, e.g. a three-month option. If, in the meantime, the price falls by more than the cost of the option, then the dealer will lose and the purchaser gain, and *vice-versa*. An option to buy is a 'CALL OPTION', an option to sell is a *put option*, and one to buy or sell is a *double option*.

Order numbers. ⇨ STANDARD INDUSTRIAL CLASSIFICATION.

Ordinal utility. A concept of UTILITY based on the idea of preference rankings, or orderings, rather than on the measurability of utility. ⇨ INDIFFERENCE ANALYSIS; INDIFFERENCE CURVE.

Ordinary share. Shares in the EQUITY capital of a business entitling the holders to all distributed PROFITS after the holders of DEBENTURES and PREFERENCE SHARES have been paid.

Organization for Economic Cooperation and Development (O.E.C.D.). The O.E.C.D. came into being in September 1961, renaming and extending the ORGANIZATION FOR EUROPEAN ECONOMIC COOPERATION. It was based on the convention signed in Paris in December 1960 by the original member countries of the O.E.E.C., plus Spain, the U.S. and Canada. In 1964 Japan also became a member. The aims of the O.E.C.D. are (a) to encourage economic growth and high employment with financial stability among member countries, and (b) to contribute to the economic development of the less advanced member and non-member countries and the expansion of world multilateral trade (MULTILATERALISM). The organization carries out its functions through a number of committees – viz. the Economic Policy Committee, the Committee for Scientific Research, the Trade Committee, the Development Assistance Committee – serviced by a large secretariat. It publishes regular statistical bulletins covering the main economic statistics of member countries and regular reviews of the economic prospects of individual members. It also publishes *ad hoc* reports of special studies covering a wide range of subjects, e.g. world POPULATION growth, agricultural surpluses, etc. The O.E.C.D. has been particularly important as a forum for the industrial countries to discuss international monetary problems and in promoting aid and technical assistance for DEVELOPING COUNTRIES. ⟳ INTERNATIONAL MONETARY FUND.

Organization for European Economic Cooperation (O.E.E.C.). After a speech by the U.S. Secretary of State, General Marshall, offering U.S. aid to post-war Europe, a conference was held in Paris in July 1947 which established a Committee of European Economic Cooperation for the coordination of the economic recovery programme of Western Europe. In April 1948, a convention was signed in Paris by the Ministers of sixteen European countries and allied representatives for Germany. The sixteen countries were Austria, Belgium, Denmark, France, Greece, Iceland, Eire, Italy, Luxembourg, the Netherlands, Norway, Portugal, Sweden, Switzerland, Turkey and the U.K. Under the agreement, multilateral trading (⟳ MULTILATERALISM) was to be re-established and a multilateral payments system and trade adjustments or restrictions reduced. Its immediate function was to propose a recovery programme and to carry it out. This meant the efficient distribution of American aid under the EUROPEAN RECOVERY PROGRAMME between 1948 and 1952. At the same time, quantitative IMPORT restrictions were steadily reduced by the O.E.E.C. The EUROPEAN PAYMENTS UNION, which was established in July 1950, was the agency through which the O.E.E.C. fulfilled its obligation to institute a multilateral payments system. In subsequent years considerable progress was made in freeing LABOUR and CAPITAL movements and payments among member countries. The O.E.E.C. opened negotiations for the setting up of a EUROPEAN FREE TRADE AREA linking the EUROPEAN ECONOMY COMMUNITY with the other member countries, but they proved abortive in the face of opposition from the E.E.C. In September 1961, to mark its widening and changing functions, the O.E.E.C. was replaced by the ORGANIZATION FOR ECONOMIC COOPERATION AND DEVELOPMENT, which included Canada and the U.S. as full members.

Ottawa Agreements. ⟳ COMMONWEALTH PREFERENCE.

Outlay. ⟳ COST.

Output budgeting. ⟳ PROGRAMME, PLANNING, BUDGETING SYSTEM.

Over capacity. ⟳ EXCESS CAPACITY.

Over-full employment. Empirical studies, especially those made in connection with the Phillips curve (⇨ A. W. H. PHILLIPS), have suggested that there is some minimum level of UNEMPLOYMENT of the LABOUR FORCE consistent with maintenance of WAGE and PRICE stability. If unemployment should fall below this level, there will tend to be wage and price INFLATION, and, correspondingly, such a level of employment of the labour force is referred to as 'over-full employment'. Essentially, it refers to a condition where DEMAND for goods and services is high relative to the maximum productive capacity of the economy, thus creating inflationary pressures in markets for goods and LABOUR. ⇨ F. W. PAISH.

Over-subscription. Where a new issue of SHARES is made and the demand for the shares exceeds the number on offer, the issue is said to be over-subscribed. It is, of course, extremely difficult for the ISSUING HOUSE to estimate precisely the price at which a share issue will be fully taken up, and new issues are usually either over- or under-subscribed. It is very common for an attractive issue to be ten times or more over-subscribed, especially because of purchases by STAGS – speculators who subscribe to new issues in the expectation that they will be over-subscribed and that dealings will begin at a PREMIUM. Very often new issues that start at a premium fall back to below the issue price as a result of PROFIT-TAKING by Stags.

Overdraft. A LOAN facility on a customer's CURRENT ACCOUNT at a bank permitting him to overdraw up to a certain agreed limit for an agreed period. INTEREST is payable on the amount of the loan facility actually taken up, and it may, therefore, be a relatively inexpensive way of financing a fluctuating requirement. The terms of the loan are normally that it is repayable on demand, or at the expiration of the agreement, and it is thus distinct from a TERM LOAN.

Overheads. ⇨ FIXED COSTS.

Over the counter market (U.S.). A SECONDARY MARKET in which unquoted SHARES are bought and sold to the general public by JOBBERS and BROKERS outside the STOCK EXCHANGE.

Overtime. The hours worked in excess of the standard number of hours of work laid down in the conditions of employment. Hourly-paid employees are normally paid at a higher rate per hour for overtime than for standard hours, and it is therefore in their interests to get the number of standard hours reduced. The amount of overtime worked fluctuates in response to movements in AGGREGATE DEMAND. However, from 1955 to 1968 the standard number of hours worked per week in the U.K. fell by about 9 per cent to just over forty hours, whereas the number of hours actually worked per week has fallen by just over 5 per cent to about forty-four and a half hours per week.

Overtrading. A firm is said to be overtrading when it has insufficient WORKING CAPITAL to meet the needs of its present level of business. For example, a firm which doubled its production, and then found that it could not meet all its current expenditure because too much CAPITAL was tied up in stocks and work in progress, would be overtrading, even though it had correctly forecast the demands for its products.

Overvalued currency. ⇨ UNDERVALUED CURRENCY.

P

Paasche Index. An INDEX NUMBER which measures the change in some aspect of a group of items over time, using weights based on current rather than past values. For example, the Paasche PRICE index finds the percentage increase of current prices over prices at some base period by dividing the total cost of the current purchases made by consumers, at today's prices, by the total cost of those same purchases at the prices prevailing at the base date. Similarly, a Paasche quantity index finds the percentage increase of current quantities purchased over quantities purchased at some base date, by dividing the total cost of the quantities currently purchased, valued at today's prices, by the total cost of the quantities purchased at the base date, again valued at current prices. In the first of these examples, the weights (⟡ WEIGHTED AVERAGE) used are current quantities purchased. In the second, the weights are current prices. A disadvantage of the Paasche Index is that because the weights are changing from year to year, comparison can only be made between any given year and the base year. ⟡ INDEX NUMBER PROBLEM; LASPEYRES INDEX.

Paid-up capital. That part of the ISSUED CAPITAL of a company that has been paid up by the shareholders. It is extremely rare among SHARES dealt with on the London STOCK EXCHANGE for the issued capital not to be paid up, and the phrase is sometimes used loosely as a synonym for issued capital to distinguish it from AUTHORIZED CAPITAL.

Paish, Frank Walter (1898–). Educated at Trinity College, Cambridge, Professor Paish was employed by the Standard Bank of South Africa Ltd, from 1921 until 1932 when he took up a post as Lecturer in Commerce at the London School of Economics. During the Second World War, he was Deputy Director of Programmes of the Ministry of Aircraft Production. From 1949 until his retirement in 1965 he was Professor of Economics (with special reference to Business Finance) at the London School of Economics. His major published works include *The Post-War Financial Problem and Other Essays* (1950), *Business Finance* (1953), *Studies in an Inflationary Economy* (1962) and *Long-Term and Short-Term Interest Rates* (1966). Professor Paish has argued that the post-war INFLATION in the

309

U.K. has been generated by EXCESS DEMAND rather than rising production costs (DEMAND PULL rather than COST PUSH). He has advocated that, as a consequence, an incomes policy (◊ PRICES AND INCOMES POLICY) is irrelevant and the right policy would be to maintain a degreee of spare capacity in the economy of over 2 per cent. The view that the British economy could not run near to full capacity without generating WAGE inflation had a strong influence over government policy in the 1960s. ◊ R. F. HARROD; PHILLIPS CURVE.

Paper profit. An unrealized MONEY increase in the VALUE of an ASSET or assets. An individual, for example, will have made a paper profit on his house if it is worth more now than it was when he bought it.

'Paradox of value'. MARGINAL UTILITY.

Parameter. A constant term in an algebraic equation. For example, in the relationship $y = 3x + 2$, the numbers 3 and 2 are parameters.

Pareto, Vilfredo Federico Damaso (1848–1923). An Italian, born in Paris, Pareto was trained as, and practised as, an engineer. He succeeded his father to a post in the Italian Railways, and in 1874 was appointed Superintendent of Mines for the Banca Nazionale, Florence. He succeeded LÉON WALRAS to the Chair of Economics in the Faculty of Law at Lausanne University in 1892. His publications include *Cours d'économie politique* (1896–7) and *Manuale di Economica Politica* (1906). He retired in 1907. He developed analytical economics from the foundation laid by Walras. He pointed out the shortcomings of any theory of VALUE in so far as it rested upon assumptions of measurable or 'cardinal' rather than ORDINAL UTILITY. He demonstrated that an effective theory of consumer behaviour and exchange could be constructed on assumptions of ordinal utility alone. Exchange would take place in a competitive MARKET between individuals such that the ratios of the MARGINAL UTILITIES of the goods traded equalled the ratio of their prices. An optimum point of exchange could be defined without the need to compare one individual's total UTILITY with another's. He defined an increase in total welfare as occurring in those conditions in which some people are better off as a result of the change, without at the same time anybody being worse off. Pareto's work in this field, coupled with the development of INDIFFERENCE CURVE analysis, invented by F. Y. EDGEWORTH, was the foundation upon which modern WELFARE ECONOMICS is based. A study of the distribution of personal incomes in an economy led him to postulate what became known as *Pareto's law*, that whatever the political or TAXA-

TION conditions, INCOME will be distributed in the same way in all countries. He noted that the distribution of the number of incomes is heavily concentrated among the lower income groups, and asserted that the number of incomes fell proportionately with the size of income. Pareto's law has not, in fact, proved valid in its strict sense. ⟡ ECONOMIC EFFICIENCY; INCOME DISTRIBUTION; E. SLUTSKY.

Pareto-optimal. ⟡ ECONOMIC EFFICIENCY.

Pareto's law. ⟡ V. F. D. PARETO.

Par rate of exchange. ⟡ EXCHANGE RATE.

Par value. The PRICE at which a SHARE or other SECURITY is issued, i.e. the FACE VALUE or NOMINAL VALUE of the INVESTMENT. A share is said to be standing above par if its quoted price on the STOCK EXCHANGE is greater than that at which the share was issued. The term is also used to describe the official EXCHANGE RATE of CURRENCIES in terms of gold and U.S. dollars, as declared to the INTERNATIONAL MONETARY FUND.

Paris Club. ⟡ INTERNATIONAL MONETARY FUND.

Partial correlation. Analysis of the CORRELATION between two VARIABLES which takes into account the fact that one or both of those variables is also correlated with some other specified variable or variables. Procedures are then used to eliminate the influence of the other variable or variables from the measure of the correlation between the two in question. The resulting correlation coefficient is known as the *partial correlation coefficient.*

Partial equilibrium analysis. The analysis of the determination of EQUILIBRIUM positions for a small part of the economy. That is, we take perhaps a single consumer, a single MARKET, or a small group of markets, and examine the determination of their equilibrium positions. Such a position is called a *partial equilibrium.* ⟡ GENERAL EQUILIBRIUM ANALYSIS.

Participation rate. The proportion of the population who are of working age, and who are part of the LABOUR FORCE of the economy, i.e. the 'economically active' part of the population. The participation rate is of interest in analysis of 'regional problems', i.e. the problems which arise out of the existence of significant differences in employment, INCOME levels, rate of economic growth, etc., between the regions of a country. In general, participation rates among men show little regional variation, but those among women are far more marked, reflecting primarily differences in regional industrial structure. Given the evidence, therefore, that women are prepared to go out to work in industry when opportunities exist, the high regional disparities suggest the existence of a significant margin of unused female labour.

Partnership. An unincorporated business formed by the association of from two to twenty persons who share RISKS and PROFITS. The legal basis of partnerships is determined by the Partnership Act of 1890. Except in a limited partnership, which, although a legal institution since 1907, is still relatively unusual in Britain, each partner is liable for the DEBTS and the business actions of the others, to the full extent of his own RESOURCES (although he is taxed as an individual). Partnerships are a common form of organization in the professions, and in businesses where CAPITAL requirements are relatively small, e.g. retail shops and other service trades. Partnerships, with sole traders ($\diamond$ SOLE PROPRIETORSHIP), i.e. self-employed persons working on their own, account for about 85 per cent of the total number of businesses. For the tax treatment of partnerships, $\diamond$ CORPORATION TAX.

Passive. An old-fashioned term for a BALANCE OF PAYMENTS deficit on CURRENT ACCOUNT.

Pawnbroker. A person who lends MONEY against a pledged article which he is free to sell if the LOAN is not repaid with INTEREST within a stated period. The article, which is a form of COLLATERAL SECURITY, might be clothing, jewellery or the tools of a man's trade. Pawnbrokers today are principally traders in used goods, and, as a CREDIT institution, pawnbroking is of very small and declining significance.

Pay-as-you-earn (P.A.Y.E.). System of collecting INCOME TAX through regular deduction by the employer from weekly or monthly earnings. Confidentiality of the taxpayer's private circumstances is preserved through the use of code numbers, which, in conjunction with tax tables, enable the employer to calculate the amount of tax he has to deduct. The system was introduced in 1944 and had been recommended by J. M. KEYNES. It is thought to be a stabilizing factor in the economy, since the tax yield automatically varies directly and rapidly with INCOME and employment, whereby the government tends to spend proportionately more tax yield in recession ($\diamond$ DEPRESSION) and less in time of high demand and employment. $\diamond$ BUILT-IN STABILIZERS.

Pay-back. The period over which the cumulative net revenue from an INVESTMENT project equals the original investment. It is a commonly used but crude method for analysing CAPITAL projects.

Its main defects are that it takes no account of the PROFITS over the whole life of the investment, nor of the time profile of the CASH FLOW. ⇨ INVESTMENT APPRAISAL.

Pay pause. ⇨ PRICES AND INCOMES POLICY.

Payment-in-kind. Payment in goods or services instead of money WAGES; made illegal by the Truck Acts. ⇨ FRINGE BENEFITS.

Payments, balance of. ⇨ BALANCE OF PAYMENTS.

Payroll tax. A TAX levied on employers' WAGE bills. It is favoured by many economists in developed economies as a means of encouraging both capital intensiveness (⇨ CAPITAL-INTENSIVE) and the more efficient use of LABOUR, and of discouraging labour hoarding. This type of tax is not used in the U.K., although authority to do so was obtained in the 1961 BUDGET as one of two 'regulators'. A flat-rate employment tax (SELECTIVE EMPLOYMENT TAX) was introduced in 1966.

Peg. ⇨ EXCHANGE RATES.

Pension funds. Sums of money laid aside and normally invested to provide a regular INCOME on retirement, or in compensation for disablement for the remainder of a person's life. Nearly all developed countries have state pension schemes, e.g. the British NATIONAL INSURANCE Scheme and Graduated Pension Scheme, but unlike these schemes, private pension schemes for which contributions receive favourable tax treatment are invariably based on ASSUR-ANCE or on managed invested funds. Pension schemes may be contributory or non-contributory by the employee; the benefits of private schemes are normally related to the length of services of the employee and the level of his salary or contributions. Pension schemes began with the Civil Service in 1832, and later spread to salaried persons in other occupations and, more recently, to wage-earners. Today pension funds have considerable economic significance and provide an important flow of funds to the CAPITAL MARKET. The pension funds of the largest corporations are often significant shareholders in other companies.

Per capita income. The total INCOME of a group divided by the number of people in the group. In comparing standards of living between economies, it is obviously more relevant to take *per capita* income than total income.

Percentile. The n'th percentile of a set of numbers, arranged in ascending order of magnitude, is that number below which *n* per cent of the numbers fall. For example, suppose that we have the numbers 1, 2, 3, 4, 5, 6, 7, 8, 9, 10, then the 80th percentile will equal 9 (since

80 per cent of the numbers lie below it), the 40th percentile will be 5, and so on.

Perfect competition. A MARKET situation in which the following assumptions hold:

(a) There is a large number of buyers.

(b) There is a large number of sellers.

(c) The quantity of the good bought by any buyer or sold by any seller is so small relative to the total quantity traded, that changes in these quantities leave market PRICE unaffected. The individual seller can therefore take the DEMAND CURVE he faces as a horizontal straight line at the going price. Similarly, the individual buyer can take the SUPPLY CURVE he faces as a horizontal straight line at the going price.

(d) Units of the good sold by different sellers are identical, i.e. the product is homogeneous. Perfect competition is sometimes distinguished from *pure competition* by three further assumptions, although pure and perfect competition are normally used as synonyms.

(e) There is perfect information, in the sense that all buyers and all sellers have complete information on the prices being asked and offered in all other parts of the market.

(f) There is perfect freedom of entry, i.e. new sellers are able to enter the market and sell the good on the same terms as existing sellers.

(g) The absence of all economic friction, including transport costs, from one part of the market to another.

The consequences of these assumptions are:

(i) The market adjusts rapidly to discrepancies between SUPPLY and DEMAND, since such descrepancies will cause price changes which are transmitted throughout the market by the process of ARBITRAGE, which relies on an unimpeded flow of information.

(ii) When an EQUILIBRIUM is achieved, it can only be at a single price.

(iii) In the LONG-RUN, there can be no profits, other than a normal competitive return (⟳ PROFIT) to the ENTREPRENEUR, because if there are, entry (⟳ BARRIERS TO ENTRY; FREEDOM OF ENTRY) takes place and they are competed away.

The assumptions underlying perfect competition are obviously 'unrealistic' in that they are not an accurate description of most real world markets. Some markets conform to some assumptions, but few, if any, conform to them all. The STOCK EXCHANGE, for example, in general conforms to the assumptions of perfect information (or nearly so), and large number of buyers. On the other hand, stringent restrictions on entry exist, and there is considerable specialization by small groups of JOBBERS in particular shares, and so the Stock Exchange is better described as a closely-knit group of OLIGOPOLIES.

Given this 'unrealism' of the assumptions, there has been considerable debate among economists over the usefulness of the theory. One result of this was the development of theories of MONOPOLISTIC COMPETITION and oligopoly in the 1930s and later. At the present time, there is still conflict of opinion on the degree of applicability of the MODEL of perfect competition. Partly this is a result of the difficulties surrounding EMPIRICAL TESTING in economics, since it is not easy to establish just how useful the perfectly competitive model is as compared to alternative theories. Partly, also, it is a result of conflict of political views, since one's belief in the efficiency of the FREE MARKET ECONOMY tends to depend on how closely one believes the markets conform, or can be made to conform, to the competitive ideal. There does seem to be a fairly general consensus of opinion, however, that first, as a limiting case (the other being absolute monopoly), the theory can give useful insights into the workings of the economy, just as a physicist might begin his study of gravity by considering an object falling in a vacuum. Extreme simplification, and then the gradual introduction of complications, may be a far more fruitful methodology than the attempt to take all the complications of the real world into account at once. Secondly, the model may give reasonably accurate predictions of the consequences of certain types of change, even if its assumptions are descriptively unrealistic. If we are interested only in predicting, and not in explaining, the details of the process by which the results come about, then, on the grounds of expediency, we may be prepared to use the theory. The cost of making a theory more realistic is generally an increased complexity, with the result that it becomes more difficult to use, and possibly less accurate, even, in its predictions. Thirdly, the perfectly competitive model fulfils certain conditions of optimal resource allocation (▷ ECONOMIC EFFICIENCY), and gives important insights into the extent to which decentralized decision-taking can be expected to lead to an economic optimum. In this respect, it acts as a standard against which to assess the efficiency of real-world economic systems.

Peril point. A term used by the U.S. Tariff Commission to describe the point beyond which TARIFF reductions would threaten the existence of domestic industry.

Personal loan. A BANK LOAN made without COLLATERAL SECURITY to a private customer for specific purposes. Personal loans are granted for a fixed period, normally up to two years, and are repaid by equal monthly instalments. Introduced first by the Midland Bank in 1958, the personal loan system was principally designed to secure for the banks a share of the expanding CREDIT business for consumer durables. Cheaper than HIRE PURCHASE, personal loans also appeal to professional persons and others as being a more discreet form of extended credit.

Personal sector. ⇨ PRIVATE SECTOR.

Petty, Sir William (1623–87). The pioneer of numerical economics. His main interest lay in public finance, and he made important contributions to monetary theory and FISCAL POLICY. His approach to these subjects contributed to the development of CLASSICAL ECONOMICS, and his work in the field of comparative statistics is in direct line of descent to the work of modern economists in the field of comparative economic statistics. His best-known work is *Political Arithmetic*, published in 1691. The so-called *Petty's law* was a remarkably far-sighted statement of the tendency for the proportion of the working population engaged in SERVICES to increase as an economy develops.

Petty's law. ⇨ SIR WILLIAM PETTY.

Phillips, Alban William Housego (1914–   ). After a number of jobs in electrical engineering, and after serving in the R.A.F. during the Second World War, Alban Phillips began lecturing in economics at the London School of Economics in 1950. From 1958 until 1967 he was Tooke Professor of Economics, Science and Statistics in the University of London. In 1968 he accepted the Chair of Economics at the Australian National University. Professor Phillips has published many articles exploring the relationships between the MULTI-PLIER and accelerator in mathematical MODELS (⇨ ACCELERATOR-MULTIPLIER MODEL) with various time lags, and has applied the engineering technique of closed-loop control systems to the analysis of MACROECONOMIC relationships.

In an article in *Economica* in 1958, Professor Phillips set out empirical evidence to support the view that there is a significant relation between the percentage change of money wages and the level of UNEMPLOYMENT. The lower is unemployment, the higher is the rate of change of wages. This relationship, which became known as the *Phillips curve*, has attracted considerable theoretical and empirical analysis. Its main implication is that, since a particular level of unemployment in the economy will imply a particular rate of wage increase, the aims of low unemployment and a low rate of INFLA-TION may be inconsistent. The government must then choose between the feasible combinations of unemployment and inflation, as shown by the estimated Phillips curve, e.g. 3 per cent unemployment and no inflation, or $1\frac{1}{2}$ per cent unemployment and 8 per cent inflation, etc. Alternatively, it may attempt to bring about basic changes in the workings of the economy, e.g. a PRICES AND INCOMES POLICY, in order to reduce the rate of inflation consistent with low unemployment. In the post-war years, the relation between unemployment and inflation has not been sufficiently stable to permit exact judgements to be made, however. In particular, the situation in 1970, with both relatively high unemployment and extremely high wage increases, represents a point well off the Phillips curve – though Professor Phillips has himself pointed out that this phenomenon is to be expected at the end of a wages freeze.

Phillips curve. ⟡ A. W. H. PHILLIPS.

Physical controls. Direct controls on production and CONSUMPTION, licensing of buildings or IMPORTS, and the rationing of goods, are examples of physical controls. These controls are alternatives to the use of monetary or fiscal measures (⟡ FISCAL POLICY) that control production and consumption less discriminately through the price mechanism (⟡ PRICE SYSTEM). ⟡ QUOTAS.

Physiocrats. A group of eighteenth-century French economists, led by F. QUESNAY, who later became known as the Physiocrats or '*Les Économistes*'. They believed in the existence of a natural order and regarded the state's role as simply that of preserving property and upholding the natural order. They held that agriculture was the only source of WEALTH and therefore this sector should be taxed by *l'impôt unique*. In this, and in their advocacy for free trade, their views were directly opposed to those of the mercantilists (⟡ MER-CANTILISM). In their belief in LAISSEZ-FAIRE, they had much in common with, and certainly influenced, British CLASSICAL ECON-OMICS, and especially ADAM SMITH. Quesnay's *Tableau Économique*, published in 1758, has in it the origins of modern ideas on the circulation of wealth and the nature of interrelationships in the economy. ⟡ R. CANTILLON; H. GEORGE; J. S. MILL.

Pigou, Arthur Cecil (1877–1959). A pupil of ALFRED MARSHALL, whom he succeeded to the Chair in Political Economy at Cambridge in 1908, Pigou continued in this chair until he retired in 1944. His major publications include *Principles and Methods of Industrial Peace* (1905), *Wealth and Welfare* (1912), *Unemployment* (1914), *Economics of Welfare* (1919), *Essays in Applied Economics* (1923), *Industrial Fluctuations* (1927), *The Theory of Unemployment* (1933) and *Employment and Equilibrium* (1941). His work on monetary theory, employment and the NATIONAL INCOME, which was in the tradition of the CLASSICAL SCHOOL, led him into controversy with J. M. KEYNES. He was the first to enunciate clearly the concept of the real balance effect, which, as a consequence, became known as the *Pigou effect*. The Pigou effect is a stimulation of employment brought about by the rise in the real value of LIQUID balances as a consequence of a decline in prices – as the real VALUE of WEALTH increases, so CONSUMPTION will increase, thus increasing income and employment. This was one of the processes by which the classical MODEL envisaged that full-employment EQUILIBRIUM could be obtained as a result of a reduction in real wages. Although his work on MACROECONOMICS was partly superseded by Keynes, he made a lasting contribution with his original work in WELFARE ECONOMICS. He strongly resisted the belief that practical policies based on propositions from welfare economics were impossible, because interpersonal comparisons of UTILITY cannot be made. He argued that, though this may be true for individuals, it was possible to make meaningful comparisons between groups. His distinction between private and social product now plays an important role in the formation of government economic policy in the field of PUBLIC EXPENDITURE.

Pigou effect. ◊ A. C. PIGOU.

Pink Book. Informal name for the annual publication, *United Kingdom Balance of Payments*. The Pink Book appears in the late summer each year, and gives estimates of the BALANCE OF PAYMENTS in detail over the previous eleven years. Quarterly and more recent estimates of the balance of payments appear in the *Monthly Digest of Statistics* and elsewhere.

Placing. The sale of a new issue of SHARES or STOCK (◊ NEW ISSUE MARKET), usually to INSTITUTIONAL INVESTORS, by a financial intermediary, such as a firm of stockholders, acting on behalf of the company issuing the shares. This method of 'private placing' of shares minimizes the cost of a new issue for small firms. If the shares are quoted on the STOCK EXCHANGE, a proportion of the issue must be made available to the general public.

Planned economy. An economy in which the basic functions of RE-SOURCE ALLOCATION are carried out by a centralized administrative process, as opposed to a price mechanism ($\Diamond$ PRICE SYSTEM). Decisions on the total outputs of all goods in the economy are taken by an administrative body, and these decisions may reflect to varying extents the wishes of consumers, and the perceived need to expand particular sectors of the economy more rapidly than others, e.g. heavy industry, armaments industries, export industries. At this stage, of course, consistency must be achieved between outputs of FINAL PRODUCTS and outputs of the INTERMEDIATE PRODUCTS required to produce them. Similarly, the total requirements for LAND, LABOUR and CAPITAL must not exceed the total amount available. The 'plans' or output programmes are then communicated to the individual production units – factories, plants and farms – and these units are expected to fulfil their plans with the resources which have been allocated to them; indeed, incentives often exist for output plans to be over-fulfilled, since this represents greater PRODUCTIVITY of resources than was envisaged in the plan. INCOME DISTRIBUTION is determined centrally, since wages and salaries are set by the administrative machinery (there are, of course, no RENT, PROFIT or INTEREST earners, apart from the state). This extreme form of centralized economic organization is most closely approached in the U.S.S.R. and China, but even these economies do not correspond perfectly to the description given above, since there are certain important sectors, notably agriculture, in which PRIVATE ENTERPRISE and some elements of a MARKET mechanism still operate. A planned system was the most obvious form of economic organization for any economy which wanted to eliminate the characteristics of the capitalist economy ($\Diamond$ CAPITAL-ISM). In addition, it permits the economy to be run in a way which corresponds to particular objectives, e.g. the rapid expansion of heavy industrial sectors at the expense of consumer goods. Such political imposition of priorities is rather more difficult in a capitalist system. Finally, an administrative process of allocation may be the only way to secure ECONOMIC DEVELOPMENT in an economy which does not possess the necessary institutions, skills and *mores* for a capitalist system to work. On the other hand, the major defects of a centralized system (assuming one does not regard the absence of private enterprise as in itself a defect) lie in its possible inefficiency as a means of allocating RESOURCES. In any industrialized economy, the scale of the problem is very large. Inevitably, the planning process requires a large BUREAUCRACY with the resulting problems of securing administrative efficiency faced by any large organization. Costly mistakes may occur, and the rigidities in the system may mean that they remain long uncorrected. Because the system is not sensitive to the detailed wishes of consumers, a planned economy is probably better suited to an economy attempting to industrialize rapidly than to a high mass-consumption economy. This fact, among other things, may account for the fact that the wealthier Socialist economies in Eastern Europe are beginning to develop methods of giving greater discretion to managers of production units, and even to experiment with price mechanisms which would enable CONSUMERS' PREFERENCES to be more accurately measured.

Ploughing back. ◊ SELF-FINANCING.

Point elasticity. ◊ ELASTICITY.

Poll tax. A TAX levied equally on each person in the community.

Population. 1. The number of people living in any defined area, such as London or the U.S.S.R. **2.** In statistics, a term applied to any class of data of which counts are made or samples taken, e.g. car population.

The stastistical study of the characteristics of human populations is called *demography*. While total population statistics derived from the registration of births and deaths and from CENSUSES of population are reasonably accurate in advanced countries, the population of many DEVELOPING COUNTRIES, e.g. China, Saudi Arabia, can only be estimated within wide margins of error because the necessary administrative machinery is not available. Projections of population, even for advanced countries, are subject to large margins of error. In 1959, the U.K. population for the year 2,000 was officially forecast at fifty-eight million, the 1966 forecast for the year 2,000 was seventy-five million and in 1971 it was for sixty-six million. The difficulty arises principally from instability in BIRTH RATES. World population is now growing very rapidly, even in the U.S. and Western Europe, where it was previously thought it would decline. In England and Wales, the overall population has increased at 0·6 per cent per annum since 1961 and was estimated at 48,815,000 in 1971. Although food production is currently expanding more rapidly than population, the fears of a world food shortage, first raised by T. R. MALTHUS in the nineteenth century, are again present. In certain developing countries, excessive rates of population increase are creating acute hardship and inhibiting economic growth. ◊ POPULATION, CENSUS OF.

Population, census of. In the U.K., a count or census of the number of inhabitants was taken every ten years between 1801 and 1971 (except in 1941), and is now taken every five years. Enumerators visit every house in areas assigned to them, leave census forms, which they later collect and check on the accuracy of the answers. Information is collected on place of residence, age, sex, marital condition, occupation and certain supplementary information on living conditions, education and occasionally other matters. All advanced countries have regular censuses, but many DEVELOPING COUNTRIES are now in the process of organizing them for the first time. It is not possible to obtain information accurately by other means. Calculations based on births, deaths and migration have not proved, in the past, to be very precise means of estimating, except as a means of interpolation between censuses. Annual estimates of the present and future population are prepared and published by the government actuary in consultation with the registrar-general.

Portfolio. The collection of SECURITIES held by an investor.

Positive economics. That part of economics concerned with propositions about what is, rather than what ought to be. That is, it is concerned with developing hypotheses which are capable of being refuted by objective factual evidence, e.g. that if the RATE OF INTEREST rises, the DEMAND for MONEY will fall; that if INVESTMENT increases, NATIONAL INCOME will rise; that firms produce at the output level at which PROFIT is maximized. These are all positive propositions, as opposed to the normative type of proposition: e.g. UNEMPLOYMENT ought to be lower; an economic policy should be carried out if the people who gain can compensate the people who lose and still be better off. The essence of a positive proposition is, therefore, that it is concerned with matters of fact, not matters of values and ethics. ⟡ WELFARE ECONOMICS.

Post Office Savings Bank (P.O.S.B.). ⟡ SAVINGS BANKS.

Post-War Credits. During the Second World War, the British government reduced certain personal allowances against INCOME TAX and credited the additional tax for repayment to the taxpayer when the war was over. The repayment of these forced LOANS has been very gradual because of the potentially inflationary effects. Men over the age of sixty and women of fifty and over were recently able to claim repayment with $2\frac{1}{2}$ per cent per annum INTEREST since 1959 on sums withheld, but plans were announced at the end of 1971 to repay all post-war credits in the following year.

321

Prebisch, Raúl D. (1901–   ). Economic adviser to Argentina and U.N. Economic Commission for Latin America and Secretary-General of the UNITED NATIONS CONFERENCE ON TRADE AND DEVELOPMENT, at Geneva in 1964. At this conference he argued that there is a permanent tendency for the TERMS OF TRADE to shift against agricultural products, and that it was in the interests of the DEVELOPING COUNTRIES to industrialize behind protective TARIFFS. He also made proposals for improving the export incomes or primary producers, for increased aid and for an expansion in trade in EXPORTS of manufactured goods from the developing countries.

Precautionary motive. A motive for holding MONEY which arises out of the possibility of unforeseen or imperfectly anticipated needs for expenditure. A need for money which can only be met by selling some non-money form of holding WEALTH, e.g. a SHARE, a BOND, may involve the holder in a loss, perhaps because of unfavourable MARKET conditions, cost penalties or transactions costs. Alternatively, it may involve borrowing, and thus incurring INTEREST costs. Hence, given that future needs for money cannot be predicted with complete certainty, some margin over the most likely required money sum will have to be held. This part of the individual's money holding then arises out of a precautionary motive.

Preference shares. Holders of preference shares take precedence over the holders of ORDINARY SHARES, but after DEBENTURE holders, in the payment of DIVIDENDS, and in the return of CAPITAL if the issuing company is liquidated ($\diamond$ LIQUIDATION). Preference shares normally entitle the holder only to a fixed rate of dividend, but participating preference shares also entitle the holder to a share of residual PROFITS. Preference shares carry limited voting rights and they may be redeemable or not ($\diamond$REDEEMABLE SECURITIES). *Cumulative preference shares* carry forward the right to preferential dividends, if unpaid, from one year to the next. From the investor's point of view, preference shares lie between debentures and ordinary shares in terms of RISK and INCOME, while to the issuing company they permit some flexibility in distribution policy at a lower cost than debentures. Preference shares account for a small proportion of issues and are tending to diminish in importance.

Preferential duty. $\diamond$ COMMONWEALTH PREFERENCES; TARIFFS, IMPORT.

Premium. 1. The difference, where positive, between the current PRICE or VALUE of a SECURITY, or CURRENCY, and its issue price or PAR VALUE. **2.** A regular payment made in return for an INSURANCE policy.

Premium Savings Bonds. A BOND first introduced by the U.K. government in 1956. Instead of being distributed directly to bondholders, the INTEREST payable is put up as prize money which is won in a draw of the serial numbers of the bonds outstanding.

Present value. The VALUE now of a sum, or sums, of MONEY arising in the future. Money now is worth more than money in the future, both because of uncertainty and because it could be invested now to produce a greater sum in the future. The present value of money in the future is calculated by DISCOUNTING it at a RATE OF INTEREST equivalent to the rate at which it could be invested. Thus £105 in a year's time has a present value of £100 if the interest rate is 5 per cent per annum. The net present value of an investment is the difference between the CAPITAL cost of an investment and the present value of the future CASH FLOWS to which the investment will give rise. It is defined as:

$$\text{net present value} = \frac{R_1}{(1 + r)} + \frac{R_2}{(1 + r)^2} + \ldots + \frac{R_n}{(1 + r)^n} - C_0$$

where $R_1 R_2 \ldots R_n$ are gross PROFITS arising in years 1, 2, ... n, C_0 is the present value of capital expenditure, and r is the annual interest rate (assumed constant throughout the period). The calculation of net present values is an important part of INVESTMENT APPRAISAL. ⟡ DISCOUNTED CASH FLOW; INTERNAL RATE OF RETURN.

Price. The quantity of MONEY which must be exchanged for one unit of a good or SERVICE. In addition, economists often use price in a broader sense to refer to anything, whether money or some COMMODITY, which has to be paid, e.g. in a BARTER economy, the price of a bride may be twenty-five cows. ⟡ PRICE SYSTEM; PRICE THEORY.

Price control. The fixing of prices by government statutory order in order to prevent PRICE rises in an inflationary situation. The U.K. government imposed price control during the Second World War, together with a system of rationing It is a temporary measure applicable to special conditions only; it does not in itself cure INFLATION. ⟡ PRICES AND INCOMES POLICY.

Price discrimination. This is said to exist when different buyers or groups of buyers are charged different prices for the same good. The reason for price discrimination is that PROFITS are higher than if a uniform price is charged to all buyers where the price ELASTICITY of demand is not the same in all MARKETS. For price discrimination to be successfully used, however, it must be possible to prevent resale of the good between consumers, otherwise it would pay buyers who bought at lower prices to resell to buyers who buy at higher prices, and such ARBITRAGE would eventually cause the prices charged to each group of buyers to converge.

Price-earnings (P/E) ratio. The quoted price of an ORDINARY SHARE divided by the most recent year's EARNINGS per share. The P/E ratio is thus the reciprocal of the earnings YIELD and a measure of the price that has to be paid for a given income from an EQUITY share. A company whose 25p ordinary shares were quoted at £1.00 on the STOCK EXCHANGE and which, in the previous year had earnings of 10p per share, would have a P/E ratio of 10 to 1, i.e. the price of every one new penny in earnings would be ten new pennies, or the earnings yield would be 10 per cent. The price of earnings will vary with the stock markets' assessment of the risks involved. Thus a reasonably large company with a good earnings record might have a P/E of 15/1 or more, but a company with a poor record might have a P/E ratio of considerably less than that.

Price elasticity of demand. ⟡ ELASTICITY.

Price elasticity of supply. ⟡ ELASTICITY.

Price freeze. ⟡ PRICES AND INCOMES POLICY.

Price index. ⟡ INDEX NUMBER.

Price level, average. The general level of PRICES of goods and SERVICES in the economy as a whole. ⟡ MACROECONOMICS.

Price maintenance. ⟡ RESALE PRICE MAINTENANCE.

Price mechanism. ⟡ PRICE SYSTEM.

Price support (U.S.). A system of agricultural support by which MARKET prices are fixed at above FREE MARKET levels and the U.S. government purchases unsold surpluses, thus supporting the PRICE and raising farmers' INCOMES. ⟡ FARM PRICE REVIEW.

Price system. The system of RESOURCE allocation based on the free movements of prices. In an economy in which MARKETS are permitted to work without outside intervention, the decisions taken by individual buyers and sellers are coordinated and made consistent with each other by movements in prices. Thus, if buyers wish to purchase more than sellers wish to supply, PRICE will rise. As price rises, this causes buyers to reduce the quantities they wish to buy, and sellers to increase the quantities they wish to sell, until, at some particular price, these quantities are equal, and the separate decisions of buyers and sellers are thus made consistent. Similarly, if sellers wish to sell more than buyers are prepared to take, price falls, causing sellers to reduce the quantities they wish to sell, and buyers to increase the quantities they wish to buy, until the quantities are again equal, and decisions are consistent. If every good, SERVICE and FACTOR OF PRODUCTION in the economy is sold on such a market, then we can see how the movements in prices bring about consistency of decisions or plans of all buyers and sellers. This mechanism by which movements in prices coordinate individual decisions is known as the price system.

Several things should be noted. First, the process of coordination is quite decentralized. No single central authority collects information on buyers' decisions and sellers' decisions, finds the level at which they are consistent and then transmits information on the necessary sales and purchases to individual buyers and sellers. Whatever one's view of the ethics of centralization, a decentralized system is, other things being equal, likely to be more efficient as a coordinating device; simply because it saves the costs of a two-way transmission of information, it may operate more quickly and with fewer mistakes. Secondly, however, we must take care not to identify too readily the workings of the idealized price system with the workings of any actual FREE MARKET ECONOMY. Many frictions and imperfections may exist in the real world which may be judged to tilt the balance of efficiency from the decentralized price system to a centralized PLANNED ECONOMY – although state ownership of the means of production by no means precludes the use of a price system to solve the technical problem of resource allocation. Finally, even if markets in the real world worked smoothly, without frictions and imperfections, the price system does not solve all the problems of resource allocation. Some goods, often called PUBLIC GOODS, cannot be bought and sold on markets. The price system does not take into account EXTERNALITIES, and so does not ensure that the socially optimal level of an activity is in fact achieved. The ability to buy goods and services through the price system depends on one's INCOME, and this may create social problems. The conditions under which the price system will bring about an optimal allocation of resources (▷ ECONOMIC EFFICIENCY) forms a major area of study of WELFARE ECONOMICS.

Price theory. That part of economics concerned with analysing the ways in which prices are determined in a FREE MARKET ECONOMY, and the role they play in solving the problems of RESOURCE allocation. The central concept of PRICE theory is the MARKET. Since the essential elements in a market are the behaviour of buyers, the behaviour of sellers, and the ways in which these interact, the study of markets is normally organized into 'sub-theories': (a) a theory of the behaviour of buyers, or the theory of DEMAND; (b) a theory of the behaviour of sellers, or the theory of SUPPLY, in which the theory of the FIRM plays a central role; and (c) a theory of market behaviour, which examines how prices are determined by the interaction of buyers and sellers in various states of the environment – PERFECT COMPETITION, MONOPOLISTIC COMPETITION, OLIGOPOLY and MONOPOLY, ⟡ INDIFFERENCE ANALYSIS; A. MARSHALL.

Prices and Incomes, National Board for. ⟡ NATIONAL BOARD FOR PRICES AND INCOMES.

Prices and incomes policy. Generally, a policy for restraining increases in PRICES and INCOMES in the interests of price stability. The persistent upward trend in prices during the post-war period in Europe has given rise to doubt that a high level of economic activity can be maintained with price stability without recourse to some direct control of incomes. This situation has probably arisen from the increased importance of collective wage bargaining in the post-war period, as well as from the existence of a number of social and economic factors tending to support high levels of AGGREGATE DEMAND. In the past, countries have preferred to rely mainly upon monetary and fiscal measures (⟡ FISCAL POLICY), but the adoption of an incomes policy was recommended by the ORGANIZATION FOR ECONOMIC COOPERATION AND DEVELOPMENT in 1962 as a useful and desirable means for controlling rising prices. In Britain, a policy of relating incomes to productivity has been in operation since 1965 and until 1970 was given statutory force in the Prices and Incomes Act 1966. The principal reason for concern about rising prices in Britain has been their effect upon BALANCE OF PAYMENTS equilibrium rather than the social or economic dangers of INFLATION. The provisions of the incomes policy in Britain did not involve coercion, except during a limited period of 'standstill', but the Act contained powers that could be invoked if voluntary cooperation did not fulfil the objects of the Act. Under the Act, notice had to be given to the government of any proposed increase, and these could then be referred to the NATIONAL BOARD FOR PRICES AND INCOMES for examination. The implementation of a prices and incomes policy is, of course, an interference with the workings of the price mechanism (⟡ PRICE SYSTEM), and in practice there are considerable difficulties to overcome if misallocation of resources is to be avoided. ⇲ R. F. HARROD; F. W. PAISH.

Pricing policy. The rules adopted by a firm or public enterprise, which determine the PRICES it sets. For example, it is often argued that PUBLIC ENTERPRISES should adopt MARGINAL COST PRICING policies. In analysing the pricing policies of PRIVATE SECTOR firms, economists predict that, if a firm's objective is to maximize PROFITS, its pricing policy will consist of setting price in such a way that MARGINAL COST equals MARGINAL REVENUE. In PERFECT COMPETITION, where price and marginal revenue coincide, the firm will thus adopt a marginal cost pricing policy. In imperfect competition, however, price exceeds marginal revenue, and hence it will exceed marginal cost. In practice, a firm might simply adopt the pricing policy: VARIABLE COSTS plus a MARK-UP; though if the mark-up is responsive to MARKET conditions, this may well give much the same result as that predicted by the economist.

Prime costs. Strictly, VARIABLE COSTS plus administrative and other FIXED COSTS that can be avoided in the short or long term if there is no output, even while the firm remains in business. Often used loosely as a synonym for variable costs. ⇲ SUPPLEMENTARY COSTS.

Prime rate (U.S.). The RATE OF INTEREST charged by COMMERCIAL BANKS to first-class-risk corporate borrowers for short-term LOANS. The prime rate is the basis of the whole structure of commercial interest rates in the U.S. The rate applies only to, perhaps, the top fifty U.S. corporations; other corporations pay higher rates.

Prior charges. DEBENTURE and PREFERENCE shareholders have a prior claim over ORDINARY shareholders to PROFITS or CAPITAL repayments. The amount of these claims are known as prior charges on the company.

Private company. A type of business organization that permits a limited number of shareholders to enjoy LIMITED LIABILITY and to be taxed as a company. Unlike the PUBLIC COMPANY, a private company may not offer SHARES for public subscription, but unlike a PARTNERSHIP, and if it requires the protection of limited liability, it is obliged to file accounts. Smaller private companies are exempted from certain of the so-called *disclosure requirements*, e.g. a company with a turnover of less than £50,000 is not required to publish its turnover. Prior to 1967, *exempt private companies* (companies with not more than fifty shareholders) were not required to publish accounts at all. The vast majority of all companies in Britain are private companies, and about 80 per cent of these were classed as exempt until that category was abolished in the 1967 Companies Act. In 1970, the number of private companies registered in Britain was 542,858, although many were virtually inactive. ⟡ COMPANY LAW; CLOSE COMPANY.

Private enterprise. Private economic activity, as opposed to government economic activity, or PUBLIC ENTERPRISE. More generally, private enterprise means an economic system in which CAPITAL resources and other property are owned by individuals jointly, or in association, and in which production is undertaken for private PROFIT. All modern economies are, in fact, mixed systems of public and private economic activity (⟡ MIXED ECONOMY). ⟡ K. MARX; WELFARE ECONOMICS.

Private net product. A term first used by A. C. PIGOU for the net NATIONAL INCOME or product, to distinguish it from the SOCIAL NET PRODUCT.

Private sector. That part of the economy not under direct government control. Beyond the productive activities of PRIVATE ENTERPRISES, the private sector also includes the economic activities of non-profit-making organizations and private individuals, these sometimes being referred to as the *personal sector*.

Probabilistic sample. ⟡ RANDOM SAMPLE.

Probability. The likelihood of occurrence of some particular event. More formally, the probability of the occurrence of some event may be represented by a number lying between zero and one, and this number is called the *probability of the event*. A probability of zero would imply that the event stands no chance whatsoever of happening. A probability of one implies that the event is certain to happen. Although, once probabilities have been assigned to events, there is a very well-worked-out body of mathematical theory concerning manipulations with probabilities and their applications to real problems, there is still considerable debate about the philosophical basis of probabilities.

Producer's surplus. The excess of total receipts by firms supplying some good, over the total COST incurred by them in supplying it. Essentially, it arises because, as output of an industry expands, MARGINAL COSTS rise, perhaps because less efficient FACTORS OF PRODUCTION have to be brought into use. Since PRICE will rise in line with marginal costs, intra-marginal firms, which are using more efficient INPUTS, will make a surplus. However, since this surplus arises out of the existence of efficient specialized inputs, the owners of those inputs may in the long-run be able to appropriate the surplus, so that it may accrue not to the 'producers' or owners of the firms, but rather to the owners of the inputs. In this respect, therefore, the term has precisely the same meaning as QUASI-RENT. ⬦ A. J. E. J. DUPUIT.

Product differentiation. ⬦ DIFFERENTIATION, PRODUCT.

Product, marginal. ⬦ MARGINAL PRODUCT.

Product-moment correlation coefficient. ⬦ CORRELATION.

Production, census of. A full CENSUS of all major manufacturing, mining, construction and public utility industries has been carried out in the U.K. on a regular official basis since 1910. These censuses give information about employment, outputs and INPUTS of each industrial sub-group. The last full census was taken in 1968. Since 1968, comprehensive information has been obtained annually by means of SAMPLE surveys. Census information is essential for much official statistical work, such as the national accounts (⬦ SOCIAL ACCOUNTING) and the index of industrial production (⬦ INDEX NUMBER).

Production, factors of. ⬦ FACTORS OF PRODUCTION.

Production function. A mathematical relationship between the quantity of output of a good, and the quantities of INPUTS required to make it. It is written as: $q = f(x_1 x_2 \ldots x_n)$, where q is output, $x_1 x_2 \ldots x_n$ are inputs (say LABOUR, machinery, raw materials, etc.), and $f(\quad)$ is the mathematical notation for 'is a function of', i.e. 'is related to' or 'depends on'. Thus, the equation would read: the quantity of output of the good depends on the quantities of the inputs x_1 (say labour), x_2 (machinery), x_3 (raw materials) and so on. This is, of course, a very general statement. The next step is to specify a precise mathematical form for the equation. For example, we might consider that the relation between output and inputs is best described by a LINEAR equation, such as: $q = a_1 x_1 + a_2 x_2 + \ldots + a_n x_n$, where $a_1 a_2 \ldots a_n$ are numbers which tell us by how much output increases if the input to which they are attached increases by one unit, all other inputs remaining the same. Alternatively, we might consider the relation best described by a multiplicative function of the form:

$$q = a_0 x_1^{b_2} x_2^{b_3} \ldots x_n^{bn}$$

which is often called the COBB-DOUGLAS PRODUCTION FUNCTION. Many other equation forms exist, and could be chosen. Choice of a particular equation form is important, since different equations have different mathematical properties and involve different assumptions about the technological characteristics of the production process being described. In fact, in choosing a particular equation form, the aim is to achieve a good compromise between simplicity and ease of manipulation on the one hand, and accuracy in describing the technological relationships on the other. Production functions may be specified for the individual firms, in which case they are useful for deriving the COST CURVES of firms, and their DEMAND CURVES for FACTORS OF PRODUCTION; and they may relate to the economy as a whole, in which case they are useful in GROWTH THEORY, the theory of INCOME DISTRIBUTION and the theory of INTERNATIONAL TRADE.

Production possibility curve. ⟡ TRANSFORMATION CURVE.

Production, theory of. The branch of economics concerned with analysing the determinants of the firm's choice of quantities of INPUTS, given its PRODUCTION FUNCTION, the PRICES of the inputs and the level of output it wishes to produce. The theory is based on the hypothesis that the firm will wish to use that set of quantities of the inputs which minimizes the overall cost of producing a given output. Then, by varying output, it is possible to construct the output-COST relationships which are the basis for much of the theory of the FIRM. In addition, the analysis in production theory forms the basis for the theory of marginal productivity (⟡ INTERNAL RATE OF RETURN) and the determination of FACTOR prices. ⟡⟡ ECONOMIES OF SCALE; FACTORS OF PRODUCTION; DIMINISHING MARGINAL PRODUCTIVITY, LAW OF; ISOQUANT, all of which are important concepts in production theory.

Productive efficiency. ⟡ ECONOMIC EFFICIENCY.

Productivity. The 'productiveness' of a FACTOR OF PRODUCTION, measured by expressing output as a ratio to the amount of INPUT required to produce it (⟡ AVERAGE PRODUCTIVITY); or by expressing the change in output as a ratio to the change in amount of input required to bring it about (⟡ INTERNAL RATE OF RETURN).

Products, joint. ⟡ JOINT PRODUCTS.

Products final. ⟡ FINAL PRODUCTS.

Profit. It is important to distinguish clearly between the definitions of profit which are used in accounting calculations in firms, and the definitions of profit made in economic theory. In many ways, the distinction reflects that made between accounting and economic definitions of COSTS. In accounting terms, we can define:

(a) *Gross profit:* Total sales revenue, less payments of wages, salaries, rents, fuel and raw materials, bills, etc. This therefore represents the difference between receipts and money outlays incurred directly in carrying on the operations of the firm.

(b) *Net profit:* Gross profit, less INTEREST on LOANS and DEPRECIA-TION. Thus, net profit is the residual VALUE arrived at after deducting all MONEY costs. After deduction of tax, it represents the surplus available for distribution to the firm's owners as INCOME, and as a source of reserves and funds for new INVESTMENT.

The economic concept of profit need not quite correspond to that of the accountant, because the economist would deduct IMPUTED COSTS as well as money outlays. If the firm owned its own LAND and buildings, the rents which the firm would have had to pay if it had to lease them will be part of the accountant's profit figure and would not be separately identifiable, whereas the economist would deduct a sum equal to the RENT which could be obtained if the land and buildings were let out to the highest bidder, i.e. he would deduct the 'imputed' rent. Some firms might be making an accounting profit, but a negative profit (loss) in the economic sense. This might arise, for example, where a firm is operating in premises purchased a long time ago, but which have risen substantially in value through, say, urban development, and which if newly leased or rented would be prohibitively costly.

Economics distinguishes between two types of profit.

(a) *Normal profit:* Profit is regarded as the income which accrues to the ENTREPRENEUR, i.e. the residual left after payment of all opportunity COSTS to the INPUTS he employs. The entrepreneur need not devote his energies to the particular line of business he is in: he could just as well devote them to some other activity, and the best return he could obtain in some alternative line of business or activity is the opportunity cost to him of remaining in the activity he is in. Then normal profit is defined as that profit which is just sufficient to induce the entrepreneur to remain in his present activity, that is, it is equal to the opportunity cost of remaining in that activity. It follows that if actual profits are less than normal profits, the entrepreneur will switch to a more profitable activity; on the other hand, if profits exceed normal profits, we would expect entrepreneurs in other activities to move into the one in question. The essential point about normal profit is that it is not a surplus over all costs, but is rather the cost of the services which the entrepreneur provides.

(b) *Super-normal profit:* Profit over and above normal profit, also referred to as *excess profit*. If entry into an activity is perfectly free, then, in the long run, super-normal profits would be zero, due to the competition of entrepreneurs attracted to the activity by the prospect of higher incomes than they were currently earning. Thus, super-normal profits are either a SHORT-RUN, DISEQUILIBRIUM phenomenon, or the result of BARRIERS TO ENTRY. This suggests the role of super-normal profits in the processes of adjustment of a FREE MARKET ECONOMY as being an indicator of 'resource deficiency' – they indicate that RESOURCES are relatively more scarce than in other areas in the economy which are just earning normal profits, and at the same time provide the attraction which, in the absence of entry barriers, leads to the appropriate expansion in scale of resources devoted to that particular activity. ⬦ F. H. KNIGHT.

Profit-and-loss account. ⬦ DOUBLE-ENTRY BOOKKEEPING.

Profit, falling rate of. The early classical economists (⬦ CLASSICAL ECONOMICS) believed that it was a feature of the economic system for the general rate of PROFIT to decline. ADAM SMITH argued that CAPITAL accumulation took place at a faster rate than the growth of total output. Although the absolute level of profits rose, competition lowered the RATE OF RETURN on capital. For RICARDO, the decline of the general rate of profit was induced by the decline in the marginal productivity (⬦ INTERNAL RATE OF RETURN) of LAND, to which all profits were linked. MARX took up ideas similar to Smith's, and predicted a fall in the rate of profit because of an intensification of competition between capitalists (⬦ CAPITALISM). There would follow, he concluded, a strong pressure to reduce REAL WAGES.

Profit taking. The sale of SHARES on the STOCK EXCHANGE in order to realize CAPITAL appreciation. When share prices rise and then fall back again as sellers appear, including those who bought the shares in the expectation that the price would rise, the fall off in prices is said to be the result of profit taking. ⬦ STAG.

Programme, planning, budgeting system (P.P.B.S.). An approach to the activities of central and local government and other non-profit-making operations which attempts to take into account the objectives it is desired to achieve, the RESOURCES available, and the way these all interrelate in such as way as to use limited resources in the most effective way. It proceeds by (a) breaking down broad programmes (health, defence, education, etc.) into detailed sub-programmes; (b) devising methods of measuring the level of output of the sub-programmes, and of evaluating the resources required to provide this output; (c) clarifying the objectives laid down by the policymakers in respect of the broad programmes, and possibly sub-programmes; (d) finding the least-cost ways of meeting these objectives; (e) clarifying the 'opportunity costs' (◊ COST) of these objectives – e.g. one extra university implies fifty fewer primary schools – and thus in turn helping to formulate future policy objectives. It is thus an attempt to introduce rational methods of management into an area where considerable difficulties of measurement and evaluation exist.

Progressive tax. A TAX which takes an increasing proportion of IN-COME as income rises.

Project analysis. ◊ INVESTMENT APPRAISAL.

Project appraisal. ◊ INVESTMENT APPRAISAL.

Propensity to consume. ◊ AVERAGE PROPENSITY TO CONSUME; MARGINAL PROPENSITY TO CONSUME.

Propensity to import. A relationship between INCOME and IMPORT levels. We would expect the DEMAND of a HOUSEHOLD for foreign goods to depend on its income, just as does its demand for domestically produced goods. Similarly, we would expect firms' demands for foreign goods – raw materials, machine tools, components, etc. – to depend on their output. The whole economy's demand for imports thus depends on NATIONAL INCOME.

(a) *The average propensity to import:* the ratio of the total value of imports to national income. It is the proportion of national income spent on imports.

(b) *The marginal propensity to import:* the proportion of an increase in national income which is spent on imports. For instance, if national income increased by £100, and imports increased by £20, then the marginal propensity to import would be $\frac{£20}{£100} = \frac{1}{5}$.

The marginal propensity to import is a useful concept in two ways. First, if it can be accurately measured, and if it is relatively constant over time, then it can be used to predict the increase in imports which will result from an increase in income. To continue the above example, if the marginal propensity to import is estimated as $\frac{1}{5}$, and national income is expected to increase by £10 million, then we can predict that imports will increase by £2 million, and this may be very useful from the point of view of control of the economy and the BALANCE OF PAYMENTS. Secondly, the marginal propensity to import determines, among other things, the value of the MULTIPLIER, and so an estimate of it will be required if we are going to be able to predict the effects on national income of a change in INVESTMENT, government expenditure (✧ BUDGET), exports or TAXATION.

Though, in the short-run, the average and marginal propensities to import may be taken as relatively constant, it must be remembered that they reflect demands for foreign goods by firms and households, and therefore are influenced by (a) relative prices of foreign and domestic goods; (b) tastes; and (c) technology and other factors, any or all of which may change over time.

Propensity to save. ✧ AVERAGE PROPENSITY TO SAVE; MARGINAL PROPENSITY TO SAVE.

Property currency. Until 1964, any U.K. resident wishing to buy property overseas could only do so by first selling an overseas property. Transactions were then allowed to take place through the investment currency market. However, because overseas property was subject to special controls, a market in property currency was established in 1965 separately. Property currency was foreign currency, e.g. 'property dollars', obtained by selling overseas property, and returned to a pool. Any U.K. resident wishing to buy property had to buy foreign CURRENCY from this pool. Because the latter was limited, a PREMIUM considerably above the official exchange rate had to be paid. The market was abolished in 1970 and merged into the investment currency market. ✧ DOLLAR POOL.

Proportional tax. A TAX which is levied at the same rate, at all INCOME levels. Hence it is intermediate between a PROGRESSIVE TAX and a REGRESSIVE TAX.

Protection. The imposition of TARIFFS or QUOTAS to restrict the inflow of IMPORTS. Arguments in favour of protectionism (✧ PROTECTION) and against FREE TRADE have their origin in the earliest periods of economic discussion, but became paramount during the Mercantilist era. (✧ MERCANTILISM). The arguments take many forms. Domestic industries, especially agriculture, must be maintained at a high level in case foreign sources are cut off during a war. Similarly, key industries which have a significant defence role should be protected to avoid reliance on a foreign supplier. In conditions of EXCESS CAPACITY, protection increases employment by switching demand away from foreign to domestic production, and, through an increase in the surplus on the BALANCE OF PAYMENTS, enables aggregate INCOME to be raised through the MULTIPLIER effect. Protection also enables new industries to develop to an optimum size – the INFANT INDUSTRY ARGUMENT. Protection can be used as a counter to DUMPING and as a retaliatory measure against other countries' restrictions. The case for protection for the DEVELOPING COUNTRIES has been put forward by Professor PREBISCH. The developing countries have experienced a long-run decline in their TERMS OF TRADE. Their demand for imported manufactures grows much more rapidly as their REAL INCOMES rise than does the advanced countries' demands for their exports with a consequent pressure on their balance of payments. Protection can improve their terms of trade by causing a reduction in the price of their imported manufactures arising from their reduced demand, and it can also be used as a means for allocating the limited supply of FOREIGN EXCHANGE. ⟡ CUSTOMS UNION; GENERAL AGREEMENTS ON TARIFFS AND TRADE; IMPORT RESTRICTIONS; TARIFFS.

Public company. An incorporated business enterprise that may offer SHARES for public subscription. In 1970, 16,639 public companies were registered in Great Britain; 10,270 of these had share capital, and about half of these are quoted on the London or a provincial stock exchange. The number of active quoted companies, however, hardly exceeds 3,000. ⟡ COMPANY LAW.

Public debt. ⟡ NATIONAL DEBT.

Public deposits. Sums standing to the CREDIT of government departments in various accounts at the BANK OF ENGLAND. The main account is the EXCHEQUER, but the National Debt Commissioners, the Inland Revenue and other departments maintain small CASH balances, and all of them are shown on the bank's published accounts under this single heading.

Public enterprise. Economic activity in a MIXED ECONOMY carried on by the state, as opposed to PRIVATE ENTERPRISE. ⟡ NATIONALIZED INDUSTRIES.

Public expenditure. Spending by central government, local authorities and PUBLIC ENTERPRISES on goods and SERVICES (including CAPITAL formation), SUBSIDIES and grants and DEBT servicing. In 1970/1, total U.K. public expenditure on capital and CURRENT ACCOUNT amounted to over £22,000 million, excluding current expenditure on goods and SERVICES, on operating account of public enterprises.

Public finance. A branch of economics concerned with the identification and appraisal of the effects of government financial policies. It attempts to analyse the effects of government TAXATION and expenditure on the economic situations of individuals and institutions, and to examine their impact on the economy as a whole. It is also concerned with examining the effectiveness of policy measures directed at certain objectives, and with developing techniques and procedures by which that effectiveness can be increased. ⟐ BUDGET; COST-BENEFIT ANALYSIS; FISCAL POLICY; PRO-GRAMME, PLANNING, BUDGETING SYSTEM.

Public goods. Goods which, because they cannot be withheld from one individual without withholding them from all, must be supplied communally. For example, it would not be possible to exclude any one individual from 'consuming' national defence, or street lighting, or general police protection. Unless this exclusion could be made, a private ENTREPRENEUR would not undertake to supply these services, because he would not have the power to force the community as a whole to pay him, and he could not exclude anyone who did not pay him from consuming the good. Since the state can raise revenues by TAXATION, it alone can finance the provision of public goods. Strictly speaking, however, this definition relates only to 'pure' public goods. Many of the goods supplied by the state could in principle be supplied privately, and some indeed are, the best examples being housing, hospitals, education and specific police protection. The non-pure, or 'quasi' public goods, are supplied by the state and financed out of taxation because it is considered that their quality and/or quantity of supply would be inadequate under private provision. Since, however, the extent to which a good is a public good is then a matter of degree, there is room for genuine political debate about the appropriate means of provision.

Public ownership. ⟐ NATIONALIZED INDUSTRIES.

Public sector. The combination of central government, local authorities, the NATIONALIZED INDUSTRIES and public corporations. The public sector of the economy is very important, and tending to increase in size in all western industrialized countries. Public consumption of goods and services amounts to over one fifth of the GROSS NATIONAL PRODUCT in both the U.S. and Britain as well as in most western European countries. ⟐ PUBLIC EX-PENDITURE.

Public Works Loan Board. A board responsible for administering the provision of long-term government LOANS in the U.K., mainly to local authorities who find it difficult to raise money on the market or to finance their CAPITAL requirements from the RATES.

'Pump priming'. ⟐ DEFICIT FINANCING.

Purchase tax. An indirect tax (⟐ DIRECT TAXATION) levied at different percentage rates for different COMMODITIES on their wholesale prices. It is intended that this tax will be abolished in the U.K. on the introduction of a VALUE ADDED TAX in 1973.

Purchasing power parity theory. A theory which states that the EXCHANGE RATE between one CURRENCY and another is in EQUILIBRIUM when their domestic purchasing powers at that rate of exchange are equivalent. For example, the current rate of exchange of £1 = $2·40 would be in equilibrium if £1 will buy the same goods in the U.K. as $2·40 will buy in the U.S. If this holds true, purchasing power parity exists. The theory has its source in the mercantilist (▷ MERCANTILISM) writings of the seventeenth century, but it came into prominence in 1916 through the writings of the Swedish economist, Gustav Cassel (1866–1945). The basic mechanism implied by the theory is that, given complete freedom of action, if $2·40 buys more in the U.S. than £1 does in the U.K., it would pay to convert pounds into dollars and buy from the U.S. rather than in the U.K. The switch in demand would raise prices in the U.S. and lower them in the U.K., and at the same time lower the U.K. exchange rate until equilibrium and parity is re-established. Cassel interpreted the theory in terms of changes in, rather than absolute levels of, prices and exchange rates. He argued that the falls in the FOREIGN EXCHANGE MARKETS in the post-war period were a result of INFLATION due to unbalanced BUDGETS increasing the quantity of MONEY. In practice, the theory has little validity, because exchange rates, which are determined by the DEMAND and SUPPLY of currency in the foreign exchange markets, are related to such forces as BALANCE OF PAYMENTS disequilibria, CAPITAL transactions, SPECULATION and government policy. Many goods and SERVICES do not enter into international trade, and so their relative prices are not taken into account in the determination of the exchange rate. Moreover, it is impossible to measure satisfactorily what purchasing power a currency in one country has relative to that in another because of the difficulty of determining the appropriate mix of commodities, and also of measuring their average price level. This means that international comparisons of standards of living, etc., based on current exchange rates have to be interpreted with great care. ▷▷ L. E. VON MISES.

Pure competition. ▷ PERFECT COMPETITION.
Pure monopoly. ▷ MONOPOLY.
Put option. ▷ OPTION.
Pyramiding. ▷ HOLDING COMPANY.

Q

Quantitative restrictions. ▷ QUOTAS.
Quantity equation. ▷ QUANTITY THEORY OF MONEY.
Quantity of money. ▷ MONEY SUPPLY.
Quantity theory of money. A theory that states the relationship between the quantity of MONEY in an economy and the PRICE level. This long-established but still controversial theory begins with the identity (known as the 'Fisher equation', after the economist I. FISHER): $MV = PT$, where M is the stock of money, V is the INCOME VELOCITY OF CIRCULATION of money, P is the average PRICE LEVEL, and T is a measure of the flow of real goods and SERVICES, i.e. the flow of REAL INCOME. This is an identity, because the left-hand side measures the total money value of transactions over a given period, i.e. the stock of money multiplied by the number of times it has circulated through the economy financing transactions, while the right-hand side measures the total money value of goods sold. Since the total money value of transactions is necessarily the same as money value of goods sold, the two sides of the equation are equal by definition. However, it is hypothesized: (a) T is constant, because the economy is at full EMPLOYMENT, and will always remain there; and (b) V is a constant, being determined by certain institutional features of the economy, e.g. time intervals between wage and salary payments, which determine the extent to which the spending pattern of buyers coincides with the requirements for money of sellers. (These features change only very slowly over time, and so can be taken as constant in the SHORT RUN.) Then we could rewrite the above identity as the equation $M = \dfrac{T}{V}P$, which, since T/V is a constant, implies that changes in the stock of money are associated with proportionate changes in the price level. This relationship is the core of the quantity theory of money.

Several important policy recommendations flow from this simple theory. It suggests that INFLATION can be controlled by the monetary authorities (▷ MONETARY POLICY) through control of the quantity of money in existence. Alternatively, if a certain rate of growth in T, real income, is anticipated, then this can be achieved without inflation by allowing the quantity of money in the economy to increase at the same rate, but no faster.

Although the macroeconomic theory of J. M. KEYNES ($\Diamond$ MACRO-ECONOMICS) was concerned very much with showing that the level of real income, T, could not be assumed to remain constant at the full-employment level, it nevertheless retained the quantity theory of money in the form of the TRANSACTIONS DEMAND FOR MONEY, which is a component of the overall demand for money. The quantity theory was heavily criticized in the 1950s and early 1960s, however, and, in the U.K., the RADCLIFFE COMMITTEE virtually abandoned it as a basis for economic policy. Criticism centred on the alleged constancy of V. Because of the existence of quasi-money ($\Diamond$ 'NEAR' MONEY), and because of the ingenuity of non-bank FINANCIAL INTERMEDIARIES in developing and extending forms of CREDIT, it was argued that variations in the money value of total expenditure and income need not bear any stable relationship to variations in the quantity of money. For example, if the quantity of money was held constant in order to keep prices level, expenditure might still be increased, if consumers withdrew money from, say, BUILDING SOCIETY accounts, or HIRE PURCHASE companies expanded their lending. Thus, it was argued, what matters are the determinants of desired expenditure, and the total LIQUIDITY in the economy. This leads logically to a 'KEYNESIAN' view of economic policy, which concentrates on the determinants of AGGREGATE DEMAND, and stresses FISCAL POLICY rather than MONETARY POLICY as methods of controlling the economy.

The quantity theory has been regaining support recently largely as a result of the work of M. FRIEDMAN at the University of Chicago. As a result of these refinements, it can be said that the theories of the DEMAND for money, based on a quantity theory of money approach, do not differ a great deal from the theories based on the Keynesian framework. The relative emphasis on the practical importance of the MONEY SUPPLY, and the nature of policy recommendations, still differ significantly between the two approaches however, and there are enormous difficulties in the way of testing the theories empirically. The controversy has considerable practical importance, and the greater emphasis placed on monetary policy by the U.K. authorities in 1969 was probably the result of pressure from the INTERNATIONAL MONETARY FUND authorities, who have been much influenced by the MONEY SUPPLY school.

Quasi-money. ⇨ 'NEAR' MONEY.

Quasi-rent. A return to a firm or FACTOR OF PRODUCTION which is a PROFIT in the SHORT-RUN, but which becomes a true COST in the LONG-RUN. 'Rent' in this context is ECONOMIC RENT, not a payment for land or a dwelling (⇨ RENT). It generally arises because certain FACTOR prices may be fixed over the short-run, but are renegotiated in the long-run. Suppose, for example, a shop is located on a particular site, and its rent is fixed on the basis of a ten-year lease. Half-way through the duration of the lease, a new housing estate is built near by, and the amount of business done, and the profits the shopkeeper makes, treble. When the time comes for renegotiation of the lease, the owner of the site, if he wants to maximize his monetary gain, could raise the rent to equal the PRESENT VALUE of the future stream of profits from the shop, since this is the maximum amount the shopkeeper would pay rather than leave the shop (note that his 'salary' or opportunity cost as a shopkeeper is included in costs, and so are not a part of profit). Either the shopkeeper can pay this new rent, or leave, and so the greater profits have now been turned into a genuine opportunity cost. What were profits in the short-run have become costs in the long-run, and such temporary profits, arising essentially because the system is not in long-run EQUILIBRIUM, are known as quasi-rents.

Quesnay, François (1694–1774). A surgeon by profession, he held the post of secretary of the French Academy of Surgery and edited its official journal. He became physician to Madame de Pompadour. His major economic works appeared in various articles in the *Encyclopédie* in 1756 and 1757, and in the *Journal de l'agriculture du commerce et des finances* in 1765 and 1767. The *Tableau Économique* and *Maximes*, a commentary on the *Tableau*, were both published in 1758. The *Tableau* set out three classes of society, and showed how transactions flowed between them. The three classes were (a) landowners, (b) the farmers and farm-labourers and (c) others, called the 'sterile class'. Only the agricultural sector produced any surplus value, the rest only reproducing what it consumed (⇨ MARX). He anticipated MALTHUS's fear of underconsumption arising from excessive SAVINGS. Net INCOME would be reduced if the flows in the *Tableau* were interrupted by delays in spending. This was the first attempt to construct a MACROECONOMIC input-output MODEL of the economy (⇨ INPUT-OUTPUT ANALYSIS). In fact, progress in this field had to await the application of MATRIX ALGEBRA and computerization ($\diamond$ W. W. LEONTIEF). Quesnay suggested a single tax, '*l'impôt unique*', on the net income from land, arguing that by so doing the nation would save tax-collecting costs. Only agriculture yielded a surplus, and therefore it bears all taxes ultimately anyway ($\diamond$ H. GEORGE; J. S. MILL). He was the central figure in the group of economists called the PHYSIOCRATS, who flourished in France between 1760–70.

Quota sample. A SAMPLE which is carried out on the basis of a 'stratification' of the population ($\diamond$ STRATIFIED SAMPLE), but, unlike a stratified sample, the items within each stratum are not then selected by a SIMPLE RANDOM SAMPLE procedure, but rather by the interviewers themselves as they conduct the survey. Each interviewer would have a specified number of items, e.g. HOUSE-HOLDS, individuals, shops, firms, etc., of each kind, e.g. households and individuals by social class, shops by type of trade, firms by size, which he would have to interview, but the actual choice of the items is left to him. In the stratified sample, on the other hand, an objective procedure is used to select the items which the interviewer must then visit. The advantage of a quota sample is that it is generally cheaper: it avoids the costly process of drawing a simple random sample within each stratum of items; on the other hand, it may be biased and unreliable, since the interviewers will still have consider-able discretion in choosing items even within the limits set by the quotas for the strata, and so conscious or unconscious biases may exist ($\diamond$ RANDOM SAMPLE). In actual practice, because of its lower costs and greater speed, quota samples are by far the most prevalent form of sample.

Quotas. The quantitative limits placed on the importation of specified COMMODITIES. The PROTECTION afforded by quotas is more certain than can be obtained by raising import TARIFFS as the effect of the latter will depend on the price ELASTICITIES of the imported commodities. Quotas, like tariffs, can also be used to favour pre-ferred sources of supply. Quotas have virtually disappeared among industrial trading countries, except for primary products. $\diamond\!\!\!\diamond$ GENERAL AGREEMENT ON TARIFFS AND TRADE; IMPORTS.

Quoted company. $\diamond$ PUBLIC COMPANY.

Quotation. The privilege granted to the issuer of a SECURITY by the STOCK EXCHANGE Council of placing the price of that security on the official list. Only public companies fulfilling certain require-ments designed to safeguard the investing public are granted quota-tions ($\diamond$ PUBLIC COMPANY).

R

Radcliffe Report. The Committee on the Working of the Monetary System was set up in May 1957, under the chairmanship of Lord Radcliffe, with wide terms of reference. It published its report in August 1959. Its members were Professor A. K. Cairncross, Sir Oliver Franks, Lord Harcourt, W. E. Jones, Professor R. S. Sayers, Sir Reginald Verdon Smith, George Woodcock and Sir John Woods. The report received considerable critical acclaim for the high standard of its description of the U.K. financial system and its institutions. At the same time, however, it gave rise to some criticism that the report had not given sufficient weight to the importance of regulating the quantity of money (⟡ MONEY SUPPLY) as part of economic and financial policy. In the late 1960s, the U.K. government became increasingly criticized (especially by economists in the U.S. and other advisers to the INTERNATIONAL MONETARY FUND who were particularly influenced by the work of M. FRIEDMAN) for following too closely the recommendations of the Radcliffe Report, which were embedded in the U.K. TREASURY'S and BANK OF ENGLAND'S philosophy. The Radcliffe Report had concluded that monetary policy should give priority to controlling the LIQUIDITY of the monetary system, and not the quantity of money in the system: 'Rejecting from among such measures [i.e. monetary measures to control INFLATION] any restriction of the supply of money, we advocate measures to strike more directly and rapidly at the liquidity of spenders. We regard a combination of controls of CAPITAL issues, bank advances and CONSUMER CREDIT as being most likely to serve this purpose.' Reasons for taking this view were the 'theoretical difficulties' of identifying 'the supply of money' and the 'Haziness that lies in the impossibility of limiting' the INCOME VELOCITY OF CIRCULATION. Nevertheless, the report did not dismiss the quantity of money as unimportant, but rather believed that given proper control of liquidity it would look after itself. 'Although we do not regard the supply of money as an unimportant quantity, we view it as only part of the wider structure of liquidity in the economy.' In external policy, the report came down in favour of fixed EXCHANGE RATES. 'It would be more difficult if there were no fixed rate to be defended, to keep domestic costs in line with costs abroad, and the need to devalue might result from the very ease with which the external value of the currency could be adjusted.' The report gave support to the need to strengthen the INTER-NATIONAL LIQUIDITY position, and saw much merit in strengthening the I.M.F. along the lines of the KEYNES PLAN. ⟨⟩ MACMILLAN COMMITTEE; SPECIAL DRAWING RIGHTS.

Random sample. Any method of taking a SAMPLE by which each member of the POPULATION of items has a known chance of being included in the sample. A special case of a random sample is a simple random sample, whereby each item in the population has an equal chance of being included in the sample, and therefore all possible samples of a given size (number of items) have an equal chance of being selected. It is important to distinguish between the meaning of random here, and its meaning in everyday usage. An intuitive interpretation of the phrase 'a random sample of voters' would be that one goes out on to the street and questions the first, say, twenty people one meets, or picks out twenty people 'at random'. This is not, however, a random sample, since we do not know what chance each member of the population (the people of voting age in a particular constituency) had of being chosen, and it is quite possible that many of them had no chance at all. A random sample, properly defined, may well in fact be the result of a careful calculation, and there may be a very precise specification of how many of which types of item are to be included in the sample. The word 'random' is therefore clearly not being used in the sense of 'haphazard' or 'fortuitous', but rather in the more specialized sense of 'probabilistic' (in fact *probabilistic sample* is the term given in the U.S. to random sample). The importance of devising a random sample is that, only if a definite PROBABILITY of being included in the sample is assigned to each item in the population, can the probable error in using the information derived from the sample to make statements about the population be estimated. An incidental, but important, advantage of random sampling is that by specifying beforehand which types of item, or even exactly which items, are to be included in the sample, on the basis of an objective procedure, the inevitable biases which arise from an on-the-spot choice of the sample are avoided. Thus, an interviewer may unconsciously select better-dressed people, or flats on lower floors, in a sample which is supposedly to be chosen at random, and such unconscious biases may influence the results in ways which cannot be estimated. For particular types of sampling

343

procedure based on the idea of a random sample, ◇ STRATIFIED SAMPLE and SIMPLE RANDOM SAMPLE.

Rate of interest. The PRICE of borrowed MONEY. In general, if a sum of money is lent for a specified period of time, the amount which is repaid by the borrower to the lender will be greater than the amount which was initially lent. It is convenient to have a standardized way of expressing this PREMIUM, and hence we define the rate of interest to be the difference between what is lent, and what must be repaid after a specified period, expressed as a proportion of the amount lent. Thus, if £100 is lent and £105 is repaid after one year, then the yearly interest rate is $\dfrac{£(105 - 100)}{£100} = 0.05$, or, in percentage terms, 5 per cent. If £105 were to be repaid after six months, then 0·05 or 5 per cent would be the six-monthly interest rate. The time period should always be carefully specified, e.g. a six-monthly interest rate of 5 per cent is not equivalent to yearly interest rate of 10 per cent (◇ COMPOUND INTEREST). Normally, interest rates are calculated for a year, and, when a time period is not specified, a yearly period is generally implied.

It is an over-simplification to talk about 'the' rate of interest. At any one time, there will be a whole set of different interest rates, each associated with a particular form of lending: bank DEPOSIT ACCOUNTS; BUILDING SOCIETY deposits; short-term government debt (TREASURY BILLS); long-term government debt; industrial DEBENTURES; etc. The reason for differences in these interest rates can be suggested by considering the reasons for the existence of interest rates: why should interest rates exist? There are several reasons:

(a) *Time preference:* Money which is lent generally represents SAVING, i.e. a sacrifice of CONSUMPTION at the present time. The lender is, in effect, postponing consumption, from the present to some time in the future. Simply as a fact of human psychology, people generally prefer to consume now rather than later, and hence must be paid something to induce them to postpone consumption. The stronger their preference for present as opposed to future consumption, the more they must be paid to induce them to postpone consumption, i.e. the higher must be the rate of interest. ◇ TIME PREFERENCE.

(b) *The possibility of illiquidity:* Lending money generally implies exchange of money for some ASSET which is not money – in the sense that it is not universally acceptable as a payment for goods and services, e.g. a treasury bill, a BOND, a building society account book, etc. If, within the duration of the loan, the lender should require money in excess of the amount he has available, he must either convert his asset into money, or borrow. The ease with which he can do the former depends on the asset in question. For example, he may have to wait for one month before he can receive some of his money from a building society. On the other hand, there may not be a time delay, if a well-organized MARKET exists for the asset, e.g. the STOCK EXCHANGE, the GILT-EDGED SECURITY market, but, at the same time, he may be forced to sell the asset for less than he paid for it, i.e. lent, and so sustains a capital loss. Alternatively, he might borrow, in which case he must himself pay a rate of interest. Thus, the fact that the lender is exchanging a liquid asset, money, for a less liquid asset, involves him in the risk of loss should the need for liquidity subsequently arise. In making the loan, therefore, the lender must be compensated for this risk, and this makes for the existence of an interest rate.

(c) *The possibility of default:* The lender may not be absolutely sure that the borrower will in fact repay the loan – he may in fact fail to repay, i.e. default. Hence, this risk will also make for a positive interest rate. Again, however, the extent of the risk depends on the type of loan being made.

(d) *Inflation:* The three factors just mentioned would make for a positive rate of interest, even if the general level of prices was expected to remain constant over the duration of the loan. We would call a rate of interest determined on such a basis the 'real rate of interest' (cf. the REAL WAGE). However, if the price level were expected to rise by, say, 3 per cent over the duration of the loan, then, in real terms, the sum lent is worth 3 per cent less when it is repaid. If inflation is anticipated, therefore, the lender will wish to take this fall in the value of money into account by raising the rate of interest by enough to offset it – in this case by three percentage points.

The above factors suggest why positive rates of interest exist. Further, since different types of loan have different characteristics in respect to some at least of those factors, we have a partial explanation for differences in interest rates. The rate of interest paid on any type of loan is essentially a price – the price which is paid for the use of that money. Hence, economists have discussed the determinants of the levels of interest rates in terms of DEMAND and SUPPLY: the demand for loans by firms wishing to invest, and the supply of SAVINGS available for lending. The demand for loans is determined by the marginal productivity of capital (⟡ INTERNAL RATE OF RETURN). J. M. KEYNES, however, stressed also the role which the demand for money to hold as an asset, in expectation of changes in prices of paper assets (bonds), plays in determining the rate of interest. ⟡ INTEREST, ABSTINENCE THEORY OF; INTEREST, CLASSICAL THEORY OF; INTEREST, NATURAL RATE OF; INTEREST, PRODUCTIVITY THEORIES OF; INTEREST, TIME PREFERENCE THEORY OF; LIQUIDITY PREFERENCE.

Rate of return. Usually, net PROFIT after DEPRECIATION as a percentage of average CAPITAL EMPLOYED in a business. One of a number of FINANCIAL RATIOS used to measure the efficiency of a business as a whole, or particular INVESTMENT projects. The rate of return may be calculated using profit before or after TAX, and there are a number of other variations of the concept. Profit may be defined as net of tax but not of depreciation and interest, i.e. profits available for EQUITY shareholders or as operating profit, i.e. to exclude investment income and CAPITAL GAINS. Capital employed may be defined to exclude LOAN CAPITAL in which case the return measured is that on equity capital; sometimes WORKING CAPITAL is excluded. The use of simple rates of return in the analysis of alternative investment projects is open to the serious criticism that it does not take account of the incidence of capital outlays and earnings, and hence does not allow for the time value of money (⟡ INVESTMENT APPRAISAL). Strictly speaking, the rate of return on capital employed in a business does not measure the return to capital alone or the efficiency of the use of RESOURCES by that business, since the returns to each of the FACTORS OF PRODUCTION cannot be separated out. However, in normal circumstances a firm which is earning a long-term rate of return lower than its cost of capital (⟡ CAPITAL, COST OF) could be said to be using resources inefficiently.

Rate of technical substitution. The rate at which one INPUT can be substituted for another along an ISOQUANT. Just as an isoquant is closely analogous to an INDIFFERENCE CURVE, so the rate of technical substitution is exactly the same kind of concept as the MARGINAL RATE OF SUBSTITUTION. Hence, see the latter for detailed discussion.

Rate of time preference. ⟡ TIME PREFERENCE.

Real capital. ⟡ CAPITAL.

Real income. INCOME measured in terms of the real goods and

SERVICES it can buy. It can be calculated by dividing MONEY income by a suitable INDEX of prices.

Real terms. Strictly speaking, real terms as opposed to MONEY terms refers to the physical, tangible characteristics of a phenomenon. Since the physical characteristics of many goods and SERVICES cannot be measured or compared directly, measurements in money terms are adjusted to an approximation of real terms by correcting for the changes in the purely monetary aspects of the measurements. For example, in order to calculate NATIONAL INCOME, goods and services are valued at their money prices, and these values aggregated. In order to find how real income has changed over time, however, i.e. how the physical flow of goods and services has changed, it is necessary to correct for the changes in prices. This is done by deflating by an appropriate INDEX NUMBER of PRICES.

Real wages. A wage rate will normally be expressed in money units per unit of time, e.g. £20 per week, or £1,200 per year, etc. However, we may be interested in knowing the purchasing power which a given money wage implies, and hence we define the real wage as the money wage divided by an INDEX NUMBER of the overall price level. This adjustment is known technically as DEFLATION. Hence, if money wages rose by 5 per cent while the price level also rose by 5 per cent, the real wage would remain unchanged, implying that the volume of goods and SERVICES which can be bought with the new money wage is equal to that which could be bought with the old. Note that 'real' is used as the opposite of monetary, not the opposite of imaginary. ⟡ MONEY ILLUSION.

Receiver. ⟡ BANKRUPTCY.

Recession. ⟡ DEPRESSION.

Reciprocal demand. ⟡ EQUATION OF INTERNATIONAL DEMAND.

Reciprocity. The practice, sometimes called 'fair trade' or 'beggar-my-neighbour policy', by which governments extend to each other similar concessions or restrictions in trade. It is reflected in U.S. trade policy in the Reciprocal Trade Agreements Acts of 1934 and the Trade Expansion Act of 1962, which made the KENNEDY ROUND OF TRADE NEGOTIATIONS under the GENERAL AGREEMENT ON TARIFFS AND TRADE possible.

Redeemable securities. STOCK or BONDS that are repayable at their PAR VALUE at a certain date, dates or specified eventuality. Most fixed-interest SECURITIES are redeemable, though CONSOLS bear no redemption date. ORDINARY SHARES and some PREFERENCE SHARES are irredeemable. ⟡ REDEMPTION DATE.

347

Redemption date. The date at which a LOAN will be repaid or release given from other obligations. ⟡ REDEEMABLE SECURITIES.

Redemption yield. ⟡ YIELD.

Reducing balance. A means of recording DEPRECIATION expenses in which the original COST of an ASSET is 'written down' by a fixed fraction each year. In this way, the amount of depreciation allowed falls each year: e.g. a machine costing £500 could be written down by 20 per cent per annum, i.e. £100 in the first year and then 20 per cent on its written down value of £400, i.e. £80 in the following year, and so on. A rate can be chosen to write down an asset to an expected residual value in a chosen period of years, e.g. five years and £50, which in our example would require an annual depreciation rate of about 53 per cent. Although the reducing-balance system gives a lighter depreciation charge in later years when maintenance and repair costs as well as risk of OBSOLESCENCE may be higher (as opposed to the straight-line method, where equal depreciation is charged every year), it is unlikely to accord very closely with actual depreciation. However, the taxation authorities in Britain and other countries base TAX allowances for certain CAPITAL investment on a reducing balance.

Re-exports. The exports of imported COMMODITIES without significant alteration. For instance, tea is imported into the U.K. in bulk and repacked into small lots which are sold overseas. In 1968, total U.K. re-exports reached a value of £218 million – compared with exports of £6,176 million – of which food, beverages and tobacco accounted for £32 million, hides and furs £37 million, machinery and transport equipment £61 million and non-ferrous metals £21 million. Since January 1970, statistics of re-exports have not been separately identified.

Regional Economic Planning Boards. ⟡ REGIONAL ECONOMIC PLANNING COUNCILS.

Regional Economic Planning Councils. In 1964, the U.K. government established planning councils and boards to coordinate and develop economic policy for the economic regions of England, Wales and Scotland. The councils consist of part-time members, being local-government officials, industrialists and trade unionists who have a special interest in regional affairs. The chairmen and members are appointed by the Secretary of State for Economic Affairs in the English regions, and the Scottish and Welsh Secretaries of State in Scotland and Wales. These councils are purely advisory. The planning boards are staffed by civil servants from the government departments concerned with regional policy. The boards help the councils to elaborate plans for their regions, coordinate government policy on a regional basis and prepare studies from time to time of regional development.

Regional employment premium. An addition to the SELECTIVE EMPLOYMENT TAX refund payable to manufacturing firms in the DEVELOPMENT AREAS. It came into operation in September 1967 for a specified period of at least seven years at a rate of £1·50 per week per man, 75p per week for women and 47½p for girls.

Registrar of Restrictive Practices. ⟡ RESTRICTIVE TRADE PRACTICES ACTS.

Regression analysis. A set of statistical techniques, the purpose of which is to quantify the relationship between two or more VARIABLES. The object of this may be to permit quantitative prediction, or forecasting; or simply to apply the techniques of STATISTICAL INFERENCE to find whether or not the variables can be expected to be closely related in the population of items under study. It also permits different hypotheses about the forms of the relationship, and the variables which should be included in it to be tested. In these respects, it is clearly of considerable importance in economics, and, in fact, is the major tool of ECONOMETRICS. Much of econometric theory has been concerned with the theoretical problems arising out of the application of classical regression MODELS, based on certain quite stringent assumptions, to economic data for which those assumptions do not necessarily hold. Most of 'applied' econometrics is concerned with the measurement and testing of economic relationships using regression techniques. Precisely as in CORRELATION, to which it bears a very close relation, regression analysis is concerned with measuring statistical association only, and does not in itself imply causation. ⟡ AUTO-CORRELATION; LEAST SQUARES REGRESSION; MULTICOLLINEARITY.

Regression model. ⟡ REGRESSION ANALYSIS.

Regressive tax. A TAX which takes a decreasing proportion of INCOME as income rises.

Rent. The PRICE paid per unit of time for the services of a DURABLE GOOD, and, in particular, LAND and buildings. Thus, we speak of the rent of a house or of a piece of land. But, in addition, one may rent a computer, rather than buy it outright, or rent a television set, and the payments for this will be referred to as rents or rentals. In economics, the term rent is often given a more specific meaning (⟡ ECONOMIC RENT). ⟡⟩ QUASI-RENT; D. RICARDO.

Rental. ⟡ RENT.

Rentier. A supplier of CAPITAL who is paid in the form of INTEREST and DIVIDENDS. He does not, however, supply entrepreneurial services – he does not participate in managing the firm (⟡ ENTRE-PRENEUR). The word is French in origin, and is derived from '*rente*', meaning interest (not the English RENT, meaning, *inter alia*, the payment for LAND).

Repressed inflation. INFLATION which exists when the state of the economy is essentially inflationary – AGGREGATE DEMAND for goods and SERVICES exceeding the AGGREGATE SUPPLY, and so, other things being equal, PRICES tending to rise – but when the rise in prices is not allowed to happen. An example would be a perfectly effective PRICES AND INCOMES POLICY, which prevented prices of goods, services and FACTORS OF PRODUCTION rising. Most economists would argue that if the underlying DISEQUILI-BRIUM of aggregate supply and demand is allowed to remain un-corrected, inflation will not be repressed for long, since no adminis-trative mechanism will be sufficiently comprehensive to control the tendency for prices (including wages) to rise in one way or another. ⟡ WAGE DRIFT.

Resale price maintenance (R.P.M.). The practice whereby a manu-facturer requires the distributors of his product to resell at certain PRICES, or at not less than minimum prices, which he has set for his products. There have been four major U.K. governmental in-quiries into the practice to determine whether or not it was in the public interest. The inquiries of 1920 and 1931 both came out in favour of continuing to allow manufacturers to follow the practice. The arguments in favour were that price fixing set PROFIT margins which ensured fair returns, both to the manufacturer and the dis-tributors for their services, and that no government had the right without very good reason to interfere with the freedom of private citizens to make contracts. In 1949, the LLOYD JACOB REPORT appeared, and in 1955 the MONOPOLIES COMMISSION'S report on *Collective Discrimination – A Report on Exclusive Dealing, Aggregated Rebates and other Discriminatory Trade Practices*. They recommended that R.P.M. collectively enforced by manufacturers should be made illegal, although individual manufacturers should be permitted to continue the practice. In 1951, the labour government published a White Paper which rejected the Lloyd Jacob Report and recom-mended the general abolition of R.P.M. with certain exceptions. The Report of the Monopolies Commission served as the basis for the

RESTRICTIVE TRADE PRACTICES ACT of 1956. This Act specifically prohibited the collective enforcement of R.P.M. and set up the Restrictive Practices Court to decide each individual case on its merits. Restrictive agreements had to be registered. The manufacturer could, under the Act, take a price-cutting retailer to court, even if there was no explicit contract between them, and the court could issue an injunction restraining the retailer. In 1964 the Resale Prices Act was passed by the Conservative government, under which all resale price agreements were assumed to be against the public interest unless it could be proved otherwise to the court. Many manufacturers, especially after sweets and shoes had been rejected by the court, decided to terminate their agreements rather than remain on the register and be required to present a costly case to the court. Only ethical drugs, proprietary medicines and books have been approved by the Court. (▷ NET BOOK AGREEMENT).

Research and development (R. & D.). Basic research, i.e. research without a specific commercial objective; applied research, i.e. research with a commercial objective or the pursuit of an invention; and development work, i.e. the perfection of an invention, the work of turning research into products or processes, including the improvement of existing products. R. & D. expenditure is growing rapidly, both in the PRIVATE SECTOR and PUBLIC SECTOR, and is a matter of great relevance to economic policy because of its contribution to INNOVATION.

Reserve currency. A CURRENCY which governments and international institutions are willing to hold in their GOLD AND FOREIGN EXCHANGE RESERVES and which finances a significant proportion of INTERNATIONAL TRADE. The prerequisites for these two conditions are normally that: (a) the value of the currency must be stable in relation to other currencies; (b) the currency is that of a country which holds an important share of world trade; (c) there exists an efficient FOREIGN EXCHANGE MARKET in which the currency may be exchanged for other currencies; and (d) the currency is convertible (▷ CONVERTIBILITY). The dollar and the pound sterling have continued in their historic roles as leading reserve currencies, although in recent years their positions have been undermined because of persistent BALANCE OF PAYMENTS deficits in both the U.S. and the U.K., which gave cause for SPECULATION as to their long-term exchange value *vis-à-vis* gold. The Swiss franc and the Deutsche Mark, because of their stability, have many of the characteristics of reserve currencies. ⇔ INTERNATIONAL LIQUIDITY; STERLING AREA.

Resource allocation. ⇔ ECONOMIC EFFICIENCY; RESOURCES.

Resources. These are the 'agents' or FACTORS OF PRODUCTION used in an economy or firm to produce and distribute goods and SERVICES. They are conventionally classified into: LAND, LABOUR and CAPITAL, where each of these is a generic name for a possibly large set of productive services. The category 'land' includes natural resources, properties of soil and waterways, or simply its ability to be built upon. 'Labour' is a term which summarizes the services of both manual and non-manual labour, the services yielded by a broker in bringing two parties together, as well as those yielded by a machine operative or road-digger. Finally, the category 'capital' refers to the services provided by machinery, buildings, tools, and other productive instruments which are goods made to produce other goods, which considerably increase the PRODUCTIVITY of land and labour, and which are only obtained by sacrificing current consumption possibilities. In certain problems, the distinctions between categories may not be rigidly applied, e.g. a highly skilled worker may be better regarded as a capital good than as a unit of labour, and tortured debate about the essential difference between factors is unnecessary.

The most important characteristic of resources is that they are relatively scarce – scarce, that is, relative to the total flow of goods and services which society would like to produce with them. This relative scarcity correspondingly creates a need for allocation, and the study of the way in which capitalist economies (⇔ CAPITALISM) carry out this process of resource allocation has long been the main preoccupation of MICROECONOMICS.

Restriction, exchange. ⇔ BALANCE OF PAYMENTS.

Restrictive Practices Court. ⇔ RESTRICTIVE TRADE PRACTICES ACTS.

Restrictive Trade Practices Act. The Restrictive Trade Practices Act of 1956 was based on the recommendations of the MONOPOLIES COMMISSION'S 1955 report on *Collective Discrimination – A Report on Exclusive Dealing, Aggregated Rebates and other Discriminatory Trade Practices*. This Act required the registration of all agreements between two or more firms, whether buyers or sellers, which contain restrictions on PRICES, quantities or quality of goods traded or on channels of distribution. It set up a Restrictive Practices Court, serviced by five judges and up to ten laymen and a

registrar of agreements. The court is required by the Act to assume
that each agreement is against the public interest unless it could be
shown to have advantages on reference to seven explicit factors:
(a) that the restriction is necessary for public safety; (b) that it
confers specific and substantial benefits or advantages on consumers;
(c) that it neutralizes monopolistic or restrictive activities of others;
(d) that it is necessary in order to be able to negotiate fair terms with
strong buyers or sellers; (e) that removal of the agreement would
lead to significant regional UNEMPLOYMENT; (f) that removal
would reduce EXPORT earnings; and (g) that it is necessary to support other restrictive practices which are in the public interest. Under
the Act the required agreements are legal until the court has dis-
approved them. Under the 1956 Act, only agreements of 'No
substantial economic significance' could be exempted from appearing before the court, and even this could be achieved only by their
removal from the Register. Only just over a hundred agreements
have been exempted in this way. In 1968, a second Restrictive
Trade Practices Act was passed by which agreements could be
exempted from court proceedings as a result of a Board of Trade
directive. The Board of Trade used its powers for the first time in
March 1969 when it exempted twenty-eight agreements from court
action. The Act also gave the Board of Trade (now the Department
of Trade and Industry) powers to call certain information agreements for registration which were excluded from the previous Act.
⇨ RESALE PRICE MAINTENANCE.

Retail price index. An INDEX NUMBER of a series of PRICES paid by
consumers for the goods they typically buy. It is also often referred
to as the 'cost of living index'. As with any other price index number, the retail price index is constructed by choosing a set of items,
finding the current prices of those items, expressing these as percentages of their prices in some BASE PERIOD and then calculating
a WEIGHTED AVERAGE of these 'price relatives'. The index is
intended to provide as accurate a representation as possible of changes
in the cost to HOUSEHOLDS of the range of goods which they normally buy. This involves, first of all, careful choice of which items to
include, the aim being to obtain as representative a set as possible.
Secondly it involves choosing an appropriate set of weights to use
in calculating the weighted average of price relatives. These weights
must reflect the importance of the items in the family BUDGET.
We would expect items on which households spend a relatively
large proportion of their INCOMES to be weighted more heavily

than items on which little is spent, since a given proportionate price rise in the former set of items will have a much bigger effect on the family's 'cost of living' than the same proportionate price rise on unimportant items. The weights must also be changed to reflect significant changes in the composition of family expenditure, if the price index is to give an accurate representation of changes in the cost of living. To help decide on which items to include, and what weights to assign, the government department responsible for the index conducts at regular intervals a family expenditure survey. This survey attempts to find how households typically divide their expenditure up between different goods, and this information then suggests which items should be included and what weights should be attached. As with any index number, the retail price index need not give an exact description of the changes in the cost of living of any one family. If one's expenditure pattern is significantly different from the average, or one buys from shops which sell at prices significantly above or below the average, then one's own 'cost of living index' would be different. Nevertheless, the retail price index gives a useful, concise picture of the broad movement of an important set of prices over time. ⇕ GROSS NATIONAL PRODUCT DEFLATOR.

Retail trade. The final link in the chain of distribution from the manufacturer to the final consumer. The retail outlet may be based on stocks (⇕ INVENTORY) located at the point of final sale whether in a large department store or a barrow in a market. Alternatively, it may, like mail order houses, centralize its stocks. The CENSUS of Distribution of 1966 showed that there are just over 500,000 establishments carrying out retailing in Great Britain. This is equivalent to about one shop for every thirty-six HOUSEHOLDS. About two and a half million people are employed in the retail trade, i.e. about 10 per cent of the total number of people in employment. The number of retail establishments fell by about 9 per cent between 1950 and 1966.

Retained earnings. Undistributed PROFITS. ⇕ SELF-FINANCING.

Retentions. Undistributed PROFITS. ⇕ SELF-FINANCING.

Return on capital employed. ⇕ RATE OF RETURN.

Return on investment. ⇕ RATE OF RETURN.

Returns to scale. The increases in output which result from increasing the whole scale of some production activity. Suppose that the quantities of all the INPUTS used in producing a given output of a particular good are increased by the same proportion, e.g. 50 per cent. Then, if output increases by a greater proportion, e.g. 55 per cent, returns to scale are said to be increasing; if output increases in the same proportion (50 per cent), then returns to scale are said to be constant; and if output increases by a smaller proportion, e.g. 45 per cent, returns to scale are said to be decreasing. Thus, returns to scale refer to the way in which output changes when the whole scale of input changes. The nature of returns to scale will clearly influence the way in which costs of production vary with scale of output. If returns to scale are increasing, then a given proportionate change in output requires a smaller proportionate change in quantities of inputs, and we would therefore expect COSTS to rise less than proportionately with output, implying a fall in cost per unit of output, i.e. a fall in AVERAGE COST. Similarly, decreasing returns to scale imply increasing average costs. Since they relate to changes in all inputs, returns to scale are necessarily a LONG-RUN concept.

The usefulness of the concept of returns to scale lies in its role as a classifying device. It provides a convenient way of classifying particular types of technological condition. For a discussion of the reasons for increasing and decreasing returns to scale, ⟡ ECONOMIES OF SCALE and DISECONOMY. Note that returns to scale refer to the relationship between input and outputs, while economies of scale relate to the relationship between cost and output, so that only those sources of economies and diseconomies of scale which are based on the input-output relationship (⟡ INPUT-OUTPUT ANALYSIS) are also sources of increasing and decreasing returns to scale respectively.

Revaluation. ⟡ DEVALUATION; EXCHANGE RATE.

Revealed preference. An analysis of consumer behaviour based only on the information on choices actually made by the consumer in various price–income situations. A particular INCOME level and set of PRICES will determine for the consumer a particular set of 'bundles' of goods he could purchase. If, in that situation, we observe that he chooses one particular bundle, that bundle is then 'revealed preferred' to all the other bundles which were attainable. Another price–income situation will lead to (in general) another bundle being revealed as preferred. By making certain quite plausible assumptions about the consistency of the choices of the consumer in the various price–income situations, it is possible to prove some of the important propositions in consumer DEMAND theory, without having to assume measurability of UTILITY, or even that INDIFFERENCE CURVES can be constructed. The revealed preference approach was first formulated by P. A. SAMUELSON.

355

Revenue reserves. ⟡ COMPANY RESERVES.

Reverse take-over. The acquisition or 'TAKE-OVER' of a public company by a private company. Often also used to refer to the acquisition of a company by another, smaller, one.

Reverse yield gap. ⟡ YIELD GAP.

Ricardo, David (1772–1823). The son of Jewish parents who were connected with the MONEY MARKET, firstly in the Netherlands, and later in London, Ricardo had little formal education. At the early age of fourteen, however, he was already working in the money market himself. It was James Mill (the father of J. S. MILL) who persuaded Ricardo, himself diffident about his own abilities, to write. Nevertheless, Ricardo succeeded in making a fortune on the STOCK EXCHANGE, sufficient for him to be able to retire at forty-two. Not surprisingly, many of his earlier publications were concerned with money and banking. In 1810, he published a pamphlet on *The High Price of Bullion, a Proof of the Depreciation of Bank Notes*; in 1811 appeared the *Reply to Mr Bosanquet's Practical Observations on the Report of the Bullion Committee*; and in 1816 *Proposals for an Economical and Secure Currency*. However, his work on monetary economics did not have the originality or exert the influence comparable to his studies in other branches of economics. In 1815, he published his *Essay on the Influence of the Low Price of Corn on the Profits of Stock*, which was the prototype for his most important work. This first appeared in 1817 under the title of *The Principles of Political Economy and Taxation*, a work which was to dominate English CLASSICAL ECONOMICS for the following half-century. In his *Principles* Ricardo was basically concerned 'to determine the laws which regulate the distribution (between the different classes of landowners, capitalists and labour) of the produce of industry'. His approach was to construct a theoretical MODEL which abstracted from the complexities of an actual economy so as to attempt to reveal the major important influences at work within it. His economy was predominantly agricultural. With DEMAND rising as a result of increasing POPULATION, and a level of subsistence which tended, by custom, to rise also over time, more and more less-fertile LAND had to be brought into cultivation. The return (in terms of the output of corn) of each further addition of CAPITAL and LABOUR to more land fell (⟡ MARGINAL PRODUCTIVITY, LAW OF DIMINISHING). This process continued until it was no longer considered sufficiently profitable to bring any additional plots of land under cultivation. However, COSTS and PROFITS must be the same on all land, whether or not it was marginal. Labour cost the same wherever it was applied. If profits were higher at one place than at another, it would encourage capital to be invested at the place of high return, until by the process of diminishing returns, profit fell into line with profits elsewhere. Therefore, as costs and profits were the same throughout, a surplus was earned on the non-marginal land, and this was RENT (shaded in diagram).

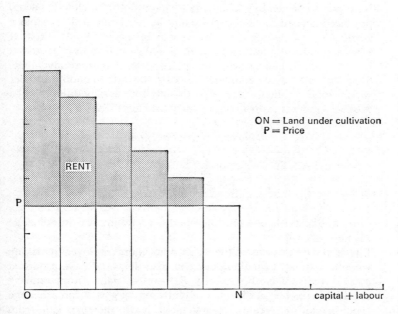

ON = Land under cultivation
P = Price

RENT

The consequence of this was that, as the population expanded and more less-fertile land was brought into cultivation, profits became squeezed between the increasing proportion of total output which went in rent and the basic minimum level of subsistence allocated to the wages of labour. Ricardo assumed that prices were determined principally by the quantity of labour used during production (▷ labour theory of value under VALUE, THEORIES OF). However, he recognized that capital costs did nevertheless also have an influence on prices and that the effect of a rise in wages on relative prices depended on the proportion of these two FACTORS OF PRODUCTION in the various COMMODITIES. With a rise in wages, CAPITAL-INTENSIVE goods became cheaper relative to LABOUR-INTENSIVE

357

goods, with a consequent shift in the demand and output in favour of the former ($\diamond$ RICARDO EFFECT). In the theory of INTERNATIONAL TRADE, Ricardo stated explicitly for the first time the law of comparative costs. This law can best be illustrated by means of the example of two countries (A and B) producing two commodities (say cloth and wine). If the relative cost of cloth to wine is the same in both countries, then no trade will take place because there is no gain to be had by exchanging wine (or cloth) for cloth (or wine) produced abroad for that produced at home. Trade will take place where cost differences exist. These can be of two kinds. First, if wine is cheap in A and cloth in B, A will specialize in wine and B in cloth, and exchange will take place to their mutual advantage. Secondly, the law of comparative costs states the condition under which trade will take place, even though both commodities may be produced more cheaply in one country than another.

Man-hours per unit of output

Country	Wine	Cloth
A	120	100
B	80	90

Country B exports one unit of wine to A, and imports in exchange $\frac{120}{100}$ units of cloth.

If Country B had devoted the eighty man-hours employed in making wine for exports to making cloth instead, it would have produced only $\frac{80}{90}$ units of cloth. Country B therefore gains from trade by the difference ($\frac{120}{100} - \frac{80}{90}$) units of cloth. As long as B can exchange wine for cloth at a rate higher than $\frac{80}{90}$, it will therefore gain from the trade. If Country A exports a unit of cloth to Country B, it will obtain in exchange $\frac{90}{80}$ units of wine. If the hundred man-hours required by A to produce a unit of cloth had been devoted to the home production of wine, only $\frac{100}{120}$ units of wine would be obtained. The gain from trade therefore is ($\frac{90}{80} - \frac{100}{120}$) units of wine. Provided therefore A can exchange cloth for wine at a rate higher than $\frac{100}{120}$, it will gain from the trade. Within the range of exchange of wine for cloth of $\frac{120}{100}$ and $\frac{80}{90}$ both countries therefore benefit.

The law of comparative costs survives as an important part of the theory of international trade today. Otherwise Ricardo's main contribution is the analytical approach of theoretical model building which has contributed substantially to economists' methodological tool-kits. ⇨ EQUATION OF INTERNATIONAL DEMAND; HECKSCHER-OHLIN PRINCIPLE.

Ricardo effect. F. A. HAYEK argued that, if the PRICES which firms received for their outputs increased more than the COSTS of their raw materials and wages, the average rate of PROFIT on CAPITAL employed per year increased more for those firms with a short than for those with a long turnover period. This can best be illustrated by a simple arithmetical example. If the rate of profit per year is 5 per cent, £100 of capital will yield £105 in one year and £110 in two years (approximately, ignoring COMPOUND INTEREST). If output prices rise by, say, 1 per cent, the YIELD rises to £6 for one year and to £11 in two years. The rate of profit, therefore, rises to 6 per cent per annum for the capital which can be turned over in one year, but only to $5\frac{1}{2}$ per cent per annum for capital with a two-year turnover period. Consequently, in a boom, when COMMODITY prices rise faster than wages, firms are discouraged from investing in capital goods industries because of the long production time required. This reaction is called the Ricardo effect because of its affinity to Ricardo's argument that, if REAL WAGES fall, firms tend to substitute LABOUR for machinery. This conclusion contrasted sharply with J. M. KEYNES's views based on the principle of the accelerator (⇨ ACCELERATION PRINCIPLE).

Rights issue. An offer of new SHARES to existing shareholders. A company will offer the 'rights' in a certain proportion to existing holdings, depending upon the amount of new EQUITY capital it wishes to raise. Thus, in a 'one for one rights issue', each shareholder would be offered a number of new shares equal to the number he already holds. To ensure that the issue is taken up, the new shares are offered at well below the market price of the existing shares. The choice of the discount below the ruling price is not as critical in normal circumstances as is often supposed, because when the rights issue is announced the market price of the shares will adjust to the market's view of the value of the rights price. Rights issues are a relatively cheap way of raising CAPITAL for a quoted company since the costs of preparing a brochure, UNDERWRITING commission or press advertising involved in a new issue are avoided. ⇨ NEW ISSUE MARKET.

Risk. A particular decision or course of action is said to be subject to risk when there is a range of possible outcomes which could flow from that decision or course of action. As strictly defined in economics (a definition owed to F. H. KNIGHT), risk exists when objectively known PROBABILITIES can be attached to these outcomes, and is thus distinguished from UNCERTAINTY, where there is a plurality of outcomes to which objective probabilities cannot be assigned. Thus, the decision to accept a gamble involving the toss of a coin, or the purchase of a PREMIUM SAVINGS BOND, is a decision subject to risk, since there is more than one possible outcome (heads, tails; win a prize, do not win a prize). Does the bet: heads I win, tails you lose, involve risk? The answer perhaps depends on the likelihood of the coin falling on its edge, but in general we would say it did not involve risk, since there is only one possible outcome – I win. Note that the term risk is being defined at once more broadly and more narrowly than in its everyday usage. A 'risky situation' in everyday terms is generally one in which one of the outcomes involves the decision-taker in losses – a businessman would not feel he was 'taking a risk' if an investment had two outcomes, one of which resulted in a PROFIT of £10,000, the other of which resulted in a profit of £5,000. Yet, on the strict definition, this is a situation involving risk. On the other hand, the fact that objective probabilities often cannot be assigned, means that many situations which in practice are called 'risky' are, on the strict definitions, really subject to uncertainty, not risk. ⟪ BERNOULLI'S HYPOTHESIS.

Risk capital. Long-term funds invested in enterprises particularly subject to RISK, as in new ventures. Sometimes used as a synonym for EQUITY capital, it is also used instead of the term *venture capital*, a somewhat more precise term meaning CAPITAL provided for a new business undertaking by persons other than the proprietors. Neither term is unambiguous, since all capital except that secured by fixed assets is at risk, and even extensions to existing business may be described accurately as a new venture. Venture capital is provided by private investors and by institutions such as the MERCHANT BANKS. There are also a number of specialized venture capital institutions, such as the Industrial and Commercial Finance Corporation.

Robbins, Lionel, Baron Robbins of Clare Market (1898–   ). Lord Robbins became a lecturer at the London School of Economics after graduating there. After a brief period as lecturer at New College, Oxford, in 1924, and again from 1927 to 1929, he was appointed in 1929 to the Chair of Economics at the London School of Economics, a position he held until 1961. During the Second World War he was, from 1941 to 1945, director of the economics section of the Cabinet Office. Since 1961 he has been chairman of the *Financial*

Times newspaper. He chaired the Committee on Higher Education. An economist in the tradition of the English CLASSICAL SCHOOL, in *An Essay on the Nature and Significance of Economic Science*, which appeared in 1932, he defined economics as 'a science which studies human behaviour as a relation between ends and scarce means which have alternative uses'. Economic analysis should beware of including propositions based on value judgements; that is it should be a scientific logical process without ethical or moral overtones. His other publications include *The Great Depression* (1934), *Economic Planning and International Order* (1937), *The Economic Problem in Peace and War* (1947), *The Economist in the Twentieth Century* (1956), *Robert Torrens and the Evolution of Classical Economics* (1958), *Politics and Economics* (1963) and *The Evolution of Modern Economic Theory* (1970).

Robertson, Sir Denis Holme (1890–1963). He was a reader in economics at Cambridge University from 1930 until his appointment to the Sir Ernest Cassel Chair at the London School of Economics in 1938. In 1944, he succeeded A. C. PIGOU to the Chair of Political Economy at Cambridge University. During the Second World War he was adviser to the TREASURY. His most important publications include *A Study of Industrial Fluctuations* (1915), *Banking Policy and the Price Level* (1926), *Essays in Monetary Theory* (1940) and *Britain in the World Economy* (1954). In 1957, he was appointed to the Council on Prices, Productivity and Incomes (◇ COHEN COMMITTEE).

Robinson, Joan Violet (1903–). Educated at Girton College, Professor Robinson took up a post as assistant lecturer at Cambridge University in 1931, becoming reader in 1949. She was elected to the Chair of Economics in 1965 on the retirement of her husband, Professor E. A. G. Robinson. Economic theorists in the 1920s were much concerned with the problem of the meaning of a theory of VALUE based on PERFECT COMPETITION. In particular, it was felt of doubtful validity to assume a situation in which there were so many firms supplying a COMMODITY, that none of them individually could affect the PRICE – in face of the existence of the economies of large-scale output. Professor Robinson broke out of the analytical framework of perfect competition and built up her analysis on the basis of firms in 'IMPERFECT COMPETITION'. Each firm had a MONOPOLY in its products which was based on the preferences of consumers (◇ CONSUMER PREFERENCE), in spite of the existence of very close substitutes produced by other firms. (◇ E. H. CHAMBERLIN, who developed similar ideas simultaneously and independently.)

These ideas were set out in her book *Economics of Imperfect Competition*, published in 1933. Her other published works include *An Essay on Marxian Economics* (1942), *Accumulation of Capital* (1956), *Essays on the Theory of Economic Growth* (1963), *Collected Economic Papers* (3 vols. 1951, 1960 and 1965), *Economics: An Awkward Corner* (1966). The 'awkward corner' of the last was the present-day confusion of 'partial LAISSEZ-FAIRE'. Government economic controls are confined to the regulation of aggregate EFFECTIVE DEMAND, and the allocation of the country's economic RESOURCES is left to FREE MARKET competition. There is, however, no more reason to suppose that competition efficiently allocates available resources, given the political and social aims of society, better than it can regulate AGGREGATE DEMAND.

Roll-over. ◊ CORPORATION TAX.

Roskill Commission. A Royal Commission set up in 1968 under Lord Roskill to report on the best location in England of a third London Airport. The commission reported in January 1971 in favour of Cublington, Bucks., with a note of dissent by Professor Buchanan in favour of Foulness on environmental grounds. The report is noteworthy in economic terms for its use of COST-BENEFIT ANALYSIS.

Rostow, Walt Whitman (1916–). Educated at Yale, and at Oxford, as a Rhodes Scholar, Rostow served during the Second World War in the Office of Strategic Services, and was the assistant chief of the Division of German-Austrian Economic Affairs of the U.S. Department of State from 1945–6. He was Pitt Professor of American History at Cambridge University for 1949–50, and Professor of Economic History of Massachusetts Institute of Technology from 1950 to 1965. He was appointed special assistant to the President in 1966. His major publications include *The Process of Economic Growth* (1952) and *Stages of Economic Growth* (1960). In the latter, he postulated that societies passed through five stages of economic development: (a) the traditional society; (b) the preconditions for take-off; (c) the take-off, when growth becomes a normal feature of the economy; (d) the drive to maturity; and some sixty years after take-off begins, (e) maturity, reached in the age of high mass CONSUMPTION. ◊ ECONOMIC GROWTH, STAGES OF; GROWTH, THEORY OF.

'Roundabout' methods of production. ◊ BÖHM-BAWERK; CAPITAL.

S

Sales promotion. ⟡ ADVERTISING.

Sample. In everyday terms, a sample is simply a quantity of something which has been selected as representative of that thing. A wine-taster takes a sample of a particular type of wine and tastes it in order to evaluate the whole vintage. In economic and social research, however, a sample is given a somewhat more restricted meaning; rather than being just a 'part' of some 'total' quantity known technically as the 'population', it is rather a part which must be selected by certain statistical methods designed to ensure that the items selected for the sample are really representative of the population as a whole. Thus, the term 'sample' should strictly only be applied to a properly chosen set of items. (For discusion of what constitutes 'proper' choice, ⟡ QUOTA SAMPLE; RANDOM SAMPLE; SIMPLE RANDOM SAMPLE; STRATIFIED SAMPLE.) The purpose of a sample is to provide some sort of information about the population from which it is selected. Since the sample is only some part of the population, if follows that we would expect some inaccuracy. For example, by questioning a sample of voters, it might be found that 30 per cent of the sample intended to vote for Party A, 50 per cent of the sample intended voting for Party B, and 20 per cent for other parties. On the other hand, if an election were held, we might well get shares of 33, 49 and 18 per cent respectively, simply because a sample is unlikely to give a perfect representation of the population. However, if the sample is properly designed, the size of the likely error is kept to a minimum and it is possible to calculate and specify the size of the likely error. Furthermore, it is possible to find how varying the number of items included in the sample affects the size of the likely error.

The advantages of taking a sample, even if the information gained is not likely to be perfectly accurate for the whole population, are often substantial. In the extreme case, where evaluating the sample actually destroys the items (tasting wine, testing a machine or component to destruction), it is quite clear that the relevant information can only be gained from a sample. In economic and social research, however, the relevant consideration is the relation between the size of the sample and the cost and quality of the information-gathering procedure. The larger the sample, the greater the number of question-naires, interviewers, etc., and the greater the COST of analysing the data.

Samuelson, Paul Anthony (1915–). Professor Samuelson was appointed to the Chair of Economics at Massachusetts Institute of Technology in 1940. He served in the U.S. Treasury for seven years after the end of the Second World War. His publications include *Foundations of Economic Analysis* (1947), *Readings in Economics* (1955) and *Linear Programming and Economic Analysis* (1958). Samuelson developed the HECKSCHER-OHLIN PRINCIPLE by showing how an increase in the PRICE of a COMMODITY can raise the INCOME of the FACTOR OF PRODUCTION which is used most intensively in producing it (⟡ CAPITAL-INTENSIVE). This led to his formulating the *factor price equalization theorem*, which states the conditions under which, as FREE TRADE in commodities narrows differences in commodity prices between countries, in so doing the prices (incomes) of factors of production are also brought into line. In other words, free trade is a substitute for the free mobility of factors of production. Professor Samuelson has made important contributions to the development of mathematical economics, general EQUILIBRIUM theory and the theory of CONSUMER BEHAVIOUR. To free the latter from what he considered to be the constraint of the traditional concept of UTILITY, he invented REVEALED PREFER-ENCE. In macroeconomic theory (⟡ MACROECONOMICS), he was, in an article in 1939, the first to formulate the interaction between the accelerator and the multiplier (⟡ ACCELERATOR-MULTIPLIER MODEL). In 1970, he was awarded the Nobel Prize for Economics.

Saturation point. A level beyond which the *relative* absorption of a product or service is not expected to increase. It is defined in terms of a ratio, e.g. ownership of refrigerators per household or per hundred persons. Once the saturation point is reached, the growth of demand slows down to levels determined by population growth and replacement, although in some cases predictions of saturation points have been falsified by the emergence of multiple ownership, e.g. of cars and television sets. ⟡ MARKET SHARE.

Saving. Not spending INCOME on CONSUMPTION. Thus, income which is not spent on consumption (and which is not taxed) is by definition saved. An important thing to note about this definition is that it is rather wider than conventional usage of the word: it is not necessary for an income-earner to place money in a savings account, or buy some kind of ASSET, to be saving in the sense used here. Simply leaving money in a CURRENT ACCOUNT, or in a jar on the mantelpiece, as long as it represents non-spending of current income, is saving. Economists choose this definition because the important feature of saving, thus defined, is that it represents money which, having been paid out as income to HOUSEHOLDS by business firms, etc., is not returned to them in the form of expenditure on goods and SERVICES. If there were not some other source of expenditure on goods and services, therefore, to 'make up for' the amount saved, firms would find that they were producing too much, and would therefore reduce production, implying in turn a fall in income and employment. In fact, another source of expenditure does exist, and this is INVESTMENT. If the amount invested just equals the amount saved, income and employment will show no tendency to change, i.e. they will be in EQUILIBRIUM. On the other hand, if investment is less than saving, total expenditure will be inadequate to maintain the previous level of output, income and employment, and the latter will tend to fall. If, however, investment were greater than saving, expenditure must be more than enough to maintain the previous levels of income, etc., and the latter will tend to rise. Thus, we can say that for income and employment to be in equilibrium, expenditure on investment must be just equal to saving or non-expenditure on consumption. This is the basis of the theory of INCOME DETERMINATION developed by J. M. KEYNES. The economic definition of saving can only be fully understood in that context.

Savings banks. Banks which accept INTEREST-bearing DEPOSITS of small amounts. The Post Office Savings Bank is the best known. Trustee savings banks antedate the P.O.S.B. and were established to encourage saving by people with low INCOMES. The first trustee savings bank was opened in Scotland in 1810. The trustee banks are managed by bodies of local trustees, are non-PROFIT-making and since 1965 have been permitted to issue CHEQUES. The P.O.S.B. was set up in 1861. It has a centralized accounting system, but allows depositors to make deposits or withdrawals, recorded in a deposit book, at some 20,000 post offices. With the Post Office GIRO system and a number of different savings-incentive schemes, the Post Office now offers a range of services approaching those of the COMMERCIAL BANKS.

Say, Jean-Baptiste (1767–1832). A practical businessman, Say developed an interest in economics and began lecturing in the subject in 1816. In 1819, he was appointed to the Chair of Industrial Economy at the Conservatoire National des Arts et Métiers. In 1831, he was appointed Professor of Political Economy at the Collège de France. His most important published works are *Traité d'économie politique*, which appeared in 1803, and *Cours complet d'économie politique pratique*, which was published in 1829. Although he can claim some credit for the introduction of the concept of an ENTREPRENEUR into economic theory, and also the division of the fundamental FACTORS OF PRODUCTION into three – LAND, LABOUR and CAPITAL – his fame and notoriety spring from his '*loi des débouches*', or 'law of markets'. It is probable that his 'law' would not figure so prominently in economics today had not J. M. KEYNES accused the CLASSICAL ECONOMISTS of being gravely misled by accepting it as the pivot of their macroeconomic theory (⟡ MACROECONOM- ICS). According to Keynes, the law said that the sum of the values of all COMMODITIES produced was equivalent (always) to the sum of the VALUES of all commodities bought. By definition, therefore, there could be no underutilization of RESOURCES; 'supply created its own demand'. However, there is some considerable doubt about what Say actually meant. Several versions have been put forward; some are incontrovertible platitudes, such as in barter a seller must also be a buyer, and if a good is sold somebody must have bought it. Probably the most meaningful interpretation is that of Keynes, but only as a condition which must be satisfied for EQUILIBRIUM to exist. ⟡ L. WALRAS.

Say's law of markets. ⟡ J.-B. SAY.

Scarce currency. Synonym for HARD CURRENCY.

Scarcity. A condition where there is less of something than people would like to have if it cost nothing to buy. Thus this word is used in economics in a relative sense. Most people would say that there were many motor-cars about, and that they were hardly scarce in the usual sense of the word; but since there is certainly not enough to give everyone who wants one a motor-car, we can say that they are, relatively speaking, scarce. Similarly, since the total quantity of goods and SERVICES which people would like to have far exceeds the amount which the economy's resources are capable of producing, we can say that there is a scarcity of resources (even though the economy might have a very large LABOUR force, many factories, etc.). The importance of the existence of scarcity is that it gives rise to a need to allocate the available RESOURCES among alternative uses. If this allocation is done through a FREE MARKET, capitalist system (⟡ CAPITALISM), rather than through a centralized command economy (⟡ PLANNED ECONOMY), then scarcity will necessarily imply positive prices for goods. Air does not have a PRICE because it is not relatively scarce: everyone has as much as he wants; food has a price because it requires resources – LAND, LABOUR, machinery, seed, fertilizer, etc. – which are relatively scarce, and could be used to produce other things.

Schedule D. ⬦ INCOME TAX.

Schedule E. ⬦ INCOME TAX.

Schuman Plan. ⬦ EUROPEAN COAL AND STEEL COMMUNITY.

Schumpeter, Joseph Alois (1883–1950). In 1919, he was appointed Professor of Economics at Czernowitz, subsequently moving to Graz. He was appointed Minister of Finance in the Austrian Republic for a short period after the First World War. From 1925 until 1932, he held the Chair of Public Finance at Bonn. From 1932, until his death, he was at Harvard University. His major publications include *Theory of Economic Development* (1912), *Business Cycles* (1939), *Capitalism, Socialism and Democracy* (1942) and *History of Economic Analysis*, which appeared posthumously and unfinished in 1954. He built up a theory of the TRADE CYCLE which was based on three time periods: (a) short, (b) medium and (c) long, to each of which he attributed different causes. He tested his theory against actual fluctuations from the eighteenth to the twentieth century. Although it was reasonably successful, he was doubtful of the predictive efficiency of his theory for future periods. He attempted to work out a theory of economic growth and fluctuation around an explicit recognition of the contribution of technical INNOVATION. He tried to argue that, without the latter, an economy would reach a static EQUILIBRIUM position of a 'circular flow' of goods with no net growth. He emphasized the evolutionary nature of the capitalist system (⬦ CAPITALISM). He argued that under MONOPOLY capitalism, firms would place less emphasis on PRICE competition, but would increasingly compete in technical and organizational innovation, thus sending 'gales of creative destruction' through the economic system. He predicted that capitalism would evolve gradually into Socialism.

Scrip issue. An issue of new SHARES to shareholders in proportion to their existing holdings made, as distinct from a RIGHTS ISSUE, without charge. A scrip or bonus issue does not raise new CAPITAL. It is merely an adjustment to the capital structure which capitalizes reserves, usually consisting of past PROFITS. The word 'scrip' is an abbreviation of 'subscription certificate'. ⬦ CAPITALIZATION.

Seasonal adjustment. A numerical alteration to TIME SERIES data to allow for the fact that the values of the data for a particular period of time are normally subject to influences peculiar to that period of time. Removal of these influences, if accurately done, then permits the underlying tendency in the data to be discerned.

Seasonal unemployment. UNEMPLOYMENT due to the seasonal nature of activity in some trades, e.g. unemployment in the building industry increases in winter.

Second Best, Theory of. An area of economics concerned with the analysis of situations in which PERFECT COMPETITION does not prevail throughout the economy, or, for some reason, the state of the economy which would result from a perfectly competitive EQUILIBRIUM cannot be achieved. The most important proposition of the theory is that, if some part of the economy does not attain the perfectly competitive equilibrium position, e.g. because of MONOPOLY, it need not be optimal for any other sector of the economy to attain that position. Rather, optimality may require that the other sectors of the economy adopt positions which diverge from the perfectly competitive one. This apparently rather abstract proposition, first advanced by R. G. Lipsey and K. Lancaster, has, in fact, very important implications for such subjects as the pricing of NATIONALIZED INDUSTRY outputs, and optimum TARIFF policies in INTERNATIONAL TRADE. For example it, may imply that nationalized industries should not adopt MARGINAL COST PRICING; or that FREE TRADE is not an OPTIMUM policy.

Secondary market. A MARKET for the resale and purchase of SECURITIES or other titles to property or COMMODITIES outside the organized exchanges or primary markets. Examples are the secondary MORTGAGE market in the U.S., where holders of mortgages who need funds can dispose of their holding before maturity. The *secondary stock market* is that in unquoted securities dealt with by private placings and dealings among BROKERS, MERCHANT BANKS and other persons and institutions. ⧫ OVER THE COUNTER MARKET.

Secular trend. A consistent underlying tendency to change in a particular direction, this tendency being the result of long-term forces. Thus, there might be a secular trend towards increasing UNEMPLOYMENT in a region, as a result of a gradual shift of DEMAND away from the products in which the region specializes, this shift being in turn a result of steadily changing tastes and technology. Secular trends are to be distinguished from shorter-term fluctuations resulting from fashion changes, the TRADE CYCLE, seasonal demand fluctuations, etc.

Securities. 1. In the widest sense, documents giving title to property or claims on INCOME which may be lodged, e.g. as SECURITY for a BANK LOAN. **2.** Income-yielding paper traded on the STOCK EXCHANGE or in SECONDARY MARKETS. Usually a synonym for STOCKS and SHARES. An essential characteristic of a security is that it is saleable. The main types of security are: (a) *Fixed interest:* DEBENTURES, PREFERENCE SHARES, stocks and BONDS (including all GOVERNMENT SECURITIES and local authority securities); (b) *Variable interest:* ORDINARY SHARES; (c) *Other:* BILLS OF EXCHANGE, ASSURANCE policies. Securities may be REDEEMABLE or IRREDEEMABLE. ⟡ EQUITIES; GILT-EDGED SECURITIES.

Security sterling. Under the Exchange Control (Blocked Accounts) Order of 1948, EXCHANGE CONTROL regulations were imposed on the disposal of the proceeds of sale of sterling SECURITIES and ASSETS by non-residents of the STERLING AREA. Under these restrictions, proceeds of such sales were credited to blocked accounts which could only be used to purchase sterling securities. Sterling in these accounts was transferable between non-residents, and was quoted generally at a discount below the official spot EXCHANGE RATE of sterling. In April 1967, the Chancellor of the EXCHEQUER cancelled the 1948 Order and merged the security sterling market with that of the official FOREIGN EXCHANGE MARKET which was freely convertible for non-residents.

Select Committee on Estimates. A select committee of the British House of Commons, whose purpose is to examine whichever of the ESTIMATES of projected government expenditure it thinks should be examined. Its purpose is essentially to find if any economies may be achieved, consistent with the policies implied in the estimates.

Selective Employment Tax (S.E.T.). A TAX which came into operation in the U.K. in September 1966 with the intention of 'encouraging economy in the use of labour in services and thereby making more labour available for the expansion of manufacturing industry'. There was also the idea that PRICES of manufactures to the consumer were distorted relatively to those of SERVICES because the incidence of taxation, as a result of the PURCHASE TAX system, fell relatively heavier on the former than the latter. Mainly because of administrative reasons, all firms were required to pay S.E.T.

S.E.T. was calculated originally at the following rates per week per employee: for men 25s. (£1.25), for women 12s. 6d. (62½p) for boys (under eighteen) 12s. 6d. (62½p) and for girls (under eighteen) 8s. (40p). These taxes were refunded in full to employers in the non-taxable industries, such as agriculture and the NATIONALIZED INDUSTRIES, and were returned with a premium to manufacturers. The premium subsidies were 7s. 6d. (37½p) per week for men, 3s. 9d. (19p) for women and boys and 2s. 6d. (12½p) for girls. The construction and services industries receive no rebates. In November 1967, the premium to manufacturing industries was cancelled, except for firms in the DEVELOPMENT AREAS, for which the premium was continued until 1970. In April 1968, the tax was increased by 50 per cent with effect from September 1968. In April 1969, S.E.T. was increased further by 28 per cent with effect from July 1969. The new rates were then: men 48s. (£2.40), women and boys 24s. (£1.20) and girls 16s. (80p). In 1971, the rates were halved and the government announced its intention to replace S.E.T. by a VALUE ADDED TAX in 1973. ⇨ NATIONAL INSURANCE; REGIONAL EMPLOYMENT PREMIUM.

Self-financing. CAPITAL generated from INCOME. A firm which is self-financing is generating its INVESTMENT funds from internal sources, i.e. the ploughing back of retained PROFITS (or retentions), and DEPRECIATION, as opposed to external borrowing. A quoted company has the choice of financing fixed CAPITAL formation or increasing its stocks and work in progress or acquiring other companies or SHARES in them, either by borrowing on the STOCK EXCHANGE (or from other sources, including banks), or by using undistributed income. If it borrows, it will have to pay INTEREST or DIVIDENDS and issuing costs on new issues. If it uses undistributed income, it is choosing to pay its ordinary shareholders a lower dividend, i.e. to distribute less of its income. Unquoted companies do not have the alternative of new issues of shares, although they may take further EQUITY from private sources and borrow from other sources. In fact, the bulk of capital expenditure is financed from internal sources. The new capital funds of U.K. industrial and commercial companies were £4,737 million in 1968, of which £2,543 million was devoted to gross domestic fixed-capital formation, £611 millions to financing increases in stocks and work in progress and the rest to acquiring financial ASSETS. Almost 70 per cent of these capital funds were provided from undistributed income, and only just over 10 per cent from capital issues by quoted companies.

(The remainder came from BANK LOANS, MORTGAGES and capital transfers.)

Self-financing ratio. INVESTMENT funds derived from undistributed INCOME as a proportion of total investment funds in any accounting period. ⟡ SELF-FINANCING.

Self-liquidating. A low-RISK financial transaction or LOAN which incorporates a procedure for simultaneous termination and clearing indebtedness. A HIRE PURCHASE transaction is self-liquidating in that regular payments culminate in a final instalment which clears the DEBT. More generally, the term is applied to any form of finance to fill a temporary shortfall of funds, e.g. BILLS OF EXCHANGE, or a bridging loan by a bank to a customer in the process of selling one house and buying another.

Selling costs. COSTS incurred in MARKETING and distributing a product, including the costs of advertising, sales promotion, packaging, salesmen, etc.

Senior, Nassau William (1790–1864). Educated at Oxford University, Senior was called to the Bar in 1819 and became a Master in Chancery in 1836. In 1825, he was appointed the first Drummond Professor of Political Economy at Oxford. He held this position twice, the first time until 1830 and the second from 1847 to 1852. He served on many Royal Commissions. His major work on economics was an *Outline of the Science of Political Economy*, which appeared in 1836. He is remembered mainly for his abstinence theory of INTEREST. Interest was a reward for abstaining from the unproductive use of SAVINGS. The creation of new capital involved a SACRIFICE. A positive return must therefore be expected to make the sacrifice worthwhile. Senior can be regarded as one of the first pure theorists in economics. He attempted to elaborate economic theory on the basis of deductions from elementary propositions.

Separation of ownership from control. In its earliest form, business was owned and managed by the same people. Social and technological development led to the development of the JOINT-STOCK COMPANY in the seventeenth century to meet the need for larger amounts of CAPITAL. This began the process of the separation of ownership from control that continued with the introduction of LIMITED LIABILITY for both PUBLIC COMPANIES and PRIVATE COMPANIES, and the gradual emergence of the modern giant corporation, in which none of the directors or managers have more than a minority financial interest. This process has given rise to the possi-

371

bility that the interests of those who control business and those who own it may conflict, a subject of continuing controversy among economists since the publication of *The Modern Corporation and Private Property* by A. A. Berle and G. C. Means in 1932. ⇔ FIRM, THEORY OF; J. K. GALBRAITH.

Serra, Antonio (15? – 16?). A Neapolitan writer in the mercantilist tradition (⇔ MERCANTILISM), who was the first to analyse and fully use the concept of the balance of trade, both visible and invisible. He explained how the shortage of precious metals in the Neapolitan kingdom was a result of a deficit on the BALANCE OF PAYMENTS. In so doing, he rejected the idea, current at the time, that the SCARCITY of money was due to the unfavourable EXCHANGE RATE. The solution was to be found in the encouragement of EXPORTS.

Services. Consumer or producer goods which are mainly intangible and often consumed at the same time as they are produced. The services of an orchestra, a telephone call or a teacher are intangible and are consumed as they are produced. However, financial services or the work of a computing bureau are partially tangible in form, e.g. a computer print-out sheet. Service industries are usually LABOUR-INTENSIVE and the measurement of net output (⇔ VALUE ADDED) and PRODUCTIVITY presents special difficulties. ADAM SMITH, like the PHYSIOCRATS and the mercantilists (⇔ MERCAN-TILISM) and others before him, did not believe that service industries contributed to the creation of national wealth. Even today, because service industries make only an indirect contribution to visible exports or military capability, or for other real or imagined reasons, economic policy is usually biased in favour of manufacturing industry or agriculture in most developed countries (⇔ SELECTIVE EMPLOY-MENT TAX).

Servicing debt. ⇔ DEBT.

Share. One of a number of equal portions in the NOMINAL CAPITAL of a company entitling the owner to a proportion of distributed PROFITS and of residual VALUE if the company goes into LIQUIDA-TION, a form of SECURITY. Shares may be fully PAID-UP or partly paid, VOTING or non-voting (sometimes called 'A' shares). ⇔ ORDINARY SHARES; PREFERENCE SHARES; STOCKS.

Share certificate. A document showing ownership of SHARES in a company. ⇔ TRANSFER DEED.

Shareholders' interest. ⇔ NET WORTH.

Share indices. INDEX NUMBERS indicating changes in the average prices of SHARES on the STOCK EXCHANGE. The indices are constructed by taking a selection of shares and 'weighting' (▷ WEIGHTED AVERAGE) the percentage changes in prices together as an indication of aggregate movements in share prices. Roughly speaking, a share index shows percentage changes in the MARKET value of a PORTFOLIO compared with its VALUE in the base year of the index. Index numbers are published by several daily papers and weekly journals. ▷▷ FINANCIAL TIMES ACTUARIES SHARE INDICES; FINANCIAL TIMES STOCK INDICES; TIMES SHARE INDEX.

Share options. ▷ OPTION.

Short-dated securities. ▷ DATED SECURITIES.

Short-run. A time period within which a firm is not able to vary all its FACTORS OF PRODUCTION. There will, in fact, be several 'short-runs', of varying lengths, corresponding to the particular possibilities which the firm has of varying particular INPUTS. For example, in the very short run, say one week, the firm may not be able to change the amounts of any of the inputs it uses (although it could, perhaps, increase LABOUR inputs by increasing overtime working in a period less than this). Over a month, however, it may be able to expand its LABOUR FORCE and increase the flow of raw materials. Over a year, it may be able to increase all its inputs, except, perhaps, certain types of machinery, which perhaps take two years to obtain and install. Hence, the 'short-run' for the firm will be anything less than two years. However, the firm may itself have it within its power to shorten the short-run by incurring higher costs. For example, the firm could rent the machinery, at a premium, and so obtain it in less than two years; or the firm may pay more to shorten the delivery time. This means that what is the short-run to a firm is as much an economic as a technological question. More generally, the term 'short-run' may be applied to any time period not long enough to allow the full effects of some changes to have operated. ▷▷ LONG-RUN; A. MARSHALL.

Short-run cost curves. Curves showing the functional relationship between SHORT-RUN total costs, AVERAGE COSTS and MARGINAL COSTS and output. They are a useful analytical tool in the theory of the FIRM.

Short-term capital. ▷ BUSINESS FINANCE.

Short-term gains. ▷ CAPITAL GAINS.

Simple interest. ▷ COMPOUND INTEREST.

Shortfall assessment. ▷ CORPORATION TAX.

Simple random sample. A RANDOM SAMPLE in which each item in the population has an equal chance of being included in the sample. Thus, suppose the population to be sampled consists of twelve students, and we wish to find, by taking a sample of three students, the average annual expenditure on books. If we want to take a simple random sample, we could number the students from one to twelve, write each number on a separate piece of paper, put them into a bag and draw out three pieces. The numbers on them would then identify the three students for our sample. Each piece of paper has the same chance of being selected; any other procedure which has the property of giving the items in the population an equal chance of being included would be suitable, and choice of a procedure depends on its cost and convenience. A simple random sample shares the general properties of random samples in being independent of human judgement and therefore of the biases this might impart, and in permitting the size of the likely error in generalizing from sample to population to be estimated. However, there may well be situations in which, although we wish to retain the properties of the random sample, we do not want each item in the population to have the same chance of being selected – we may wish to have consistently more of one type of item than another in our sample. This then requires a STRATIFIED SAMPLE. ⟡ CLUSTER SAMPLE.

Simulation. The use of a MODEL of some activity or process to examine the way it works, and to solve problems associated with it. The model may be a physical construction; e.g. the stresses to which an aeroplane design may be subject can be examined by simulating its flight by means of a scale model in a wind tunnel. More generally, however, a mathematical model of the system concerned will be constructed, and a computer used to reproduce the essential workings of the system. In this latter sense, simulation has come to play a very important role in OPERATIONS RESEARCH. The reason for its use is, of course, that it is generally much cheaper to construct a model, physical or mathematical, than to operate the process itself. ⟡ MONTE CARLO METHOD

'Single-tax party'. ⟡ H. GEORGE.

Sinking fund. ⟡ AMORTIZATION.

Sismondi, Jean Charles Léonard Simonde de (1773–1842). A Swiss historian and economist, who after a period in exile in England, began lecturing at Geneva Academy in 1809 on history and economics. His economic works include *Richesse Commerciale* (1803), *Nouveaux Principes d'économie politique* (1819) and *Études sur l'économie politique* (1837). Sismondi argued against the doctrine of

LAISSEZ-FAIRE in favour of state intervention. He recommended UNEMPLOYMENT and sickness benefits, and pension schemes for workers. Along with T. R. MALTHUS, he attacked D. RICARDO for not recognizing the possibility of economic crisis developing from underconsumption. He tried to emphasize the dynamic nature of the economic process, compared with the comparative statics of Ricardo (⍰ COMPARATIVE STATIC EQUILIBRIUM ANALYSIS), and was the first to use sequence analysis as an analytical device. Increased output in one period, he argued, is faced with a level of INCOME generated by a lower level of output in the previous period. Total demand falls short of the available supply. Lags in the economic system, therefore, could give rise to underconsumption.

Size distribution of firms. A description of the size pattern of firms in an industry or economy. It is constructed, first, by choosing some suitable measurement of size (total sales, number employed, NET ASSETS, etc.), and then by establishing size classes, e.g.:

number employed: less than 10
11 – 20
21 – 50
51 – 100
and so on.

Then, the number of firms falling within each size class is calculated, and these numbers are tabulated against the size classes. This then gives the size distribution of firms. ⍰ CONCENTRATION RATIO; FREQUENCY DISTRIBUTION.

Slump. ⍰ DEPRESSION.

Slutsky, Eugen (1880–1948). He was appointed a professor at Kiev University in 1918, where he remained until 1926. In 1934, he accepted a post at the Mathematics Institute of the Academy of Sciences of the U.S.S.R., where he remained until his death. He published an article in the Italian journal *Giornale degle Economiste* in 1915 on consumer behaviour. In this article he showed how the concept of ORDINAL UTILITY could be used to build a theory of consumer behaviour of the same scope as that of A. MARSHALL, but without the underlying assumption of the measurability of UTILITY. However, the article lay unnoticed until J. R. HICKS and R. G. ALLEN rediscovered it in 1934. In his book *Value and Capital*, Hicks applied Slutsky's name to the mathematical formulae which illustrate how a consumer would react to PRICE and INCOME changes (⍰ CONSUMER BEHAVIOUR, THEORY OF; V. F. D. PARETO).

375

Slutsky did little further work in economic theory, but made important contributions to statistics and PROBABILITY theory which are of relevance to economics. He emphasized the danger of assuming causes for observed fluctuations in TIME SERIES by showing how regular cycles could be generated in the derivation of MOVING AVERAGES from a series, even though the latter was made up of random numbers. He also made important advances in the study of serial CORRELATION.

Smith, Adam (1723–90). A Scotsman, brought up by his mother at Kirkcaldy, he became a student under Francis Hutcheson at Glasgow University at the age of fourteen and won a scholarship to Oxford, where he spent six years until 1746. He lectured at Edinburgh University from 1748 to 1751. From 1751 until 1763 he was at Glasgow, first in the Chair of Logic and a year later the Chair of Moral Philosophy, which he took over from Hutcheson. From 1764 to 1766 he toured France as the tutor to the Duke of Buccleugh. His major work on economics, *An Inquiry into the Nature and Causes of the Wealth of Nations*, appeared in 1776. This work of Adam Smith's became the foundation upon which was constructed the whole subsequent tradition of English CLASSICAL ECONOMICS, which can be traced from D. RICARDO through A. MARSHALL to A. L. PIGOU. Smith was primarily concerned with the factors which led to increased WEALTH in a community, and he rejected the PHYSIOCRATS' view of the pre-eminent position of agriculture, recognizing the parallel contribution of manufacturing industry. He began his analysis by means of a sketch of a primitive society of hunters. If it cost twice the labour to kill a beaver as it does a deer, one beaver would exchange for two deer. LABOUR was the fundamental measure of VALUE, though actual PRICES of COMMODITIES were determined by SUPPLY and DEMAND on the MARKET (◊ RICARDO and MARX). There were two elements in the problem of increasing WEALTH: (a) the skill of the LABOUR FORCE and (b) the proportion of productive to unproductive labour. (According to Smith, the SERVICE industries did not contribute to real wealth.) The key to (a) was the DIVISION OF LABOUR. To illustrate his point, he quoted the example of the manufacture of pins. If one man were set the task of carrying out all the operations of pin manufacture – drawing the wire, cutting, head-fitting and sharpening – his output would be minimal. If, however, each man specialized on a single operation only, output would be increased a hundredfold. The size of the output need only be limited by the size of its market. The key to (b) was the accumulation of CAPITAL. Not only did this enable plant and machinery to be created to assist labour, but it also enabled labour to be employed. Capital for the latter was the wages fund (⟡ WAGE FUND THEORY). The workers must be fed and clothed during the period of production in advance of the INCOME earned from their own efforts. Smith believed that the economic system was harmonious and required the minimum of government interference (⟡ LAISSEZ-FAIRE). Although each individual was motivated by self-interest, they each acted for the good of the whole, guided by a 'hidden hand' (⟡ INVISIBLE HAND) made possible by the free play of competition (⟡ B. DE MANDEVILLE). Free competition was the essential ingredient of the efficient economy. However, from his *Wealth of Nations* it is clear that not only did his scholarship range widely over the fields of history and contemporary business, but that, at the same time, he was a very practical man. He was quite aware, for instance, of the forces which were at work to limit competition: 'People of the same trade seldom meet together even for merriment and diversion, but the conversation ends in a conspiracy against the public, or on some contrivance to raise prices' (Book one, Chapter X, Part 2). In his discussions of PUBLIC FINANCE, he laid down four principles of TAXATION, viz. (a) equality (taxes proportionate to ability to pay), (b) certainty, (c) convenience, and (d) economy. ⟡ D. HUME.

Social accounting. The presentation of the NATIONAL INCOME and expenditure accounts in a form showing the transactions during a given period between the different sectors of the economy. The tabulations are set out in the form of a MATRIX showing the source of INPUTS of each sector or part of sector and the distribution of their outputs. The production sector, for instance, shows for an industry how much of its inputs were bought from other home industries, how much it imported and how much it spent on WAGES, salaries and DIVIDENDS. At the same time, it shows how much of its output it sold to other industries, how much it exported and how much was consumed by private individuals or the government sector. These transactions of the producers' sector are counterbalanced by corresponding transactions of the other sectors. For instance, the personal sector shows the value and sources of INCOMES earned from the producers' sector and others, and the way these incomes are spent on the outputs of the various industries, or on IMPORTS or are saved. Much work on the development and

377

analysis of these MACROECONOMIC statistics for economic prediction is being undertaken at Cambridge University under the direction of Professor J. R. Stone. ⟡ INPUT-OUTPUT ANALYSIS; W. LEONTIEF.

Social benefits. A term sometimes used in two senses: (a) All the gains in welfare which flow from a particular economic decision, whether or not they accrue to the individual or institution taking the decision, i.e. the total improvement in welfare of the society as a whole, *including* the decision-taker. (b) Those gains which accrue not to the individual or agency taking the decision, but to the rest of society. Thus, 'social' benefits are contrasted to 'private' benefits. In this sense, social benefits are equivalent to beneficial EXTERNALITIES or 'spillover' effects. The first sense is probably the more widely used.

Social capital. The total stock of CAPITAL possessed by the economy as a whole. This includes not only the buildings, machinery, etc., which are used in producing marketable outputs, but also those which are engaged in producing goods and SERVICES which are not marketed, e.g. hospitals, schools, defence equipment, etc.

Social cost. COSTS of some activity or output which are borne by society as a whole, and which need not be equal to the costs borne by the individual or firm carrying out that activity or producing that output. Social costs therefore consist of the opportunity costs of RESOURCES used in some activity, together with the value of any loss in welfare, or increase in costs, which that activity causes to any other individual or firm in the economy. Thus the social cost of a motor-car journey exceeds the private cost by the amount of the increase in costs to other motorists caused by an increase in congestion, and the costs of providing the road facilities (which are not reflected in the cost to a motorist of an additional journey); the social cost of building a factory in an area of high UNEMPLOYMENT is less than the private cost to the extent that workers are employed who would otherwise be unemployed, and therefore have zero opportunity costs, and so on. The idea of social cost is closely related to the idea of EXTERNALITIES: if the opportunity costs of resources are correctly reflected in their MARKET price, then social costs differ from private costs by the amount of the value of any external economies and DISECONOMIES conferred ⟡ A. C. PIGOU.

Social credit. Major C. H. Douglas, a Scottish engineer, developed this scheme during the 1930s. He argued that the distribution of the real WEALTH of the community by means of earned INCOMES was inequitable, and, in addition, that INFLATION was endemic because of the abuse of the CREDIT-creating privileges of the banks. Manufacturers were forced to raise PRICES of goods for final CONSUMPTION in order to redeem LOANS from banks, even if they were raised on CAPITAL goods only. Douglas proposed the setting up of industrial banks owned by LABOUR into which industry paid WAGES, salaries and DIVIDENDS and through which the state reimbursed the industry with a given proportion of the amount to which its prices, fixed by the state, fell short of total costs. The government would pay out dividends directly, or as price rebates, and these would eventually entirely replace wages. The movement gained some support in Canada, and the party won the election of 1935 in Alberta. Attempts by the party to put the theory into practice were, however, frustrated by the Federal government and the Supreme Court. The latter's views were upheld by the Privy Council meeting in London in 1947.

Social overhead capital. ⟡ INFRASTRUCTURE.

Social welfare. The well-being of the community as a whole. In general, economics takes this as being entirely determined by the preferences of the individuals within the society. It is not regarded as something which is inherently measurable, since, if the UTILITY of an individual is not measurable, how can that of a group be? Rather, we can only say that, given two situations, 'society' prefers one situation to another, or is indifferent between them. If we wish, we can then say that social welfare is greater in one situation than another, or is the same, but this is not implying the intrinsic measurability of social welfare. The difficulty then is to establish criteria by which to say that 'society' prefers one situation to another, or is indifferent between them. For a discussion of this, ⟡ SOCIAL WELFARE FUNCTION and COMPENSATION PRINCIPLE. ⟡ COST-BENEFIT ANALYSIS; A. C. PIGOU; WELFARE ECONOMICS.

Social welfare function. A preference ranking placed by society on a set of alternative economic situations. Thus, it allows us to say that, e.g., a situation in which there is a 45 per cent CORPORATION TAX and a PROGRESSIVE TAX system is preferred by society to a situation in which company PROFITS are untaxed and the same tax rate is applied to all INCOMES. However, on what basis may such a ranking be derived? The answer must be that it is determined by the government of the society, which explicitly or implicitly makes choices between alternative economic situations. In a democratic society, ultimately the formulation of the social welfare function will be influenced by the wishes of individuals in the society, and, in fact, a full analysis of the social welfare function really requires an analysis of political as much as economic behaviour.

Soft currency. A CURRENCY whose EXCHANGE RATE is tending to fall because of persistent BALANCE OF PAYMENTS deficits or because of the building up of speculative selling of the currency in expectation of a change in its exchange rate. Governments are unwilling to hold a soft currency in their FOREIGN EXCHANGE RESERVES. In the immediate post-Second World War period, all European currencies were 'soft' on account of their imbalance of trade with the U.S. The opposite expression is 'HARD CURRENCY' or 'scarce currency', as exemplified by the dollar in the post-Second World War situation. ⇨ INTERNATIONAL MONETARY FUND.

Soft loan. A LOAN bearing either no RATE OF INTEREST, or an interest rate which is below the true cost of the CAPITAL lent. It is the policy of the INTERNATIONAL BANK FOR RECONSTRUCTION AND DEVELOPMENT working through its affiliate, the INTERNATIONAL DEVELOPMENT ASSOCIATION, to give 'soft' loans to DEVELOPING COUNTRIES for long-term capital projects.

Sole proprietorship, sole trader. A business owned by one man. The majority of small firms are sole traders or PARTNERSHIPS. ⇨ BOLTON COMMITTEE; COMPANY LAW.

Sources and uses of funds. An accounting statement describing the CAPITAL flows of a business. Sources of funds are PROFITS from trading operations, DEPRECIATION provisions, sales of ASSETS and borrowing, including capital issues. Uses of funds are purchase of fixed or financial assets (including CASH), and distribution of INCOME. ⇨ SELF-FINANCING.

Special deposits. Cash deposited at the BANK OF ENGLAND by the CLEARING BANKS in response to a special directive. The scheme which was introduced in 1958, although it did not become effective until 1960, was designed to provide a mechanism for reducing bank lending by reducing their LIQUIDITY RATIO. The banks were instructed to increase their gross deposits at the Bank of England (part of their LIQUIDITY base) by a certain percentage. The banks receive interest on the special deposits at approximately the current TREASURY BILL rate. Besides the clearing banks, the scheme also applies, on somewhat different terms, to the Scottish banks. Theoretically, the requirement for special deposits appears to be a powerful method for reducing bank lending, since it operates directly on the CASH RATIO of the banks and quite small percentage increases in deposits should have a significant effect on bank advances. However, the banks could offset the increase in deposits by reducing their holdings of government BONDS and, in practice, the importance of an announcement of a requirement for special deposits is that it is a signal of the intention of the monetary authorities to squeeze CREDIT. Until 1971, these authorities continued to rely on a direct limitation on bank advances, as they did in 1957 before special deposits were introduced, and on other means of controlling credit. From 1971, a new system of CREDIT CONTROL was introduced. Special deposits continue in force, but do not form part of the reserve assets of the new system. ⇨ CREDIT SQUEEZE.

Special drawing rights (S.D.R.s). There has been growing concern during the past decade that a shortage of INTERNATIONAL LIQUIDITY could become sufficiently acute as to prevent the continued growth of INTERNATIONAL TRADE. The instruments for financing international trade are predominantly the RESERVE CURRENCIES, such as dollars and sterling, and gold. Dependence on the latter, as J. M. KEYNES pointed out, is an anachronism which had been successfully terminated as far as domestic economies were concerned. The problem of depending on the former is that the supply of these currencies is regulated by their countries' BALANCE OF PAYMENTS deficits or surpluses. The deficit on the U.S. balance of payments has been an important source of the flow of LIQUIDITY into CENTRAL BANK reserves. The difficulty, of course, was that the persistent deficits led to doubts about the maintenance of the currency's EXCHANGE RATE and made central banks less willing to hold dollars. In the mid 1960s, indeed, it was declared policy of France to sell dollars for gold. This problem came to a head in August 1971, when the U.S. government imposed various measures to correct its balance of payments deficit. In December 1971, the dollar was devalued by about 10 per cent. The 'Group of Ten' (⇨ INTERNATIONAL MONETARY FUND) countries agreed that discussions should be held to review the whole problem of international liquidity. However, clearly the disadvantage of these sources for LIQUID assets for transacting trade was that their supply was quite arbitrary. J. M. Keynes had put forward the idea of an international currency, to be called BANCOR, regulated by a central institution (⇨ KEYNES PLAN). This idea was turned down then for fear that the creation of liquidity would generate INFLATION. In July 1969, the 'Group of Ten' agreed to establish S.D.R.s, which are similar in principle to Keynes's original idea, and their agreement was ratified in the I.M.F. The S.D.R., each unit of which is linked to gold and equivalent to 1$ U.S. at the gold rate of exchange of $35 per oz. (or about $1·09 at the rate of exchange of $38 an ounce), is an entry in a member country's bank balance with the I.M.F. At the beginning of 1970, a total of $3,414 million worth of S.D.R.s were distributed, and $2,949 million in 1971 and $2,951 million in 1972. A decision will be made later about the size of the distribution for 1973 and 1974. These sums are distributed to each member country in proportion to its I.M.F. quota. There are certain restrictions on their use. A member must retain in its reserves at least 30 per cent of its original allocation, and, *per contra*, can refuse to receive S.D.R.s if its holding is over three times its original allocation. Although S.D.R.s have a gold guarantee, they also receive INTEREST from the I.M.F. The U.K. received $410 million in S.D.R.s at the beginning of 1970, used $65 million of them in part settlement of her I.M.F. debts and received a further $300 million in 1971.

Specialization. ⟡ DIVISION OF LABOUR.

Specie points. The limits between which the EXCHANGE RATE between two CURRENCIES on the GOLD STANDARD fluctuated. For instance, before the First World War the same amount of gold could be bought in London for £1 and in New York for $4·87, and therefore the par rate of exchange was £1 for $4·87. If the pound fetched less than $4·87 in London, it would pay a merchant to ship gold to the U.S. to settle his DEBTS provided the cost of freight and INSURANCE were less than the difference between the par rate and the London rate. Therefore in practice the rate never fell by an amount more than the cost of shipment. Similar forces applied in reverse to prevent the rate rising by an amount in excess of the cost of shipment.

Specific tax. ⟡ TAX, SPECIFIC.

Speculation. Buying and selling with a view to buying and selling at a PROFIT later when PRICES have changed. ⟡ ARBITRAGE; BEAR; BULL; STAG.

Speculative motive. A motive for holding MONEY which arises from the possibility that the money VALUE of other forms of WEALTH may change. Thus, suppose an individual can hold his wealth either in BONDS or in money. If he expects the PRICE of bonds to fall in the future, he will wish to switch from bonds to money, i.e. he will sell his bonds. This is because a fall in the price of bonds clearly involves him in a loss of wealth (the price of all other goods and

SERVICES remaining unchanged). On the other hand, if he expects the price of bonds to rise, he will reduce his holdings of money and buy bonds. Since his desire to hold money is therefore related to his EXPECTATIONS of the variations in value of other ASSETS, and the way in which he can take advantage of them, this part of the individual's money holdings are said to be determined by the speculative motive. ⟡ LIQUIDITY PREFERENCE; PRECAUTIONARY MOTIVE; TRANSACTIONS MOTIVE.

Spot market. A MARKET in which goods or SECURITIES are traded for immediate delivery, as distinct from a FORWARD MARKET. 'Spot' in this context means 'immediately effective', so that *spot price* is the price for immediate delivery.

Spot price. ⟡ SPOT MARKET.

Spot sterling. ⟡ FORWARD EXCHANGE MARKET.

Stabilization policy. The name given to the measures which governments take to reduce the amplitude of cyclical fluctuations. Left to themselves, FREE MARKET capitalist economies (⟡ CAPITALISM) tend to exhibit over time cyclical fluctuations in NATIONAL INCOME and employment. The determinants of the timing and amplitude of these fluctuations are analysed in that part of economics known as the theory of the TRADE CYCLE. Thus, as the economy approaches the 'peak' of a cycle, there is rapid wage and price INFLATION, IMPORTS rise relative to EXPORTS, and BALANCE OF PAYMENTS deficits occur. On the other hand, in the 'trough' of a cycle, UNEMPLOYMENT is undesirably high, particularly in certain regions which typically have unemployment rates of twice the national average. Hence, the aim of stabilization policy is to restrain the economy when it is nearing the peak of the cycle, and to stimulate the economy when it approaches the trough. Because of the alternation between restraint and stimulation which the policy implies, it has earned the name 'STOP-GO' in its post-war British manifestation.

The principal instruments of stabilization policy are MONETARY POLICY and FISCAL POLICY, and the policy is facilitated by the existence of BUILT-IN STABILIZERS. Stabilization policy is not so straightforward and simple as its description might suggest. Not only are there limitations arising out of the bluntness of the instruments available, but the imperfections in the information available to the managers of the economy also create serious difficulties. These imperfections may interact with certain time-lags which exist within the system, so that stabilization policy may actually be destabilizing. Thus, we could divide the overall time period which elapses between the time an event requiring correction occurs, and the time a corrective measure takes effect, into three phases: (a) the time between occurrence of the event and recognition that corrective action is required (this depends, among other things, on the time-lags in information flow); (b) the time between recognition of the need for action, and actually taking action (which depends on the speed with which the policy-making processes work, the administrative arrangements for putting policy into effect, etc.); and (c) the time between the action, and the impact of that action on the VARIABLES under consideration (which depends on the time-lags in the institutional and behavioural relationships in the economy). Given the existence of these time-lags, it is generally pointless to take action to correct something which is currently happening. Rather, current events must be used to predict future events, and then the policy measures must be designed to influence these. But this, of course, involves the difficulty that the future can never be predicted completely accurately. But, even worse than this, the knowledge of the present is based on estimates of national income magnitudes – CONSUMPTION, INVESTMENT, exports, imports, etc. – and since these estimates are known to contain (sometimes considerable) errors, knowledge of the present is also extremely imperfect. Thus, predictions about an uncertain future have to be made on the basis of an incompletely known present. The costs of inappropriate policies may be high. Suppose, e.g., that measures designed to restrain 'overheating' in the economy come into effect just as the economy is past the peak and beginning to turn down. The measures will then accelerate the downturn, and cause INCOME and employment to fall farther and faster than they might otherwise have done. It is considerations such as this which make stabilization policy more of an art than a science at the present time.

Stag. A speculator (⟡ SPECULATION) who subscribes to new issues in the expectation of selling his allotment of SECURITIES at a profit when dealings in them begin. ⟡ NEW ISSUE MARKET.

'Stand-by' arrangement. ⟡ INTERNATIONAL MONETARY FUND.

Standard deviation. A statistical measure of the extent to which a set of numbers are dispersed about their arithmetic mean (⟡ AVERAGE). It is the square root of the VARIANCE. An advantage of the standard deviation is that, whereas the variance will be measured in terms of the square of the units of measurement of the original set of numbers, the standard deviation is measured in terms of the original units. Thus, if we found the variance of a batsman's scores over a season, it would be in units of 'runs squared', while the standard deviation will be in runs. Clearly, the latter is easier to interpret in everyday terms. The formula for the standard deviation is:

$$\text{standard deviation} = \sigma = \sqrt{\frac{1}{n} \sum_{i=1}^{n} (x_i - \bar{x}^2)}$$

where x_i is the i'th number and $\bar{x}$ is the arithmetic mean. Everything said on the relation between the variance and the degree of dispersion of numbers about their mean also applies to the standard deviation.

Standard Industrial Classification (S.I.C.). A categorization of economic activity used in compiling and presenting official statistics. It consists of 181 *Minimum List Headings*, e.g. '*471. Timber*, grouped into twenty-seven *Order Numbers*, e.g. '*II. Mining and Quarrying*. First introduced in 1948, and revised in 1958 and 1968, the British S.I.C. system follows the same principles as the International Standard Industrial Classification (I.S.I.C.) issued by the United Nations.

Standard rate. ⟡ INCOME TAX.

State planning, or central planning. Usually refers either to the activities of central government in MIXED ECONOMIES, in preparing schemes for production or INVESTMENT in NATIONALIZED INDUSTRIES, or that of economic planning authorities in countries where all the means of production and distribution are owned by the state. Since the Second World War, developments in the methods of demand management (⟡ FISCAL POLICY), and the increased importance of the PUBLIC SECTOR, have also led to the increasing use of *indicative planning*, which may not necessarily involve executive action by the state. In the early 1960s detailed national economic plans were prepared for the British economy. These related private and public industry, and formulated targets for EXPORTS, national product and investment and other economic aggregates. The purpose of these plans is to identify problems and bottlenecks in the economy and, through disseminating information, to help to give coherence to private economic decisions and to speed up economic growth. Today all developed countries, and most DEVELOPING COUNTRIES, carry out some form of economic planning and forecasting, ranging from virtually complete state planning in the

U.S.S.R. to semi-indicative planning in France, indicative planning in Britain, and minimal planning exercises in Western Germany. The state in all countries must, of course, plan its own economic activities and its policies on demand management and other monetary and fiscal matters. Increasingly, western countries are also developing more complex planning intervention in the determination of the industrial structure of the PRIVATE SECTOR by means of MONOPOLY policy on the one hand, and bodies to stimulate small business, or encourage rationalization of industry into larger units, on the other. ⟫ INDUSTRIAL REORGANIZATION CORPORATION.

Statistical inference. That branch of statistics which is concerned with the making of general statements about a group or 'POPULATION' of items, on the basis of imperfect information about that group. For example, we may be interested in trying to know in advance who will win the next General Election. By taking a RANDOM SAMPLE of voters, we may obtain information on voting intentions, but this information is imperfect, since it does not describe with certainty what all the voters will in fact do. Nevertheless, it is possible to generalize about the population on the basis of the sample. The techniques of statistical inference are primarily concerned with the question of the degree of confidence which can be placed on the generalizations and the margins of error which may be involved. In this, they rely heavily on methods of PROBABILITY theory. Since it is rarely possible, especially in economics, to obtain perfect information about the group of things under study, yet it is desired to examine relationships, test hypotheses and make measurements for the group as a whole, techniques of statistical inference have become extremely important.

Steady-state growth. A state in which the rates of growth of the VARIABLES in an economic system, e.g. a MARKET or an economy, remain constant over time. Thus, suppose we have an economy consisting simply of firms and HOUSEHOLDS (no government, no foreign trade), where firms receive consumers' expenditure in return for goods and pay this back to households in return for productive SERVICES; households spend part of what firms pay them on CONSUMPTION expenditure, and save the rest; and firms spend on new INVESTMENT exactly the same amount as households save. If, now, NATIONAL INCOME, consumption expenditures, SAVING and investment expenditures were all growing at, say, 5 per cent per annum, every year without change, then we would say that the economy was in steady-state growth. It need not be the case that the growth rate of all the variables is the same, although theory tells us that in our simple MODEL they would be, but the growth rate of each variable must be constant through time for steady-state growth to exist. The steady-state situation is generally the starting-point in the analysis of most models of economic growth. It therefore fulfils much the same role as the concept of EQUILIBRIUM in static theory: as a useful theoretical abstraction which need hardly ever be realized in practice.

Sterling area. The sterling area has its origins in the supremacy of the U.K. in the INTERNATIONAL TRADE and finance of the nineteenth century. The pound sterling became the most convenient CURRENCY in which to settle international BALANCES OF PAYMENTS, and London the leading centre for raising the finance required to open up the new colonies. The sterling area, however, remained only a loose association of countries until the U.K. went off the GOLD STANDARD in 1931. At that time, these countries had to choose between linking their currencies to gold or to sterling. With the outbreak of the Second World War in 1939, the area became more formalized by the acceptance of EXCHANGE CONTROL in respect of transactions with non-sterling area members. Up to this time, the sterling balances held by the members of the sterling area in London were relatively small, and approximately matched by the GOLD AND FOREIGN EXCHANGE RESERVES held by the U.K. The U.K., however, had to liquidate much of its foreign ASSETS to pay for the war, so that by 1945 the gold and foreign exchange reserves were depleted. At the same time, the sterling balances had risen to the extent that the reserves were only a small proportion in comparison. The Exchange Control Act of 1947 defined the sterling area as a list of 'scheduled territories', and the area discriminated against trade with 'HARD CURRENCY' areas, particularly the U.S., against the background of the inconvertibility of sterling. In the 1950s, exchange control was eased and the area became less discriminatory (⟡ GENERAL AGREEMENT ON TARIFFS AND TRADE). However, the fact that the reserves of the U.K. must serve for the area as a whole, and that these reserves have remained small relative to the sterling balances, has led in recent years to the generation of considerable fluctuations in the U.K. reserves. After the sterling devaluation of 1967 and the INTERNATIONAL LIQUIDITY crises at that time, the sterling area countries began to convert their sterling balances into other currencies. In 1966, the BANK FOR INTERNATIONAL SETTLEMENTS arranged a currency swap agreement with the U.K., which was renewed in 1967 and 1968. This in effect lent foreign exchange to the U.K., not to finance its balance of payments deficits, but to offset the violent short-term movements in her reserves resulting from movements in the sterling balances. After 1967, this was obviously insufficient. The so-called 'Basle facility' was made available in 1968, and was designed to support a permanent drop in the sterling balances. An amount of $2,000 million is available to the U.K. for a period of ten years, which the U.K. can draw on, for repayment in six or ten years, if the sterling balances fall below a certain agreed level. At the same time, the U.K. has given dollar guarantees on official sterling area holdings of sterling in exchange for member countries' agreement not to let the sterling content of their reserves fall below an agreed proportion.

Sterling balances. ⟡ STERLING AREA.

Stock. 1. A particular type of SECURITY, usually quoted in units of £100 value rather than in units of proportion of total CAPITAL, as in SHARES. Stock, or stocks and shares, have now become synonyms with securities, and the original distinction between shares and stock has become blurred. The term stock, however, is now coming to mean exclusively a fixed-interest security, i.e. loan stock in a company or local or central government stock. **2.** An accumulation of a COMMODITY. ⟡ INVENTORY.

Stock analysis. ⟡ INVENTORY ANALYSIS.

Stock exchange. A MARKET in which SECURITIES are bought and sold. There are stock exchanges in most capital cities, as well as in the largest provincial cities in many countries, and over twenty in Britain. The principal stock exchange in Britain is known as the Stock Exchange, and is located in Throgmorton Street in the City of London; the New York stock exchange is located in and is known as Wall Street. Continental European exchanges are often referred to as *Bourses* (Fr.). The economic importance of stock exchanges is that they facilitate SAVING and INVESTMENT, first through making it possible for investors to dispose of securities quickly if they wish to do so, and secondly in channelling savings into productive investment. Ready marketability requires that new issues (⟡ NEW ISSUE MARKET) should be made or backed by reputable borrowers or institutions, that information should be available on existing securities, and that there should be both a legal framework and market rules to prevent fraud and sharp practice. Stock exchanges have their own rules and conventions, but their functioning depends also on the existence of company and other law and FINANCIAL INTERMEDIARIES, such as the ISSUING HOUSES.

The British Stock Exchange, founded in 1773, developed from informal exchanges in coffee houses in the City of London. It is managed by a council of members. There are some 3,500 members, who alone may deal or even enter the floor of the exchange. STOCKBROKERS act as agents for the public, and buy from and sell to JOBBERS. Members are formed into a declining number of companies and there are now only 192 broking firms and ninety-one jobbing firms on the London exchange. Business is conducted entirely by word of mouth, and although jobbers and brokers keep their own registers and may record details of a 'bargain' (as all transactions are called) on the official list, they are not obliged to do so. Even today there are no official statistics of the volume of transactions, although prices at the exchange are widely available in the press. The market value of the securities quoted on the exchange is about £120 billion, of which rather more than half are foreign securities.
  ⇨ ACCOUNT; MARKET; SECONDARY MARKET; SHARE INDICES.

Stock jobber. ⇨ JOBBER.

Stock-sales ratio. ⇨ INVENTORY TURNOVER.

Stock split. An issue of new SHARES to shareholders without increasing total CAPITAL. The object of a stock split is to reduce the average quoted price of shares to promote their marketability.

Stock turnover. ⇨ INVENTORY TURNOVER.

Stockbroker. A member of the STOCK EXCHANGE, who buys and sells SHARES on his own account, or for non-members, in return for a COMMISSION on the PRICE of the shares. ⇨ BROKER.

Stockholm Convention. ⇨ EUROPEAN FREE TRADE ASSOCIATION.

Stop-go. The description given to economic policy in the U.K., particularly during the 1960s. The government used fiscal and monetary controls (⇨ FISCAL POLICY and MONETARY POLICY) to reduce AGGREGATE DEMAND, and so to preserve the EXCHANGE RATE, which tended to come under severe pressure during boom conditions in the home market. These controls, together with the underlying TRADE CYCLE movements, produced subsequent periods of stagnation and rising UNEMPLOYMENT, which, in turn, encouraged the government to stimulate the economy, and so a return to boom conditions. ⇨ STABILIZATION POLICY.

Strategy. A term used in the theory of GAMES to describe the set of choices a player will make in each possible set of circumstances.

Stratified sample. A type of RANDOM SAMPLE which is designed by first classifying the overall population into sub-groups or strata according to some principle, and then taking a SIMPLE RANDOM SAMPLE within each stratum. Its purpose is to ensure that the sample is, in fact, representative of the various groups which make up the POPULATION, a property which a simple random sample need by no means possess. For example, in order to design a sample to estimate the expenditure on house RENTS of families, we might divide the total population into broad income groups, decide on the sample size appropriate for each group, and then choose the families according to the same procedure as would be used for a simple random sample. If this were not done, it might be the case that the sample chosen might, by chance, contain an over-representative figure for one income group, and an under-representative figure of another, and thus the estimate of AVERAGE expenditure on rent per HOUSEHOLD would be biased upward or downward as the case may be. In designing a stratified sample, we need some information about the population to be available before the sample is carried out. This information is then used to increase the representativeness of the sample. The stratified sample is still a random sample, since each family (or item in the population) has a known chance of being selected. The basis of the stratification, or the 'stratification factor', is chosen so as to be relevant to the problem in hand. For example, in studying voting intentions, it would be useful to stratify by social class, but probably not by sex. As well as increasing the representativeness, and therefore accuracy, of the sample, stratification may also be used, because it is of interest to see how the results differ between the strata, e.g. how voting intentions vary between social classes or rent expenditures between income groups.

Structural unemployment. UNEMPLOYMENT created by some basic long-term change in the demand or technological conditions in an economy, e.g. unemployment of coal miners as a result of the decline in demand for coal. Such unemployment will often tend to persist for a long time, since it tends to be heavily localized and the unemployed workers have the 'wrong' type of skills. The attempt to reduce such unemployment is at the root of the location of industry policy of the U.K. government, and the establishment of retraining centres.

Subsidiaries. Companies legally controlled by other companies. Although a shareholding of less than 50 per cent may be sufficient to control a company effectively, it is not correctly described as a subsidiary unless between 50 and 100 per cent of the SHARES are owned by another. Companies may choose to retain subsidiaries rather than to integrate them fully into their own organizations for a variety of reasons – e.g. the desire to allow local participation, a wish to conceal business connection or to avoid the cost and complication of integrating an acquired company.

Subsidy. In general, payment by government to an industry to prevent its decline or an increase in its PRICES. The term *cross-subsidy* is also used within a single industry when the profits from one activity are used to keep prices down in another. ⟡ FARM PRICE REVIEW.

Subsistence theory of wages. ⟡ WAGE FUND THEORY.

Substitutes. Two goods are substitutes if a rise in the price of one causes an increase in DEMAND for the other. This substitute relationship arises because the goods perform a similar function or serve a similar taste. However, we can generally think of a whole spectrum of substitution possibilities for a particular good, and so we often refer to 'close' substitutes or 'weak' substitutes. For example, a Bentley would be a close substitute for a Rolls-Royce, but a minicar would not. The closer are the available substitutes for a product, the greater, other things being equal, will be its price ELASTICITY of demand.

Substitution effect. The change in the quantity demanded of a good which results purely from a change in its PRICE relative to the prices of other goods. Thus, suppose that a consumer pays a price of 10p per unit for a good X, and that then its price falls to 5p. It has now become more attractive to him relative to its SUBSTITUTES, and so the consumer will tend to buy more of that and less of the others. The overall change in his demand for X will also, however, depend on the INCOME EFFECT.

'Sun-spot' theory. ⟡ W. S. JEVONS.

Super-normal profit. ⟡ PROFIT.

Supplementary costs. A now little-used synonym for FIXED COSTS or OVERHEADS.

Supply. The quantity of a good or SERVICE which sellers desire to sell at a given PRICE.

Supply curve. A curve relating quantity of a good supplied to PRICE. We can distinguish between the *supply curve* of an individual firm and the *market supply curve*. The latter is obtained by summing individual firm supplies at each price. The supply curve is generally depicted as rising from left to right, indicating that more will be supplied at a higher price. ⟡ A. MARSHALL.

Supply services. An item in the British BUDGET consisting of expenditures which are estimated annually and voted in Parliament. It includes expenditure by government departments, such as defence, agriculture, including SUBSIDIES, the National Health Service, etc.

Surplus value. ⟡ K. MARX.

Surtax. An additional tax on higher incomes levied on net income after certain deductions, such as earned income relief or approved pension scheme contributions. Surtax is charged according to a sliding scale at rates varying from 10 to 50 per cent. For 1971–2, surtax will not be charged where surtaxable income does not exceed £2,500 and is limited to an average rate of 40 per cent. Surtax is payable on 1 January following the year of assessment. ⟡ INCOME TAX.

T

'Tableau Économique'. The table by which QUESNAY analysed the circulation of WEALTH in the economy by setting out the different classes of society. The table showed how the '*produit net*' produced by the agricultural sector circulated between the owners of the LAND, the tenant farmers and other classes, such as artisans and merchants. Only agriculture produced any net additions to wealth; all other activities were 'sterile'. The table showed, too, how output is annually reproduced. The sterile classes were essential in that they created the necessary demand for the agricultural sector. ⇨ R. CANTILLON; W. LEONTIEF; PHYSIOCRATS.

Take-off in economic development. ⇨ ECONOMIC GROWTH, STAGES OF.

Take-over. The acquisition of one company by another. Take-overs are sometimes financed by paying CASH at an offer PRICE in excess of the MARKET price of the SHARES, but, more frequently for large acquisitions, by the exchange of shares or loan STOCK, possibly with some cash adjustment, issued by the acquiring company for the shares of the acquired company. The term 'take-over' is normally used to imply that the acquisition is made on the initiative of the acquirer and without the full agreement of the acquired company; as distinct from a MERGER. ⇨ REVERSE TAKE-OVER.

Tap issue. An issue of TREASURY BILLS to government departments and others at a fixed PRICE and without going through the MARKET; as distinct from a tender issue (⇨ TENDERS).

Tariffs, import. Taxes imposed on commodity IMPORTS. They may be levied on an *ad valorem* basis, i.e. as a certain percentage of VALUE; or on a specific basis, i.e. as an amount per unit. Their purpose may be solely for raising revenue, in which case the home-produced product corresponding to the import would bear an equivalent compensatory tax. However, import duties are generally applied for the purpose of carrying out a particular economic policy, and in this context may be used to serve many functions:

(a) To reduce the overall level of imports by making them more expensive relative to their home-produced SUBSTITUTES, with the aim of eliminating a BALANCE OF PAYMENTS deficit. ⇨ DEVALUATION.

(b) To counter the practice of DUMPING by raising the import price of the dumped commodity to its economic level.

(c) To retaliate against restrictive measures imposed by other countries (⟡ RECIPROCITY).

(d) To protect a new industry until it is sufficiently well established to compete with the more developed industries of other countries (⟡ INFANT INDUSTRY ARGUMENT).

(e) To protect 'key' industries, such as agriculture, without which the economy would be vulnerable in time of war.

Tariffs may be either preferential or non-discriminatory. For instance, under COMMONWEALTH PREFERENCE, which was confirmed by the Ottawa Agreements in 1932, imports into the U.K. originating in the Commonwealth attract lower duties than those coming from non-Commonwealth countries; similarly, in respect of members compared with non-members of the EUROPEAN FREE TRADE ASSOCIATION and the EUROPEAN ECONOMIC COMMUNITY. However, it was an accepted principle, under the MOST-FAVOURED NATION CLAUSE of the GENERAL AGREEMENT ON TARIFFS AND TRADE, that tariffs should be non-discriminating, and any concessions agreed between two or more countries should automatically be extended to all. It has, however, been accepted that this principle may be waived in the interests of the DEVELOPING COUNTRIES. Since the end of the Second World War, through the G.A.T.T., significant progress has been made in the reduction of tariff levels by means of a series of negotiations, of which the KENNEDY ROUND, concluded in July 1967, was the latest.

Taussig, Frank William (1859–1940). Apart from a period from 1917 to 1919 when he was chairman of the U.S. Tariffs Commission, Taussig spent his whole career at Harvard University. His works on economics include *Tariff History of the United States* (1888), *Wages and Capital* (1896), a textbook, *Principles of Economics* (1911), and *International Trade* (1927). An economist in the tradition of RICARDO and MARSHALL, Taussig attempted to relate his theory to established statistical data.

Tautology. ⟡ HYPOTHESIS.

Tax. ⟡ TAXATION.

Tax, ad valorem. An indirect TAX which is expressed as a proportion of the PRICE of a good – hence it is 'by value'.

Tax avoidance. Arranging one's financial affairs within the law so as to minimize taxation LIABILITIES, as opposed to *tax evasion,* which is failing to meet actual tax liabilities through, e.g., not declaring INCOME or PROFIT.

Tax base. The object to which the TAX rate is to be applied, e.g. INCOME, WEALTH, the PRICE of a good.

Tax burden. The amount of MONEY which an individual, institution or group must pay in TAX. It should include all costs to the taxpayer which he incurs in paying the tax, e.g. the net of tax cost of employing an accountant to complete a tax form.

Tax, 'cascade'. ⇨ TURNOVER TAX.

Tax equalization account. ⇨ COMPANY RESERVES.

Tax evasion. ⇨ TAX AVOIDANCE.

Tax impact. The point on which the burden of a TAX initially bears. ⇨ TAX INCIDENCE.

Tax incidence. The point at which the TAX BURDEN ultimately rests. For example, the imposition of a specific tax on a COMMODITY may cause firms to increase PRICE by the amount of the tax. If consumers do not reduce their purchases, the entire burden of the tax will have been shifted on to them. ⇨ TAX IMPACT; TAX, SPECIFIC.

Tax, progressive. ⇨ PROGRESSIVE TAX.

Tax, proportional. ⇨ PROPORTIONAL TAX.

Tax, regressive. ⇨ REGRESSIVE TAX.

Tax, specific. An indirect TAX which is expressed as a given absolute sum of MONEY per unit of the good.

Tax, turnover. ⇨ TURNOVER TAX.

Tax yield. The amount of MONEY which results when the rate of TAX is applied to the MONEY value of the TAX BASE, minus the costs of collecting the tax.

Taxation. A compulsory transfer of MONEY (or occasionally of goods and SERVICES) from private individuals, institutions or groups to the government. It may be levied upon WEALTH or INCOME, or in the form of a surcharge on PRICES. In the first case, it would then be called a DIRECT TAX; in the latter, an *indirect tax*. Taxation is one of the principle means by which a government finances its expenditure. ⇨ CORPORATION TAX; ESTATE DUTY; INCOME TAX; PUBLIC GOODS; A. SMITH.

Technical Development Capital Ltd (T.D.C.). A subsidiary institution formed in 1962 by the Industrial and Commercial Finance Corporation (⇨ MACMILLAN COMMITTEE), with a number of banks and INSURANCE companies to invest in technical developments and INNOVATIONS.

Tenders. Offers to supply at a fixed PRICE. A DISCOUNT HOUSE tendering for an issue of TREASURY BILLS, for example, will offer to take up so many bills at a certain price.

Term loan. A bank advance for a specific period (normally three to ten years) repaid, with INTEREST, usually by regular periodical payments. Term loans are common practice in the U.S. commercial banking system for business finance, and for larger borrowings the LOAN may be syndicated, i.e. the provision of funds and the interest earned are shared between several banks. Similar facilities are available in Britain, mainly from subsidiaries of the COMMERCIAL BANKS or other institutions such as the Industrial and Commercial Finance Corporation (▷ MACMILLAN COMMITTEE), but OVERDRAFTS are the most common form of BANK LOAN, and are a cheaper form of finance. Unlike an overdraft, the interest of a term loan is fixed and the loan cannot be recalled in advance of its maturity date.

Terms of trade. The ratio of the INDEX OF EXPORT prices to the index of IMPORT prices. An improvement in the terms of trade follows if export prices rise more quickly than import prices (or fall more slowly than import prices). The U.K., together with other developed countries, has experienced a long-run improvement in its terms of trade because of a fall in relative prices of primary commodities. This movement has, in fact, given rise to concern in so far as it imposes losses on the DEVELOPING COUNTRIES, and various proposals have been put forward for schemes to compensate the primary producing countries for their losses (▷ UNITED NATIONS CONFERENCE ON TRADE AND DEVELOPMENT). In the decade following 1958, import prices to the U.K. rose by only about 6 per cent, whereas export prices rose by about 14 per cent, giving an improvement in the terms of trade of about 8 per cent. This means that the same quantity of exports would buy 8 per cent more imports at the end compared with the beginning of the period.

Theories of value. ▷ VALUE, THEORIES OF.

Theory of distribution. ▷ DISTRIBUTION, THEORY OF.

Theory of the firm. ▷ FIRM, THEORY OF.

Theory of games. ▷ GAMES, THEORY OF.

Theory of income determination. ▷ INCOME DETERMINATION, THEORY OF.

Theory of production. ▷ PRODUCTION, THEORY OF.

Theory of second best. ▷ SECOND BEST, THEORY OF.

Thünen, Johann Heinrich von (1783–1850). A member of the land-owning Prussian class of *junkers*, after completing his education at agricultural college he attended the University of Göttingen. For the remainder of his life he farmed his estate at Mecklenburg. The first volume of his work *Der isolierte Staat in Beziehung auf Landwirtschaft und Nationalökonomie* was published in 1826, and part one of volume two in 1850. The rest of volume two and volume three appeared in 1863. He used his farm as a source of facts for his theoretical work in agricultural economics. He built a theoretical MODEL which he used to find the important factors which determined the most profitable location of various branches of agriculture in relation to their sources of DEMAND. In so doing, he devised a theory of RENT similar to that of RICARDO. He set out a theory of DISTRIBUTION based on marginal productivity, using calculus, which was considerably ahead of his own time, and he could be considered one of the founders of MARGINAL ANALYSIS. ⟪⟫ LOCATION THEORY.

Thornton, William Thomas (1813–80). ⟫ WAGE FUND THEORY.

Tied loan. A LOAN granted by one country to another on condition that the debtor uses the loan to buy goods or SERVICES from the creditor country.

Tight money. ⟫ DEAR MONEY.

Time deposit (U.S.). Money in a bank account for which the bank may require notice of withdrawal, usually of up to three months. ⟪⟫ DEPOSIT ACCOUNT.

Time preference. A person's preference for current as opposed to future CONSUMPTION. Suppose we asked an individual the following question: 'If you were to give me £1 today, in exchange for a promise to pay you a sum of money in one year's time, what would that sum of money have to be to compensate you for the loss of the current consumption?' We stipulate that the sum of money is certain to be paid, and that there is no INFLATION. We mean by the word 'compensate' that we wish to leave the individual feeling just as well off as if he hadn't given up the £1 – no more and no less. Then, his answer will tell us the degree of his time preference. If, for example, our individual replied: 'One pound and twenty-five pence', then he is showing a preference for current as opposed to future consumption: £1 now is worth more than £1 in the future, and in fact it is worth 25 per cent more, since he requires £0·25 more than the amount he is giving up to leave him feeling just as well off. On the other hand, if he had answered '£1', then he clearly is indifferent between consuming now or in the future, since he feels equally well off by consuming £1 in the future as £1 now. Finally, if he had said 'seventy-five pence', then he is showing a preference for future as opposed to current consumption, since £0·75 worth of consumption in one year's time is worth to him as much as £1 of consumption now.

We can make this idea more precise by defining the 'rate of time preference', which is a kind of subjective RATE OF INTEREST. Let us take the two numbers in our time preference experiment, namely the £1 given up now, and the sum required to be paid in compensation. Taking the ratio of the latter to the former in each example given above, we can write:

$$\text{(a)} \quad \frac{£1·25}{£1} = (1 + 0·25)$$

$$\text{(b)} \quad \frac{£1}{£1} = 1$$

$$\text{(c)} \quad \frac{£0·75}{£1} = (1 - 0·25)$$

We now define in these three examples the consumer's rate of time preference as the number, in the form of an interest rate, which expresses the individual's relative evaluation of future and current consumption. In the first case, the individual required to be paid 25 per cent more than he gave up to compensate him for postponing consumption. In the second case, nothing extra had to be paid. In the third case, 25 per cent less had to be paid. Thus, 25 per cent, 0 and −25 per cent are the rates of time preference in the respective cases. Clearly, the larger the value of this subjective interest rate, the more highly is current consumption valued relative to future consumption.

An individual's rate of time preference will depend to a large extent on his tastes and personality, which in turn could depend, *inter alia*, on his age and social situation. In addition, it will depend on the total amount of INCOME he currently has, and the amount he expects in the future. One might expect, for example, an individual who expected his income to double in the near future to have a high rate of time preference – a pound's worth of consumption now is more valuable to him than it will be later; conversely, if he expects a falling income, then he will tend to have a low or even negative rate of time preference – consumption later will have a high value relative to consumption now. Generally, we can say that the higher is current relative to future income, the lower will be the rate of time preference, while the lower is current relative to future income, the higher will be the rate of time preference. Note also that although, in the example used above, a time period of one year was chosen, a rate of time preference can be defined for any time period.

The concept of time preference plays an important part in the theories of CAPITAL, of SAVING, and hence of the rate of interest. The nature of its role can be suggested by the following propositions: an individual will postpone consumption and lend on the CAPITAL MARKET as long as the rate of interest exceeds his rate of time preference. If his rate of time preference increases as the quantity lent increases, then his total saving is determined by equality between the rate of interest and his rate of time preference. If firms invest up to the point at which the RATE OF RETURN on INVESTMENT is equal to the rate of interest, then, in EQUILIBRIUM, the rate of time preference will equal the rate of return on investment. ⇨ I. FISHER.

Time series. The values taken by some VARIABLE over several consecutive periods of time. ⇨ CROSS-SECTION ANALYSIS.

Times covered. ⇨ DIVIDEND COVER.

Times Share Index. An index of prices of SECURITIES on the London STOCK EXCHANGE published daily in *The Times* newspaper, together with average DIVIDEND and earnings YIELDS. It is now based on 2 June 1964. ⇨ FINANCIAL TIMES ACTUARIES SHARE INDICES; FINANCIAL TIMES STOCK INDICES; INDEX NUMBER.

Trade barrier. A general term covering any government limitation on the free international exchange of merchandise. These barriers may take the form of TARIFFS, QUOTAS, IMPORT DEPOSITS, restrictions on the issue of IMPORT LICENCES or stringent regulations relating to health or safety standards. ⇨ PROTECTION.

Trade bill. ⇨ BILL OF EXCHANGE.

Trade credit. The CREDIT extended by business firms to other business firms. It may occur explicitly through the issue of a BILL OF EXCHANGE, or may arise from the delay of receipts and payments for services performed. It can have an important influence on economic policy, because it is in total an important source of finance, comparable, for instance, with bank credit and, at the same time, it does not come under the direct control of the authorities as does the latter. ⇨ FACTORING.

Trade cycle. Regular oscillations in the level of business activity over a period of years. In the post-war years, the trade cycle has been controlled to the point where absolute downward movements in the level of output have been largely eliminated in the western industrial economies. The trade cycle has, in consequence, been replaced by the recession (⟡ DEPRESSION), in which temporary pauses in the advance of total output occur and are followed by a resumption in growth. Although sharp downward movements in output and employment have been largely eliminated, a steady upward progression with full employment (⟡ EMPLOYMENT, FULL) has proved elusive in 'free-enterprise economies'.

Considerable attention has been given to the Trade Cycle phenomenon by economists, culminating in the work of SAMUELSON, HICKS, Goodwin, PHILLIPS and Kalecki in the late 1940s and the 1950s. Most explanations of the existence and nature of the cycle are based on the determinants of business investment, and its effects, through the MULTIPLIER process, on the level of NATIONAL INCOME. The accelerator theory of investment (⟡ ACCELERATION PRINCIPAL), in conjunction with the multiplier, can be used to show that the adjustment of the level of investment to the rate of change of sales gives rise to cyclical fluctuations in national income. ⟡ ACCELERATOR-MULTIPLIER MODEL; INCOME DETERMINATION, THEORY OF; STABILIZATION POLICY.

Trade discount. The percentage below the published retail PRICE at which a manufacturer sells to his distributors (wholesale or retail) or at which a wholesaler sells his goods to a retailer. In addition, further discounts are sometimes given on a scale related to the quantities of the goods taken. A '*concealed*' *discount* is one granted by a manufacturer or wholesaler to favoured customers and not made publicly known to prevent accusations of unfair trading. ⟡ RESALE PRICE MAINTENANCE.

Trade diversion and trade creation. ⟡ CUSTOMS UNION.

Trade investments. SHARES held by one company in another; normally minority holdings in customers or suppliers.

Trading stamps. Coupons given by a retailer to a customer according to the VALUE of goods purchased. The trading-stamp firm sells the stamps to the retailer and redeems them by exchanging them for goods or CASH when presented by the retailer's customer. The trading-stamp firm makes a PROFIT from selling the stamps to the retailer at a price greater than their value and from the fact that not all of their stamps are redeemed. The retailer benefits in so far as he would lose business if his rival gives stamps. The customer benefits only in so far as he likes collecting stamps, the financial benefit being generally small, and in any case being a cumbersome method of getting a TRADE DISCOUNT. The Trading Stamps Act of 1964 made it illegal to sell stamps without a cash value.

Transactions demand. ⟡ TRANSACTIONS MOTIVE.

Transactions motive. A motive for holding MONEY which arises from the use of money as a medium of exchange. Since receipts and payments are rarely perfectly synchronized, an individual will generally need to hold a stock of money to meet expenditures, even when those expenditures can be perfectly foreseen. For example, one may receive one's salary at the end of each month, but make expenditures more or less continuously over the following month. Hence, a steadily dwindling stock of money must be held to make these transactions. If, on the other hand, all expenditures were made simultaneously with receipts, there would be no need to hold a money balance. ⟡ PRECAUTIONARY MOTIVE; SPECULATIVE MOTIVE.

Transfer costs. The COSTS incurred in transporting raw materials and finished products between raw-material sources and factory on the one hand, and factory and MARKET on the other. They should include all costs of achieving these physical transfers, including loading and unloading costs, administrative costs, etc., and not simply freight charges.

Transfer deed. A legal document by which ownership of SECURITIES is transferred from the seller to the buyer. In Britain, it is no longer necessary for both parties to sign such a document when disposing of a share. The seller gives his authority to the issuer of the security to remove his name from the records while the buyer's BROKER simply informs the issuer of the purchaser's name.

Transfer earnings. The earnings of a FACTOR OF PRODUCTION which are just sufficient to keep it in its present employment. Any excess of actual earnings over transfer earnings is known as ECONOMIC RENT. Not to be confused with TRANSFER PAYMENTS.

Transfer payments. Payments which are not made in return for some productive service; e.g. payments made by the state to needy individuals which, in effect, transfer INCOME from wealthier sectors of the population to the poorer. Examples are old-age pensions, UNEMPLOYMENT benefit and widows' pensions. They are not a payment in return for productive services, but rather represent an income redistribution. Likewise TAXATION is a transfer payment to the government. Whenever it is desired to measure income generated by some kind of INVESTMENT, or by the economy as a whole, transfer payments must be excluded, since they do not arise from the production of new goods and SERVICES. The treatment of transfer payments is of importance in several areas of economics, particularly in COST-BENEFIT ANALYSIS and NATIONAL INCOME determination. ⇩ NATIONAL INSURANCE.

Transformation curve. A curve which shows how one good, say X, can be 'transformed' into another good, say Y, by reducing output of X, and transferring the RESOURCES thus saved into production of Y. It is drawn on the assumption that resources in the economy are fixed in total, and so shows the alternative combinations of X and Y that are technically feasible. An example of a transformation curve is shown in the figure.

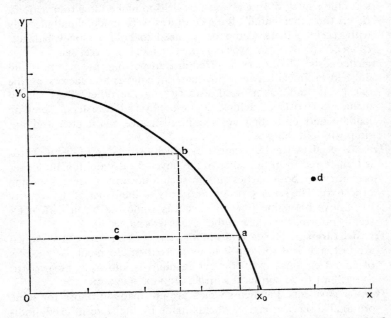

The curve shows that, if all resources are devoted to Y, a total of Y_0 can be produced; if all resources are devoted to X, a total of X_0 can be produced; or some intermediate combination of X and Y can be produced, e.g. such as that at a or b. It is also possible to produce at a point within the transformation curve, e.g. at c, which implies that resources are not being used fully, or with full efficiency, since it is possible to have more of both goods by being on the transformation curve at, e.g., b. On the other hand, it is not possible to be at a point such as d, since this is outside the transformation curve – it requires more resources or greater efficiency than are in fact possessed. The shape of the curve is due to the operation of the law of DIMINISHING RETURNS. It represents the fact that as X is reduced from X_0 by small, equal amounts, the increases in Y get smaller and smaller because the resources being released from X are encountering diminishing returns when they are moved into Y, and similarly if we reduce Y from Y_0.

The transformation curve is an important analytical device in several areas of economics, particularly in GENERAL EQUILIBRIUM theory, WELFARE ECONOMICS and INTERNATIONAL TRADE theory. It is also useful in pointing up some basic economic lessons, e.g. in an economy with a fixed quantity of resources and a given technology it is not possible to have more of one thing without having less of another. The curve is also sometimes referred to as the *production possibility curve*.

Treasury, The. Managed by the Chancellor of the EXCHEQUER, this British government department coordinates national economic policy (including MONETARY POLICY), and controls PUBLIC EXPENDITURE. Some of the Treasury's functions passed to the DEPARTMENT OF ECONOMIC AFFAIRS when it was set up in 1964, but returned to it in 1969 when the D.E.A. was closed. Also, prior to the establishment of the Civil Service Department in 1970, the Treasury was responsible for the management of the Civil Service, but the Civil Service Department has now taken over this role.

Treasury bills. Instruments for short-term borrowing by the government. The bills are promissory notes to pay to the bearer (usually) £5,000 ninety-one days from the date of issue. The bills are issued by tender to the MONEY MARKET and to government departments through TAP ISSUES. TENDERS are invited every week from bankers, DISCOUNT HOUSES and BROKERS for amounts varying between £100 and £200 million. On the one hand, treasury bills provide the government with a highly flexible and relatively cheap means of borrowing MONEY to meet its fluctuating needs for CASH. On the other hand, the bills provide a sound SECURITY for dealings in the money market, and the BANK OF ENGLAND, in particular, can operate on that market by dealing in treasury bills. Commercial bills (▷ BILL OF EXCHANGE) have declined in importance, but treasury bills, which date from 1877, now account for the bulk of national FLOATING DEBT, the amount of these bills outstanding in non-government hands being of the order of £950 million in March 1971.

Treasury deposit receipt (T.D.R.). An instrument of compulsory government borrowing from the COMMERCIAL BANKS during the Second World War. The T.D.R.s were, in effect, unmarketable TREASURY BILLS bearing a RATE OF INTEREST of 1⅛ per cent. First issued in 1940, they reached a total of £1,800 million by 1945, after which they were gradually replaced with treasury bills.

Treasury notes. In denominations of £1 and 10s. (50p), these, also known as *currency notes*, were issued to replace the gold coins withdrawn in Britain in 1914. At that time the lowest denomination of BANK OF ENGLAND notes (◊ BANK-NOTE) was £5, and the two kinds of CURRENCY complemented one another until 1928, when treasury notes were amalgamated with the Bank of England issue. ◊ FIDUCIARY ISSUE.

Treaty of Rome. ◊ EUROPEAN ECONOMIC COMMUNITY.

Treaty of Stockholm. ◊ EUROPEAN FREE TRADE ASSOCIATION.

Truck System. ◊ FRINGE BENEFITS.

Trust. 1. MONEY or property vested with an individual or group of individuals to administer in the interests of others. Trusts of this kind are usually set up to continue interests in accordance with the general instructions of the initiator and to protect them from outside interference. Thus people set up trusts or appoint trustees to administer their estates after their death. Certain newspapers are administered by trusts. Banks act as trustees for a fee, and a similar service is provided by the Public Trustee, established in 1908. The term is a legal one. **2.** Financial trusts are also established for commercial purposes where particular protection is required against fraud, e.g. UNIT TRUSTS or INVESTMENT TRUSTS. **3.** (U.S.) A very large amalgamation of firms. ◊ ANTI-TRUST.

Trustee Savings Banks. ◊ SAVINGS BANKS.

Turgot, Anne Robert Jacques, Baron de l'Aulne (1727–81). Educated for the Church, he became an abbé at the Sorbonne in Paris, but then took up a career in the Civil Service, where he remained for the rest of his life. He was the Administrator of the District of Limoges from 1761 to 1774, when he became Secretary of State for the Navy. For a short time, he held the post of Controller of Finance. His economic work appeared in *Réflections sur la formation et la distribution des richesses*, published in 1726. In this work he gave a clear analysis of the law of DIMINISHING RETURNS. He demonstrated how more and more applications of a FACTOR OF PRODUCTION (CAPITAL) to a constant factor (LAND) will first increase then decrease the return at the margin. He was the first to equate capital accumulation with SAVING, a view which became a central feature of CLASSICAL ECONOMICS.

Turnover. The total sales REVENUE of a business.

Turnover tax. A TAX levied as a proportion of the PRICE of a COMMODITY on each sale in the distribution chain; also called a *cascade tax*. ⇨ VALUE ADDED TAX.

U

Unavoidable costs. ⟡ FIXED COSTS; MARGINAL COSTS.

Uncalled capital. AUTHORIZED CAPITAL issued to the public, but not called (⟡ CALL) and not PAID-UP CAPITAL.

Uncertainty. One of a number of terms defined much more narrowly in economics than in everyday usage (others are INVESTMENT, COST and PROFIT). The classical definition of uncertainty, first given by F. H. KNIGHT, is that uncertainty exists when there is more than one possible outcome to a particular course of action, the form of each possible outcome is known, but the chance or PROBABILITY of getting any one particular outcome is not known. If the probabilities of actually obtaining certain outcomes are known, then this situation is one of RISK, not uncertainty. For example, suppose I make a bet with you that if I toss a coin, and it falls heads, I pay you £1, while if it falls tails, you pay me £1. To you, there are two possible outcomes of the decision to play this game: receiving £1, paying £1. If the coin has not been tampered with in any way, we can say that the chances of its falling heads are fifty-fifty, i.e. there is a probability of 0·5 that it will be heads or tails. Since the probabilities of the outcomes are known, this is therefore a situation of risk. Suppose, however, instead of tossing a coin, I had made the bet contingent on whether or not the next motor-car which passes us has an *A* or an *E* in its registration number. Since you are not likely to know the probabilities of these two events, the problem facing you is one of uncertainty (though if you were able to calculate these probabilities, it would become one of risk). Risk can be insured against (⟡ UNDERWRITING); uncertainty cannot.

Undated securities. SECURITIES not bearing a REDEMPTION DATE or OPTION, hence IRREDEEMABLE SECURITIES.

Underdeveloped country. ⟡ DEVELOPING COUNTRY.

Undervalued currency. A CURRENCY whose EXCHANGE RATE is below either its FREE MARKET level or the EQUILIBRIUM level which it is expected to reach in the LONG-RUN. The German Deutsche Mark became undervalued in the 1950s when the German BALANCE OF PAYMENTS was in persistent surplus. To correct this, the Deutsche Mark was revalued in 1961 from DM 4·00 to DM 4·20 to the U.S. dollar. Conversely, an *overvalued currency* may develop as a consequence of balance of payments deficits. This was the experience of the U.K. when sterling became overvalued in terms of the dollar at the fixed par rate of exchange and sterling was devalued in 1967 (⟡ DEVALUATION). ⟡⟡ INTERNATIONAL MONETARY FUND.

Underwriting. The business of insuring against RISK. An underwriter in return for a COMMISSION or PREMIUM agrees to bear a risk or a proportion of a risk. Specifically, an underwriter is a member of Lloyds, who joins with others to underwrite the risk of damage or loss to a ship or cargo – if the ship sinks and is not recoverable he will pay a proportion of the cost of the loss to the insured – but the term is generally used to describe the basic activity of INSURANCE. An ISSUING HOUSE also underwrites directly or indirectly a new issue of SHARES – if the public do not take up the whole issue, the balance will be taken up by the underwriters.

Unemployment. A situation which exists when members of the LABOUR FORCE wish to work but cannot get a job. It is therefore used in the sense of 'involuntary' unemployment, rather than the voluntary decision on the part of someone to choose leisure rather than work and, probably, a higher INCOME. Most post-war governments have taken it as a prime object of policy to keep aggregate national unemployment at a minimum. This minimum was at one time thought to be at 2 per cent of the labour force, but throughout the 1950s and 1960s, 1·5 per cent has come to be considered normal (⟡ BEVERIDGE). Work done by such economists as A. W. PHILLIPS and F. W. PAISH suggest that such a policy objective is, in fact, inconsistent with the objectives of a low rate of wage and price INFLATION, and stable BALANCE OF PAYMENTS. This points to the need either for basic structural changes in the economy, so as to make the goals consistent, or a revision of one or more of them. Several 'types' of unemployment have been distinguished, for which ⟡⟡ CYCLICAL UNEMPLOYMENT; DISGUISED UNEMPLOYMENT; FRICTIONAL UNEMPLOYMENT; SEASONAL UNEMPLOYMENT; STRUCTURAL UNEMPLOYMENT.

Unemployment rate. A measure of the extent of UNEMPLOYMENT of the LABOUR FORCE at any particular time. In Britain, it is calculated by taking a count of the National Insurance cards lodged with government labour exchanges at a particular point in time and expressing the result as a percentage of the total labour force. In other countries, the unemployment rate may be based on statistics collected by other means and using other definitions, such as

SAMPLE surveys in the U.S., and the figures may not be strictly comparable. However, the sample survey method is shortly to be adopted in Britain.

Unilateral flow. ⟡ BILATERAL FLOW.

Unit cost. ⟡ AVERAGE COSTS.

Unit trust. An organization which invests funds subscribed by the public in SECURITIES, and in return issues units which it will repurchase at any time. The units, which represent equal shares in the trust's investment PORTFOLIO, produce INCOME and fluctuate in value according to the INTEREST and DIVIDENDS paid and the STOCK EXCHANGE prices of the underlying INVESTMENTS. The trustees which actually hold the securities are usually banks or INSURANCE COMPANIES, and are distinct from the management company. The subscriber to a unit trust does not, unlike a shareholder in an INVESTMENT TRUST, receive any of the PROFITS of the organization managing the trust. Management derives its income from an initial charge and regular service charge as a percentage of the income of the trust's investments. Unit trusts are strictly controlled by the Department of Trade and Industry, which must give its approval to a trust before units can be offered to the public, and which sets maximum management charges and generally supervises the operation of the trusts. Unit trusts were introduced in Britain as long ago as 1930, but they have grown particularly rapidly since the late 1950s. The number of unit holdings more than doubled between 1963 and 1968, and there are now approaching 200 unit trusts in existence in Britain. Unit trusts are directed particularly at the investor with small sums at his disposal. Units are easily purchased and resold, and risks are widely spread, it being usual for holdings of any one security to be kept below 5 per cent of the total. The investor also benefits from expert management, although the performance of the trusts varies enormously. Trusts may be fixed or flexible, i.e. their PORTFOLIO may remain the same or be altered as market conditions dictate. Some unit trusts specialize in small companies or BLUE CHIP shares, others in COMMODITIES or foreign companies. Some are designed to maximize income, others CAPITAL growth. The latter offer the option of distributed or reinvested income, and there are also trusts incorporating life insurance which can be subscribed to by regular payments.

United Nations Conference on Trade and Development (U.N.C.T.A.D.). A conference convened in 1964 in response to growing anxiety among the DEVELOPING COUNTRIES over the difficulties they were

408

facing in their attempts to bridge the standard of living gap between them and the developed nations. A further full meeting was held in 1968 and a third meeting is planned for 1972. The then Director-General of U.N.C.T.A.D. Professor R. D. PREBISCH, summed the problem up in his report *Towards a New Trade Policy for Development*. The growth rate of 5 per cent per annum which was required for the developing countries to make progress in terms of REAL INCOME per head, implies a required IMPORT growth of 6 per cent. However, the trend rate of growth of their EXPORTS has been only about 4 per cent in value, and this has been reduced to the low figure of 2 per cent because of the deterioration in their TERMS OF TRADE. If this relationship continues, they will suffer chronic BALANCE OF PAYMENTS deficits which will lead to a worsening in their economic welfare. The problem, therefore, could be tackled on two fronts: (a) through measures to offset the deterioration in the terms of trade, and (b) to promote their exports. The terms of trade approach could be through INTERNATIONAL COMMODITY AGREEMENTS, which would be designed to prevent primary prices from falling and through compensatory finance arrangements. Many compensatory financing schemes had been put forward before the convening of U.N.C.T.A.D., but had not generally got beyond the proposal stage. An exception is the compensatory facility of the INTERNATIONAL MONETARY FUND, which came into operation in 1963. It is, however, available in principle to all members of the fund. It extends LOANS to finance short-term balance of payments deficits caused by a fall in exports below trend. The loan is limited to a proportion of the member's I.M.F. quota. The U.N.C.T.A.D. recommended that the I.M.F. should study the possibilities of extending this facility. Professor Prebisch suggested that the developed countries which benefited from the terms-of-trade shift should contribute to a fund which would be used to reimburse the losers. Professor J. E. Meade has suggested that the transfer should be between the importers and exporters of primary COMMODITIES and based on the movement of price levels above or below agreed limits. A report by the Group of Experts of U.N.C.T.A.D., *International Monetary Issues and the Developing Countries* (1965), linked the problem with INTERNATIONAL LIQUIDITY. They proposed that the I.M.F. should be authorized to increase LIQUIDITY by the issue of certificates, distributed in proportion to agreed quotas to the developed countries in exchange for their CURRENCY. This currency would then be lent through the INTERNATIONAL BANK

FOR RECONSTRUCTION AND DEVELOPMENT to the developing countries. Many of the proposals aired in U.N.C.T.A.D. are still under discussion. Professor Prebisch had suggested that the developing countries should be free to combine to discriminate against imports of manufactures from the developed countries, and at the same time the latter should give preferences (⇨ INFANT INDUSTRY ARGUMENT). The distaste felt by the developing countries for the MOST FAVOURED NATION CLAUSE of the GENERAL AGREEMENT ON TARIFFS AND TRADE was recognized by that institution. A new chapter to the G.A.T.T. was added in 1956 on trade and development, which called for the reduction of TARIFFS and QUOTAS on developing countries' exports. It became possible for preferential duties to be given to imports from developing countries without having to extend these preferences to all the contracting parties of G.A.T.T. Finally, in 1970, agreement was reached by which the developed nations in the EUROPEAN FREE TRADE ASSOCIATION and the EUROPEAN ECONOMIC COMMUNITY, and the U.S. gave preferences in specified manufactured goods to the developing countries. This agreement came into force in 1971 for a period of ten years, subject to annual review.

United Nations Relief and Rehabilitation Administration (U.N.R.R.A.). An emergency organization established towards the end of the Second World War to supply the basic food and clothing, raw materials and machinery requirements of the countries of Western Europe which had suffered extensive war damage. The organization was particularly active in Greece, Italy, Yugoslavia, Austria, Czechoslovakia, Poland and the Ukraine. It was financed by the British Commonwealth and the U.S., and extended its aid to the Pacific on the conclusion of the war there. It was only intended as an emergency operation and could not do more than ease the immediate shortage of necessities. It was wound up officially in August 1946, and the major task of rehabilitation was taken over by the EUROPEAN RECOVERY PROGRAMME.

Unrequited exports. EXPORTS for which there is no reverse flow of goods or finance in payment. They take place in the settlement of past DEBTS.

User cost. 1. The cost involved in using a unit of CAPITAL, which can be thought of as the fall in its VALUE which results from its use. For example, suppose that a machine could be sold now for a maximum of £100. If it is instead used to produce some output and the result of this is to reduce the price at which it can be sold to £90,

the user cost is £10. The concept of user cost is clearly closely related
to DEPRECIATION, where the latter term is used in the economic,
rather than the accounting, sense of the word.
2. A term used in COST-BENEFIT ANALYSIS, and defined here
as the total costs incurred by users in their use of a particular facility.
These costs include SOCIAL COSTS as well as private costs. For
instance, in carrying out an INVESTMENT APPRAISAL of capital
expenditure on a road, the alternative costs to the traffic *using* the
road and its alternatives are evaluated. These costs not only include
the costs of petrol and wear and tear of vehicles, but also the time
taken in travelling along the alternative routes.

Utilitarianism. The philosophy by which the purpose of government
was the maximization of the sum of UTILITY, defined in terms of
pleasure and pain, in the community as a whole. It was not hedonistic
(▷ HEDONISM) in so far as pleasure could include, for instance,
the satisfaction of helping others. The purpose of government
was to ensure the 'greatest happiness of the greatest number'.
It implied that utility could be measured and interpersonal comparisons made. Its chief advocate was JEREMY BENTHAM.

Utility. The classical definition of utility is that it is the satisfaction,
pleasure, need-fulfilment, etc., derived from consuming some quantity
of a good. It is thus essentially a psychological thing which is in-
capable of measurement in absolute units. The concept of utility
lay at the heart of the classical theory of DEMAND, in the form of
the law of diminishing MARGINAL UTILITY, until the 1930s,
when J. R. HICKS and R. G. D. ALLEN rediscovered and extended
the work of E. SLUTSKY and V. F. D. PARETO on INDIFFERENCE
ANALYSIS. The objection was that if utility were essentially un-
measurable, it was invalid to construct a theory which proceeded
as if it could be measured. Demand theory was therefore recast in
terms of ORDINAL UTILITY, i.e. the consumer was assumed simply
to be able to rank quantities of goods on the basis of preference
(▷ CONSUMER'S PREFERENCE) or indifference. Then, to say that
some combination of goods has a 'greater utility' than some other
combination simply means that the consumer prefers the first
combination to the second. Though most of the results of demand
theory are unchanged, this interpretation of utility as preference,
rather than as some 'crude hedonistic calculus', is held to have put
the theory on a much sounder footing. ▷ REVEALED PREFERENCE.

V

Value. 1. The total UTILITY which is yielded by the object in question. This is often referred to as its 'value in use'. **2.** The quantity of some other COMMODITY for which the object in question can be exchanged. This is then referred to as its 'value in exchange'. Thus, if the other commodity is MONEY, the value of the object is its PRICE. If the other commodity is fur coats, the value of the object is the number of fur coats for which it can be exchanged.

In most economic contexts, the term 'value' is used in sense **(2)**. Thus, 'value theory' could just as well be termed PRICE THEORY, and consists of the analysis of what determines the EQUILIBRIUM rates of exchange between commodities directly, or between commodities and money.

Value added, or net output. The difference between TOTAL REVENUE of a firm, and the cost of bought-in raw materials, services and components. It thus measures the VALUE which the firm has 'added' to these bought-in materials and components by its processes of production. Since the total revenue of the firm will be divided among CAPITAL CHARGES (including DEPRECIATION), RENT, DIVIDEND payments, WAGES and the costs of materials, services and components, value added can also be calculated by summing the relevant types of cost. Although 'value added' and 'net output' are often used synonymously, net output in the CENSUS OF PRODUCTION is calculated by subtracting the value of materials purchased (allowing for stock changes) from the value of each industry's sales. Payments for *services* rendered by other firms, e.g. R. & D. (RESEARCH AND DEVELOPMENT) work, hire of machinery, are not deducted, so that in this technical sense, 'net output' is distinguished from 'value added', a term sometimes used to describe the contribution of an industry to the GROSS DOMESTIC PRODUCT. ⟡ VALUE ADDED TAX.

Value added tax (V.A.T.). A general tax (⟡ TAXATION) applied at each point of EXCHANGE of goods or SERVICES from primary production to final consumption. It is levied on the difference between the sale price of the goods or services (outputs) to which the tax is applied and the cost of goods and services (INPUTS) bought in for use in its production. The cost of these inputs is taken to include all charges, including all taxes except V.A.T. itself. The method of payment and

412

collection is as follows. Each trader sells his outputs at a price increased by the appropriate percentage of V.A.T. He is then liable for the payment of the tax so obtained from his customers, but can claim a refund of any V.A.T. included in the invoices for the inputs which he himself purchased from his suppliers. His customers do likewise, and so on down to the final consumer. At each point of exchange the tax is passed on in the form of higher prices. Being at the last point in the chain of exchange, the final consumer bears the whole tax. The traders within the chain do not bear any tax but act as collecting agencies. It is planned to introduce V.A.T. in the U.K. in 1973, because it is the form of INDIRECT TAXATION applied in the EUROPEAN ECONOMIC COMMUNITY and is the basis of contribution to the community budget. It will replace the existing indirect taxes such as PURCHASE TAX and SELECTIVE EMPLOYMENT TAX. Basic foodstuffs, housing and EXPORTS will probably be excluded from the tax. V.A.T. may be applied to different goods or services or in different industries at different rates, including zero and exempt. The difference between the latter two is that only with the former can refunds be claimed. ⇨ TURNOVER TAX.

Value judgement. A statement of opinion or belief which is not capable of being falsified by comparison with fact. It is therefore, essentially a NORMATIVE rather than a POSITIVE statement. Thus, the statement, 'UNEMPLOYMENT should not exist', is a value judgement, while the statement, 'Unemployment does not exist', is not. In economics, the desirability of the clear distinction of value judgements from positive analysis is always stressed. Where the object is to understand and make predictions about actual economic phenomena, opinions and beliefs may only obscure the issues, e.g. if one is trying to analyse the role of excess PROFITS in the mechanism of RESOURCE allocation (⇨ ECONOMIC EFFICIENCY) in a FREE MARKET ECONOMY, or to predict the consequences of a 45 per cent CORPORATION TAX on this process, it helps to put to one side one's belief that profits are iniquitous/virtuous. This is not to say, however, that economists should not make value judgements, or make prescriptions about the objectives of economic policy. Indeed, some of the most successful 'positive' economists have been the most vocal advocates of particular policy objectives, e.g. J. M. KEYNES. Rather, it is simply to argue that value judgements must not be allowed to obscure analysis of what is, as opposed to what ought to be. This is, in essence, simply part of scientific method, but is something which is especially difficult to achieve in economics. ⇨ L. C. ROBBINS.

Value, theories of. There have been three broad approaches to the analysis of VALUE in use or exchange in economic theory. (a) *General use theories:* Theories which were based on the assumption that the value of a commodity was related to the use to which it could be put. ⟡ F. GALIANI. (b) *Labour theory:* Value is interpreted as reflecting the cost of production measured in terms of LABOUR time absorbed. ⟡ K. MARX; D. RICARDO; A. SMITH. (c) *Marginal utility theory:* The UTILITY of the final small increment in DEMAND and SUPPLY determines the value of COMMODITIES in exchange. ⟡ H. H. GOSSEN; W. S. JEVONS; MARGINAL UTILITY; A. MARSHALL; M. E. L. WALRAS.

Variable. A number capable of taking different VALUES. In mathematics, a variable is regarded simply as a general abstract concept, with no necessary real-world counterpart (thus one solves an equation for the variables x, or y, which are not any particular things). In any applied science such as economics, however, variables are usually identified with real-world things of interest, e.g. CONSUMPTION and INVESTMENT will be regarded as variables in a MODEL of INCOME DETERMINATION.

Variable costs. Costs which vary directly with the rate of output, e.g. LABOUR costs, raw-material costs, fuel and power. Also known as *operating costs, prime costs, on costs* or *direct costs*.

Variable proportions, law of. ⟡ DIMINISHING RETURNS, LAW OF.

Variance. A number which measures the extent to which a set of numbers are dispersed about their arithmetic mean (⟡ AVERAGE). It is defined as: the average of the sum of the squares of deviations from their mean of a given set of numbers. The bigger the variance, the greater the dispersion of the numbers. Given a set of numbers, $x_1, x_2, \ldots x_n$, we may have calculated their mean as an average or representative value, a measure of the 'central tendency' of the numbers. It is then useful to consider the extent to which the numbers are dispersed about the mean. For example, suppose we have the three numbers 100, 101, 102. Then their mean is: $\bar{x} = \dfrac{100 + 101 + 102}{3} = \dfrac{303}{3} = 101$. On the other hand, suppose we have the three numbers: 31, 71, 201. Then their mean is also: $\bar{x} = \dfrac{31 + 71 + 201}{3} = \dfrac{303}{3} = 101$. Clearly, in the first case, the numbers are far more closely grouped around their mean than in the second case, and so we would tend to say that the mean is a far better representation of the whole set of numbers than in the second case. Therefore, given that we might often wish to use the mean to tell us something about a set of numbers, it would appear to be useful to have another number, which would tell us how widely or narrowly the numbers are clustered around the mean.

A seemingly obvious way to get such a measure might be to subtract the mean from each number and add up the differences. The larger this sum, the more widely must the numbers be dispersed about their mean. The trouble with this measure is that the sum of the differences will always be zero. For example:

$$100 - 101 = -1 \qquad\qquad 31 - 101 = -70$$
$$101 - 101 = 0 \qquad\qquad 71 - 101 = -30$$
$$102 - 101 = 1 \qquad\qquad 201 - 101 = 100$$
$$\ 0 = \text{Total} \qquad\qquad \ 0 = \text{Total}$$

This is not an accident of the numbers chosen – it is a property of the mean that this is always so. The problem therefore has not been solved. The solution proposed by statisticians is to take the square of the difference between the mean and each number, and then to sum these squared differences. This trick of squaring the difference solves the problem, because the square of a negative number is always a positive number, and the square of a positive number is also always a positive number, and hence the sum of these squared differences must be a positive number. Thus, to the above calculations, we can add:

$$(-1)^2 = 1 \qquad\qquad (-70)^2 = 4,900$$
$$(0)^2 = 0 \qquad\qquad (-30)^2 = 900$$
$$(1)^2 = 1 \qquad\qquad (100)^2 = 10,000$$
$$\ 2 = \text{Total} \qquad\qquad \ 15,800 = \text{Total}$$

Clearly, the greater the differences between the numbers and the mean, the greater the squares of these differences, and so the greater the sum of these squares.

However, our problem of finding a single number to summarize the degree of dispersion of a set of numbers about their mean has not yet been solved. By simply summing the squares of the differences, we run the risk that the sum may be large, not because the numbers are widely dispersed about their mean, but because there are many numbers. Thus, suppose we have a set of 1,000 numbers, 500 of which are equal to 1 and 500 of which are equal to 3. Their mean is then 2. Each number is only one unit away from the mean, and we would say that the numbers were closely clustered about their mean, yet the sum of the squared differences is equal to 1,000, i.e. $500 \times (-1)^2 + 500 \times (1)^2$. Clearly, what we need is some measure of the 'average' difference, i.e. some way of allowing for the numbers of values involved. This is done by dividing by the number of values. In the above example, we would divide by 1,000; in the previous example, we would divide by 3. Hence we have arrived at a procedure for finding a number which summarizes the extent to which a set of numbers are dispersed about their mean. This number is called the variance, and it is defined by the formula:

$$\text{Variance} = \sigma^2 = \frac{1}{n} \sum_{i=1}^{n} (x_i - \bar{x})^2$$

where x_i is the i'th number, $\bar{x}$ is the mean, and n is the number of values, $x_1 \, x_2 \ldots x_n$. This formula says succinctly: calculate the difference between each number and the mean; square these differences; sum these squared differences; divide this sum by the number of numbers, i.e. by n. The greater dispersion of the numbers about their mean, the greater will be the differences between each and the mean, and so the greater the value of the variance.

To illustrate how we might use the variance in practical situations, suppose we were told that two companies had each, over the past ten years, paid out on average a DIVIDEND of 10 per cent, i.e. the mean dividend was 10 per cent, but that the variance of dividend payments of one company was four times that of the other, i.e. the dividend payments of one were much more dispersed about the average than the other, being in some years much higher but in other years much lower. Then, if we attach importance to consistency or stability of dividends, we should choose the share with the lower variance. Examples of the applications of the variance to all fields which involve numerical data and its analysis are numerous.

One slight problem which occurs when an attempt is made to give a variance an everyday interpretation is that, since it involves the squares of numbers, it must be expressed in terms of the squares of the units in which those numbers are measured. Thus, if we were calculating the variance of a set of weights measured in pounds, then the variance would be measured in 'pounds squared' or 'square pounds'. However, this problem can easily be overcome by defining the STANDARD DEVIATION as the square root of the variance.

Veblen, Thorstein Bunde (1857–1929). ⇨ CONSPICUOUS CONSUMPTION.

Vector. A set of numbers, arranged in a row or column. Thus, we have the row vector: (3 2 0); and the column vector:

$$\begin{pmatrix} 3 \\ 2 \\ 0 \end{pmatrix}$$

These vectors are three-dimensional, because they have three components, the three numbers 3, 2, 0. If we let $a_1 a_2 \ldots a_n$ stand for any n numbers, then we can define the n-dimensional row vector: $(a_1 a_2 a_3 \ldots a_n)$; and the n-dimensional column vector:

$$\begin{pmatrix} a_1 \\ a_2 \\ . \\ . \\ . \\ a_n \end{pmatrix}$$

where n can be any positive number greater than 1. Just as basic elementary operations of addition, subtraction and multiplication have been defined for ordinary numbers, so mathematicians have framed rules for carrying out these operations with vectors. Much of economic theory, and particularly GENERAL EQUILIBRIUM theory, can be translated into terms of vectors and a related concept, the MATRIX. Such a translation permits considerable simplification and clarification. In addition, the development of the mathematical theory of vectors and matrices has stimulated some extremely important innovations in economics, most notably INPUT-OUTPUT ANALYSIS, which is based entirely on the algebra of matrices and vectors.

Velocity of circulation. ⟡ INCOME VELOCITY OF CIRCULATION.

Venture capital. ⟡ RISK CAPITAL.

Vertical integration. The undertaking by a single firm of successive stages in the process of production of a particular good. The petroleum industry is a good example of a vertically integrated industry. The major firms undertake exploration, drilling and extraction, transport of crude oil to refineries, refining into petroleum, fuel oils, etc., transport to distribution outlets (filling stations and garages), and ownership of those outlets. There are several advantages arising from vertical integration, the extent of these varying from industry to industry, and, within limits, presumably determining the degree of vertical integration. There may be technical advantages to be gained from physical proximity of successive processes, e.g.

417

iron-ore smelting and the production of steel and steel products. Important advantages may arise out of greater security and stability, and improvements in coordination between stages of production, which comes about if control is centralized. In addition, a firm may be able to eliminate excessive PROFITS of a seller or buyer, or carry out the relevant operation more efficiently, by itself taking over the operation. Or the firm may have to integrate vertically from sheer necessity – there may be no other firm capable of supplying the raw material, component or service efficiently enough and to the required specifications. Finally, vertical integration may simply represent a very profitable INVESTMENT, particularly if the product is sold to other buyers.

Viner, Jacob (1892–   ). ⬦ CUSTOMS UNION.

Visible balance. The BALANCE OF PAYMENTS in VISIBLE TRADE, i.e. IMPORTS, EXPORTS and RE-EXPORTS.

Visible trade. INTERNATIONAL TRADE in merchandise, IMPORTS, EXPORTS and RE-EXPORTS. ⬦⬦ INVISIBLES.

Voting shares. EQUITY shares entitling holders to vote in the election of directors of a company. Normally all ORDINARY SHARES are voting shares, but sometimes a company may create a class of non-voting ordinary shares if the holders of the equity wish to raise more equity capital but exclude the possibility of losing control of the business. PREFERENCE SHARES are rarely, and DEBENTURE shares never, voting shares.

W

Wage drift. The tendency for wage EARNINGS to exceed wage rates gives rise to wage drift, measured as the difference between wage earnings and rates. This difference will consist of overtime earnings and special bonuses not provided for in the general agreement which establishes the wage rates for a particular class of workers. Since wage earnings are, on the one hand, what determine the spending power of a large group of consumers, and, on the other, the costs of producing goods and services, it is these rather than wage rates which influence the rate of INFLATION. The significance of wage drift therefore lies in the fact that, to the extent that it exists, control of inflation through restraint on wage rates is ineffective. In general, government control can only really be exercised over wage rates: overtime working, special bonuses, etc., tend to be determined at the place of work and hence are very difficult to supervise. The extent of wage drift therefore shows the degree of failure of a policy of wage freeze (◇ PRICES AND INCOMES POLICY). However, some economists would argue that wage drift is a desirable thing. If wage rates are pegged at particular levels, then they are not able to fulfil their functions as prices in indicating situations of scarcity, and eradicating these by rising and attracting more LABOUR. If the extent of wage drift does, in fact, measure the degree of labour scarcity at particular places, then wage earnings will be fulfilling their role as PRICES, and this is desirable from the point of view of market efficiency. Thus, it would not necessarily be desirable to eliminate wage drift entirely.

Wage freeze. ◇ PRICES AND INCOMES POLICY.

Wage fund theory. ADAM SMITH took over from the PHYSIOCRATS the idea that wages are advanced to the workers in anticipation of the sale of their output. Wages could not be increased unless the CAPITAL destined to pay them was increased. Capital, in turn, was determined by SAVINGS. The CLASSICAL ECONOMISTS developed their theory of wages around these ideas. In the short run, there was a given number of workers and a given amount of savings to pay their wages. The two together determined the average wage. In the long run, the supply of LABOUR was related to the minimum of subsistence needed to sustain the LABOUR FORCE. (This subsistence level was not simply physiological; it was related to a standard of living accepted by custom.) If the wage rate rose above this, the population increased; if it fell below, it contracted. In the long run, the level of the demand for labour was determined by the size of the wages fund, and this, in turn, by the level of savings. This meant that, as J. S. MILL put it, 'the demand for COMMODITIES is not the demand for labour'. If you increased CONSUMPTION you reduced savings and therefore the wage fund. PRODUCTIVITY did not influence REAL WAGES, what mattered was the level of PROFITS, for savings depended on profits. The argument assumed that savings flowed into fixed capital and variable (wage) capital in equal proportions so that what MARX called the organic composition of capital remained constant. RICARDO worried about this point in his analysis of the effect of machinery on employment. Investment by-passed the wages fund and the demand for labour was reduced. W. T. Thornton criticized the wages fund doctrine on the grounds that wages were determined by SUPPLY and DEMAND in the market. J. S. Mill accepted some of Thornton's points and admitted that the wages fund idea might be more appropriate in the context of a discontinuous production process (akin to seed-time to harvest) rather than a continuous flow of output, which was the true state of affairs. There was some popular confusion at the time, because it was thought the economists meant there existed a definite fund available for wages so that there was no hope of workers obtaining higher average earnings.

Wage rates. ⟡ EARNINGS.

Wages, bargaining theory of. ⟡ BARGAINING THEORY OF WAGES.

Wall Street (U.S.). The New York STOCK EXCHANGE.

Walras, Marie Esprit Léon (1834–1910). A mining engineer by training, he accepted the offer of a newly created Chair of Economics in the Faculty of Law at Lausanne in 1870. He held this post until he was succeeded by PARETO upon his retirement in 1892. His publications include *Éléments d'économie Politique Pure* (1874–7), *Études d'économie Sociale* (1896) and *Études d'économie Politique Appliquée* (1898). One of the three economists to propound a MARGINAL UTILITY theory in the 1870s, he set out the theory of diminishing marginal utility and showed how PRICES at which COMMODITIES exchanged are determined by the relative marginal utilities of the people taking part in the transaction (⟡ JEVONS, MENGER and GOSSEN). He also constructed a mathematical MODEL of general EQUILIBRIUM as a system of simultaneous equations in which he tried to show that all prices and quantities are uniquely determined. This is regarded as one of the foremost achievements in mathematical economics, of which Walras is considered the founder.

Washington Agreement. An agreement concluded with the U.S. in December 1945, under which $25,000 million of Lend-Lease aid to the Commonwealth was written off and the U.K. was granted a long-term loan of $3,750 million. The agreement was approved by the U.S. Senate in July 1946. The sterling value of this drawing in 1945 was £931 million by the end of 1970, but with two sterling DEVALUATIONS in the meantime, the amount outstanding had risen to £1,208 million ($2,899 million). ⟡ EUROPEAN RECOVERY PROGRAMME.

Waste product, ⟡ BY-PRODUCT.

Wasting assets. ASSETS with strictly limited, though not necessarily determinate, lives, e.g. a mine, timber lands or a property on lease. Wasting assets have many of the characteristics of CURRENT ASSETS, but they are normally included under fixed assets.

Watering stock. The issue of the nominal capital of a company in return for less than its money value, thus overstating the capital of the company and reducing its apparent return on capital (⟡ RATE OF RETURN).

Ways and Means Advances. Advances to the CONSOLIDATED FUND made by the BANK OF ENGLAND (⟡ NATIONAL DEBT).

Wealth. The wealth of an individual is his total stock of tangible or intangible possessions which have a market VALUE. This implies that they must be capable of being exchanged for MONEY or other goods, i.e. the ownership in them must be capable of being transferred. It also implies that we not only include physical possessions, such as a house, STOCKS and SHARES, bank accounts, etc., but also his business and professional connections, together with the value of particular skills which he may possess. These latter forms of wealth have a market value in the sense that they can be exchanged in the relevant MARKET. If it is desired to distinguish between the tangible and intangible types of wealth, the terms *human wealth* and *non-human wealth* are often used (⟡ CAPITAL and HUMAN CAPITAL). A basic property of wealth is that it is a means of generating INCOME, i.e. income is often regarded as the return on wealth. It follows that the value of a stock of wealth is given by the PRESENT VALUE of the flow of income it generates.

'Wear and tear' allowances. ⟡ CAPITAL ALLOWANCES.

Weights. ⟡ WEIGHTED AVERAGE.

Weighted average. A form of arithmetic mean ($\Diamond$ AVERAGE) constructed by first multiplying each number by a number designed to reflect its importance on some criterion, summing the resulting products and then dividing by the sum of the numbers used as weights. The object of 'weighting' the numbers is simply to obtain an overall average which correctly reflects the differing relative importances of the constituent items. For example, suppose that we want a number which shows the average change in the cost of providing oneself with the basic necessities of life between now and some past period. We could choose the set of items which we take to be the basic necessities, find by how much their PRICES had changed and calculate a straightforward arithmetic mean. Assume that there are three goods involved, and the current prices as percentages of the earlier prices are 120, 115 and 125 respectively. The simple mean of these is $\dfrac{120 + 115 + 125}{3} = 120$. However, if we want our average to give an accurate representation of the change in our cost of living, we should take into account differences in the relative importance of these goods. For example, if we spent most of our INCOME on the second good, whose current price is only 115 per cent of its earlier price, our cost of living has obviously risen by less than if we spent most of our income on the third good, whose price is 125 per cent of its former value. In fact, taking a straightforward unweighted average implicitly assumes that each item has exactly equal importance, or, in this example, that a third of one's income is spent on each good. Instead, suppose that 30 per cent of income is spent on the first good, 60 per cent on the second and only 10 per cent on the third. It seems natural then to weight each percentage by its share of total expenditure, and to obtain the weighted average as:

$$\frac{\left(\dfrac{30}{100}\right) \times 120 + \left(\dfrac{60}{100}\right) \times 115 + \left(\dfrac{10}{100}\right) \times 125}{\dfrac{30}{100} + \dfrac{60}{100} + \dfrac{10}{100}} = \frac{36 + 69 + 12 \cdot 5}{1}$$

$$= 117 \cdot 5$$

This is lower than the previous value, because the smallest percentage has the largest weight, and *vice versa*. Where the weights to be used are expressed as percentages or proportions, the denominator in the calculation will generally be equal to one, and this can be used to simplify calculations. This need not always happen, however. Suppose we thought that the relative importance of the three percentages could be best expressed by the weights 3, 12 and 1. That is, we regard the first percentage as three times more important than the third, and the second as four times more important than the first. Then we would construct our weighted average as:

$$\frac{3 \times 120 + 12 \times 115 + 125}{3 + 12 + 1} = \frac{360 + 1380 + 125}{16} = \frac{1865}{16} = 117$$

Clearly, the greater the differences in the values of the items, the greater the sensitivity of the final average value to choice of particular weights. ⟡ INDEX NUMBER; INDEX NUMBER PROBLEM; RETAIL PRICE INDEX.

Welfare economics. That branch of economics concerned firstly with defining ECONOMIC EFFICIENCY; secondly with evaluating the economic efficiency of particular systems of RESOURCE allocation; and finally with analysing the conditions under which economic policies may be said to have improved SOCIAL WELFARE. The first two sets of problems are approached by defining the conditions which are necessary for a maximum of economic efficiency to be achieved, and then by examining the degree to which actual systems, e.g. the PRICE SYSTEM, fulfil these conditions. The third set of problems is approached by defining tests or criteria which may be applied to proposed changes to decide if they represent improvements in welfare or not. ⟡ COMPENSATION PRINCIPLE; COST-BENEFIT ANALYSIS; A. C. PIGOU.

Wicksell, Knut (1851–1926). Educated at Uppsala University in Sweden, where he studied mathematics and philosophy, he was appointed to the Chair of Economics at Lund in 1904, a post he held until 1916. His major publications include *Über Wert, Kapital und Rente* (1893), *Finanz theoretische Untersuchungen* (1895) and *Geldzins und Güterpreise* (1898). A synthesis of his work was published in 1901 and 1906 with the English title of *Lectures on Political Economy*. He assimilated the GENERAL EQUILIBRIUM analysis of WALRAS with the work of BÖHM-BAWERK and worked out a theory of DISTRIBUTION based on the new MARGINAL ANALYSIS of JEVONS, WALRAS and MENGER. In addition, he had a significant influence on monetary theory. He pointed out that high RATES OF INTEREST often coincided with high prices, which was contrary to what current theory predicted. He drew attention to the significance of the relative level of interest rates rather than their absolute level. Prices were related to the difference between changes in the real or natural rate of INTEREST (which was determined by the expected rate of PROFITS) and the money rate. The CENTRAL BANK had an important influence over the price level through its operations on the discount rate (◊ BANK RATE). These theories were incorporated into his theory of the TRADE CYCLE. (◊ INTEREST, NATURAL RATE OF).

Wieser, Friedrich von (1851–1926). He succeeded MENGER to the Chair of Economics at Vienna University in 1903 after a period at Prague University. His most important works include *Über den Ursprung und die Hauptgesetze des Wirtschaftlichen Wertes* (1884), *Der Natürliche Wert* (1889) and *Theorie der gesellschaftlichen Wirtschaft* (1914). He developed a law of costs which became known later as the principle of opportunity COST. FACTORS OF PRODUCTION will be distributed by competition such that, in EQUILIBRIUM, the value of their marginal outputs will be equal. The costs of production of any COMMODITY reflect the competing claims in other uses for the services of the factors needed to produce it. The law became an important element in the theory of RESOURCE allocation (◊ ECONOMIC EFFICIENCY).

Winding up. ◊ LIQUIDATION.

Window dressing. A practice of the British CLEARING BANKS prior to 1946, in which, in their half-yearly BALANCE SHEETS, their CASH RATIO was shown to be substantially higher than it was at other times of the year. At the time, the banks wished to show that their cash ratio was about 11 per cent although they normally operated at nearer to 8 per cent. To achieve the desired figure for the purposes of the accounts, the banks temporarily called in MONEY AT CALL AND SHORT NOTICE from the MONEY MARKET. In fact, an 8 per cent operating cash ratio was quite adequate, and since 1946 the published figures have reflected this.

Working capital. That part of current ASSETS financed from long-term funds. ◊ CURRENT RATIO.

World Bank. ◊ INTERNATIONAL BANK FOR RECONSTRUCTION AND DEVELOPMENT.

X

X-efficiency. The term given to denote general managerial and technological efficiency. That is, the efficiency with which a firm uses INPUTS, solves its organizational problems and undertakes all its activities at minimum cost. In economic theory it is usually argued, as a corollary of PROFIT maximization, that firms will operate with the maximum x-efficiency. More recently, however, it has been pointed out that when firms are insulated from competition, this may not be the case. ⟐ ECONOMIC EFFICIENCY; FIRM, THEORY OF; MONOPOLY; OLIGOPOLY.

Y

Yield. The INCOME from a SECURITY as a proportion of its current market price. Thus, the *dividend yield* is the current DIVIDEND as a percentage of the market price of a security. The *earnings yield* is a theoretical figure, based on the last dividend paid as a percentage of the current market price. The *redemption yield* is normally applied only to fixed-interest securities, and is the interest payment over the remaining life of the security, plus or minus the difference between the purchase price and the redemption value, i.e. it is the earnings yield adjusted to take account of any CAPITAL GAIN or loss to redemption. With fixed-interest securities, the nominal interest, or COUPON, is unlikely to be the same as the actual yield. An IRREDEEMABLE SECURITY in the form of a government bond having a flat yield of 3 per cent with a PAR VALUE of £100, but a market price of £50, provides an earnings yield of 6 per cent. The earnings yield will fluctuate with the price of the security, rising as security prices fall, and *vice versa.* ⟡ GILT-EDGED SECURITIES.

Yield gap. The difference between the YIELD on ORDINARY SHARES and the yield on GILT-EDGED SECURITIES, e.g. 2½ per cent irredeemable CONSOLS. If the latter exceeds the former, it is called the *reverse yield gap.* A reverse yield gap appeared for the first time in 1959.

Z

Zero-sum game. A situation in the theory of GAMES in which the gains and losses of the 'players' sum to zero for every possible choice of STRATEGIES. For example, suppose there are only two players, Firm *A* and Firm *B*, which between them control 100 per cent of the MARKET for a particular product. Whatever increase in market share which Firm *A* might gain will be exactly equal to the loss suffered by Firm *B*. The importance of this type of game is that the players are in pure conflict.